Greek Tragedy

Greek Tragedy and Comedy

F. L. LUCAS

THE VIKING PRESS
New York

VIKING COMPASS EDITION
First published in 1968 by The Viking Press, Inc.
625 Madison Avenue, New York, N.Y. 10022

Distributed in Canada by
The Macmillan Company of Canada Limited
SBN 670-00227-5
Library of Congress catalog card number: 68-17108
Printed in U.S.A.

Originally published in 1954 by
The Macmillan Company (New York)
under the title Greek Drama for Everyman
Fifth printing March 1975

To Sir Herbert Grierson

"That a man could hardly be better employed than in interesting students in the best of Greek and Latin literature, I have never doubted." —H. W. GARROD

CONTENTS

PREFACE

Quince. *Bless thee, Bottom! bless thee! thou art translatęd!*
Bottom. *I see their knavery; this is to make an ass of me.*
A Midsummer Night's Dream.

OF GREEK TRAGEDY there survive, apart from fragments, thirty-three plays (with an imposing total of some 50,000 lines)—seven by Aeschylus, seven by Sophocles, and nineteen by Euripides (if we include the satyric *Cyclops* and the doubtful *Rhēsus*). Of Greek comedy we possess eleven plays by Aristophanes, one play (since 1959) and lengthy fragments of Menander.

This volume contains translations of Aeschylus' *Prometheus* and *Agamemnon*, Sophocles' *Antigone* and *Oedipus the King*, Euripides' *Hippolytus* and *The Bacchae*, and Aristophanes' *Clouds*; secondly, summaries, with extracts, of the other thirty-seven plays; thirdly, what seemed the best fragments of lost plays, both by these dramatists and by others. The introductions and notes, necessarily brief, are of course meant, not for the Greek scholar, but for the ordinary English reader who cares for poetry and wishes to travel through a great age long gone.[1]

This inclusion of extracts and fragments may be questioned. Yet Lamb's *Specimens of the English Dramatic Poets* has become a classic. And I see no answer to the eighteenth-century good sense of d'Alembert's 'Observations sur l'Art de Traduire' (*Œuvres*, 1822, iv, 38): '*La troisième loi arbitraire que les traducteurs ont subie, c'est la contrainte ridicule de traduire un auteur d'un bout à l'autre. Par là le traducteur, usé et refroidi dans les endroits faibles, languit ensuite dans les morceaux éminens. Pourquoi d'ailleurs se mettre à la torture pour rendre avec élégance une pensée fausse, avec finesse une idée commune? Ce n'est pas pour nous faire connaître les défauts des anciens qu'on les met dans notre langue, c'est pour enrichir notre littérature de ce qu'ils ont fait d'excellent.*'

About methods of translation there can never be general agreement. Personal tastes are too violent and too various. Still, it may save *some* misunderstanding to state at least one's aims.

On translation at large I warmly share the views of that great scholar Walter Headlam (*A Book of Greek Verse*, 1907, p. ix): 'Not a few of these

---

[1] I have tried to help the non-classical reader with the less familiar proper names, where there seemed any chance of mispronunciation. In such cases long vowels are marked by a line above them; an accent means that the syllable is short, but *stressed* in English (this has, of course, nothing to do with Greek accents which marked *pitch*). *E.g.* Stēsíchorus. Final *-e* is always pronounced, and pronounced long.

originals have been described as "untranslatable." It is a term that piques one: but I think it is applied too readily; and, once applied, a term like that is apt to be repeated lightly and become a superstition. . . . Translation with success is always possible when in the translator's language there exists a native form and manner corresponding: when there exists no such model, then, but only then, translation may perhaps be sometimes called impossible. . . . There is surely no more close affinity, historical and spiritual and artistic, than between the great dramatic speech of Aeschylus and Sophocles and the heroic language and blank verse of our Elizabethan Dramatists and Milton.'

As regards metre, then, it would follow that the iambics of Greek drama (with six feet) are best rendered in the iambics of English blank verse (with five feet, or five and a half). True, Professor Gilbert Murray has persistently preferred the rhymed heroic couplet. He is one of our very few verse-translators who are also poets (sometimes, indeed, I find him better than his originals); his renderings may seem often too free, too romantic, or too Swinburnian, but they have music and style of their own; and few men have done so much to keep Greek poetry a living influence in England. None the less I have never felt happy about his rhymed dramatic dialogue. Like Dryden, he here seems to be attempting something alien to the English temperament. What in French can become a stately convention, in English tends to leave a sense of unreality and artifice.

For Greek iambics, then, I believe in English blank verse. But 'blank verse' means many things. One can write:

> Whether 'tis Nobler in the minde to suffer
> The Slings and Arrowes of outragious Fortune;

or

> Whether it is more ethical to tolerate with equanimity
> All the unpleasant contingencies of contemporary existence.

This second sort of metre and style has in recent years acquired a certain vogue, even for translating Greek tragedy. Whether it is beautiful or barbarous would be vain to argue. (Mr Micawber would have loved it.) But one *can*, I think, reasonably argue that its nonchalance of rhythm is no very faithful equivalent for the religiously formal strictness of Greek tragedy, whose iambics obey far more rigid and elaborate rules than any English blank verse. Indeed I imagine they can have been no easier to compose than the *ottava rima*, rhyme royal, and sonnet-sequences in which Swinburne had the whimsy to write parts of his play *Locrine*. Even the looser metres of Attic comedy are difficult compared with English prosody. But Greek art was not labour-saving. They did not groan about 'the bondage of rhyme'; they accepted, with grace, yet stricter bondages.

Therefore, I think, the translator's blank verse should not be too loose.

On the other hand, much English blank verse since Milton seems to me
monotonously stiff.   The metre of *Paradise Lost* was magnificent marble
for Milton's own purposes; but does it not lack the flesh-and-blood elasticity
which the best Elizabethans and Jacobeans attained, here by shortened
lines, there by extra syllables—especially by feminine endings?   Fletcher,
for example, was capable of using these last (excessively, I feel) for four
lines out of every five in a play, or even for sixteen consecutive verses; but,
since Milton, feminine endings have come often to be regarded with a sort
of misogynist distrust.   This can be seen in the blank-verse poems of the
eighteenth century, then of Wordsworth, Tennyson, Browning, or Arnold;
and again in such nineteenth-century dramas as *Prometheus Unbound* and,
still more, *Merope* or *Atalanta* (though Browning with typical waywardness
flew to the opposite extreme in his *Agamemnon,* and tagged a feminine
ending on to every single line—with effects, to my ear, quite horrible).
Landor remains a happy exception.   So, still more, does Beddoes.   Though
poor at plot or character, he seems to me almost alone of our dramatists
since Dryden in writing really beautiful, yet dramatic, blank verse.

With the lyrics of Attic drama there again arises the question: to rhyme
or not to rhyme?   But *here*, I think, the answer is: 'Rhyme.'   I have
tried both.[1]   But I am driven to the general view that, apart from iambics,
trochaics, and anapaests, the rhymeless metres of Greek are too remote
from English for successful imitation.   Repeated attempts have been
made; the results usually seem ingenious, but hateful—a chaos of eccentricities, where the reader remains uncertain how, even, the things should
be read.   *Vers libre*, on the other hand, tends to be shapeless and quickly
boring.   Only rhyme can give, I feel, what these lyrics need—impetus,
inevitability, variety.   Naturally it proves vastly more laborious;[2] but that
has to be put up with.   Here again I find myself anticipated by Headlam
(pp. xvii–xviii): 'Had Milton only known the true construction of Greek
Choral Song, we may be sure that instead of the mistaken imitations in the
Samson Agonistes he would at least have given us inventions no less beautiful than the stanza of the *Hymn on the Nativity*. . . .   Valuable, however,
as rhyme is, it makes translation very much more difficult.   Indeed with
Choral lyrics, such as these of Aeschylus and Sophocles, when what you
are to say is limited by the original, and how you may express it is limited
by rhyme; when what is said has so much meaning and significance, and
there is a pair of *strophes* to be matched with periods corresponding and

---

[1] *E.g.* unrhymed version of the *Antigone* chorus on Man (332–75) in *The Oxford Book
of Greek Verse in Translation,* p. 365; rhymed version here.   Anapaests I have here
sometimes rhymed, sometimes not.
[2] As the man of letters observes in Fielding's *Amelia* (viii, 5): 'Rhymes are difficult
things; they are stubborn things, sir.   I have been sometimes longer in tagging a couplet,
than I have been in writing a speech on the side of the opposition, which hath been
read with great applause all over the kingdom.'

both shaped with rhyme into organic stanzas capable of being sung—I do not know another task which makes so heavy a demand on all resources.'

But, though using rhyme, I have tried to preserve something of the original form by keeping, usually, the same number of lines, and roughly the same line-lengths, as the Greek. (It will be remembered that the exact line-divisions of choruses are often a matter of dispute, and may vary widely in different editions.)

After metre, diction. Here too, our own age, while it has gained by the progress of scholarship, is at a certain disadvantage in dealing with classic writers such as Homer, Aeschylus, Sophocles, or Virgil. Much modern literature hates tradition, strict form, grace, and dignity; about which it tends to feel like Walt Whitman, when urged to bind his work in vellum: 'Pshaw! Hangings, curtains, finger-bowls, china-ware, Matthew Arnold!' This reaction against 'Victorianism' may in part be healthy; but like most reactions it has gone too far. At all events it is a falsification to render by go-as-you-please metres and hail-fellow-well-met colloquialisms that deliberate loftiness which Greek tragedy gradually evolved. 'Tragedy,' says Aristotle (*Poetics*, ch. iv), 'was long in acquiring its solemn dignity'; and he dismisses with curt contempt a certain Aríphrades who, anticipating Wordsworth, criticized tragic poets for *not* talking like ordinary men. Recall too the rage of Aeschylus in *The Frogs* against the more realist and democratic style of Euripides:

Poor wretch, can you not see
That souls high-wrought, and mighty thought, must speak with majesty,
And heroes whose line is half-divine need words with a nobler air,
Just as their dress has a lordliness beyond our common wear?

(1058–61.)

Yet even Euripides used a proportion of poetic words such as many moderns would deride.[1]

And so when a modern translator, however excellent in other respects, makes the Chorus of *Agamemnon* observe to the agonized Cassandra: 'That refrain is hackneyed,' at a phrase so 'hackneyed' I seem to see a gesture of disgust from the ghost of Aeschylus.

We do it wrong, being so Majesticall.

And when a modern poet, however gifted in other ways, makes Turnus cry: 'Aeneas, where are you off to? Don't welsh on your marriage-contract,' a deeper melancholy seems to settle on the phantom face of Virgil.

I am not in favour of going to the opposite extreme and calling cowherds 'kine-wardens.' But there exists, I think, a mean between the

[1] In the lyrics, even of Euripides, prose words are said to be only forty-one per cent.

vulgar and the stilted.[1]   And if anyone finds the ancients linguistic snobs, that is a matter of taste; but it is not a translator's business to reform his authors.   One might as well act *Antigone* in shorts and sweaters.   Indeed it would be less misleading.   For no one would suppose it represented the original.

Finally let me quote Headlam once more (p. xx): 'No fault, perhaps, is commoner, and none, probably, is harder to avoid, than *over-translating*. The translator's love for the original is fond and jealous, and he is inclined, I fancy, to regard the details with a somewhat feverish and exaggerating eye, which fixes too intently on single words and tends to magnify them out of due proportion.'   This is a salutary warning for translators; and also, if I may venture to say so, for translators' critics.

In fine, I believe that the first duty of a classical translator is simply to aim at giving sensitive readers the same sort of *pleasure* as they would get from reading the original with a reasonable knowledge of classics.   Translations are not made for scholars.   Scholars do not need them; and it is only human that they should tend to dislike them.

The translator's second duty, I think, is to be true to the spirit, the personality of his author.   Chapman, for example, was untrue to Homer's personality when he made him 'conceited'; Pope, when he made him a too correct man of the world; Samuel Butler, when he made him slightly vulgar. For Homer was too wise to be merely clever; was wider than men of the world; and was aristocratic in feeling—so that, though he shows sympathy even for Polyphemus when the blinded Cyclops talks to his ram, he has none for the demagogue Thersites.

Third comes the duty of being true also to the spirit, the atmosphere of an author's period.   This does not mean affected archaism, or the equivalent of Gothic garages; but it means respecting the past.   If the original gives me a feeling of venerable antiquity, I am as little grateful as Aladdin for having my old lamp replaced by some garishly up-to-date article, with all the magic gone.   Our predecessors romanticized; we vulgarize.   It is no great improvement.   Unfortunately many persons have no sense of history and believe, like Bernard Shaw,[2] that the past was populated by the same people, merely wearing different clothes.   Actually

---

[1] A typical problem is whether to use 'thou' or 'you.'   Most translations keep rigidly to one or other.   But there are passages of ancient dignity, especially in Aeschylus, where 'you' seems an impoverishment, as it would in *Job* or *Samson Agonistes*; there are passages of modernist realism, especially in Euripides, where 'thou' seems 'tushery,' as it would in *Caesar and Cleopatra*.   It seems better to use 'thou' or 'you' according to the needs of the context, with the full freedom of Shakespeare or Webster.   (That is to say, though 'thou' is, in general, more familiar, superior, or poetic, this rule is readily sacrificed by them to euphony.)

[2] Cf. his letter from the Levant to Ellen Terry (12th Oct. 1899): 'However, I am at least quit of Athens, with its stupid classic Acropolis and smashed pillars.'   The habit of dancing derisively on conventional attitudes easily becomes itself a conventional attitude.

our own grandfathers seem already in some ways extraordinary and incomprehensible. The differences of the past and its strangeness are as important as its likenesses and its familiarity. This indeed is the charm of travelling in time; but some of us are like the type of British tourist who used to bawl for his native bacon and eggs under the shadow of the Capitol or in the Piazza of Saint Mark.

Fourth—but, to my mind, only fourth—stands the need for fidelity in detail; important though this too remains. Excessive licence can be nearly as bad as excessive literalism.[1] It turns translation into a different thing— adaptation. Much as I admire FitzGerald, I can see no justification for inserting passages of his own in Omar and Aeschylus. One should neither add, nor omit, anything essential without saying so. As a rough-and-ready rule, a translation seems to me too free if it could not conceivably be retranslated to give the original text.[2]

For the rest, if readers, dissatisfied with these pages, are goaded to learn Greek and read the originals, a large part of my purpose will have been attained.

In introductions and notes I have included a certain amount of critical comment; here too I should like to hazard a word on general principles. Every year sees new interpretations of Greek drama, as of Shakespeare. But, with certain brilliant exceptions, many of them leave me unhappy and unconvinced. It is perhaps the doom of poets to be torn asunder by wild professors. But too minute criticism of drama is particularly dangerous, because here the gulf yawns so wide between the audience watching the swift traffic of the stage and the solitary student under his lamp. Midnight oil gives a very different illumination from footlights—often it proves a mere will-o'-the-wisp. With a poem, if you wrest some abstruse meaning from it by reading it sixty-nine times, you can at least argue that the poet *meant* it to be read sixty-nine times. Optimistic of him; but not impossible; some poets are capable of anything. But no sane dramatist expects any member of his audience to go to sixty-nine performances. A Greek dramatist was quite lucky if his play was performed *once*. And though Greek plays, like Elizabethan, were also read,[3] the Athenians were no great readers. They were very busy; they talked incessantly; and they had no printing. True, production could sometimes make clear in the theatre points that are obscure in the text. But on the whole, just as jokes that

[1] A fault of the last century rather than of ours; so that Labouchère could perfidiously praise Bohn's series as having finally shown up the classics. Housman has preserved a pleasant Homeric specimen (quoted in *The Oxford Book of Greek Verse in Translation*, p. xcvii): 'They cut off his ears with the sharp brass; but he, injured in his feelings, went about, enduring that calamity with frantic mind.'

[2] It has to be recalled that in Greek the emphasis tends to lie at the beginning of the sentence; in English, at the end. This entails frequent changes of order in translating.

[3] Cf. p. 429.

take ten minutes to see are usually poor jokes, so dramatic points that take centuries to see are usually pointless.[1] In plays like *Oedipus* and *Othello* the dramatist successfully relies on audiences being blind to glaring impossibilities; the critic who expects them to seize impalpable nuances knows little of the stage.

The Duke of Wellington had a supreme, and wise, contempt for 'clever devils.' Cleverness has been the ruin of many writers, from Ovid and Seneca to Meredith and Shaw; but it has probably been the ruin of still more critics. Naturally the impulse is strong in many of us, if we cannot write *Hamlet*, to rewrite it. But when this leads to such revelations as that Hamlet 'is an element of evil in the state of Denmark' amid 'the healthy bustle of the court,' I must own that I begin to have doubts. New shades of meaning are thrilling to the discoverer; but such shades are too often ghosts. Stage-plays remain practical things which have to contend, on their way to the hearer's brain, with a multitude of obstacles and distractions. Actors cannot whisper. And just as the critic of Shakespeare should, in my belief, remain perched in imagination among the noisy groundlings, the flaunting gallants, the bustling alarums and excursions of the Globe, so the interpreter of Greek drama must constantly ask himself: 'What would this mean, not to the scholar poring in his study, but to a sensible man sitting on a hard seat in the open air of a Greek spring (not always very clement), along with fourteen thousand others, for six or seven hours at a stretch?'

Few poets have been scholars; and not all scholars are qualified by temperament to deal with poets. Indeed it is hard not to question sometimes whether universities are always very happy places for pursuing the arts (as distinct from pure learning). The arts are sometimes pursued there so relentlessly that they drop dead. As the gentle malice of Goldsmith once observed: 'If criticism could have improved the taste of a people, the Germans would have been the most polite nation alive.' In restoring classical or Shakespearian texts scholarship has done wonders; let us be grateful; but in expounding them it has sometimes been wonderful in a different way. Too often it has tumbled into the bottomless pit of the false profound. Great architecture is not built with gimlets. Therefore I have here fought shy of subtle explanations. For I believe that the criticism of Greek drama needs to follow the spirit rather of the realist Johnson than of the gifted, but preposterous Verrall.[2]

[1] See, for example, p. 128.
[2] Cf. Napoleon's wise words at St Helena, which are no less true of much criticism than of much history: '*On donnera souvent beaucoup de profondeur, de subtilité de ma part à ce qui ne fut peut-être que le plus simple du monde; on me supposera des projets que je n'eus jamais.... Souvent on alambiquera, on tordra ce qui fut tout-à-fait naturel et entièrement droit ... et de là encore la fable convenue qu'on appellera l'histoire. ... Du reste, dans leurs affirmations positives ils se montreront plus habiles que moi, qui, très-souvent, aurais été très embarrassé d'affirmer avec vérité ma pleine et entière pensée.*' (Las Cases, *Mémorial de Sainte-Hélène*, 1821-3, vii, 239-42.)

NOTE

In rendering the plays here translated in full I have been mainly indebted to the following editors: for *Prometheus* to P. Mazon and George Thomson; for *Agamemnon* to W. Headlam, Mazon, G. Thomson, and E. Fraenkel; for *Antigone* to Sir Richard Jebb and P. Masqueray; for *Oedipus the King* to Jebb, Masqueray, and Sir John Sheppard; for *Hippolytus* to L. Méridier and G. Murray (Oxford Text); for *The Bacchae* to E. L. Dodds; for *The Clouds* to W. J. M. Starkie, B. B. Rogers, and V. Coulon. I should also like to express my debt to my brother, D. W. Lucas, for helpful and tactful criticisms, as well as to his book *The Greek Tragic Poets*; and my thanks to the Clarendon Press for permission to reprint passages from my translation of *Medea*, published by them in 1924.

Unless otherwise stated, tragic fragments here translated are from A. Nauck, *Tragicorum Graecorum Fragmenta*, 1889; and comic fragments from T. Kock, *Comicorum Atticorum Fragmenta*, 1880-8.

CHRONOLOGICAL TABLE

B.C.	*Tragedy*	*Comedy*
600	Arion of Corinth (*c.* 600) ('Tragic' choruses)	
	Thespis wins tragic prize (*c.* 534)	
	Aeschylus b. (*c.* 525)	
	Phrynichus (fl. *c.* 510–470)	
	Pratinas of Phlius (fl. *c.* 500)	

TABLE

Thought, Literature, and Art	Greek History	Events elsewhere
	Solon (c. 639–559) legislates at Athens (c. 594)	
Thales (c. 624–546)		Nebuchadnezzar (605–562) takes Jerusalem (597)
Stēsíchorus (c. 610–550)		
(Heroic legends in lyric)		Servius Tullius king of Rome (578–534)
		Croesus king of Lydia (560–546)
	Peisistrătus tyrant of Athens (c. 561–556, 546–527)	
		Cyrus, king of Persia, conquers the Medes (550)
	Persia conquers the Greeks of Asia Minor (545)	Cyrus conquers Lydia (546)
Pythagoras (fl. c. 530)		Cyrus takes Babylon (538)
		Tarquinius Superbus king of Rome (534–510)
		Cyrus d. (529)
		Cambyses, king of Persia, conquers Egypt (525)
		Dareius king of Persia (521–485)
		Zerubbabel rebuilds the Temple (520–516)
	Athens freed from tyranny of Hippias (510)	Rome freed from Tarquins (510)
		Buddha (c. 560–c. 480)
Hēraclītus (fl. c. 500)		Confucius (551–479)

B.C.	Tragedy	Comedy
500	Aeschylus' first production (c. 500)	
	Sophocles b. (c. 496)	
	Phrynichus, *Fall of Milētus* (c. 494)	
		Epicharmus (c. 530–440)
		Official comic contests introduced at the Dionysia (486)
	Euripides b. (c. 485)	
	Aeschylus' first victory (484)	
	Phrynichus, *Phoenician Women* (c. 476)	
	Aeschylus, *Persians* (472)	
	Sophocles' first victory (468)	
	Aeschylus, *Seven against Thebes* (467)	
	Aeschylus, *Oresteia* (458)	
	Aeschylus d. in Sicily (456)	
	Euripides' first production (455)	
		Aristophanes (c. 450–c. 385)
		Cratīnus (c. 484–19)
		Comic contests introduced at the Lēnaea (c. 442)
	Sophocles, *Antigone* (c. 441)	
	Euripides' first victory (c. 441)	
	Sophocles general (440)	
	Euripides, *Alcestis* (438)	
	Euripides, *Mēdēa* (431)	
	Tragic contests introduced at the Lēnaea (c. 432)	Sophron, Syracusan writer of mimes (c. 470–400)
	Euripides, *Hippolytus* (428)	Aristophanes' first play performed (427)

Thought, Literature, and Art	Greek History	Events elsewhere
	Ionian revolt from Persia (499–494)	
	Marathon (490)	
Aegina pediments (c. 490)		
		Xerxes king of Persia (485–464)
Parménides (c. 520–455) Pindar (c. 518–438)	Thermopylae and Salamis (480) Persian defeat at Plataea (479)	
Anaxágoras (c. 500–428) Temple of Zeus at Olympia finished (c. 456)	Ephialtes in power at Athens, Areopagus reduced to a court of justice (463–461)	
		Decemviri at Rome (451–450). Laws of the Twelve Tables.
Building of Parthenon (447–433) Protágoras (c. 485–411) Heródotus (c. 484–429)		
		Nehemiah builds walls of Jerusalem (445)
Socrates (469–399)	Peloponnesian War between Athens and Sparta (431–404) Plague at Athens (430) Pericles d. (429)	

	Tragedy	*Comedy*

Tragedy	Comedy
Euripides, *Hecuba* (c. 424) Euripides, *Suppliants* (c. 422)	Aristophanes, *Acharnians* (425), *Knights* (424), *Clouds* (423), *Wasps* (422), *Peace* (421) Eupŏlis (c. 445–10)
Euripides, *Trojan Women* (415)	
Euripides, *Electra* (c. 413)	Aristophanes, *Birds* (414)
Euripides, *Helen* (412) Sophocles appointed *Pro-boulos* (412)	
	Lysistrata (411) *Thesmophoriaʒūsae* (411)
Sophocles, *Philoctētes* (409) Euripides, *Orestes* (408) Euripides, *Bacchae* (c. 407) Euripides d. (c. 406) Sophocles d. (c. 406)	
	Frogs (405)
Sophocles, *Oedipus at Colōnus* produced (c. 401)	

Tragedy	Comedy
	Ecclesiaʒūsae (c. 392 or 389?) *Plutus* (388)

Thought, Literature, and Art	Greek History	Events elsewhere
Democritus (*c.* 460–370)		
Thucydides (*c.* 455–400)		
	Cleon killed at Amphípolis (422)	
	Peace of Nícias between Athens and Sparta (421)	
	Athens conquers Mēlos (416)	
	Athenian expedition against Syracuse (415)	
	Athenian disaster at Syracuse (413)	
Tīmotheus, musical innovator (*c.* 450–*c.* 360)		
	Athens surrenders to Sparta (404)	
	Thrasybūlus restores democracy at Athens (403)	
	Socrates executed (399)	Rome takes Veii (396)
		Rome taken by the Gauls (390)
Plato (*c.* 429–347)		
Praxíteles (fl. *c.* 360)	Philip king of Macedon (359–336)	
Demosthenes (384–322)		
Aristotle (384–322)		

B.C.	*Tragedy*	*Comedy*
350		

Philēmon (*c.* 361–260)
Menander (342–291), first pro-
    duction (321)

Menander, *Rape of the Locks*
    (*c.* 313)

Thought, Literature, and Art	Greek History	Events elsewhere
		First war of Rome with Samnites (343–341)
	Philip defeats Athens and Thebes at Chaeronēa (338)	
	Alexander king of Macedon (336–323)	
Lysippus (fl. c. 330)	Alexander invades Persia (334)	Second Samnite War (327–304)
	Alexander d. (323)	
	Antípater of Macedon defeats the Greeks at Crannon (322)	
Epicurus (342–271)	Demetrius Poliorcētes adulated with divine honours at Athens and lodged in the Parthenon (307–304)	

PART ONE

GREEK TRAGEDY

INTRODUCTION[1]

Som time let Gorgeous Tragedy
In Scepter'd Pall com sweeping by,
Presenting Thebs, or Pelops line,
Or the tale of Troy divine.

Milton.

THE SETTING

In its staging the fifth-century Attic theatre was extremely simple: but its
setting was of a magnificence unsurpassed.

Tiers of wooden benches; a round dancing-floor, some sixty feet across,
backed by a wooden stage-building—that was all. Yet above towered the
wall of the immemorial Acropolis, over which, in place of the older temple of
Athena burnt by the Persians, from 447 B.C. there began to climb, white
against the blue Mediterranean sky, the columns of the Parthenon; and
the Athenian who looked from that Acropolis, as the old Aegeus had once
stood to watch for the sail of his son Theseus returning from the perils of
the Cretan Labyrinth, saw around him one of the great landscapes of the
earth. To north-east, behind Lycabettus, the graceful triangle of Mount
Pentélicus hid the battle-field of Marathon; to northward, beyond the
Colōnus of Sophocles, the sullen ridge of Mount Parnes walled Attica
from the tragic Thebes of Oedipus and Antigone; to westward lay the
sea-girt Salamis of Ajax and Xerxes, the mountains of the hated Mégara,
and the distant citadel of that Corinth where Mēdēa slew her children;
south-east rose the peak of Aegīna, ancient kingdom of Achilles' grandsire
Aeăcus, flanked fifty miles away, past sacred Epidaurus, by the crest of Mount
Arachnaeon, whose signal-beacon once blazed the fall of Troy to the
dwellers in the Argive Plain beyond; and finally, southernmost of all,
there jutted out that rugged promontory of Troezēn where Phaedra had
loved Hippolytus in vain. On every side of an ancient Athenian lay these
scenes of a legendary past; and, also, the challenge of a threatening future.
He lived dangerously—between memory and menace. For him the 'old
unhappy things' were not far off: the battles of 'long ago' might return
to-morrow. The hill-tops of his enemies looked in upon his very market-
place—as if in sight of central London loomed the frontiers of Germany
and of Russia. Aeschylus, ten years after fighting at Marathon, of which

[1] For a brief general introduction to the land and literature of Greece, see my *Greek
Poetry for Everyman*, pp. xxv–xxx.

he seems to have been prouder (as Scott would have been) than of writing eighty plays, saw the Acropolis itself taken and its temples laid in ashes. In the year of his *Oresteia*, 458, an inscription commemorates the dead of one Attic tribe (containing perhaps three thousand citizens) fallen within twelve months on six different fronts, from Aegīna to Egypt. Just as the stage of Athens was lit, not by footlights, but by the morning sun, so tragedy and life there remained vividly and terribly close. It was a vastly smaller world than ours, yet often more filled with a sense of greatness. For the free individual had not yet become a specialized animalcule, lost amid the millions of a giant-state, bustling about the drab termitaries of modern cities on a suicidally overbreeding earth.

All this need not blind us to the shadows in the picture. Fifth-century Athens had its share of evils—its aggressiveness, its demagogy, its slavery. Not long after the climax of the Persian Wars there appear already the first symptoms of decline. Even at its best, I feel, Attic drama was never to regain the supreme heights of Homer, or to rival those of Shakespeare. Like Shakespeare, indeed, it is singularly uneven; at its worst, it too can be 'sad stuff.' Yet here where past and present, Nature and Art, joined hands in a setting of sculptured mountain, limpid air, and resplendent sea; where thought and action moved, for a brief space, so fast and brilliantly together, was surely a fit scene for the birth of western tragedy, with its eternal theme of the magnificence, yet unhappiness, of man.

ORIGINS

This problem fills whole shelves of controversy: here it can only be touched in outline.[1]

The patron-god of Tragedy was Dionysus; its Attic cradle, the village of Icária at the foot of Mount Pentélicus; its parent, the choral lyric of the Dorians (though the individual characters, which emerged from the choral group, spoke the iambics of more individualist Ionia); and, lastly, the plots enacted by these characters came almost wholly from the legends of the Heroic Age.

First, Dionysus. Few races have valued reason so much as the Greeks; but they were too reasonable to ignore the power of the non-rational—too intelligent to become as narrowly intellectual as some minds of the eighteenth-century Enlightenment. For this non-rational side of the human spirit they created an immortal symbol—Dionysus.

He was no 'plumpie Bacchus, with pink eyne,' no mere deity of

---

[1] For fuller accounts see the *Oxford Classical Dictionary* (1949), 'Tragedy'; D. W. Lucas, *The Greek Tragic Poets* (1950); for a detailed discussion of the evidence, A. W. Pickard-Cambridge, *Dithyramb, Tragedy and Comedy* (1927).

wine-bibbers; he was the god of other growths besides the grape. His worshippers adored him as *Dendrites*, 'God of Trees'; *Anthios*, 'Lord of Flowers'; *Eukarpos*, 'Fair of Fruits.' He was associated with generation and the phallus, with bull and goat, with the half-divine, half-bestial wildness of Satyrs and Sileni. Legend linked him not only with birth, but with death also. He was a slain god, torn limb from limb by the Titans (as his worshippers tore their victims—as Lycurgus, Orpheus, and Pentheus were torn), and yet in the end rising again from the tomb. But above all he was the giver of ecstasy.

If the maxims of Apollo were 'Nothing too much' and 'Know thyself,' the worshipper of Dionysus found, on the contrary, like Blake, beauty in exuberance, wisdom in excess; he strove, not to know, but to forget himself. In fine, Dionysus has become a symbol of the recurrent nostalgia of civilized man for the lost, untamed wildness of his childhood and the childhood of the race—of the dreams and fantasies that rise from the more primitive, less conscious levels of the soul. '*Il faut nous abestir pour nous assagir.*' [1]

Names may change; but Dionysus remains still one of the most potent forces in man's life—the god of romantic dreamer and daemonic enthusiast. Pater has pictured his medieval resurgence in *Denys l'Auxerrois*. And never was he more terrible than to-day, in our century of fanaticisms.

In Homer he is barely mentioned. Perhaps this newer divinity of the people was less congenial to that aristocratic world—too alien to the spirit of those great epics, which seem still to breathe the keener air of the North and to be in some ways nearer to the heroic Scandinavia of Edda and Saga than to the emotional Mediterranean. Originally connected with Thrace and with the Phrygians (who had crossed from Thrace to Asia Minor), Dionysus seems to have reached Greece, especially Boeotia and Attica, both by land from the northward and by sea across the Aegean. The tales of ancient kings who perished, like Lycurgus and Pentheus, in resisting his fanatical worship may contain a core of truth. On the other hand, some popular, anti-aristocratic despots of the historic period thought it good policy to do him honour. Paradoxically enough, those who would understand this God of Unreason from whom the earliest Greek tragedy was supposed to have sprung, will get their most vivid picture of him from almost the latest of our extant tragedies—*The Bacchae* of the rationalist Euripides.

Next, the choric origins. Tragedy grew from some type of choral lyric—according to Aristotle (though some modern scholars dissent), from the dithyramb. This form, in its beginnings specially associated with Dionysus, is first mentioned by Archílochus of Paros (*c.* 700–650 B.C.). In two vigorous trochaic tetrameters (the quantitative equivalent of the metre of *Locksley Hall*, and used for dialogue by early Greek tragedy, till almost wholly replaced by the six-foot iambic), Archílochus implies that he

[1] Montaigne.

improvised while the Chorus answered him—perhaps with a refrain; and that he improvised better in his cups, inspired by Dionysus himself.

> *I* can lead Lord Dionysus' dithyrambic song divine,
> When my spirit staggers smitten by the lightnings of his wine.

But it was the less individualist Dorians who perfected choral dance and song. About 600, Aríon of Corinth (a real poet, despite his legendary escape from murderous seamen on a dolphin's back) appears to have developed some kind of 'tragic' lyric. Similar performances flourished in neighbouring Sícyon; and its despot Cleisthenes (*c.* 600–570) transferred, we are told, to the popular Dionysus certain 'tragic' choruses in honour of Adrastus, that legendary King of Argos who attacked Thebes in the generation before the Trojan War. How such choruses passed from the Dorian states to Attica remains obscure; but the partly Dorian origin of tragedy is supported by the survival of Dorian dialect-forms in the lyrics of our Attic dramatists.

Even the exact meaning of *tragoidia* ('goat-song,' from *tragos,* 'goat') is disputed. The name may have arisen because the Chorus were originally dressed in goatskins; or dressed like goats; or because a goat was sacrificed; or because a goat was once the prize.

Thirdly, the Attic beginnings. Legend told that Dionysus on reaching Attica chose Icárius of Icária (a village even now called 'Dionysos,' in a valley north-east of Pentélicus) to make known among the people the blessings of wine. So Icárius drove about in his chariot dispensing the new gift; but was slain by certain shepherds who supposed, when they grew drunk, that he had poisoned them. His daughter Erígone, helped by his dog Maera, found his body buried beneath a tree; and hanged herself in despair from a branch. Dionysus set Icárius in Heaven as Arcturus, Erígone as Virgo, Maera as the Dog-star; and punished the Athenians with an epidemic of madness which made their daughters hang themselves, like Erígone, until the shepherds' crime was expiated by a festival in honour of the dead.

In the sixth century Thespis, said to have been likewise a native of Icária, is related to have given drama its real start by inventing an 'answerer' or actor (*hypócrites,* whence our 'hypocrite'—a man who 'acts' in real life) to conduct dialogue with the Chorus-leader. He is also credited with introducing masks, enabling one actor to play many parts (though these *may* have been part of the original dress of the Chorus); and the iambic trimeter for dialogue.

Plutarch tells that, after seeing Thespis act, the old lawgiver Solon (anticipating Plato's distrust of poetic fiction) angrily asked the dramatist if he was not ashamed to tell such lies in public; and predicted that this sort of deception would soon pass from entertainment into real life. Sure enough, by making his politics sufficiently melodramatic (it is easy to think of modern parallels), Peisistrătus soon afterwards became tyrant of Athens. But the new dictator favoured the drama. He founded in honour of Dionysus the festival of the Great or City Dionysia; and under him, about 534, Thespis is said to have won the prize at a tragic contest in Athens itself.

For the rest of the sixth century the development of tragedy remains obscure. The predecessors and older contemporaries of Aeschylus are now little more than names (though it is worth noting that it apparently took him a full sixteen years to win his first victory). Pratinas of Phlius (c. 500) concentrated on burlesque satyric dramas (that is, with satyr-choruses). Phrynichus (fl. c. 510–470) produced a play on the Persian capture of Milētus, which brought on him a fine for waking painful memories; another play, The Phoenician Women, on the defeat of Xerxes, like Aeschylus' later Persians; and another, Alcestis, in which Apollo saved the life of his benefactor, King Admētus, by making the Fates drunk (a state which history might suggest to be not uncommon with them). He is also credited with originating women characters.

Early in the fifth century Aeschylus added a second actor; then Sophocles a third. At three—some may feel, unfortunately—the number stopped; except that a fourth actor seems needed in Oedipus at Colōnus.[1] It also became the rule that each poet should exhibit three tragedies, followed by a satyric drama.

Fourthly, the Heroic Legends. For its plots Greek tragedy, unlike comedy, almost always took stories from the Heroic Age; as medieval drama, similarly born from religious ritual, took its stories from the Bible or the lives of saints.[2] Already the Sicilian Stēsíchorus (c. 610–550) had used the legends of epic—for instance, that of Clytemnestra and Orestes—as themes for his choral lyrics. Now, just as Apollo by a wise and tolerant compromise had once given his stormy younger brother a share in his own Delphic shrine, so it may be said that Dionysus gave Apollo a place in his theatre. For in dramatizing these heroic tales, with their stress on wisdom, measure, and self-control, tragedy made room, beside its Dionysiac passion, for that other, disciplined side of the Greek character that we may call Apolline; and so could rise from a rustic festival to the statuesque dignity and heart-searching thought of Aeschylus.

One may, however, regret that this restriction of subjects became so rigid. The tales of Greek mythology are indeed amazing both in their

[1] A curious, but, I think, tiresome convention has long established itself of prefixing that ugly little word 'the' to titles of all Greek plays. 'The Suppliants' is rational; but why 'the Agamemnon'? One does not usually say 'the Hamlet' (except in such phrases as 'the Hamlet of Shakespeare'). The habit is now strong; but it seems worth an effort to break it.

[2] One may compare the passion of Romantics for the Middle Ages. The Attic dramatists were separated from the Heroic Age by a similar interval of seven or eight centuries. Distance lends dignity; and gives freedom.

quantity and in their quality. Often, one may feel, these original legends
are really finer poetry than their Attic dramatizations. There must have
lived marvellous imaginations before Homer. All the same one could wish
that Greek tragedy had dealt more often with real life, as in *The Persians* or
in that play on Candaules of which a strange fragment has recently come
to light in Egypt.[1] There were tragedies enough in Greek history. As it
is, the plots of the Attic theatre leave a certain sense of monotony and
repetition. One does not altogether envy the Athenian who might in the
course of his life be presented with play after play on Oedipus or Orestes,
Pentheus or Mēdēa.[2] By over-cultivating this limited field Attic tragedy
hastened its own exhaustion.

Last, and very far from least, there had breathed already in Homer, more
fully, I feel, than ever again till Shakespeare, the very spirit of tragedy.
In this sense, whatever he really meant by it, Aeschylus could well call his
own works 'helpings from the great banquets of Homer.' (It is hard to
realize how much drama, both tragic and comic, is already contained in
Greek epic. Half *The Iliad*, it is said, consists of speeches.) Here too
there is already a deep sense of life's tragic irony. Helen in her faithlessness,
Agamemnon in his arrogance, Achilles in his pride, all gain their heart's
desire; and, gaining it, find they have brought ruin, not only on others, but
also on themselves. But there is more than irony. Greater still is Homer's
pity:

> Thinking how Man is most hapless of all that comes to birth
> In the blue deep's abysses, or over endless earth:
> How all that he toils to build, God breaks for evermore,
> As a child its own sand-castle, playing on the waste seashore,
> And for all at last, in silence, there waits the gaping grave—
> For the warrior in the carnage, the sailor in the wave,
> For women's beauty, and lads unwed, and old men's weary years,
> And maidens in their springtide, with young hearts fresh to tears:
> And yet, though as yestereven's clouds all memories melt away,
> How brave, how bright with beauty, Man's brief and bitter day.

Tragedy is largely based, not so much, as Aristotle said, on life's pity and
terror, as on its pity and yet splendour. Here is something for even the
Gods to watch; and when in *The Iliad* (vii, 58–61) Athene and Apollo
perch in the shape of eagles on a great oak-tree amid the Trojan Plain,

---

[1] See p. 350.
[2] The names are known of 141 tragic poets, and of 387 tragedies. These include 12
on Oedipus; 7 on Mēdēa, 7 on Tēlephus, and 7 on Philoctētes; 6 on Alcmaeon and 6 on
Thyestes (W. Schmid and O. Stählin, *Geschichte der Griechischen Literatur*, i, ii, 87).
French classical tragedy, however, was similarly persistent. In two hundred years,
from the middle of the sixteenth century onwards, it produced a dozen plays on the
Labdacidae and over 20 on the Atreidae. '*Il semble en vérité*,' says Brunetière, '*qu'on
éprouvait tous les dix ans le besoin de voir Clytemnestre assassiner Agamemnon.*'

'joying in the spectacle of man,' we may see there already a foreshadowing of the tragic audience. For though Homer, curiously enough, sometimes sees his gods as comic, he makes his gods see men, not as jests, but as figures of tragedy.

DRAMATIC FESTIVALS

The two main dramatic festivals were the Lēnaea (Feast of the Wine-press) in January, when the vintage was finally complete; and the Great or City Dionysia at the end of March, when life was reviving with the spring. But the Lēnaea was devoted mainly to comedy (though tragedies also were performed then from about 432 B.C.): the main tragic festival was the City Dionysia. There were also Rural Dionysia, with dramatic perform-ances, in the townships of Attica.

At the City Dionysia the proceedings were probably as follows. Some days before the festival there was a preliminary procession of the choruses and actors of the three competing poets. (It was on this occasion, in 406, that Sophocles is said to have brought on his Chorus in mourning for the death of his rival Euripides.) A herald then announced the poets' names and the titles of their plays.

Probably on this same day the image of Dionysus was also taken in procession from his temple beside the theatre to a point near the Academy on the road from Eleuthĕrae, by which he had once reached Athens from the north; and brought back by torch-light amid carnival revelry to the theatre itself, where his priest would occupy the central seat of honour during the performances.

On the first day of the festival proper there were dithyrambic con-tests between choruses each fifty strong—five of men, five of boys.

On the next three days a tragic tetralogy [1] was performed each morning; and during the Peloponnesian War a comedy, apparently, each afternoon.[2]

It has been calculated that this festival might employ over seven hundred singers (if no one sang in more than one chorus)—a wealth of amateur musical activity more easily pictured by a Welsh than an English mind. Anyone acquainted with amateur actors (even though the ordinary citizen performed only in choruses) will realize what an intensely critical audience the Athenians must have made.

Poets wishing to compete at the Great Dionysia applied to a magistrate, the *archon eponymos,* who assigned choruses to a selected three—a heavy responsibility. We hear of a chorus being granted to a mediocrity,

[1] A 'tetralogy' ('group of four pieces') consisted of three tragedies (a 'trilogy') followed by a satyric drama; compare the Elizabethan habit of following a tragedy with a jig.
[2] But see p. 366; and, for the latest views on the subject, A. W. Pickard-Cambridge, *Dramatic Festivals of Athens* (1953), ch. ii.

Gnesippus, in preference to Sophocles; but it seems strange that we do not
meet more cases of such official blunders; and that even the unpopular
Euripides was granted a chorus so often.   The main expense of producing
each play was imposed, as a sort of surtax, on some rich citizen—the
chorēgos.[1]   In earlier times, though not always later, the dramatist was his
own producer.   The three prizes (in money, with an ivy-wreath in addition
for the winning poet) were awarded by taking at random five of the verdicts
given by ten judges, themselves chosen by lot from a selected list.   A
curious system, but the festival was religious—perhaps it behoved the gods
to influence the lots; certainly these helped to exclude the undue influence
of men.

THEATRE AND PRODUCTION [2]

The main thing about stage conventions is that they should be fairly
simple; flexible; and quickly forgotten.   For that they should be forgotten
is vital.   Nor is this usually hard.   Neo-classic critics used to argue, in
support of the Unities, that no one can imagine sitting for years in the
theatre, or being transported leagues while he sits there.   In fact, with a
little habituation, the dullest audience finds no difficulty.   A child picks
it up at once.   Similarly we gaze without a qualm into rooms whose
fourth wall has been neatly removed, as if by a bomb.   Silent films could
once seem quite 'natural': now that we are used to sound films, they become
astonishingly grotesque.   The greatest difficulty in accepting artistic conventions seems to arise when they clash with other conventions previously
acquired.

In drama, the words and the actors who speak them are the essentials;
whatever diverts attention from these is self-defeating—whether it be too
elaborate and expensive scenery, mistaken efforts at excessive realism, or
eccentric innovations.   Antony and Cleopatra with live camels—Antony
and Cleopatra modernly attired in brass hat and high heels—Antony and
Cleopatra mouthing some medley of dialects supposed to be Elizabethan
English—all alike are distracting, disturbing, and tiresome.

The conventions of the Greek stage were simple; and of innovation it
grew shy to excess.   Athens did not even build a stone-seated theatre till
about 330, when her greatness was past and over Greece lay the shadow of
Macedon.

The audience was vast (say fourteen thousand); it seems to have been
lively, noisy, emotional, and demonstrative.   They ate, they applauded,

[1] Not to be confused, as in a recent translation of Sophocles, with the *Chorus-leader*
(*koryphaios*).
[2] For fuller details see R. C. Flickinger, *The Greek Theater*, 4th ed. (1936); A. W.
Pickard-Cambridge, *The Theatre of Dionysus at Athens* (1946), *Dramatic Festivals of
Athens* (1953).

they hissed, they kicked their wooden seats in disgust. It appears that women were admitted to tragedy, and probably even to comedy. From the later fifth century the poor had their admission paid for by the state. Therefore the Attic dramatists, like the Elizabethans, had a public of all classes, not of one; intelligent, but not composed of 'intellectuals'; democratic, not precious. One can understand that it should have been impressed and awed by Aeschylus; amused (rather too easily) by Aristophanes; suspicious of Euripides. That it should have made a favourite of Sophocles remains remarkable. Yet one great excellence of the Greek mind was its power to combine simplicity and subtlety; just as the lines of Greek temples are made to look perfectly straight by being, in reality, delicately curved.

For most of this large audience the actors must have been physically remote. That sense of remoteness may have been heightened, in tragedy at least, by the masked, statuesque figures of the actors themselves (though the prodigiously thick-soled buskins once attributed to them seem fabulous for our period). The acting must have depended, not, like Garrick's, on vividness and variety of facial expression, but on voice, gesture, and grouping. And as, with not more than three actors (apart from supers), the same *man*, in the same play, might have to double parts as astonishingly diverse as Ismēne and Teiresias, Alcestis or Dejaneira and Hēracles, Phaedra and Theseus, one must suppose a good deal of versatility. At first the dramatists themselves acted, like Shakespeare; but Sophocles found his voice too weak; and gradually acting became professionalized—continuing, as in our eighteenth century, to gain importance even after drama had declined.

Since, at moments, actors and Chorus could mingle freely, it seems impossible that there was a stage of any height between the circular orchēstra or dancing-floor in front and the wooden background behind. This last, probably evolved from the original tiring-house, might represent a palace, temple, or other building (or, in comedy, several two-storeyed houses); but it could easily be disguised as a natural feature, like Prometheus' rock, or the cave of Philoctētes. Some simple kind of scene-painting began with Sophocles. But changes of scene[1] were rare, since the continuous presence of the Chorus automatically imposed a broad observance of the

---

[1] Change of place from Delphi to Athens in *The Eumenides*; from hut to seashore in *Ajax*. A choric ode, like the fall of a modern curtain, could cover a lapse of time, *e.g.* the voyage from Troy to Argos in *Agamemnon*. Time, indeed, was treated with unusual freedom in the lost *Sthéneboea* of Euripides. This began at Tiryns where Sthéneboea, finding her advances rejected by Bellérophon, accused the man she loved (like Potiphar's wife, and Phaedra) to her husband, King Proetus. A long interval elapsed while Bellérophon was sent by the king to Caria, where he killed the Chimaera. He returned on the winged horse Pegasus; and, when Sthéneboea again wooed him, flew off with her on Pegasus' back and ungallantly jettisoned her in the sea. This must have occupied a second interval; after which her body was found, and Bellérophon justified himself to the widowed Proetus.

Unities of Space and Time.   (Here comedy, being more fantastic, remained more free.)

Stage-properties were few—an occasional altar (besides the permanent one in mid orchēstra), or a tomb, or images of gods.   Machinery, too, was simple—devices for imitating thunder and lightning; for lifting celestial persons from Heaven and back; for revealing the interior of the stage-building, as after Agamemnon's murder—apparently by the primitive method of pushing forth, or revolving, a platform on wheels.

Music was also unelaborate—a single flute-player to accompany the Chorus; though towards the close of the century more complicated solo-singing was developed by Euripides (and duly mocked by Aristophanes). On the other hand there could be large-scale spectacular effects, with stage crowds and chariots; particularly in Aeschylus.

Thus both Greek and Elizabethan stages were admirably simple and untrammelled.   Both the Theatre of Dionysus and the Globe breathed the open air; acted even nocturnal scenes in sunlight; and in general depended less on stage-carpenters than on the imaginative powers of their audiences. The Elizabethan apron is not wholly unlike the Greek orchēstra; but the Elizabethan inner stage with its curtains gave great advantages, both for showing interiors and for that rapid change of scenes now made possible by medieval tradition and by the absence of a chorus.   The Elizabethan theatre gained too in freedom, by being a private enterprise working all the year round; not part of a religious ritual and a fixed state-festival.   The result was something cruder, but warmer; less statuesque, but more coloured; less artistic, but more lively and multitudinous, than the drama of Athens.

Yet it must be owned that some conventions of the Greek theatre seem far from happy.   Thus it is a rule that acts of violence must take place 'off.'   This avoids Elizabethan horrors like men being flayed alive with false skins, or Gloucester's eyes slithering about the boards.   But, carried to rigid excess, it leads to a certain artificiality; and to a plethora of Messengers' Speeches.   There remains some force in the jest of the French critic Ogier (1628) that streams of messengers are more suited to a good inn than to a good tragedy.   It would seem wiser to avoid atrocious plots altogether than to conduct them partly *in camera*.

Nor can I admire that far odder Greek convention of *stichomythia* (line-for-line dialogue), which can leave a couple of characters bandying with deadly iteration the most anaemic repartees, sometimes for pages together. Unfortunate, too, is a persistent fondness, especially (but not only) in Euripides, for making characters plead their cases in set speeches, with all the quibbling sophistry of opposing counsel in a law-court.[1]   No doubt

---

[1] Even the demagogue Cleon is made by Thucydides to reproach the Athenian assembly with its unseasonable love of verbal virtuosity: 'You are simply carried away by the pleasures of the ear, and behave more like an audience sitting at a display of

this was largely due to that Athenian mania for engaging in lawsuits, or sitting on juries, at which Aristophanes laughs in *The Wasps*. But the less litigious modern often feels that such passages degrade tragic poetry into the dreariest of forensic prose. Apollo becomes Buzfuz.

But of all Greek tragic conventions perhaps the greatest difficulties to the modern mind are caused by the Chorus. It is hard, indeed, to judge it fairly, since of its dancing and singing we have only the vaguest notion. Nothing is more distressing and depressing in modern revivals than the spectacle of a dozen old gentlemen or young ladies in white sheets mopping and mowing about the stage. (One reason why one may prefer Greek tragedy in the study rather than in the theatre.) Yet if the ancient Chorus was anything like the dancing of a group of Samian girls I once watched on that island, the whole effect must have been far more restrained, stately, and graceful—and quite unlike the affected friskings and writhings sometimes seen in modern ballet. However, of all this nothing is left us now but, in effect, the *libretto*. And when one considers the literary worth of most modern *libretti*, the marvel is, not that Greek choric odes are often feeble, but that they are sometimes magnificent in their power of transporting the hearer far into the past or the future, to the ends of the earth or into the other world of universal ideas.

From the Chorus, tragedy itself had arisen; its best lyrics remain some of the finest things in Attic poetry; but, as the great century goes on, its share in the plays tends to dwindle in quantity and, after Aeschylus, often in quality also. In *Prometheus, Agamemnon,* and *The Eumenides* the Chorus is a living element; in *The Bacchae* it makes a last, vivid recovery; but on the whole this standing stage-army becomes a growing encumbrance. Clearly Euripides at times found it so; but it was too established an institution to be easily got rid of. And unfortunately this lyric, operatic element lent itself to some of the worst weaknesses of Attic tragedy—those orgies of lamentation, those ecstasies of self-pity, those interminable caterwaulings, conjugating the verb 'to be wretched' in every person, tense, and mood, which make some passages in Greek drama tediously contemptible beside the nobler restraint of Homeric epic or Icelandic saga. At crises the behaviour of the Chorus too often suggests a flock of flabbergasted, but pompous sheep. Its style, at uninspired moments, is apt to luxuriate in

---

sophists than citizens met to debate their country's policy' (iii, 38). And as they loved legal eloquence in the theatre, so they loved theatrical eloquence in the law-court. Aristophanes makes his old juryman boast:

> And if into court Oeagrus is brought, we do not set him free
> Until he has played his best tirade from the part of Niobe.

(Wasps, 579-80.)

turgid verbiage and preciosity.[1]   And its thought can descend to such
idiotic banalities and shattering platitudes as would bring hoots from an
intelligent nursery; until, indeed, one is reminded of dear Goldsmith's
summary of some of the wisdom in eighteenth-century tragedy: 'that we
should not resist Heaven's will, for in resisting Heaven's will, Heaven's
will is resisted.'

Housman's parody, *Fragment of a Greek Tragedy*, is generally taken as
mere fun; but it is also acute criticism; and it illustrates some of these foibles
so amusingly that part of it may be quoted here.

> *Chorus.* Go, chase into the house a lucky foot.
>   And, O my son, be, on the one hand, good,
>   And do not, on the other hand, be bad;
>   For that is very much the safest plan.
> *Alcmaèon.* I go into the house with heels and speed.

> *Chorus*

> STROPHE

> In speculation
> I would not willingly acquire a name
>   For ill-digested thought;
>   But after pondering much
> To this conclusion I at last have come:
>   Life is uncertain.
>   This truth I have written deep
>   In my reflective midriff
>   On tablets not of wax,
> Nor with a pen did I inscribe it there,
> For many reasons: Life, I say, is not
>   A stranger to uncertainty.
> Not from the flight of omen-yelling fowls
>   This fact did I discover,
> Nor did the Delphine tripod bark it out,
>   Nor yet Dodona.
> Its native ingenuity sufficed
>   My self-taught diaphragm.

---

[1] *E.g.* (in a recent literal version), *Agamemnon*, 995–7: 'Man's inward parts do not
vainly bode—the heart, in eddies that bring fulfilment, whirling against the mind which
is conscious of just retribution.'

The verbose laments which often mar Greek tragedy present a curious contrast to
that finer reticence with which certain characters like Prometheus or Jocasta, Dejaneira
or Eurydice, meet crises of their fate.

Finally, by its mere presence the Chorus, less and less able to act effectively itself, severely cramped all dramatic action. This point has never been better put, if we allow for humorous exaggeration, than in a letter of 1751 [1] from Gray, who certainly did not lack admiration for the ancients, to his familiar goose, Mason, who was trying to revive the classical Chorus in a play of his own. 'A greater liberty in the choice of the fable, and the conduct of it, was the necessary consequence of retrenching the Chorus. Love, and tenderness delight in privacy. The soft effusions of the soul, Mr Mason, will not bear the presence of a gaping, singing, dancing, moralizing, uninteresting crowd. And not love alone, but every passion is checked and cooled by this fiddling crew. How could Macbeth and his wife have laid the design for Duncan's murder? What could they have said to each other in the Hall at midnight, not only if a chorus, but if a single mouse had been stirring there? Could Hamlet have met the Ghost, or taken his mother to task in *their* company? If Othello had said a harsh word to his wife before *them*, would they not have danced to the window, and called the watch? The ancients were perpetually confined and hampered by the necessity of using the Chorus, and, if they have done wonders notwithstanding this clog, sure I am they would have performed still greater wonders without it.'

However, it may well be answered that it is idle wishing the Parthenon to have all the beauties of Lincoln Minster, or Lincoln Minster those of the Parthenon. Let us be thankful for both.

[1] *Correspondence*, ed. P. Toynbee and L. Whibley (1935), i, 358.

AESCHYLUS

(c. 525–c. 456 B.C.)

Who first raised up in grandeur, battlemented strong,
The deep-toned voice of Tragedy, the beetling heights of Song.

Antipater of Thessalonica (time of Augustus).

AESCHYLUS was born at Eleusis about 525, fought at Marathon (490) and Salamis (480), visited the court of Hiero at Syracuse about 470 and again in 458, and died at Gela in Sicily about 456.[1]

Of his eighty or ninety plays, seven remain—*The Suppliants, The Persians* (472), *The Seven against Thebes* (467), *Prometheus Bound,* and the *Oresteia* trilogy (458), a masterpiece written at nearly seventy.

Artistic development has a familiar, and natural, tendency to pass from a period of grandeur and energy, through a prime of balanced beauty, to a closing phase of cleverness or prettiness, realism or romance. Examples can be seen in such successions as Aeschylus, Sophocles, Euripides—Marlowe, Shakespeare, Beaumont and Fletcher—Corneille, Racine, Voltaire—Michael Angelo, Raphael, Correggio. This evolution is marked by a steady increase both in critical self-consciousness and in the need for novelty. During the earliest stage the conscious part of the mind is still upborne by a vigorous inspiration drawing freely on preconscious levels; the middle period attains a harmonious balance between conscious and less conscious thought; in decadence the reasoning intellect asserts itself too arrogantly or else, by reaction, abandons itself too blindly.

Such generalizations, however, over-simplify. It is amazing how vast an artistic development is covered by the career of Aeschylus alone. He found drama an archaic, still half-rustic ritual: he left it high tragedy. His own early work seems curiously primitive; and had we lost the masterpieces of his old age, *Prometheus* and *Oresteia,* his fame would be of quite a different order. As it is, many will find the climax of the Greek theatre, not in Sophocles, but in these two late works of Aeschylus. So some of the Romantics felt. Indeed the rise of Romanticism brought Aeschylus an audience in some ways more sympathetic than he had ever found before, even in Antiquity. For in his passionate search for righteousness he has touches of a Hebrew prophet; his Prometheus is akin to Milton's

---

[1] For his epitaph on himself see p. 111. Its authenticity has been questioned; but I do not find it easy to imagine any man but the austere poet himself either wishing, or daring, to compose an epitaph which remembers only Marathon, and says not a word to suggest that he ever composed a line. Contrast the sepulchral epigrams on Aeschylus, Sophocles, and Euripides in the *Palatine Anthology,* vii, 20–2, 36–7, 39, 40, 43–51, 411.

Satan, his Clytemnestra to Lady Macbeth; and his audacities seem less wild to us than to many of his countrymen. *They* repeated stories that he composed when drunk—or that Dionysus had appeared to the boy Aeschylus while he watched a vineyard by night. They spoke of him in not wholly approving astonishment, as 'grandiloquent to a fault,' 'a faggoter of high astounding terms,' with 'bright-helmeted clashes of high-plumed words.'[1] Similarly for the neo-classic Fontenelle he becomes '*une manière de fou, qui avait l'imagination très vive et pas trop réglée*'; for Dryden, he 'tears it upon the tripos.' But to-day we welcome his titanic qualities. And we have learned that Titans are rare.

But if his imagination has seemed at times undisciplined and uncontrolled, his character was not. 'See the difference training makes!' was his reported comment to Ion of Chios, as they watched contending boxers at the Isthmian Games. 'The man who took the blow is silent; it is the spectators that cry out.' The iron silences of his own characters[2] became famous. Aristophanes, again, can make him claim that his plays never stooped to the licence of portraying a woman in love. He remained, for fifth-century Athenians, the stern old soldier of Marathon; the somewhat aloof aristocrat, who was also a moderate democrat, hating alike tyranny and anarchy; the type of an Athens as yet untouched by decadence.

As a thinker he has perhaps been treated over-seriously by adoring professors. It seems to me a mistake to talk as if his wrestlings with the problem of evil were an advance on the calm acceptance of Homer. Homer saw that the rash and wicked often suffer; but often, also, the wise and good —the prudent Odysseus like the headstrong Achilles, the blameless Andrómache far more than the guilty Helen. In the House of Zeus, he says, there stand two jars, one of good things, one of evil; and no man can hope to taste of the good things only. Nobility must often be its own, and only, reward. Beyond that, questioning grows vain.

But Aeschylus could not so accept. Like the prophets of Israel, he agonized to find justice. If Homer has often the mysterious serenity of a sunset sea, Aeschylus recalls rather the tempestuous tossings of a mountain forest. He dislikes the idea that a man may suffer merely because the Gods are jealous of his prosperity; or merely because his fathers sinned.[3] True, Oedipus was doomed before birth by his father's folly. Yet Aeschylus gropes towards a juster compromise. A man's sin, he seems to suggest, can bring a curse, an Erinys, upon his house; but the Erinys cannot strike

[1] Cf. p. 414.
[2] *E.g.* Atossa, Prometheus, Clytemnestra, Niobe, Achilles.
[3] Cf. Ezekiel a hundred years before (early sixth century): 'What mean ye, that ye use this proverb concerning the land of Israel, saying: The fathers have eaten sour grapes, and the children's teeth are set on edge? Behold, all souls are mine; as the soul of the father, so also the soul of the son is mine; the soul that sinneth, it shall die.' (xviii, 2, 4.)

his posterity until that posterity, in its turn, has also sinned.   Yet even if
this were true, it would still remain unjust.   Aeschylus has not wholly
escaped here from older thought, which did not distinguish the responsibility of an individual from the responsibility of his group.   Why, because
of some ancestral sin, should a man be dogged by a sort of spectral Argus,
with a hundred eyes watchful to visit new transgression?   Real justice
should be the same for all.

Homer was wiser than this; as Job was wiser than that singularly un-
observant Psalmist who had never seen the righteous forsaken, or his
seed begging bread.   Either, as Aeschylus hoped, the universe is
governed by a divine wisdom, or it is not; if it *is* so governed, the problem
of evil remains a mystery; if it is not so governed, there is no problem
of evil.

More striking is the idea in *Prometheus* that God Himself can learn and
progress.   Here is foreshadowed a kind of evolution of which some moderns
have also dreamed—as Bernard Shaw imagined the Life-force struggling to
become more and more like Bernard Shaw.   And yet, in face of the irretrievable agony of all the ages since life began, some will still feel that such
ideas have more power to exasperate than to console.

But, after all, philosophers are not expected to be good dramatists: why
should dramatists be good philosophers?   It seems rash to demand it.
An intelligent playwright, like any intelligent man, must indeed face the
eternal questions; even if his answer be dim, a definite view of life can give
unity and life to his work.   But Aeschylus remains first and foremost a
poet.   It is curious that, though he may never have drawn a woman in
love, his two most moving characters are yet women—Clytemnestra and
Cassandra; and his two most effective choruses feminine also—the Daughters
of Ocean and the Eumenides.   But, as with the works of Milton, so with
his—their most impressive character is perhaps the poet himself.   Aeschylus
abides like a giant Memnon speaking in the dawn of drama.   Take that
four-line fragment of his on Death [1]—from what Greek lips but his could its
sombre dignity have come?   It is hard to imagine it written by Sophocles
or Euripides.   His genius created, as genius can, a lonely world, and a
language, of his own.

It is, as his modesty admitted, a far narrower world than Homer's; which
knows both joy and sorrow, spring and autumn, sunlight and storm, while
over that of Aeschylus seems to brood continually the gloom of towering
thunderclouds.   One may doubt whether his lost satyric dramas, though
once famous, would have much changed this dominant impression.   But
there are moments in his tragedies, like mountain gorges lit by lightning,
whose grandeur haunts posterity more than anything his two younger
rivals produced.   He seems nearer than they to wild nature—to bird and

[1] p. 110.

beast, to hill and sea.[1]   He looms up in his remoteness, to quote a typical phrase from his own *Suppliants* (794–6), like 'a sheer and goat-untrodden, far-withdrawn and lonely-hearted, eagle-haunted, beetling crag.'[2]   And if at times its peak is lost in clouds, that darkness serves only to deepen its grandeur and its mystery.

THE SUPPLIANTS[3]

And strewed one marriage-bed with tears and fire
For extreme loathing and supreme desire.

Swinburne.

Io, princess of Argos, beloved of Zeus (p. 48), wandered away to Egypt and there bore him Épaphus.   Two great-grandsons of Épaphus, named Dánaüs and Aegyptus, had respectively fifty daughters and fifty sons.   The sons wished to wed their cousins.   This mass-espousal might seem a providential arrangement for a father blessed with fifty daughters; but both Dánaüs and his daughters objected.   The idea that they thought marriage with cousins incestuous, seems baseless—after all, in historic Egypt a man could marry his sister; and even in historic Athens his half-sister on the father's side.   It appears rather that the Danaïds disliked wedding any kinsmen, because their own rights might then be sacrificed to family interest; still more, disliked their wooers as brutal; and in general, like Hippolytus, felt an excessive dislike for marriage itself.   Fleeing with their father, they landed in their ancestral Argos.

Here the play begins.   The fugitives beg protection, both as kindred and as suppliants, from Pelasgus, the old King of Argos; and, when he hesitates to risk a war for their benefit, threaten to pollute the land by hanging themselves from the images of the gods at whose altars they have taken refuge.   The embarrassed, but highly constitutional monarch finally persuades his Argive subjects to vote asylum for these violent young women.   But now enters the Egyptian herald of the pursuing cousins, with his retinue of black slaves, and tries to kidnap the Danaïds.   He is foiled,

[1] He feels for the birds frozen dead in the Trojan winter, or eagles robbed of their young; for the starving eaglet or the hound dreaming in his sleep; for the herds bellowing on the uplands of Ida.   His landscapes are not always vast like the Scythian solitudes of Prometheus or the beacon-lit darkness of the Aegean; he can flash on the mind the quiet vision of a reedy stream by a single epithet—'many-distaffed rivers.'
[2] Cf. the poet's words on popular belief (spoken through his Chorus in *Agamemnon*, 757): 'But I, *though alone*, think not with these.'
[3] This has long been thought the earliest, as clearly the most primitive, of the extant plays.   A puzzling papyrus-fragment recently published (*Oxyrhyncus Papyri*, Part xx (1952), pp. 30–1) might seem to suggest a date after 470; and this evidence is not easy to get round.

however, by the return of the Argive king; and the refugees take their way, chanting, to the hospitable city.

A curious and primitive story. But the play should be imagined rather as a spectacular opera and ballet. The Chorus of heroines was possibly fifty strong; in later works of Aeschylus it was to be twelve, before settling down, with Sophocles, to the number normal in fifth-century tragedy—fifteen. The fifty heroines may have had fifty handmaids; then there was the Argive king with his bodyguard, the Egyptian herald with his negroes —perhaps fifty of each. But spectacle, ballet, and music are lost to us; there remains the beauty of some lyrics, already full of the religious musings of Aeschylus, and recalling at times the vague archaic charm of those statues of Athenian girls found on the Acropolis, from the period before the Persian War. 'Zeus' is the very first word of the play; again and again the Chorus appeal to him, by his love for their ancestress Io, to save them from the brutality of man.

> God grant indeed that our prayers avail!
> The paths of His purpose are dim to trail;
>   Yet even through darkest night,
> With a doom as dark, it blazes forth
>   In all men's sight.
>
> Once Zeus hath nodded, His will stands fast—
> Stout wrestler never backward cast!
>   Far off beyond Man's gaze,
> Through brake and briar of forest gloom,
>   He winds His ways.
>
> Down from their hopes high-towering
>   He casts men in His might:
> No violence overpowering
>   He brings; no sword to smite.
> God striveth not, nor straineth;
>   His thought performs His will
> Straightway, while quiet He reigneth
>   In His holy Heaven still.
>
>   (86–103.)
>
> In might Almightiest,
>   O King of Kings, give ear!
> Most blest, O happy Zeus, among the Blest,
>   Protect Thy children here,
> With Thy just wrath, from men's demented pride—
> Ah, drown them in yon darkening purple tide,
>   As their curst black hull draws near!

Take Thou the woman's part!
    Recall our storied line—
How *we* too sprang from her that won Thy heart;
    Renew Thy grace divine!
On Io once (remember!) lay Thy hand;
Our race once wandered from the Argive land;
    Our blood was born from Thine.

I have turned again to the ancient ways,
    Where once in the flowering meadows fed
Io, beneath her herdsman's gaze—
    Our mother; till in frenzied dread
    Before the gadfly's goad she fled,
      Guided of Fate, through many a race,
    To brave the tide that parts the lands,
    And leave her name where Europe stands
      With Asia face to face.[1]

                  (524–46.)

In this early work drama has hardly learnt as yet to speak in dialogue. The characters still generally address the Chorus, rather than each other. But there comes a foreshadowing of the future stature of Aeschylus in the grim menace of the Egyptian herald, prophesying war:

    The God of War, he judges not *such* suits
    By witnesses!   He endeth not *such* strife
    With fines of silver!   Many a head must first
    Fall; many feet must spurn their last at life.

                  (934–7.)

But perhaps, of the whole play, the image that stands out longest in the memory is that 'lonely-hearted, eagle-haunted crag' (p. 19), from which the Danaïds dream of flinging themselves to escape dishonour, like the women of Suli two thousand years later under Turkish tyranny.

The story was completed in the two following plays of the trilogy, now lost. In *The Egyptians* the victorious sons of Aegyptus apparently forced marriage on their cousins; but on the wedding-night forty-nine of these young women, as they had sworn, cut off their bridegrooms' heads. Only one, Lynceus, was spared by his bride Hypermnestra, who broke her vow, in the famous phrase of Horace (*Odes*, iii, 11):

    Splendid in her *un*truth, a maiden noble
    Till the world's ending.

      [1] *I.e.* at the 'Bosporus'—'Ox-ford.'

Finally, in the third play of the trilogy, *The Danaïds*, this one loyal wife seems to have been brought to trial for her breach of faith, before her father and sisters; and, like Athena in *The Eumenides*, so here Aphrodite, Goddess of Love, intervened for acquittal. Of the goddess's speech on love's universality a fragment still remains.

> Love seizes the holy Heaven to pierce the Earth,
> Love makes Earth yearn for wedlock.
> So falls the rain. And by that Heavenly love
> Earth grows a mother, bringing forth for men
> Demeter's sustenance, and grass for flocks,
> While on her trees beneath the quickening showers
> Her fruits grow ripe. Through all *I* play my part.
>
> (Nauck, *Trag. Gr. Fragm.*, p. 16, fr. 44.)

So Life reasserts its ancient law; and Hypermnestra is raised above her sisters as the happy ancestress of Hēracles and that glorious race of the Hēracleidae who were to reign in Argos, Sparta, and Messēne.

THE PERSIANS

(472 B.C.; repeated at Syracuse *c.* 470)

> *A king sate on the rocky brow*
> *Which looks o'er sea-born Salamis;*
> *And ships, by thousands, lay below,*
> *And men in nations—all were his!*
> *He counted them at break of day—*
> *And when the sun set where were they?*

Byron.

The Persians, performed in 472 with the young Pericles as *chorēgos* (some four years after Phrynichus had produced his *Phoenician Women* on the same theme, probably with Themistocles as *chorēgos*), celebrates the crowning mercy of Xerxes' defeat at Salamis. It opens with a splendid energy of marching anapaests, as there enter the Elders of Persia.

> To the marches of Hellas hath passed away
> The might of Persia—her 'Faithful' are we,
> Set to keep ward on her walls well-stored,
> The wealth in each golden treasury.
> Such charge did Dareius' son, our Lord,
> King Xerxes lay
> On our seniority.

(1–7.)

But they meditate anxiously on their far king's fortunes, asking like Sisera's mother: 'Why tarry the wheels of his chariots?' They are followed by Queen Atossa, widow of the great Dareius, who is troubled by dreams and an evil omen. The Elders advise her to pray to her dead husband. Then she questions them about these unknown Greeks.

Queen. Tell me where in earth's wide region, O my friends, is Athens town?
Chorus-leader. Far it lies, towards the sunset, where our Lord the Sun sinks down. . . .
Queen. Who the shepherd of their people? Who the master of their host?
Leader. *They* are called the slaves of *no* man. Of their homage *none* can boast.[1]

(231–2, 241–2.)

One can still feel in imagination a tremor of pride run through the listening theatre.

But now a messenger bursts in, overwhelmed with disaster. The flower of Persia has perished. The only comfort is that Xerxes lives. But his greatness lies shattered on the beaches of Salamis.

Here follows the crowning passage of the play—the account, by an eye-witness of twenty-five centuries ago, of one of the decisive battles in the long struggle between East and West—a fine pendant to the epic prose of Heródotus.

Messenger. Mistress, our whole destruction was begun
  By some ill genius, some avenging spirit.
  There came a Hellene from the fleet of Athens
  With a message for thy son, Xerxes the King:
  'If there shall fall a night of pitchy darkness,
  The Greeks will hold no longer—all the crews
  Will crowd aboard their galleys and, in panic,
  This way and that run scattering to safety.'
  And Xerxes, when he heard it, little guessing
  The guile of Greece, the jealousy of God,
  Made instant proclamation to his captains:
  'Soon as from earth the last flame of the sunset

[1] There is a certain irony in comparing such passages with the statement of one of our leading authorities on Aeschylus, that watching the audience of workers in the Bolshoi Theatre at Moscow he 'realized for the first time the nature of the inspiration behind the *Oresteia.*' Less vivid imaginations may have had some difficulty in picturing the drama of Aeschylus (or Aristophanes) behind Iron Curtains, with Choruses of Secret Police; and may wonder if this red bouquet would much have pleased the old poet who fought oriental despotism at Marathon—or the millions who have enacted in forced-labour camps tragedies bitterer than Hellas ever conceived.

Dies, and the dark takes hold on Heaven's precinct,
Let our main fleet be ranged in triple line
To seal all issues of the sea-beat straits.
Others shall fetch a compass round the isle
Of Ajax.   Then, if the Hellenes find escape
By stealthy flight from the evil end that waits them,
Your heads shall pay for it.'
So he commanded, in his confidence,
With heart purblind to Heaven's purposes.
Then in obedience and discipline,
The crews prepared their meal; and by its thong
Each rower lashed his stout oar to its thole-pin.
But when the sunlight glimmered from the world
And darkness gathered, then on board there marched
The master-oarsmen, the mighty men of war;
And, sailing out to their allotted stations,
Squadron cheered squadron as they stood to sea.
So, through the night, the captains of our fleet
Kept all their galleys cruising to and fro;
Yet, though the slow night waned, the host of Hellas
Made no least move to sail off through the darkness.
But when the white-horsed Dawn lit up the world,
Then from the Greeks rolled out, triumphantly,
A chant of battle, while from the island-crags
Shrill answered Echo.   But our Asiatics
Felt their hearts fail, as all their hopes grew dim;
For not like flight it rang, that solemn paean
The Hellenes raised—rather it was the voice
Of men that rouse in confidence to war.
Then with the sudden pealing of a trumpet
Their line took fire—and instant, at command,
A crash of oars scourged the salt sea to foam
And, at full speed, their whole fleet swept in sight.
Their right wing led, in faultless order—then
All their main line of battle moved to action,
While a great shout came bursting on our ears:
'Charge home, ye sons of Hellas—for the freedom
Of your dear land—for the deliverance
Of wife and child, the graves where sleep your fathers,
The temples where they worshipped.   For to-day
These stand or perish.'   Then our Persian throats
Roared answer; and the waiting-time was done—
Ship after ship with brazen beak rammed home.

Their charge was headed by a ship of Hellas
That sheared the whole poop from a Phoenician;
Then the rest followed, choosing each her target.
At first our countering flood of Persian galleys
Made head against them; but, as our multitude
Of vessels found itself hemmed in and huddled
Thick in the narrows, where none could aid another
(Nay, ship ran foul of ship, with brazen beaks
That left whole oar-banks splintered), all this while
With cunning seamanship the keels of Hellas
Circled and struck.   Soon wrecks, and hulls capsized,
And floating corpses veiled the very sea,
And all its shores and shoals grew heaped with slain.
By now the galleys of the Persian fleet
Sought to row clear, in panic-stricken flight;
But still the Greeks, with splintered shafts of oars
And spars of wreck, kept striking—breaking backs—
As fishers strike at tunnies in their net.
All the sea-spaces rang with shrieks and wailings,
Till the dark brows of Night brought peace at last.
Not though I told thee for ten days together,
Could I recite the sum of our disasters.
But this I tell thee, Lady—never yet
In one day's space have died so many men.

                                                            (353–432.)

After further details of calamity the Elders break into a passionate oriental
lament.

Chorus. Thou hast given Persia's pride to the sword,
    To death the countless hosts of her,
        O Zeus, O Lord!
Yea, Susa and Ecbatana
    Thou hast darkened with lamentation.
Now the soft hands of women tear
Their veils, and the tears of their despair
Over their breasts are poured,
    Mid a people's desolation.
Now Persia's brides, but lately wed,
    Must wail for those that come never again;
Their youth starts up from love's soft bed,
With a sorrow that will not be comforted;
    And I too raise my mourning strain
        For the fallen of our nation.

Lo, now all Asia far and wide,   *strophe* 1.
Desolate, weeps for her sons that died;
  Xerxes led them forth—ah me!
  Xerxes slew them—misery!
Xerxes it was, with heart too blind to guide
  The galleys of the sea.
Wherefore, in older days,
  Did Persia prosper so
  Beneath Dareius' bow,
The prince of Susa's praise?

Footmen and seamen of the King—   *antistrophe* 1.
With painted eye and woven wing,
  The long ships bore them hence—ah me!
  The long ships slew them—misery!—
Ships' deadly beaks, their timbers shattering,
  And Ionia's mastery.
Scarce by a little space
  Even our Lord, 'tis said,
  By fearful tracks hath fled
Across the plains of Thrace. . . .

Now Asia's coasts no more   *str.* 3.
  The Persian power obey;
The tribute forced of yore
  They bring no more to-day;
No more in reverence now
Their heads to earth they bow;
  The Great King wanes away.

No more in each word spoken   *ant.* 3.
  Men guard their tongues.   The dread
Of Persia's yoke is broken,
  Freely men's thoughts are said.
Where, bloodstained, mid the foam,
Stands Ajax' ancient home,
  There Persia's pride lies dead.

(532–67, 584–97.)

The queen now makes her offerings to Dareius, and from his tomb behind the orchēstra the dead monarch rises, like Samuel's wraith at Endor. He hears the ill news; recognizes that the voice of prophecy is fulfilled; predicts new humiliations for the arrogance of his son; then goes his way back to the grave, bidding his old counsellors a strangely Epicurean farewell, as disillusioned as his fellow-countryman, Omar Khayyám, fifteen centuries afterwards:

> I must be gone, back to the nether gloom.
> But you, old men, farewell, and give your souls,
> Though ill the times, to the pleasures of to-day.
> For riches profit nothing to the dead.
>
> (839–42.)

Last enters the discomfited and ragged Xerxes; and the play closes in an alternation of lament between him and the Elders.

A restrained and simple drama, though it celebrates one of the most amazing triumphs ever won by a small nation against terrifying odds. Here is none of the exultation of Drayton's *Agincourt*. Not a Greek appears; not a Greek is even named;[1] though the names of Persians (often, it is said, still recognizably Iranian in form) are recited with as much zest for their thunderous sonority as Marlowe felt for the oriental names in *Tamburlaine*. Remoteness of place and manners gives, as in Racine's *Bajazet*, that dignity of distance elsewhere provided by remoteness in time. But the play's insistent moral is the punishment of pride—the pride that dared bridge the divine Hellespont, and sought to dominate the earth, and laid in ashes the temples of the gods. All this is condemned by Dareius as a departure from the wise tradition of former Persian kings. Actually Cyrus had fallen, if Heródotus is right, in trying to extend his insatiable conquests to the east; Cambyses had died mad, after brutally subjugating Egypt; Dareius himself, apart from his defeat at Marathon, had nearly perished, like others after him, by invading the elusive wastes of Russia. But Aeschylus chose to ignore these grim precedents. (Indeed in knowledge of Persian history he seems strangely vague compared with Heródotus a generation later.) Instead, he preferred the simpler contrast between the wisdom of the Old King and the folly of the Young, which might also warn his own Athens, 'Lest we forget.'

The defeat of the Armada inspired no such poetry in England. The nearest counterpart to *The Persians* is perhaps Hardy's larger picture in *The Dynasts* of that still vaster ruin which visited in its turn the vaster pride of Napoleon.[2]

---

[1] Patin compares the severity of Cato the Elder, whose history left all generals anonymous—though it did give the name of a valiant elephant!

[2] Napoleon may seem remote from Greek tragedy; it is the more interesting to find him reading aloud at St Helena the *Agamemnon* of Aeschylus, 'dont il a fort admiré l'extrême force, jointe à la grande simplicité'; and regretting that he had not had Sophocles' *Oedipus the King* performed, despite Talma's reluctance, in the ancient fashion, with Chorus and all. (Las Cases, *Mémorial de Sainte-Hélène*, iv, 108.)

THE SEVEN AGAINST THEBES
(467 B.C.)

The ancient blinded vengeance and the wrong that amendeth wrong.
William Morris.

Originally this play was preceded by two other tragedies, *Laïus* and *Oedipus*, and followed by a satyric drama, *The Sphinx*; but these three are lost.   The first tragedy told the story of Laïus, King of Thebes,[1] who disregarded the thrice-repeated warning of Delphi not to beget children; and tried vainly, when Oedipus was born, to elude his fate by having the child exposed on Mount Cithaeron.   The next play, *Oedipus*, like the extant *Oedipus* of Sophocles, presumably enacted the discovery of its hero's unintended parricide and incest.   *The Seven* shows the third generation doomed in its turn.   For the blind, deposed Oedipus had rashly cursed his sons Éteocles and Polyneices, as Lear his daughters, for dishonouring him at a feast: 'they should divide their heritage with the sword.'   Éteocles grasped the crown of Thebes; his banished brother Polyneices, marrying the daughter of Adrastus, King of Argos, sinned on *his* side by leading against his country, with the help of his father-in-law, an army containing six other famous champions.   So came 'The Seven' against Thebes.

Our play opens with Éteocles preparing to meet an immediate assault. Imperiously he calms the Chorus of panic-stricken Theban women; then a messenger details one by one which of the seven hostile heroes threatens each of the city's seven gates.   (In the original performance, we are told, as their arrogant menaces were described, a skilled dancer Telestes, one of the Chorus, gave a mimed accompaniment.)   In reply, Éteocles appoints a Theban opponent to meet each Argive.   His own words of modest confidence in each provide, for Greek ears, an edifying contrast to the bluster of the enemy.   Six enemy chiefs have been named, and six Theban opposers; but now at the seventh gate, which Éteocles presumably had always intended for himself, the messenger reveals that the adversary waiting is no other than his hated brother.   In this grim coincidence Éteocles sees suddenly the resistless working of his father's curse.   His long restraint is swept away by a burst of suicidal passion.   And though the Chorus beg him to send some other in his place, the king rushes out with a final cry to fratricide and death.

> Now since God's hand drives headlong to the issue,
> Loathed by Apollo let all Laïus' race
> Drift with the wind to doom down Hades' River! ...

[1] Genealogical table, p. 227.   Laïus had been cursed by Pĕlops, whose son Chrysippus he carried off.

For my dear father's Curse sits, black and hateful,
Beside me now, with dry and tearless eyes,
Whispering: 'Death comes better soon than late.' . . .
For us the Gods henceforward care no more;
Yet still my death can win some grace, some honour.
Why should I fawn, then, longer on my fate?

(689–91, 695–7, 703–5.)

The brothers fall by each other's hands; but at least, for the moment, Thebes is saved. (Though the sons of the Seven Champions were one day to sack it in vengeance for their fathers' fate.) A spurious final scene, influenced by Sophocles' *Antigone*, presents the two sisters, Antigone and Ismēne, disputing whether to obey the public edict that condemns the body of their traitor-brother Polyneices to be left a prey to dog and bird.

In Antiquity the play was praised as 'full of the War-god'; some would have preferred a play fuller of human beings. Vivid as may be its picture of the terrors of a besieged city, amid all the snortings and the trumpets, I wait in vain for a character to rouse my sympathy.[1] Real life, as in *The Persians*, can be more moving than this sort of pugnacious fiction, unless the fiction can include personalities as living as life itself, like Hotspur or Antony. And the workings of an ancestral curse were to find far finer treatment in the *Oresteia*.

True, some modern scholars find Éteocles the finest male character in the ancient theatre, or compare him to Homer's Hector and Achilles. Tastes are subjective. But one wonders if such critics know one end of a human being from another. I own it shocks me to think of comparing this patriotic matamore, who (apart from the fine lines just quoted) might die ten times over without my caring two straws, with the tragic gallantry and gentleness of Homer's Hector, or the burning eloquence and passionate comradeship of Homer's Achilles.

---

[1] There is, however, a vivid touch in the picture of the Seven Champions preparing for the assault:

And round Adrastus' chariot they hung,
For the parents they had left behind at home,
Mementoes of themselves, and wept the while—
And yet no sound of weakness passed their lips.

(49–51.)

PROMETHEUS BOUND

The good want power, but to weep barren tears.
The powerful goodness want: worse need for them.
The wise want love; and those who love want wisdom;
And all best things are thus confused to ill.

Shelley, *Prometheus Unbound.*

This play's date is uncertain. Enough to say that, with the *Oresteia*, it belongs to the close of the poet's career.

In legend before Aeschylus, Prometheus,[1] son of the Titan Iápetus (cf. Japhet), had been a cunning rebel who found ruin, like the Scandinavian Loki, or the Satan of Christian story, by matching his over-cleverness against the Almighty Wisdom. He tried, says Hēsiod, to cheat Zeus over the division of the sacrificial victim between gods and men—but only brought punishment on mankind.

So Zeus ordained us sorrow, and fire He hid from men.
Yet the hero-son of Iápetus stole it again
For mortals' sake, in a fennel-stalk from Zeus the wise;[2]
Then spake the Lord of Thunder, whose wrack benights the skies,
In wrath: 'O soul most subtle, Iápetīonides,
Thou hast stolen fire, and tricked me—thy heart it well may please.
Yet sorely shalt thou repent it! And men unborn! In vain!
Such a curse will I send to requite them—a curse they shall rush to gain,
Embracing in their blindness the thing that is their bane.'

(Hēsiod, *Works and Days*, 47–58; *Greek Poetry for Everyman*, p. 197.)

This curse was Woman. For now, says the misogynist legend, Zeus created Pandora, who released from her fatal jar the afflictions of mankind; and Prometheus was chained, like Loki, for eternity—or, in later versions, till freed by Hēracles. This primitive tale Aeschylus remoulded to his subtler purposes.

Hegel saw tragedy as, in essence, a conflict of discords finally resolved in a higher harmony. For him, both sides are right, yet wrong because not right enough—because one-sided in their rightness. Therefore they suffer, that from their conflicting antithesis may emerge a higher synthesis. With many tragedies this formula fails to work; as specially applied by Hegel to Sophocles' *Antigone* (p. 127), it becomes preposterous; but it does fit parts of Aeschylus, with his effort to justify the ways of God, and to

---

[1] Genealogical table, p. 113.
[2] The story is dramatized by Bridges in *Prometheus the Firegiver*.

justify them by works that sometimes close, like those of Shakespeare's last period, in reconciliation. The strife of Dánaus' daughters with their cousins ends at least in one happy wedlock; the Eumenides are reconciled at last to a new and kindlier role at Athens; but the best example is *Prometheus*, with its theme that even Providence can learn.

Already a later generation had softened the grim old legends of wars in Heaven by telling that Zeus finally forgave the conquered Titans. Now Aeschylus makes the Prometheus story more dramatic by lessening the too unequal odds between God and Rebel. Zeus here becomes neither all-mighty nor all-wise. Like the young Augustus, this young Victor of the Universe is both cruel and violent. (We may compare the contrast between the God of the Old Testament and the God of the· New.) Prometheus, on the other hand, is made a generous saviour of mankind, a seer who can defy Zeus by knowing what Zeus himself does not know—a secret that can cost even Zeus his power. Thus Aeschylus avoids a serious flaw which Milton could not escape; for in *Paradise Lost* the rebellion of Satan against absolute Omnipotence becomes incomprehensible madness— the challenge of a midge to a mammoth. And because in Aeschylus neither antagonist is perfect, Zeus can at last (again like Augustus) mellow into benign wisdom, and Prometheus learn to humble his own too headstrong pride. It will be noted that Pandora has vanished from the story. She was no longer needed. And one may suspect that Aeschylus had little taste for that side of womanhood, though the seductive Helen flits as a fatal symbol through the background of *Agamemnon*; whereas Milton, though his *Samson* recalls *Prometheus*, still kept Dalila.

The sequel, *Prometheus Unbound*, is lost; but its outlines are known. The tortured Titan had been raised again from Hades to a peak of Caucasus, where an eagle devoured his liver. But Zeus, now grown milder, had already pardoned the Titans, some of whom formed the Chorus. Hēracles, thirteenth in direct descent [1] from the Io once persecuted by Zeus, appeared as a deliverer to shoot the eagle. Prometheus, grown at last less wilful, made his peace by revealing to Zeus his great secret—that the sea-nymph Thĕtis, beloved by Zeus, was destined to bear a son mightier than his father; and so, mastering his passion, Zeus wedded her to the mortal Pēleus, to bear him the mightier Achilles. The liberated Prometheus assumed as symbols of his former fetters a wreath of willow and a ring of iron.

The third play of the trilogy is generally thought to have been *Prometheus the Fire-bearer* and may have dealt with the founding of his ritual cult at

---

[1] The scholiast on *Prometheus Bound*, 94 says that in *Prometheus the Fire-bearer* Prometheus was described as chained 'for thirty thousand years.' But the number seems impossible to take literally. Thirteen generations could not much exceed four hundred years.

Athens, where he was a patron-god of potters and honoured with torch-races.   If so, lacking these local Athenian interests, we might have felt it something of an anticlimax.

Some may find comfort in this general picture of the world's destiny (though Aeschylus was hardly an optimist).   Distantly it recalls, as already said, those modern dreams of the evolution of the Life-force, or Immanent Will, which suggested the close of Hardy's *Dynasts*.

> But—a stirring thrills the air
> Like to sounds of joyance there
> That the rages
> Of the ages
> Shall be cancelled, and deliverance offered from the darts that were,
> Consciousness the Will informing, till It fashion all things fair!

But Hardy, indomitably honest, turned in his last years from this shred of hope to stoic silence.   Even if it were true, after the agonies of endless generations since life began, could we cry light-heartedly: 'All's well that ends well'?   Ivan Karamazov was less ignoble when he 'handed God back the ticket.'   For, in the words of a fragment of the tragic poet Agathon (died *c.* 401):

> One thing not God Himself hath power to do—
> To make undone what things have once been done.

The same objection meets Shelley's *Prometheus Unbound*, with its day-dream of happy anarchy for a perfected humanity.   The quiet acceptance that closes *Candide* seems saner and truer: '*Il y a horriblement de mal sur la terre . . . cultivons notre jardin!*'

PROMETHEUS BOUND

PROMETHEUS	OCÉANUS
HEPHAESTUS	IO
FORCE	HERMES
VIOLENCE	CHORUS OF OCEAN-NYMPHS

[*A crag in Scythia, beside the earth-encircling Ocean stream. Prometheus is led in by two grim symbolic figures, Force and Violence, followed by Hephaestus, the Heavenly Craftsman.*]

Force. At last we are come to earth's extremity,
   The Scythian wilderness, by man untrod.
   Time for thee now, Hephaestus, to remember
   Our Father's bidding—bind this miscreant
   Against yon precipice of beetling crag,
   With chains of adamant, unshatterable.
   His was the hand that stole and gave to mortals
   That secret of all thy arts, bright-flowering fire;
   Now Heaven's retribution overtakes him.
   So let him learn to reverence the dominion
   Of Zeus!—and cast off his passion for mankind.
Hephaestus. Ah Force, ah Violence, the will of Zeus
   For *you* must take its course—ye falter not.
   But *my* heart fails me—must I chain by force
   A God, my kinsman, in this wintry gorge!
   And yet I *dare* not shrink.
   Fearful it were to neglect the Allfather's word.

   High-hearted son of wisely-judging Thĕmis,
   Against my will, as thine, these hands must fasten
   Thee, with bronze fetters indissoluble,
   To this forsaken crag where no man's voice,
   No human shape shall find thee evermore.
   But here the sunlight's flame shall scorch and blast
   Thy body's beauty.   Ever thou shalt long
   For starry-mantled Night to veil his glare;
   Then long no less for his radiance to scatter
   The frosts before the dawn.   For each in turn
   Shall seem the bitterer torment; and unborn
   Is the saviour of thy sorrows.

Such thy reward for loving humankind.
Thou didst them too much honour!—thou, a God,
Braving for Man's poor sake the wrath of Gods.
Therefore on this grim rock thou must keep thy vigil,
Fettered upright, with knees that crave in vain
To bend, and eyes to slumber. Ah what cries
Of anguish thou shalt utter!—yet no help
The heart of Zeus abides implacable;
And pitiless are lords new-come to power.

Force. How now, why lingering? Why this vain compassion?
Must thou not hate this God whom Gods abhor,
Him that betrayed to men *thy* holy flame?

Hephaestus. Comradeship—kinship—these have fearful power.

Force. Maybe. And yet the Almighty Father's word—
Canst thou be deaf to *that*? Not fear Him more?

Hephaestus. *Thy* heart knew never pity! Only pride.

Force. Idle are lamentations for this fellow.
Waste not thy pains on such futilities.

Hephaestus. Accurst be all the cunning of my hands!

Force. Why cursing that? Not on thy craftsmanship
Can fall the blame for this calamity.

Hephaestus. Yet I would that all my skill had been another's!

Force. All life is hard; except to rule in Heaven.
None lives at liberty, save Zeus alone.

Hephaestus. Too well I see it now—and know no answer.

Force. Why then, bestir thyself!—make fast his fetters.
Let not the Almighty Father find thee laggard.

Hephaestus. See for thyself. Here are his shackles ready.

Force. Then take them—with the full weight of thy hammer
Rivet his wrists—nail him against the rock.

Hephaestus. I do my task. It is not idly done.

Force. Come, harder, tighter still! Leave nothing loose.
This wretch is cunning to slip the straitest toils.

Hephaestus. *That* arm is fastened, inescapably.

Force. Now pin the other. Let this schemer learn
He is no match for the Almighty Wisdom.

Hephaestus. None could find fault with *that*—except the victim!

Force. Now nail him with yon wedge of adamant—
Force its relentless fang right through his breast.

Hephaestus. Ay me, Prometheus!—'tis for *thee* I groan.

Force. Again this faltering! Pity whom Zeus abhors!
Take care! Thou mayst grow sorry for *thyself*.

Hephaestus. This sight before thee is too hideous.

Force. I see but a wretch that finds fit punishment.
   But come!—now tighten the girth about his ribs.
Hephaestus. No help for it! Yet cease to shout me on.
Force. Shout?—that I *will*, and hound thee to the task.
   Now get beneath and ring his ankles tight.
Hephaestus. The labour of a moment. It is done.
Force. Hit hard, and drive the piercing shackles home.
   Stern is the Judge whose doom we execute.
Hephaestus. Thy utterance is as hateful as thy shape.
Force. Melt, tender heart! But find no fault with *me,*
   If *I* am rugged and implacable.
Hephaestus. Let us be gone. His feet are in the toils.
Force (*to Prometheus*). *Now* throne there in thy pride—*now* steal from
     Heaven
   The treasures of the Gods, to fling to mortals!
   Can *they* redeem thee from this misery!
   False was that name the Immortals call thee by—
   'Prometheus!' Truly, thou needest all thy 'forethought,'
   To twist thy way from *this* trap's craftsmanship.

                                         [They go out.

Prometheus. Aether divine, and winds so swift of wing!
   Springs of all rivers! Waves of all the seas,
   With your multitudinous laughter! Earth, All-mother,
   And thou, all-seeing circle of the Sun,
   See what I suffer—a God!—at hands of Gods!

   See with what anguish, with what dishonour,
   These lacerated limbs must wrestle
   Age after age,
   Since the new Master of the Immortals
   Hath fashioned for me His branding fetters.
   Ah for my agony—now—hereafter!
   When, when arises the destined daybreak
   Shall bid my sufferings cease?

   And yet what words are these? Whatever comes,
   Stands clear before my vision. I can suffer
   Nothing that I foreknew not. I must bear
   All that is doomed, as best I may; well knowing
   None can do battle with Necessity.
   Yet such a fate!—I cannot speak of it,
   Cannot keep silence!—yoked as I am to sorrow,
   For that privilege of power I gave to men,

The fount of flame I stole in the stalk of fennel,
Stay of their lives, and teacher of their arts.
Such was the guilt that hangs me pinioned here,
Bare to the blasts of Heaven!

[*A sound of voices.*

Ah?
What sound then? What faintness of fragrance wind-wafted?
Some god that comes?—or man?—or demigod,
To this far end of earth?
And what is it brings them? To see my sorrows?
Behold me!—a God; yet fettered in anguish!
Since Zeus now hates me—and all the Blessed
Abhor my name in the courts of Heaven—
For loving too dearly the sons of men.
But what is this rustle, close around me,
Of birds a-flutter? Of light wings whirring
Across the sky?
Fear falls upon me of all that comes.

The Chorus of Ocean-nymphs approaches through the air.

strophe 1.

Chorus. Fear nothing! For in friendship, borne swift upon the breeze,
    (Though loth was our father to give us leave to go)
        With racing wings to thy hill we came.
    Barefoot for haste we quitted our cave beneath the seas—
        At the clash of steel resounding, blow on blow,
            We cast aside our maiden-shame.
Prometheus. Alas!
    Children of Tethys the many-childed,
    Daughters of Ocean whose waters unsleeping
    Circle the world,
    Cast now your eyes on the gyves that gird me,
    Manacled fast,
    Here on this hilltop heavenward towering,
    To keep my vigil of pain.

antistrophe 1.

Chorus. I see it all, Prometheus. And dark with tears my eyes,
    In horror at these adamantine chains,
        This rock where thy tortured limbs are thrust.
    For now to the helm of Heaven lords of a new race rise;
        New laws, and tyrannous, Zeus ordains;
            And the mighty of old He treads to dust.
Prometheus. Would beneath earth His hand had hurled me,

Where Hades gathers the perished nations
In limitless Hell!
There, past escape, had His cruelty chained me,
Never a God, nor any other,
Had mocked at my misery!
But here I must hang, the stormwinds' plaything,
The laugh of my foes.

Chorus. Laugh!—can there live a God so harsh in Heaven?   *str. 2.*
    Who would not grieve with thee?—
Save Zeus alone.   Yes, *He* hath not forgiven.
    His hate, implacably,
Crushes the race of Crŏnus, and shall not find its ending,
Until at last it surfeit; or, with all odds contending,
    Some rebel wrest His sovereignty.

Prometheus. Indeed the day comes, when the Lord of Heaven
Shall learn at the last His need of me!—
Of *me*, His captive, thus tied and tortured—
To bid Him beware of a new-framed purpose
That drags His throne and His glory down.
Vainly *then* shall He seek to charm me
With soft persuasions as sweet as honey;
In vain shall He threaten.   He cannot cow me.
Never a word shall He win, till He set me
Loose from my fetters, with full atonement
For my sorrow and my shame.

Chorus. Headstrong thou art!   Too rash of tongue thine anger,   *ant. 2.*
    By misery undismayed.
But at my heart there stabs the dread of danger—
    For *thee* I am afraid.
Ah when shalt thou find harbour from the storms of tribulation?
For the soul of the Son of Crŏnus is deaf to supplication,
    The heart of *Him* no prayers persuade.

Prometheus. A savage Lord, too well I know Him,
And a law to Himself; yet He too hereafter
Shall soften at last;
The weight of peril shall break His will.
Then shall He tame His temper unbending,
Glad to sue me for reconcilement—
And I as glad to give!

Chorus-leader. But tell us now the naked truth of all.
On accusation of what wickedness
Has Zeus condemned thee to such pain and shame?
Unless there is danger, speak!

Prometheus. To speak of it, for me, is bitterness,
Bitter is silence.   Every way lies sorrow.
    That day when first there rose up wrath in Heaven
And strife of Gods with Gods
(Some eager from his throne to topple Crŏnus
And give to Zeus the kingship; some as hot
That never Zeus should reign among the Immortals),
Vainly I strove to counsel for the best
The Titan brood of Earth and Urănus—
They would not hearken.   For their stubborn courage,
Disdainful of all subtle stratagems,
By violence hoped for easy victory.
But *I* had heard my mother, Thĕmis—Earth
(For one she is, though manifold her names),
And not once only, prophesy the future,
Foretelling that no force, no violence,
But deeper guile must conquer.
Yet though of this I warned them, all my guidance
They deemed not worth one glance.
    And so, of all that offered, best it seemed
To take my mother with me and to join
The cause of Zeus—as willing He as I.
Thanks to my counsels, then, the black abyss
Of Tartarus has closed on the ancient Crŏnus,
And his confederates with him.   Such the service
For which in turn the Ruler of the Gods
Repays me here with pain and punishment.
For in all absolute rule somehow there dwells
This malady—it cannot trust its friends.
    Upon what accusation, ye have asked,
Does he treat me with such outrage?   Hear the answer.
No sooner seated on His father's throne,
To all the Immortal Gods He portioned out
Their several honours, and to each assigned
Their powers; and yet for hapless Men He cared
Nothing.   His will was to annihilate
The race at once—create, instead, a new.
There was not one rose up to cross His path
But *I*—I dared it.   *I* saved humankind,
That else His hand had hurled in ruin to Hades.
For *that* I am now bent double with these torments,
Bitter to bear, and pitiful to see.
Little I dreamed my pity for mankind

Should shut myself from pity.
Yet now from Zeus I suffer this grim correction—
A sight that brands His name!

Leader. A heart of iron he has, a frame of marble,
That does not suffer at such agony
As thine, Prometheus.   Would I had never seen
What stabs my very soul to look upon!

Prometheus. Bitter, indeed, to all that care for me!

Leader. And didst thou venture further for mankind?

Prometheus. I turned their eyes from seeing the doom before them.

Leader. And by what medicine?

Prometheus. I gave blind hopes a home within their hearts.

Leader. Truly, a blessed gift was *that* to give!

Prometheus. And fire as well I brought them.

Leader. Do those brief lives know now the bright glance of fire!

Prometheus. And thereby many an art shall yet be theirs.

Leader. So *this* was the fault that Zeus——?

Prometheus. Now visits with injustice unrelenting.

Leader. And for thy anguish is no end appointed?

Prometheus. None—until *He* shall will it.

Leader. How *should* He!—what's to hope for?   Seest not
Thine error?   Ah, 'error' is a bitter word
For thee; to me, no pleasure.   Nay, enough!
But seek from thy suffering *some* deliverance.

Prometheus. Easy enough for one that keeps his footing
Clear of calamity, to give the wretched
Advice and admonition.   I knew all,
I willed my error!—I shall not deny it—
Most freely willed it; and to succour men
Found, for myself, disaster.
And yet I own I dreamed not of pain like *this*—
Thus to hang wasting on a dizzy crag,
Alone, in an unneighboured wilderness.
Yet mourn no more for what I now endure;
Descend to earth, and listen, while I tell
Of the doom that is drawing nearer.
Grant me, oh grant me this, and share my pain.
It is *I* that suffer now.   But flitting sorrow
Swoops now on one head, now upon another.

Leader. Thou needst not to urge us.   We grant too gladly
Thy will, O Prometheus.
From the swift-soaring charger that wafted me hither
Across the pure Heaven,

Where the birds wing their ways, now with light foot descending
On earth, the stony, I set my steps.
Glad would I listen
To all the tale of thy sorrows.

> *While they alight on earth, Océanus enters above, mounted on a winged, four-legged creature.*

Océanus. To find thee, Prometheus, from far I have travelled,
    Mounted upon this wind-swift creature,
    That bends without bridle the way I will.
    Be sure that my heart is wrung with thy sorrow.
    Our kinship constrains me.
    And even although one blood did not bind us,
    Than thee there is none I hold higher in honour.
    I gloze not, nor flatter.   My actions can witness.
    Tell to me only how I shall help.
    Never shalt say that a friend was truer
    Than Océanus to *thee*.

Prometheus. Ha, what is this!   Art thou too come to gaze
    Upon my anguish?   Couldst thou dare forsake
    The stream that bears thy name, and thy sea-caves
    Sprung in the living rock, for *this* harsh land,
    Mother of iron?   Is it to see my ruin
    And suffer with my sorrow?   Then indeed
    Behold this spectacle—the friend of Zeus,
    The fellow-builder of His sovereignty—
    And with what weight of woe He bows me down!

Océanus. I see it well, Prometheus—and would advise thee
    Of what is best—all subtle as thou art.
    Learn now to know thyself.   Change your old ways
    For new.   A *new* Lord rules in Heaven now.
    But if thou wilt fling such harsh and whetted words
    Against Him, then, though high aloft in Heaven
    He sits enthroned, yet Zeus may hear, and make
    These ills that throng thee now, seem childish play.
    Unhappy, lay aside this indignation,
    And seek release from sorrow.
    Do I seem to speak a wisdom too outworn?
    Yet think, Prometheus, these are but the wages
    Of a too proud and contumacious tongue.
    Thy heart is still unhumbled.   Stubborn still
    Against misfortune, to thy present pains
    Thou art bent on adding others.
    Be schooled by me, kick not against the pricks,

Seeing that to-day One rules Omnipotent,
Harsh in His ways, to none accountable.
Now I will go to Him, and try my fortune
In hope to accomplish thy deliverance.
But thou—be quiet, and curb that violent tongue.
Know you not well, that are so over-subtle,
How retribution waits on wanton lips?

Prometheus. I count you happy, still to go unblamed,
Though once you shared in all my plans and dangers.
But now let be.　Give no more thought to this.
Move Him you cannot—*He* is not lightly moved.
And take good care you do not rue your errand.

Océanus. Ah, you are better far to teach your neighbours
Than school yourself.　The visible proof's before me.
But do not check me in my eagerness.
For I am sure, most sure, Zeus will accord me
The boon I beg Him—thy deliverance.

Prometheus. Truly I honour—shall not cease to honour—
This zeal ungrudging.　And yet spare your labour.
For labour how you might, all's labour lost,
And would avail me nothing.
No, keep you quiet, out of the way of danger.
Unhappy as I am, I would not therefore
Bring ruin on all the others that I can.
Far from it!　All too bitterly I mourn
My brother Atlas' fate, who far to westward
Shoulders the pillar of the Earth and Heaven—
A bitter burden and no sweet embrace!
And again I was torn with pity when I saw
That dweller in caverns of Cilicia,
That hundred-headed portent of destruction,
Impetuous Typhon, son of Mother Earth,
By violence overmastered, as he struggled,
God against Gods, by violence to ruin
The reign of Zeus, while from his ghastly jaws
Hissed terror, from his eyes grim lightnings glared.
In vain!　From Zeus a sleepless thunderbolt,
The headlong lightning with its breath of flame,
Smote him, and shattered all the sounding vaunts
Of his vainglory—struck to the very heart,
His thunder-blasted strength was scorched to ashes.
And now supine in all his helpless length,
Beside yon straitened sea-gate, there he sprawls

Flattened beneath the mountain-roots of Etna;
While, high above, Hephaestus hammers out
His red-hot iron amid her precipices;
Whence there shall burst hereafter streams of flame
To devastate with jaws implacable
The level fields of fertile Sicily.
So fierce a fury Typhon still shall vomit,
With shafts insatiate of fiery rain,
Though burnt now and blackened by the bolt of Zeus.
You too have seen these things.   No need of me
To teach them.   As best you may, preserve yourself.
I will endure the fate that has come upon me,
Until the heart of Zeus shall rest from wrath.

Océanus. But hast not learnt that prudent words, Prometheus,
Can heal the wild distemperature of anger?

Prometheus. In season, yes, their balm may soothe the heart:
But force no astringents on a swollen passion!

Océanus. But if in warmth of friendship one should dare—
What harm see you in that?

Prometheus. Labour that's vain, and empty-headed folly!

Océanus. My judgment ails?   Then suffer it to ail.
Best that my wisdom be accounted blind.

Prometheus. But here the fault will be accounted *mine.*

Océanus. This, then, is your plain counsel?   To turn home?

Prometheus. For fear that, pitying me, you win the hatred—

Océanus. Of this new Lord throned in omnipotence?

Prometheus. Of Him beware!   Rouse not *His* heart to anger.

Océanus. Indeed thy fate, Prometheus, stands a warning.

Prometheus. Hence then!   Begone!   Keep to those wiser thoughts.

Océanus. No need to urge me further.   I am going.
See, my winged charger beats with his flapping pinions
At the air, his yielding highway; all impatient
To stretch at ease in his own stall at home.

Océanus mounts Heavenward and flies away.

Chorus. I lament thee, Prometheus. These eyes that watch thy pain   *strophe* 1.
Are wet with tears; on these young cheeks, for thee so sorely tried,
   The drops run down like rain.
For with laws of His own, most hateful, this Zeus new-glorified
Goads at the old Gods fallen with the spear-point of His pride.

And a voice of lamenting replies from all the earth—   *antistrophe* 1.
Mourning for ancient glories gone, for thy brothers and for thee,
   Proud race of Titan birth.

Yea, throughout holy Asia, all tribes of men there be
Uplift their lamentations for *thy* calamity.

They that dwell far off in Colchis,   *str.* 2.
Maids who fearless march to war,
And the Scythian hordes bewail thee,
Where they hold earth's utmost confines, round about Maeōtis' shore;

And the Arabs, flower of manhood,   *ant.* 2.
Whose high mountain-citadel
Under Caucasus arises,
Where mid sharp-beaked spears of battle, loud and fierce their war-cries
     swell.

One alone have I seen in toil like thine—   *epode.*
Atlas, the Titan of race divine,
In his adamantine chain.
Upon his giant shoulders lies
The burden of the vaulted skies;
And, as he groans in vain,
The Ocean-breakers with their fall
Moan answer, and the great deeps call,
And Hell's black gulfs repeat his pain;
While rivers whirling towards the sea
Their waves' unsullied purity
Murmur his grief again.

During a perceptible pause Prometheus broods in silence.

Prometheus. Think it not stubbornness or arrogance,
     That holds me silent.   But my heart is gnawed
To see myself a thing of contumely.
And yet, to these new Gods, who then but I
Apportioned all their honours and their powers?
Enough of that—a tale ye know too well.
Yet hear of *human* sorrows—
How from those minds, all childish once, I made
Beings of reason, blessed with understanding.
Yet this that I say is not to blame mankind;
Only to show the goodwill of my gifts.
     In those first years, though seeing, mortals saw not,
Hearing, they heard not; but lifelong they drifted,
Lost in confusion, like dim shapes of dream.
Nothing they knew of how to work in timber,
Nor how to build with interwoven bricks

Homes that the sunlight gladdens; underground
Like feeble ants they dwelt, in lightless caves.
No certain signs they had of coming winter,
Or flowery springtime, or of fruitful summer,
Senseless in all they did; until I showed them
The rise of stars, their settings dim-descried.
And then I taught them Number, crown of knowledge,
And linkéd letters, whence comes Memory,
Mistress of crafts and Mother of the Muses.
I was the first that bowed the strength of brutes
To serve beneath yoke or saddle, and relieve
Man's limbs of heaviest labour;
The first that harnessed to the chariot
The bitted steed, pride of the rich and mighty.
It was I, no other, launched the sea-swept galley
And wove her wings of canvas. Yet—poor fool!—
I that for Man discovered such inventions
Face my own ruin devoid of all device.

Chorus-leader. Ah, bitter plight! Now, with your wisdom gone,
You wander lost; and like an ill physician,
Grown sick, you lie despairing; ignorant
What remedy can bring you health again.

Prometheus. Hear to the end. Still more will grow your wonder
At all the crafts and the contrivances
I found for men; and this the chief of all—
If sickness came, they had no healing simples,
To eat, or drink, or smear upon their bodies,
But wasted helplessly; until I taught them
How to compound the kindly drugs wherewith
Now they can counter every malady.
First was I too to fix the divers kinds
Of divination—how to know aright
The omens hid in casual utterance
Or in meetings by the wayside; to foretell,
From dreams, what haps the waking hours shall bring;
To augur from the flight of crook-clawed birds,
With clear discernment, which are favourable,
And which of evil presage—all the ways
Of every race of fowl; their mutual loves,
Their enmities, their gatherings together.
I showed men too, in beasts of sacrifice,
What hue of the entrails marks that Heaven is kindly—
Their smoothness, and the dappled shapeliness

Of gall and liver. Kindling on the altars
The thigh-bones fat-enfolded, and the chine,
I gave men guidance towards that art obscure;
Opening their eyes, where all was blindness once,
To read the future writ in signs of flame.
So much for this. And all those boons to Man
That Earth holds hidden—bronze, iron, silver, gold—
Who dares to claim he found them out before me?
Indeed, the boast were idle!
Nay, the whole truth I tell ye in a word—
It was Prometheus gave men *all* their arts.

Leader. Ah, but enough of serving men past measure,
Not recking thy own ruin! For still I dream
One day to see thee, all thy fetters broken,
In power not less than Zeus.

Prometheus. Not yet, not yet does all-fulfilling Fate
Doom *this* to be. No freedom from my chains,
Till I have bowed to endless agonies!
Frail are all arts beside Necessity.

Leader. But of Necessity who holds the helm?

Prometheus. The Fates three-formed, the unforgetting Furies.

Leader. Is Zeus less strong than these?

Prometheus. Not even He can baffle destiny.

Leader. And what is destined Him but reign eternal?

Prometheus. Of *that* ye may not learn. Seek not to know.

Leader. Thou hidest, surely, some high mystery?

Prometheus. Think of some other theme. Now is no time
To talk of *that*! In darkest secrecy
Let it be hid. On keeping that concealed
Hangs my escape from fettered ignominy.

str. 1.

Chorus. Never may *my* will clash with Zeus, the Lord of all; ah, never
Be *my* steps slow to bring the Gods the sacred blood of kine,
Where flows by the shores of Ocean my sire's eternal river!
Never (oh, firm be my resolve!) let a godless mouth be mine!

Happy enough our maiden-lot—with high hearts and uncaring   *ant.* 1.
To revel away our length of years. But I shudder when I see
Thy thousand griefs, Prometheus. Headstrong and over-daring,
Too little hast thou honoured Zeus! Too much, humanity!

Dear heart, what avails thy service? Where now lies strength to save
thee?
str. 2.
In creatures of a day? Couldst so mistake

Yon race that wanders weak as dreams, and blinded,
With frailty and impotence to bind it?
     This frame of things God founded, no plan of Man may shake.

This have I learnt, Prometheus, in gazing on thy sorrows.   *ant. 2.*
     And ah, there came back to my memory
That song—so different then!—we all stood singing
By bath and bed, when home thou camest bringing
     The bride thy gifts had won thee, our own Hēsíone.

     The maiden Io enters madly, her forehead horned like the moon.

Io. What land now?   What nation?   Who is it I see here,
Bridled and curbed mid the crags of the mountain,
Bare to the storm?
What was the sin, then, that brought thee to suffer?
Say whither on earth
My weary feet are come.
Ah!
Again the stab of the gadfly's sting!
O God!
Again comes the wraith of earth-born Argus,
The herdsman with a myriad eyes.
He dogs me, still, with his stealthy glances—
Dead, yet the grave-mound cannot hide him!
From Hell he rises to hunt me onward,
Wandering hungry for ever, along the sands of the deep.
                              [She chants.

About and about me I hear again   *strophe* 1.
His waxen pipe with its drowsy strain.
Ah where—to what world's ending—
Must I wander on alone?
What have I done, O Crŏnus' son,
That Thy yoke on my neck is thrown?
Gadfly-haunted, maddened with terror,
Why torturest me?
Burn me with fire, or whelm me in earth,
Or fling to the beasts of the sea!
Nay, listen, Lord, to my prayer!
I have wandered and suffered enow.
Where shall I find me deliverance?   Where?
I cannot know.   But Thou—
Canst Thou hear the voice of my crying?—the maiden with hornéd
     brow?

Prometheus. *I* hear indeed!   The gadfly-goaded daughter
Of Ínachus!—the face that set afire
The heart of Zeus with passion; whom Hēra's anger
Drives now to run a race that never ends.

Io (chanting). How knowest *thou* my father's name?   *antistrophe* 1.
O thou whose anguish is the same,
Unhappy as I, who art thou?—
That thy tongue can tell my birth
And the frenzied mind, by God assigned,
That goads me over earth,
Headlong leaping, sick and famished,
Condemned to fly
From Hēra's hatred?   Of all the accurst,
Who so accurst as I?
Ah, tell me, clear and sure,
What must I yet fulfil
Of suffering?   Canst thou name no cure,
No help, for all my ill?
Ah, tell a girl in sorrow, who wanders homeless still.

Prometheus. Indeed I will tell thee clearly,
With words plain-spoken—not in tangled riddles—
As friend should speak to friend.
I am Prometheus, who gave fire to men.

Io. O benefactor of all humankind,
Luckless Prometheus, why tormented so?

Prometheus. A moment since I told my unhappy tale.

Io. Ah, grant me yet this favour that I ask!

Prometheus. Ask what you will, and you shall have the answer.

Io. Say then who nailed you on this precipice.

Prometheus. It was the will of Zeus; Hephaestus' hand.

Io. But what was the transgression you atone?

Prometheus. What I have said suffices.   Ask no further.

Io. Yet tell me, too, what end to all my wanderings?
Where is the term of my unhappiness?

Prometheus. Far better not to know it, than to know.

Io. Ah, do not hide what I am doomed to bear.

Prometheus. I do not envy you this gift you crave.

Io. Then why so hesitant to tell me all?

Prometheus. I grudge not *that*.   I fear to crush thy spirit.

Io. Ah, be not careful of me past my wish!

Prometheus. So eager!   I must speak, then.   Listen now.

Leader. Stay for a moment.   Do me too a pleasure.
May we not learn from *her* lips now what ails her,

Her history of ruin heaped on ruin?
Then let her hear her coming trials from *thee*?
Prometheus. It is for thee to grant their asking, Io,
Remembering these are sisters to thy father.
Well for *thee*, too, to ease a heavy heart
With weeping, and with words that win in turn
Thy hearers' tears of pity.
Io. I cannot find it in me to refuse you.
All that you ask, plainly I will deliver:
And yet I burn with shame
Even to tell how first it all began—
This storm that Heaven has launched upon my head,
Leaving me thus unhappy and misshapen.

   Night after night, into my maiden chamber
There stalked strange shapes of dream, that to my ear
Bent murmuring with smooth whispers: 'Maid most blest,
Why cling to maidenhood?—'tis thine to be
Bride of the Highest.   Zeus Himself is stricken,
For thee, with the flame of passion, and He longs
To clasp thee in His arms.   Scorn not, my daughter,
The bed of Zeus.   To the waving grass of Lerna
Come!—where there feed thy father's flocks and kine;
Gladden the eyes of God, that yearn for thee.'

   Such were the visions nightly haunting me,
Till, in my misery, I steeled my shame
To tell my father of my darkling dreams.
At once he sent to Delphi and Dōdōna
His sacred envoys, one upon another—
What words of his, what deeds, could please the Gods?
Yet back they brought only bewildering answers,
Dark sayings of mysterious oracles—
Until, at last, there came to Ínachus
One clear and unambiguous command:
He must drive me forth, away from home and country,
God's wandering victim, to the ends of the earth.
Or else the blazing levin-bolt of Zeus
Should smite to annihilation all our race.

   Such was Apollo's oracle—my father
Obeyed and drove me from his palace-doors,
Barring them on me with a heart as sad
As was my own—yet the will of Zeus constrained him,
Like a charger that chafes in vain against the curb.
Then fell my mind distracted, and this my brow

Grew hideous with horns, and in my flesh
A gadfly plunged its sting—with frantic leaping
I fled, down towards Cerchneia's crystal stream,
Down to the spring of Lerna. But behind me
Followed the herdsman Argus, son of Earth—
Merciless in his rages, watching me
With multitudinous eyes. On him there swept
The sudden stroke of Death; but still the gadfly
Drives me, with scourge divine, from land to land,
Such is my story. If you know what yet
Remains to bear, speak out! Do not in pity
Soothe me with pleasant falsehoods. Such untruth,
To me, is foulest of all weaknesses.

Chorus. Hold, hold!—too horrible!
Never, ah never did I dream my ears
Should hear such strange, forbidding things,
My eye should see
Such suffering, terror, torture. At my heart
They stab as cold as steel.
O Fate, O Fate,
At Io's doom I shudder!

Prometheus. Too soon this outcry and this consternation!
Wait till ye hear what yet there waits behind.

Leader. Tell on, tell all. Sick souls may find a comfort
In sure foreknowledge of what's still to bear.

Prometheus. Ye have had your wish, and had it easily,
To hear from her the story of her sorrow.
Now listen what new griefs at Hēra's hand
Her youth must suffer.
And take to heart, daughter of Ĭnachus,
My warnings how thy wayfarings shall end.

    Departing hence, first towards the sun's uprising
Turn thee, across waste lands that no man ploughs.
There thou shalt find the nomad Scythians,
Far-shooting archers, housed in homes of wicker
Built, not on earth, but high on rolling wains.
From them keep far aloof, and skirt their land,
Close to the beaches moaning with the sea.
But on thy left hand leave the Chalybes,
The smithiers of steel—of these beware,
For grim they are, and inhospitable.
Then to the stream Hybristes—well so named—
Thou shalt draw near. But pass it not—the passage

Is perilous—until to Caucasus
Thou come, of all peaks highest, where that river
Vomits its violence from the mountain-peak.
Over those summits neighbouring the stars
Thy path must lie; then southward, till thou reach
The host of Amazons, haters of men,
Who shall make their homes one day in Themiscȳra,
Beside Thermōdon's banks, where sharp to seaward
Juts out the rugged jaw of Salmydessus,
Grim host to sailors, stepmother of ships.
Those Amazons shall guide thee, and right gladly,
Upon thy way to where the sea-gates narrow
At the Cimmerian Isthmus—then, undaunted,
Plunge from the shore, and swim the Maeotic Strait.
Thy passage there shall live in fame for ever
And men shall call it, in thy memory,
'The Bosporus.' And so, from Europe's bourn,
Thou shalt set thy foot in Asia's continent.

[*To the Chorus.*

What think ye now? Is not the Lord of Heaven
Tyrannical, in all His ways alike?—
This God that lusting for a mortal's beauty
Hounds her across the earth! Ay, thou hast found,
Poor maid, a brutal lover. For I warn thee
All this is scarce the prelude to thy sorrows.
Io. Woe, woe, woe!
Prometheus. Again this cry of woe! What wilt thou do
When thou hast heard the evils yet to come?
Leader. What! There remain more sorrows to foretell her?
Prometheus. One stormy ocean of calamities!
Io. Why, then, what use in living? Why have I not
Hurled myself headlong from this precipice!
Then, shattered far beneath, I might have rested
From all my labours. Better far to die,
Once and for all, than live this daily torment.
Prometheus. You would bear but ill the trials that fall on *me*,
Whom destiny denies the power to die,
And find release from sorrow.
But all my labours have *no* term appointed,
Till Zeus Himself falls from his sovereignty.
Io. How? Is it *possible* for Zeus to fall?
Prometheus. Glad, I think, *thou* wouldst be to see that day.
Io. How should I not, whom Zeus has outraged so?

Prometheus. This thing is true.   Of that you may be sure.
Io. But who shall despoil Him of His royal sceptre?
Prometheus. Himself shall spoil Himself, by scheming folly.
Io. But how?   If it is not dangerous to speak.
Prometheus. A marriage He shall make that He repents.
Io. With Goddess or mortal?   Say—if it may be said.
Prometheus. No matter which!   For *that* may not be uttered.
Io. Shall His own bride depose Him from His throne?
Prometheus. She shall bear a son yet mightier than his sire.
Io. And has He, then, no means to escape His doom?
Prometheus. None, but myself—when these my chains are loosened.
Io. But who can loose them against the will of Zeus?
Prometheus. One, it is fated, who descends from *thee*.
Io. What!   One of *my* blood thy deliverer!
Prometheus. Twelve generations pass, and then he comes.
Io. Thy prophecy grows dark to comprehend.
Prometheus. Enough.   And of *thy* misfortunes ask no more.
Io. Ah, do not promise help, and then withhold it!
Prometheus. I give thee a choice between two prophecies.
Io. What *are* they?   Make it plain, and let me choose.
Prometheus. Choose!   Shall I now reveal what further troubles
   Await thee still; or who shall set me free?
Leader. Ah, for *her* sake do one, for mine the other.
   Grudge not thy words—I beg thee—tell to *her*
   What wanderings yet remain; to *me*, thy saviour.
Prometheus. Since ye so crave it, I will not deny you,
   But answer all ye ask.
   First, thy long wanderings, Io—grave them fast
   Upon the mindful tablets of thy heart.
      Passing the strait that parts two continents,
   Turn towards the flaming borders of the East,
   Where treads the rising sun; until, beyond
   The thunders of the deep, thou comest forth
   Into Cisthēnē's plain, the Gorgon-haunted,
   Where dwell three aged women, white as swans,
   Daughters of Phorcys, sharing a single eye,
   A single tooth, between them.   Never sun,
   Nor moon by night, looks down upon their darkness;
   And close at hand there haunt three wingéd sisters,
   Abhorred of men, with hissing snakes for hair,
   The Gorgons, whom no eye may see and live.
   Therefore heed well my warning.
   Beware, no less, another grisly sight—

Those hounds of Zeus, with beaked but voiceless mouths,
The Griffins—and fear too the cavalry
Of one-eyed Arimaspians, that dwell
By the Plutonian stream with sands of gold.
From these keep far.   So shalt thou come at last
To a distant country, with a sable race
That dwells beside the River Aethiops,
Next to the very well-head of the Sun.
Follow that river's bank until thou reach
The Cataract, where out of Byblis' mountains
The Nile floods forth his clear and sacred stream.
For this shall lead thee to the land three-cornered
Of Egypt, where abides for thee, O Io,
And thy posterity your far-off home.

But if, in aught I say, you find my meaning
Doubtful or indistinct, renew your questions,
Till all stands clear before you.
I have much leisure—that I well could spare!
Leader. If any word of her unhappy journey
Remains to say, or has been left unsaid,
Speak.   But if all is told, remember *us*
And the favour that you promised.
Prometheus. Io has heard the goal of all her journey;
But now, to prove I tell no idle tale,
In witness of my words I will recount
The hardships she endured in coming hither—
Not the whole story (*that* were burdensome),
Only its latter ending.

When thou hadst reached at last the Molossian plain
And neared high-ridged Dōdōna, where there lies
The seat prophetic of Thesprōtian Zeus
And that marvel past belief, His speaking oaks—
Which hailed thee, in no riddling oracles,
But clearest speech, as doomed to be hereafter
The glorious bride of Zeus (does this awake
Thy memories?)—there frenzy fell upon thee,
Driving thee far along the coastward track
To the great Gulf of Rhea; whence again
The tempests of thy fortune drove thee back.
So in the years to come that gulf of sea
Shall bear (be sure of this) the name 'Ionian,'
Recalling to mankind thy ancient passage.

These signs I give thee that my spirit's vision

Pierces beyond the outward shows of things.
But now, returning to my former story,
To you and her I will reveal the rest.

   By the sea's edge a city stands, Canōpus,
Where at his mouth Nile heaps his silted slime;
There by the gentle touch of hand laid on thee,
And that alone, Zeus shall restore thy reason.
Then shalt thou bring to birth a dark-skinned son,
Got by the touch of God, and so by name
Called 'Épaphus,' who shall enjoy the fruits
Of all lands watered by broad-flowing Nile.
And from his race, five generations after,
Shall fifty maidens turn again to Argos,
Fleeing perforce from wedlock with their kin,
Their cousins—who, with hearts inflamed to frenzy,
In hot pursuit of that forbidden passion,
Like falcons close in chase of fleeing doves,
Shall follow; and yet those bodies that they crave,
God shall deny them.   For Pelasgia's earth
Shall greet them with midnight murder, at the hands
Of women maddened with the rage of Ares;
And every bride shall plunge her whetted dagger
Deep in the lifeblood of her lover's heart.
(Such love I wish to all my enemies!)
One girl alone shall find her purpose blunted
By tenderness—too fond to kill her husband
And deeming better to be counted coward
Than murderess.   So from her womb shall spring
A royal line in Argos.

   Too long it were to set forth all the story,
But from her race there shall be born a hero,
A glorious archer, who shall break at last
My bondage.   Such the prophecy once uttered
To me by my ancient mother, Titan Thĕmis.
But in what wise and way these things shall be,
Were long to tell; nor serves it thee to know.

Io. Eleleu! Eleleu! Again the spasm
  Of soul aflame and senses maddened—
  Fiercer it stabs than arrow stings!
  Against my breast my heart-beats hammer,
  From side to side my eyeballs whirl,
  As the blasts of madness blow my spirit
  Out of its course, and the waves of frenzy

Scatter my words, like a turbid torrent
From a tongue grown past control.

                                                              [*She rushes out.*

Chorus. Wise in his counsel was he,   *strophe.*
     Whose heart was first to weigh this truth, whose lips first spoke it loud—
     ''Tis best for a man to match with his own degree.'
     Who wins his bread, is a fool to wed with those whom a purse makes
          proud,
     Or who boast of their blood's antiquity.

     Never, ah never for me,   *antistrophe.*
     O Fates revered, may there come the day when Zeus bids *me* to His bed!
     Never may *I* be beloved of a deity!
     I shrink afraid at this girl betrayed, to a hated lover wed,
     Whom Hēra hounds by land and sea.

     Not equal-matchéd love   *epode.*
     I fear—but from above
     Bent on me ruthlessly some glance divine.
     That were a fight too vainly fought, a wealth of misery.
     And *then* what end were mine?
     From what Zeus once disposes, what flight could set me free?
Prometheus. Yet Zeus, I say, for all His stubbornness
     Hereafter shall be humbled.   Such a marriage
     He shall design, as from His sovereignty
     Hurls Him to sheer destruction.   Then at last
     Shall come to full accomplishment the curse
     Breathed by His father Crŏnus, as he fell
     From his immemorial throne.   And *no* God lives
     But I, with power to tell this Son of Crŏnus
     What can avert His doom.   But I—I know it,
     And how it could be done.   So let Him sit,
     Proud in His power to make the Heavens rumble,
     Brandishing His fire-breathing thunderbolt:
     For these shall not avail to save Him falling
     Dishonoured, by a fall intolerable.
     So terrible an adversary now
     He raises up to wrestle with Himself,
     A power portentous, irresistible,
     Armed with a flame shall turn the lightning pale,
     The roar of it out-bellowing the thunder;
     And strong enough to break the ocean-trident,

Poseidon's spear, that shakes the earth to palsy.
Then, with this doom upon Him, Zeus shall learn
How different to be sovereign, and be slave.
Chorus-leader. Surely such threats are but thy wishful dreams?
Prometheus. I speak my wishes—but I speak the truth.
Leader. Can this be true, that Zeus shall find a master?
Prometheus. Things He shall bear yet bitterer than that.
Leader. And yet how *dare* you cry such things abroad?
Prometheus. What should I fear, whose doom is not to die?
Leader. Yet *He* could inflict still sharper agonies.
Prometheus. Let Him! Whatever comes, I have foreseen.
Leader. But wise are those that bow to Adrasteia.
Prometheus. Pray! Cringe! Adore the master of the moment!
But Zeus for me is less than a thing of naught.
Let Him act His pleasure! Let Him play the monarch
This little while! Not long shall He reign in Heaven.
But here I see the messenger of Zeus,
The new Lord's lackey;
Doubtless with some new message to deliver.

Hermes enters, flying through the air.

Hermes. To you the schemer, bitterer than gall,
The thief of fire, that sinned against the Immortals,
Giving their powers to creatures of a day—
To you I speak. Our Father now commands you:
Reveal this marriage that you boast shall bring
His ruin—and say it, not in ambiguous riddles,
But clear and full. Trouble me not, Prometheus,
To make a second journey. You can see,
Zeus is not softened by such ways as these.
Prometheus. What solemn pomp, what arrogance of speech!—
As well befits a varlet of the Gods.
New—ye are new to power, and fondly dream
No sorrow scales your ramparts. Yet from thence
Have I not seen two Lords of Heaven fall?
Yes, and shall see this third that thrones there, follow
Most shamefully, and swiftly. Seems it now,
I crawl and cringe before you younger Gods?
No, I reject it. Utterly! Begone!
Back by the road you came!
You shall learn *nothing* that you ask me of.
Hermes. Think, it was just such stubbornness before
Upon your own head brought calamity.

Prometheus. All my misfortunes—of that you may be sure—
  I would not change for your servility.
Hermes. Better, no doubt, be bondsman to this rock,
  Than the Allfather's faithful messenger!
Prometheus. My insult was fitted to your insolence.
Hermes. It seems your present plight makes you grow vain.
Prometheus. Vain! What a joy, had but my enemies
  Such cause for vanity! And thou among them!
Hermes. Am *I* too, then, to blame for your disasters?
Prometheus. To sum it in a word—*all* Gods I loathe,
  All that so ill requite the good I did them.
Hermes. There speaks a mind maddened to sheer distraction.
Prometheus. Is hate of enemies madness? Be it mine!
Hermes. Prosperity would make thee past all bearing.
Prometheus. Alas!
Hermes. 'Alas'? To Zeus that word is all unknown.
Prometheus. Yet ageing Time has lessons still for all.
Hermes. It has not taught *you* yet the use of reason!
Prometheus. True!—or I should not argue with a slave.
Hermes. To our Father's questions, then, you answer nothing?
Prometheus. If I were in His debt, I would repay.
Hermes. You make mere game of me! As of a child.
Prometheus. Are you not child, and simpler than a child,
  Even to dream of learning more from me?
  There is no outrage, and no stratagem,
  Zeus can devise to wring my secret from me,
  Till I am freed from these dishonouring chains.
  So let Him hurl on me His lurid lightnings—
  With white-winged snow and subterranean thunders
  Confound in chaos all the universe!
  In vain—He shall not bend my will to tell Him
  By whom His sovereignty is doomed to fall.
Hermes. Yet think, can all this help you?
Prometheus. Long since this was foreseen, and firm resolved.
Hermes. Yet bring yourself, poor fool, still bring yourself
  To see aright your own predicament.
Prometheus. Why trouble me? As well go chide the waves.
  Dream not that terror at the will of Zeus
  Can make a woman of me—make me beg,
  With effeminate upturnings of these hands
  To Him I hate, that He will loose my chains.
  It lies not in me.
Hermes. All that I say, it seems, is said in vain.

Not all my pleadings melt thee.   Like a colt
Unbroken, with the bit between his teeth,
Still thou must strive and battle with the curb.
Thy violence trusts in its own futile cunning—
Futile indeed!   For what so impotent
As is the stubborn self-will of a fool!

   Yet think, if all my words are wasted on thee,
What storms, what vast waves of calamity
Shall whelm thee, past escape.   For first our Father
Shall shatter with thunder and His lightning's flame
This crag, and tomb thee in earth's grip of granite.
And only after aeon on aeon accomplished
Shalt thou revisit daylight.   Then shall come
A wingéd hound of Zeus, a blood-red eagle,
An uninvited, day-long banqueter,
To rend and raven thy body like a rag,
Gorging thy liver's blackness.   Hope no more
For any assuagement of that agony
Until some other God, of his own will,
Shall take thy doom upon him and descend
The gulfs of Hell, the gloom of Tartarus.

   Consider, then.   These are no idle threats,
But all too true.   Never a word of Zeus
But finds fulfilment—*His* lips cannot lie.
Look well, and weigh my warning.   What use to hold
True wisdom cheaper than such stubbornness?

Chorus-leader. Surely these words of counsel Hermes gives
  Are not untimely—when he bids you leave
  This headstrong will, and turn to wisdom.   Listen!
  The sage must blush when he falls himself to folly.

Prometheus. Too well I foreknew it, this message of menace
  He dins in my ears; but it brings no dishonour
  To suffer evil at hated hands.
  So let Him launch headlong upon me
  The coils of His forked and fiery lightning,
  And rack the Heavens with roar of thunder
  And shuddering blasts of winds in fury;
  Let Him shake the Earth from her foundations
  Before His breath, till the mad sea's surging
  Confounds the stars upon their courses;
  Let Him hurl these limbs to the murk of Hades,
  Caught in the pitiless swirl of doom—
  Yet He cannot slay me, ever!

Hermes. Such is the speech, and such the will,
  Of men that rave with minds demented.
  What are these boasts but blindest madness?
  What measure of frenzy yet remains?

                              [*He turns to the Chorus.*

  But you that share, in your compassion,
  All that he suffers, quick!—begone!
  Lest the bellowing thunder, that knows not pity,
  Leave your senses crazed and lost.
Leader. Look for another, better counsel
  And *I* may listen.   But do not vainly
  Batter my ears with words past bearing,
  Nor bid me play but a coward's part.
  Whatever comes, with *him* will I suffer.
  I was not bred with a love for traitors.
  There is no failing
  My heart so scorns as *that*!
Hermes. So be it!   Remember my words of warning,
  And when ye are caught in destruction's net,
  Blame not your fortune—no complaining
  That Zeus on your guiltless heads hath scattered
  A ruin unforeseen!
  Not by His doing, but your own,
  Not secretly, nor suddenly,
  The end will come,
  When, snared in the meshes no hand untangles,
  Your folly holds ye fast.

                  [*Hermes flies away.   Thunder and lightning.*
Prometheus. In very deed, and in word no longer,
  The Earth is shaken.
  Out of the echoing deep there bellows
  The voice of the thunder; coil on coil
  The lightning flickers; the dust-clouds whirl,
  While, face to face, from the winds' four quarters
  To battle gallop the tempest-blasts,
  And Heaven and Ocean are whirled in one.
  Clear to behold, with strides of terror,
  There gathers against me the storm of God.
  Ah, holy Mother; ah, wheeling Heaven,
  Whose light revolves upon all things living,
  See now injustice done!

                              [*He sinks into the abyss.*

> *That king*
> *Treading the purple calmly to his death,*
> *While round him, like the clouds of eve, all dusk,*
> *The giant shades of fate, silently flitting,*
> *Pile the dim outline of the coming doom.*

Browning.

A sinister destiny hung over the royal house of Argos.[1] First Pĕlops, son of the wicked Tantalus, son of Zeus, coming from Phrygia to Hellas, won the daughter of Oenomaüs, King of Elis, at the cost of her father's life. Then the son of Pĕlops, Thyestes, seduced the wife of his brother Atreus: in revenge, Atreus feasted Thyestes on the flesh of his two young sons—a horror at which the Sun turned back upon his course. And now Thyestes cursed the whole race of the Pĕlopidae. Atreus' son, Agamemnon, leading a host against Troy to regain Helen, wife of his brother Menelaus, committed in his turn a further crime. For he sacrificed his own daughter Iphigeneia to Artemis at Aulis, to appease the anger of the goddess, who stayed his fleet with adverse winds. His queen, Clytemnestra, never forgave him. She took for lover Aegisthus, son of the false Thyestes, and they plotted to murder her husband on his return from Troy.

Such is the background. The events of the play speak for themselves. But it may be worth briefly considering why many have felt it the finest work, not only of Aeschylus, but of all ancient drama. (Swinburne's hyperbole, acclaiming the *Oresteia* as 'the greatest spiritual work of man,' may be left to lovers of ecstatics.)

There seem a number of reasons. Spectacle is far from being the main thing in the theatre. But it counts. And, lover of the spectacular as he was, Aeschylus never equalled, in the other plays that remain to us, this series of scenic effects—the lonely watchman on the palace roof; the sinister Clytemnestra gazing coldly at the dawn fires of rejoicing; the triumphal entry of Agamemnon, amid guards and captives, in his chariot; the unfolding of the crimson carpets for his doomed feet; the agonized Cassandra stripping herself symbolically of the prophetic insignia with which Apollo mocks her; and, last, the tall queen erect in vengeance between the dead bodies of prophetess and king. There is too, though a

---

[1] Genealogical table, p. 115.

spectacle only for the imagination, the rush and roar of the mountain-beacons blazing the fall of Troy across the Aegean to the palace of Argos.

Such visions grow only more impressive to those who have stood beneath the Lion Gate of Mycenae, ancient already when Aeschylus was born; or looked on the golden treasures of its dead kings, found by Schliemann where they had already lain buried and forgotten for nearly a thousand years before the writing of this play.

Then there is the music and muscle of the verse, both dialogue and lyric. Perhaps the greatest speech in all Greek drama is that insidious welcome of Clytemnestra to her hated husband, as passionate in its wild imagery as the oriental Isaiah (p. 84). Indeed the whole scene strangely recalls another masterpiece of biblical style—the harlot-wife of *Proverbs* (ch. vii): 'With her much fair speech she caused him to yield, with the flattering of her lips she forced him. He goeth after her straightway, as an ox goeth to the slaughter, or as a fool to the correction of the stocks. . . . Her house is the way to hell, going down to the chambers of death.'

Nor did Aeschylus ever equal these choruses, with their visions of Iphigeneia and of Helen—of the innocent life sacrificed to the cold malignities of the State and, on the other hand, of a whole commonweal sacrificed still more wantonly to a single frivolous soul. Never did he muse so magnificently as here—on the mystery of the world, 'Zeus, whoe'er He be'; on the futile horror of war; on the captive victim, who is yet nobler in her clear vision than the blind victor who crushes her; on the forsaken husband, watched intolerably by the cold marble eyes of the statues in his empty hall.

The plot, too, though simple, is still real to us—a man coming home from war to be murdered by his adulterous wife and her lover. Such things still happen. Whereas too many plots in Greek drama (as in some Romantic writers) show a certain morbid eccentricity, in their obsession with frightful and abnormal family situations, where someone has either to marry or to murder a father, mother, brother, sister, son, or daughter. Are parricide, matricide, and incest really so interesting—at least to the conscious mind? Such things also happen. But, fortunately, not often enough to signify. Siamese twins likewise happen. One can imagine an ingenious dramatist contriving a most ingenious tragi-comedy about a pair of Siamese twins—conceive their complicated feelings if they both loved the same person; or if one loved her, and one hated. There would be only one fatal objection. Siamese twins are too rare, too abnormal, too singular.

But from this rather frequent blemish of Greek tragedy *Agamemnon* escapes (though not its two sequels, with their theme of matricide). Further, it is brilliantly heightened by symbolism and suspense. And the dramatic conflict here becomes vivid as never before. In previous extant plays of Aeschylus one party to the conflict—the sons of Aegyptus, the Greek victors of Salamis, Polyneices, Zeus—had remained behind the scenes. But here Agamemnon and Clytemnestra, Clytemnestra and Cassandra, the Chorus and Aegisthus clash face to face.

Lastly, there are its characters—often, to my mind, the most vital thing of all in drama, provided that plot, ideas, and style are adequate. (Think, for example, of Cleopatra, Shylock, Macbeth, Falstaff, Hamlet.) The characters in *Agamemnon* may seem still comparatively flat and thin beside the figures of an Ibsen or a Tchekhov. All the same, Clytemnestra lives and moves in our minds as no earlier figure on the stage had ever done. She has already some of the intricacy and mystery of life—hysterical strength of passion in crisis, nervous reaction after it, and a mixture of motives that leaves us wondering—how far was she really moved by revenge for Iphigeneia, how far by guilty love for Aegisthus? (Presumably we are meant to feel that anger for Iphigeneia began the estrangement, adultery followed, jealousy of Chryseis and Cassandra added their sting; now, with her husband's return, Clytemnestra must strike or perish.)

Cassandra, some have said, is only faintly sketched: but at least it is a sketch that our imaginations fill to a roundness far more living than many a more elaborate portrait. Even sentinel and herald, even the Chorus (apart from their too ludicrous futility at the actual moment of the murder) possess their own touches of individuality. Aegisthus is all he needs to be. Only Agamemnon seems to me not wholly satisfactory. Like Shakespeare's Julius Caesar, though he gives his name to the play, he disappoints. He remains forcible-feeble; stiff, yet weak; not great, but the shadow of greatness. As with Caesar, it has been argued that, were he more effective, he would distract too much attention from the rest of the play to himself. That seems to me more an excuse than a reason. The very living Agamemnon of *The Iliad* remains, without growing too important, far kinglier and more impressive; the ghostly Agamemnon of *The Odyssey*[1] moves me far more deeply when he tells in Hades of his murder in the hall of Aegisthus. The truth may be that Homer had a better first-hand knowledge of real princes than any Attic dramatist.

This view is not shared by all. Professor Fraenkel in his monumental edition of this play remains full of admiration for the king, whom he finds a 'true gentleman.' But one must ask whether English 'gentlemen,' even in the indulgent days of the Regency, would not have stared, if in 1814 the Duke of Wellington had arrived in triumph from Paris at Hamilton Place with a French mistress in his chariot, and asked the Duchess to see her comfortably lodged. In the play that outrage is well contrived to heighten the retribution near at hand. All the same one may feel that the death of Agamemnon would have seemed more moving, and the revenge of Orestes

---

[1] *Odyssey*, xi, 385–464; *Greek Poetry for Everyman*, p. 150.

less odious, if the King of Kings had been, as in Homer, a finer person—
rash indeed and proud, yet brave and royal and human.

Be that as it may, this tragedy was, I think, never to be outdone on the
European stage till, two thousand years later, another king murdered
through a wife's adultery, and destined to be avenged by his son, stalked
spectral along the battlements of Elsinore.

AGAMEMNON

AGAMEMNON, King of Argos
CLYTEMNESTRA, his Queen
AEGISTHUS, son of Thyestes, cousin
   of Agamemnon, and lover of
   Clytemnestra

CASSANDRA, daughter of Priam
SENTINEL
HERALD
CHORUS OF ARGIVE ELDERS

[*Night. The palace at Argos. A sentinel lies couched on its roof. Before its door is an altar of Apollo, and his image, or a conical pillar symbolizing him.*]

Sentinel. Now Heaven send relief from all my labour!—
   This year-long watch, that keeps me lying here
   On this roof of the Atreidae, like a hound,
   Couched on my elbows; till I know too well
   These starry multitudes in midnight conclave,
   And the bright lords among them, in Heaven resplendent,
   That bring to mortals wintertime and summer.
   Still must I watch and watch for the beacon-signal,
   The fiery glare that shall bring news from Troy,
   That Troy is fallen.   Thus, grown high with hope,
   Has ruled one woman's heart—bold as a man's.
   But on this couch of mine, dew-drenched, uneasy
   That no dreams haunt (for how dare *I* close eyelid,
   When Fear, not Sleep, stands always at my side?),
   If ever I *have* a mind to sing, or hum
   Some ditty as an antidote to slumber,
   It turns to a lamentation for this house,
   No longer nobly governed; as it *was.*
   Oh for that blest deliverance from labour,
   The beacon-light of victory through the gloom!

      For a while he scans the darkness. The glare of a beacon appears
      to eastward. He springs to his feet.

   All hail, thou splendour turning night to day,
   With tidings that shall set afoot in Argos
   Many a ring of dancers!
   Oho!   Oho!
   I cry aloud to the Queen of Agamemnon!—
   Up!—let her rise in haste, and through her palace
   With jubilation greet this beacon-flame,
   If truly, as it tells now, Troy is taken.

And *I* will dance myself, by way of prelude.
For *me* this beacon-fire has thrown three sixes!
My masters' dice fall lucky—mine to move!
Well, may I see this house's lord come home,
And grasp his own dear hand!   I say no more.
My tongue wags not—a great ox treads upon it.
Yet—if this house could talk,
There'd be a tale!   I choose to speak to those
That *know*; for those that know not—I forget!

> *He runs from the palace roof.   There enters a chorus of twelve
> elders of Argos.*

Chorus.   Ten years are spent
   Since Menelaus first defied,
   With Agamemnon at his side,
   King Priam to the sword's arbitrament;
   Ten years, since the two Atreidae, paired
   By Zeus with thrones and sceptres shared,
   Launched from this Argive shore
   A thousand ships to war,
   While fierce their cry of battle rung;
   As eagles, robbed of their callow young
   (So long, so vainly brooded), high
   Above their craggy eyrie soar
   On widely wheeling wings, and cry
   With desolate tongue;
   Till far aloft to some God's ear—
   Zeus, maybe, or Apollo or Pan—
   The wail of their anguish rises clear
   And roused for His creatures' sake to wrath
   He sends, slow but sure, His Erīnys forth
   Against the guilt of man.

So Zeus, whose might none may withstand,
   The Lord of Hospitality,
On Paris loosed the Atreidae's hand.
All for a wanton's sake, He planned
   To Trojan and to Greek should be
Many a bitter wrestling given,
Many a knee in the dust down-driven,
Many a spear-shaft snapped and riven,
   Ere wed at last were she.

And now?   The truth is what it is,
And Doom shall ordain the end of this;

No poured libations can abate,
No sacrifice that a man may bring,
No burnt, nor unburnt offering,
God's unrelenting hate.

To war they marched away; but we,
With *our* old limbs like children's grown,
Upon our staffs propped uselessly,
Must here at home remain.
Soft springs the marrow in the bone
Of infant's breast, to War unknown;
And as weak in our age it grows again.
When all the leaves of life fall sere,
Beneath the weight of year on year
Old men, on three legs tottering, seem
Frail as a child, faint as a dream
Flutters when dawn grows plain.

> *Clytemnestra enters, with attendants who burn incense on the altar
> before the palace.*

But tell us, thou,
Daughter of Tyndareus, Argos' Queen,
O Clytemnestra, what tidings now?
What is astir?
Comes news by some sure messenger?
Or what may these thine orders mean
For sacrifice on every hand?
Why to the Gods that guard our land,
The Gods of Heaven and of Hell,
The Gods of home and market—tell!—
Do flames from our altars skyward glare,
With smoke from the purest unguents rolled
That the store-rooms of thy palace hold,
In silent innocence of prayer?
If it be lawful to reveal,
Lady, speak it now—and heal
This heart of care,
That aches at times too bitterly!—
Though, as I see these offerings burn,
With a kindlier light my hopes return
And drive my gnawing thoughts from me.

> *The Queen does not regard them: turning away, they resume their chant.*

Yet still I am strong to tell in song   *strophe* I.
Of that fair augury

That greeted our kings, the day
They marched!   Though I be gray,
God breathes in me the passion
And power of poesy,
To tell how the Kings of Achaea,
The leagued lords of our land,
Leading the hosts of Hellas
With avenging spear in hand,
Were sped against Troy by wings of wrath.
For our sea-kings saw, at their setting forth,
Two kings of the air—one sable,
One with a tail plumed white.
Clear in men's eyes, by the palace
They settled, on the right,
With claws that tare a mountain-hare—
And the young within her womb,
Never to race on the hillside,
With their mother met their doom.
Alas!   Alas!—
And yet come good to pass!

Then he saw clear, that subtle seer   *antistrophe* 1.
Who led our host to war,
In the birds that slew the hare
The Atreidae—warrior-pair
Diverse, likewise, in spirit;
And thus the prophet swore:
'In the end, the arms ye muster
Shall take Priam's town; and Fate
Shall smite the vast herds of his people
In front of tower and gate.
If only, before your host at last
For a curb in the mouth of Troy is cast,
No wrath from Heaven darken,
Nor its lightning strike us down!
For Artemis the Maiden
With pity and with frown
Beheld that hare, before she bare
Her young, poor cowering beast,
By her Sire's winged hounds dismembered—
And she loathes the eagles' feast.'
Alas!   Alas!
And yet come good to pass!

'Fair Huntress-queen, although   *epode.*
The fierce lion's helpless cubs to thee
Be dear, and though Thou lovest so
All the young life of wild and wood—
Ah yet fulfil for us the good
Foreshadowed in this augury,
Though evil too it should portend!
And Thou, Apollo, Healer, stay
Thy sister, lest she send
Upon the ships of Greece ill winds' delay,
Demanding that to her we pay
A sacrifice our lips spew forth—
That never law can consecrate—
That braves men's wrath,
And breeds their hate!
For a curse of terror and treachery clings,
With steps that ever return again,
To haunt the house that hath seen such things—
A Wrath that remembers children slain.'

Thus did the prophet's cry forebode
Not only triumphs to be,
From that omen the eagles showed,
But doom as well for our dynasty.
Therefore sing we:
'Alas! Alas!
And yet come good to pass!'

Zeus, whoever He may be,   *str.* 2.
By that name on Him I call
(If 'tis thus He would be known).
Though I weigh infinity,
Naught my thought may grasp at all,
Save Him alone,
To lift away this load of pain
Burdening my soul in vain.

He that first was Lord of Earth,   *ant.* 2.
Mighty God of Battles—lo!
E'en His memory is dead.
He that second came to birth,
Met in turn his overthrow,
In turn is fled.

But wisdom *they* shall find that call
'Praise to Zeus, who conquers all!'

He hath shown man wisdom's ways,   *str.* 3
He hath made His ordinance plain
Unto all—'By suffering learn!'
Sleepless still, the sinner pays:
Dark memories, drop by drop, return,
Till stubborn hearts are schooled by pain.
So the stern Gods give their grace,
Holding in Heaven the helmsman's place.

Then the elder of our Kings   *ant.* 3.
Whom Achaea's host obeyed,
Durst not blame what said the seer,
Bowed to the blast of adverse things;
Since, with winds that would not veer,
Hunger on his people weighed,
Where, by Chalcis, evermore,
Turn the tides on Aulis shore.

For ceaseless gales from Strymon setting   *str.* 4.
Held them deedless, foodless, fretting,
Straggling on that shore astray.
Week on week, the tempest's power
Rent hull and hawser, while the flower
Of Argos waned away;
Until the prophet cried at last:
''Tis Artemis that holds us fast!'
And for that bitter sea
A bitterer cure he found,
That made the Atreidae weep, aghast,
With sceptres, in their agony,
Smiting the ground.

Then Atreus' elder son cried, mourning: *ant.* 4.
'Ah bitter, if I spurn this warning!
Bitter, too, to kill my child!
Pride of my house her beauty stands;
How shall a father see his hands
With maiden blood defiled,
At God's own altar! What choice to take?
My gathered fleet can I forsake?

Can I fail my loyal allies?
To lull this gale to rest,
They claim her death—their wrath will wake,
With justice, if my voice denies.
God grant the best!'

So, yoked beneath Necessity,   *str. 5*
His purpose veered; heart-hardened thus,
He let that outrage be;
Unclean, unhallowed, impious!
When guilty madness goads the brain,
It blinds to the ruin that lurks before—
He did not quail.
For a woman's sin his child was slain,
To speed his host to war,
To let his galleys sail!

They pitied not her girlish years,   *ant. 5.*
Those judges wild for war—no care
They took for all her tears,
Her cries of 'Father!'   After prayer,
That father bade his henchmen drag
And hold her, like a young kid, high
O'er the altar's face—
Drooping, with tangled robe—and gag
Those sweet lips (lest their cry
Should curse all Atreus' race).

Curbed there she lay, in dumb duress,   *str. 6.*
Low trailed in the dust her saffron dress;
But still on her slayers near
She cast in piteousness
Mute eyes of fear;
Fair as a picture, still she strove to call
Their names, as in old days
When maiden in her father's festal hall,
With girlish voice, the third libation made,
To the glad prayer that her loved father prayed,
She sang her loving praise.

What followed, I nor saw, nor tell;   *ant. 6*
As Calchas warned, so all befell;
Yet Justice orders, stern:

'By suffering, it is well
That men should learn.'
What comes, shall come.   I greet it now.   (Yet vain,
When Destiny hath planned,
To greet, or grieve!)   This dawn shall make all plain.
God turn it to the best—whate'er hath been—
As wills our rightful regent, and our Queen,
Sole stay of the Argive land.

They turn anew to her silent figure.

Chorus-leader.   In reverence, Clytemnestra, of thy greatness
I come before thee now—with honour due
To our Queen whose lord is absent, void his throne.
But why this sacrifice?   Hast thou assurance
Of some great tidings?   Or but happy hopes?
I pray thee speak—or if thy lips are sealed,
Lady, thy will be done.

Clytemnestra.   Fair breedeth fair, men say; may now a Morn
Of promise like its Mother Night be born.
Far surer than mere hopes is *my* good news.
The hosts of Argos have taken Priam's city!

Leader.   What's this!   Thy words escaped me.   Past belief!

Clytemnestra.   Troy's in Achaean hands.   *Now* am I plain?

Leader.   Such joy steals over me, it turns to tears.

Clytemnestra.   Thine eyes do honour to thy loyalty.

Leader.   What makes thee, then, so sure?   Hast any proof?

Clytemnestra.   I have.   Indeed I have.   Unless God cheats me.

Leader.   Is it some dream that awes thee to belief?

Clytemnestra.   I take no fancies of a drowsing brain.

Leader.   Then is it some light-winged rumour swells thy hopes?

Clytemnestra.   Thou ratest me no wiser than a child.

Leader.   And how long *is* it since the city fell?

Clytemnestra.   In the very night that brought this dawn to birth.

Leader.   What messenger could ever come so fast?

Clytemnestra.   Hephaestus!—that sped his flame from Ida's top,
Whence beacon after beacon hath relayed
This message-fire to Argos—first, Mount Ida
To Hermes' crag on Lemnos; then, from Lemnos,
Athos, the peak of Zeus, caught up the blaze
And swept it across the heaven, while all the sea
Was filled with fishes leaping in their joy
Up towards that pine-fed glare, gold as the sun.
It reached Mācistus' summit—him in turn

No heedless sleep nor sluggishness delayed
From hastening the signal onward. Swift its glitter
Shone afar off across Eurīpus' channel
To the warders set on Mount Messāpion;
Who with a counter-flame passed on the tidings,
Kindling a stack piled high with ancient heath.
That beacon-torch, in undiminished splendour
Bright as the moon, o'erleapt Asōpus' plain,
To wake in turn from the ridges of Cithaeron
A new relay of light. The watchers there
Rejected not the far-sent fiery call,
Kindling an even mightier conflagration
Than they had been commanded. Onward still
The splendour flashed across Gorgōpis' lake
And reached Mount Aegiplanctus with its summons
Not to delay the balefire's course ordained.
So with an eager will they sent outstreaming
A mighty beard of flame, that overflew
The promontory that guards the Sarōnic Strait
And never stooped until it reached yon height
That neighbours us, the steep of Arachnaeon.
So on this roof of the Atreidae's palace
The light leapt down, of yon far blaze on Ida
True lineal descendant.
Such was the torch-race that I had commanded,
Passing in turn from runner on to runner;
And of that team both first and last alike
Have victory.
Such is the token and the testimony
My lord hath sent from Troy.
Leader. Lady, for this I will praise Heaven hereafter;
Meanwhile, I pray, tell out thy tale again,
That I may feed my wonder to the full.
Clytemnestra. This day the Achaeans are the lords of Troy.
With cries of hideous discord now methinks
Her streets resound—such fell antipathy
As when ye mingle oil and vinegar.
There at this moment mingle shrieks and cheers
From throats of conquered and of conquerors—
The wails of women clinging to dead limbs
Of husbands and of brothers—aged men
Moaning their sons—voices that cry aloud
For loved ones lost, lost too their liberty.

Meanwhile the victors, famished after battle
And a night of roving plunder, break their fast
Upon Troy's plenty—none gives orders now,
None makes assignment—all's a lottery.
So in Troy's conquered homes they sit at ease,
Relieved at last of bitter bivouac
In dew and frost—to sleep, like men of fortune,
The livelong night off guard!

    Now if with reverence due they still shall honour
The shrines and guardian Gods of fallen Troy,
Then shall these spoilers not in turn be spoiled.
But let them not now grow greedy!   Let our people
Not turn to plundering of holy things!
For they have yet to sail back safe to Hellas,
Their race's homeward lap is still to run;
And only if they shun offence towards Heaven,
Our host may hope
(Saving some stroke of evil luck) to hush
Those curses that the dying called on them.
Such is my judgment (that am but a woman).
But may the good prevail, with naught to cloud it!
For, of life's blessings, dearest in my eyes
Is power still to enjoy them.

Leader. Lady, thou speakest wisely—like a man
Of understanding.   Trusting these clear proofs,
I will turn me back again in prayer to Heaven,
That has not grudged full blessing on our toils.

                             [The Queen withdraws.

Chorus. O Zeus our Lord!   O friendly Night
With splendours untold in thy treasury,
Across Troy towers thou hast drawn tight
A prisoning net, whence none leapt free!
So close about them all—her young,
Her men of might—
Its mesh of ruin and bondage clung.

I bow before God's punishment—
The Zeus of Hospitality!
Long since at Paris His bow He bent
And His arrow fell not short nor spent,
Nor over the starry firmament
Flew soaring aimlessly.

Well may we say: 'From God this blow   *strophe* 1.
Hath struck them!'   Well we see and know
God planned, God wrought it.   Fool is he
That cries: 'Though underfoot ill men have trod
Fair sanctities, yet God
Heeds not.'   Ah blasphemy!
Our eyes have seen the humbling
Of hearts puffed up with pride,
Grown insolent in evil,
And of houses magnified
Too much.   The better part
I deem modest contentment
In an understanding heart:
For doomed is he that, wanton
With wealth that his hands have won,
Spurns the great altar of Justice
Down to oblivion.

For thus Temptation, deadly seed   *antistrophe* 1.
Of counselling Ātē, to her need
Constrains him.   *Then* he finds no cure.
His ruin may not be hid—too grim it glows;
For tried by time he shows,
Like basest bronze, impure;
Blotched grows his soul in the testing,
And toiling all in vain
(Like a child a bird pursuing),
He sets on his land a stain.
No God heeds now his prayer,
Nay, Heaven plunges headlong
That sinner to despair.
So once to the hall of Atreides
Sailed Paris oversea,
And stole his queen, and outraged
Hospitality.

To Greece she left the trampling and the din   *str.* 2.
Of seamen mustered, warriors called to war;
And through Troy-gates, unblushing in her sin,
Lightfoot she passed; and yet with her she bore,
For dowry, death!   But sorrowing
The prophets cried, of Sparta's king:
'Woe for our royal house!   Woe for the bed
Whither of old her loving beauty came!

Lonely he sits—with no word of blame,
With mind bemused, with honour fled;
But mistress still in his hall shall be
That phantom face from oversea.
Fair marble shapes watch round him—
Lovely, yet loathed are they.
For hungry eyes their beauty dies;
And Love has passed away.

'Before his heartsick vision, shapes of dream   *ant.* 2.
Hover with happiness bestowed in vain.
For, ah, what vanity, when before us seem
To stand our hearts' desires—yet glide again,
Between our hands, that cannot keep,
Fast fleeting down the paths of sleep!'
Such sadness broods within the king's abode,
Such griefs to bear, and heavier griefs than these;
And now, through every home in Greece,
What tears for men that down the road
To far-off war they watched depart!
Ay, *here* are thoughts to wring the heart.
For they pass, the remembered faces;
And in the place of men,
The arms they bore and their dust—no more—
Homeward return again.

Yea, thus deals Ares, money-changer grim,   *str.* 3.
Who holds His scales where clashes spear on spear.
A pinch of dust for the living limb—
Dust purged in flame, with many a tear
Weighed down, yet light within the urn—
Is all that He sends again
From Troy, to those that loved them well.
Wailing, the mourners praise their slain—
How one in fight was stern,
How nobly his comrade fell.
'Yet all through the wife of another!'
They mutter, while creeps abroad
Anger against the Atreidae
That drew the sword.
So many by Troy have found them,
In their beauty, graves at last;
The land that hates them hides them,
Yea, holds her conquerors fast.

Dread is a people's murmured discontent— *ant.* 3.
Like the ban of a city's curse, it bringeth doom;
I dread to hear the accomplishment
Of ills that as yet lie veiled in gloom.
On those whose hands have loved to slay
The eyes of the Gods are set,
And on the wicked whose luck seems fair
The dark Erīnyes follow yet,
To wear his life away—
Till he darkens to despair,
And lies, past help, with the perished.
Woe to too great renown!
For the gaze of God grows jealous
To smite it down.
Nay, mine be a bliss unenvied!
No city's sack I crave;
As I crave that never victor
May trample *me* for slave.

Of the glad news brought by the beacon-flame *epode.*
   Fast now from street to street
Flies rumour. And yet—was it truth that came?
Who knows? Or by the Gods are we beguiled?
What man so crazed of wit, or such a child,
   That he will set his soul aflare
   With beacon-fires—and then despair
     When all is proved a cheat!
     'Tis women's way to cry
Rejoicings, ere the fact itself be clear.
So credulous of what they hold most dear,
Their wishes widen, and too fast they fly;
Yet tales by women told as swiftly disappear.

Leader. Now we shall know what mean these fiery signals,
   These conflagrations kindling flame from flame,
   Whether they tell the truth or, like a dream,
   This light that flashed its gladness fooled our hopes.
   For here from the shore I see there comes a herald,
   Brows wreathed with olive. And the thirsty dust,
   Next sister unto mud, that covers him,
   Is sign of no dumb errand. *He* will bring us,
   Not by the smoky glare of faggots kindled
   High on the hills, but by plain word of mouth

Surer rejoicing or—but hence the thought
That things could fall less fairly!
May all that follows crown the first good tidings.
If any prays not thus for the weal of Argos,
Let his disloyalty reap its own reward!

> *There enters the Herald of Agamemnon. Bowing down, he kisses the ground.*

Herald. Ancestral earth of mine own Argive land,
At last, in the light of this tenth year, I find thee!
Broken so many hopes—yet *this* fulfilled!
For never I dared to trust that here in Argos
My dust should share the happy sleep of home.
Hail, land beloved!   Hail, sun that shines on it;
And Zeus, its highest Lord; and Pytho's King,
Far-shooting with Thy arrows—aimed, I pray,
Never again at *us*!
Enough we felt Thy wrath beside Scamander,
O Lord Apollo—draw Thou nigh us *now*
As Healer and as Saviour.
To all of you I call, O Host of Heaven;
And chiefly to my own protector Hermes,
Herald beloved, by heralds reverenced;
And to the Heroes—ye who sent us forth,
Bless this returning host the spear hath spared!
Halls of our kings, all hail!   Walls long beloved!
Seats of our mighty!   Gods that front the dawn!
Now, of all times, with bright and sunlit faces
Greet fair our lord that rides, at long last, home.
For unto you and all this people here,
Lightening the darkness, comes King Agamemnon!
Give him good welcome, as in truth is fitting
For him that hath digged down the walls of Troy
With the mattock of the justice-dealing Zeus;
Whereby her earth is broken utterly
And, rooted up, all seed of Ilios dies.
So heavy a yoke the elder son of Atreus
Hath cast on Troy, and now is come again
With happy fortune, worthiest to be praised
Of all that live to-day; since neither Paris,
Nor yet that city his accessary,
Can boast to have harmed us more than they have suffered.
For yon proved thief and robber has both lost
His plunder and cut off in utter ruin

The house of his own father, and all Troy.
So Priam's sons paid twofold penalty.
Leader. Joy to thee, herald of the Achaean host!
Herald. 'Tis mine!—though the Gods sent *death* now, I were happy.
Leader. So hard hast thou wrestled with the love of home?
Herald. So hard, that my eyes are dim with tears of joy.
Leader. Sick, suffering heart!—and yet a happy sickness!
Herald. How shall I take thy meaning?
Leader. Because the love ye bore, was love returned.
Herald. Argos so craved us?   As we craved for Argos?
Leader. So deeply, that often my darkened spirit groaned.
Herald. But why your gloom?   *That* was the army's curse.
Leader. My saving remedy hath long been silence.
Herald. How?   Our lord absent, hast thou dreaded *others*?
Leader. So much, that *now,* like thee, I could die happy.
Herald. Ay, we have triumphed.   And yet, in those long years,
Though we could call ourselves in many ways
Fortunate, sore we suffered!   (Who, save Gods,
Can live untouched by sorrow all his days?)
For if you knew our hardships!—our rough quarters,
Ill bedded on our galleys' crowded gangways . . .
Or, on the Trojan shore (more hateful still!),
To live encamped beneath a hostile rampart,
Drenched with the constant curse of rain from Heaven,
And dews of the field, that swarmed our clothes with vermin!
Those winters, too, that Ida's snows made bleak
Past bearing, while the very birds fell dead—
Those burning heats of noon, when every wind
Sank, and without one ripple slept the sea!
But what use grieving now?   The pain is past,
And past for all our dead the slightest wish
To rise back, ever, to this earth again.
What use to tell the roll-call of our fallen
And sadden the living with old griefs remembered?
Farewell, for me, all our calamities!
To us survivors of the Argive host
What we have won outweighs all we have suffered.
Therefore with vaunts that wing by land and sea,
Well may we boast before the sun's bright face:
'The Argive armies, mastering Ilios,
Have nailed these spoils, to hang in ancient glory,
Upon the temples of the Gods of Greece.'
After such tidings, needs must men cry honour

To Argos and her leaders.   Thank we too
The grace of Zeus that wrought it!   There's my tale.
Leader. Thy words have overcome me—freely I own it;
Age abides ever young enough to learn.
Rich news is this to me—yet most it touches
Queen Clytemnestra and our royal house.

                                                    [*Clytemnestra enters.*

Clytemnestra. Long since, I sang my chant of jubilation,
When that first fiery herald of the night
Proclaimed that Troy was taken and overthrown.
Yet some rebuked me: 'Trust mere beacon-signals
For proof that Ilios is put to sack!
How lightly a woman's heart is lifted up!'
Such talkers made my wit seem wandering;
But none the less I offered sacrifice,
And at my woman's word throughout the city,
This side and that, men raised the shout of gladness,
And, in the temples, first with incense fed,
Then quenched, the fragrant flame.
       And now what need from thee of a longer story?
The King himself shall tell me all of it.
But let me hasten to prepare my welcome
For my honoured lord's return.   What happier day
For a wife's eyes, than when she flings her gates
Wide for her husband, safely home from war
By God's own keeping?   Back!—and thus tell my lord.
Quick let him come, the darling of this land!—
And, coming, find the wife beside his hearth
As faithful as he left her—of his house
The trusty watch-dog, foe to all his foes,
And in all else the same—each seal he left,
Through the long years unviolated still.
Pleasure in other men, or lightest touch
Of ill repute—I know as little of them
As how to dip the tempered steel of war!
       Such vaunt is mine.   And there's no shame to make it
For an honourable woman.   It is *true*!

                                                    [*She goes out.*

Leader. So she has said.   And, well interpreted,
Thou must perceive it is a seemly speech.
But tell me, herald—it is of Menelaus
I long to hear.   Is *he* in your company,
Safely returned, that lord beloved in Argos?

Herald. I cannot tell a falsehood with fair semblance,
  Even for those I love.   Too brief its fruit.
Leader. Ah that thy news could be both good and true!
  Yet if not both—truth cannot long be hid.
Herald. Know, then, he is vanished from the Achaean host—
  He and his ship.   So stands the naked truth.
Leader. Did you see him sail alone from Ilios,
  Or did some storm strike the whole fleet and part ye?
Herald. Like a master-bowman, thou hast hit the mark
  And summed in those brief words a long disaster.
Leader. What rumours passed among your mariners?—
  That he lives yet, or has perished?
Herald. No clear report—there is no one that knows,
  Saving the Sun that fosters all things living.
Leader. How came it, then, this storm that Heaven's anger
  Sent on the fleet?   What was the end of it?
Herald. Ill is it to pollute a day of blessing
  With tongue of evil tidings.   Such affliction
  Suits not with Heaven's praises.
  When comes a messenger with darkened brow
  To tell his city of some fell disaster—
  Its host destroyed, alike with public ruin
  And mourning in many a home for warriors slain
  By that two-headed goad that Ares loves,
  His twin spears crimsoned with their double havoc—
  Then such a one, bowed with calamity,
  May lift such strains to Hell's Erīnyes.
  But, bringer of glad tidings of salvation
  To a city rejoicing in her happiness,
  How can I blend my good news with such evil?—
  Tell of this storm that came not, sure, without
  God's wrath on the Achaeans?
  For those two once inveterate enemies,
  Fire and the sea, grown now conspirators,
  Revealed their covenant by shattering
  The hapless host of Argos.
  With night there rose an evil-surging swell,
  And gales from Thrace crashed galley against galley;
  Till, butted hard amid the rage of winds
  And thunderous rain, from sight our vessels vanished
  Beneath the whirling lash of that grim shepherd.
  But when there rose the clear light of the sun,
  Before us stretched the Aegean Sea, a field

Whose flowers were wrecks and bodies of Achaeans.
As for our own ship, with her hull undamaged
Some God—no power of man!—by intercession,
Or secret aid, preserved her, with His hand
Guiding her helm.   Upon her deck sat Fortune
With kindly will to save us, suffering her
Neither to founder in the surge at anchor,
Nor drive on the reefs to shoreward.

Thus, then, escaped from death amid the deep,
Though fair the day above us, still distrusting
Our own good luck, we gave up all our hearts
To grief to feed on, for the evil plight
Of our hard-battered fleet.

And now, if among them any yet are breathing,
Doubtless they talk of *us* as gone to death,
While we so guess of *them*.   God send the best!
For Menelaus—hope, above all things,
His safe return!   At least, if any gleam
Of sun still sees him looking on the light,
Some chance abides that Zeus, not yet desiring
To destroy the House of Atreus, may dispose
His home-coming.   And now ye have heard the truth.

                     [*The Herald goes out.*

Chorus. Whose the tongue that called her so—   *strophe* 1.
    Called her all too fittingly?
Was it One we do not know,
    Prophet of the doom to be,
Named that woman, born to breed
    Bridal strife and clash of steel,
'Helen'?   Ah, a Hell indeed
    For ships and men and commonweal!—
A name by Doom decreed!

From her curtained bower to sea she crept
And with giant-lips the West Wind blew;
But thickly her armoured hunters flew
(Though dim the trail of her fleeing oar)
To where upon the leafy shore
Of Símoïs the lovers leapt—
So willed the Fiend of War.

Thus, for Troy, implacably,   *antistrophe* 1.
    Wooing turned at last to woe.

Retribution bade it be—
    What She willeth, falleth so.
She hath claimed (though years were long),
    For the Zeus that holdeth dear
Hearth and home, the price of wrong
    From Paris' race, that chanted clear
Queen Helen's bridal-song.

With her hymns of gladness turned to pain,
King Priam's ancient capital
Learns now to wail aloud—to call:
'Ah Paris, for thy fatal bed!'—
To cry a dirge, uncomforted,
For all her gallant children slain,
Her blood in sorrow shed.

Thus in his home a man once bred   *str.* 2.
The offspring of a lion, torn
From its mother's breast—a thing milk-fed,
Still in its life's first morn,
Playmate of many a child—
And on it the old men smiled.
Often about their breasts it clung,
Tame as a babe; and soft its eye
As it licked their hands with a fawning tongue,
To quiet its hunger's cry.

But the years, that gave it strength, laid bare   *ant.* 2.
The nature of its breed of old,
Repaying all their fostering care
With slaughter in flock and fold.
Mid blood-splashed walls the beast
Gorged its unbidden feast;
In helpless anguish they stood to see
How there it ravened and it slew;
Doom's minister God bade it be
For the home where long it grew.

So first it seemed there came to Ilios city   *str.* 3.
A soul whose windless calm no storms would shake;
A wealth of tranquil loveliness;
Love's flower—so sweet, the sense must ache;
Soft eyes, whose glances bless.

But then, a change!   To that bridal-hymn
She gave a bitter end and grim.
The God of Guests sent her to be
But joyless, loveless company;
On the House of Priam He bade her leap,
A Fury—for Troy's brides to weep.

Long among men has lived an ancient saying—   *ant.* 3.
That, coming to full years, Prosperity
Not childless dies, but makes to grow
For generations yet to be,
From Weal, unending Woe.
But I, though alone, think not with these—
I deem man's own Impieties
Beget in turn new deeds of ill,
Like in nature, but waxing still.
For where a house loves Righteousness,
From sire to son Luck grows not less.

But Pride that the years have hardened bringeth forth,   *str.* 4.
Sooner or later, in its time's full age
A ruinous younger Pride, a child of Wrath,
    Whose demon rage
Scorns holy things, puts sword and spear to scorn—
Black ruin for the house where it was born,
    Foul as its parentage.

Yet Justice shines in huts by smoke defiled,   *ant.* 4.
Honours the hearts where righteousness abides;
From gilded walls that hands unclean have piled
    Her glance She hides;
Scorning the coin of counterfeited praise,
And turning back Her steps towards purer ways,
    All things to their goal She guides.

> *Agamemnon enters in his chariot, with Cassandra, preceded
> and followed by his guards.*

Leader. Tell me, O King, thou son of Atreus,
    Sacker of Troy,
How shall I speak to thee?   How do thee homage,
Not overshooting, not falling short
Of the honour thy due?
Many there are, transgressors of justice,
That turn from the truth to follow fair-seeming;
And all are ready to shed their tears

Over the wretched, although within them
Their hearts are untouched by the tooth of sorrow;
While for the happy they feign rejoicing,
With features unsmiling enforced to mirth.
But the *good* shepherd, who knows his sheep,
Is not beguiled by the liar's look,
That feigns a loyalty never felt,
And fawns with a watery love.
Of old, as I watched thee (I will not hide it)
Levy thy hosts for the sake of Helen,
My heart beheld thee in shape ungracious,
As a blind pilot of evil counsel,
That paid for a willing wanton
Lives of men.
Yet now, with a loyalty not of the lips,
And true goodwill, I remember the adage:
'Well is all labour whose end is well.'
But of those thou hast left home-keeping in Argos,
Time shall show thee, if well thou weigh them,
The faithful—*and* the false!

Agamemnon. To Argos, first, due greeting, and her Gods,
Who lent their help to my safe coming home,
And to my vengeance on the city ruled
By Priam. In that trial 'twixt him and me
There were no voices spoke—yet Heaven heard:
And, with one mind, the high Gods cast their votes
In the red urn of carnage—ruin for Troy
And slaughter for her people! All in vain
The opposing urn of mercy saw each hand
Draw near—then pass beyond it. Now the reek
Still makes a landmark of Troy's fallen towers;
Still lives that storm of ruin; still embers dying
Roll their smoke rich with opulence consumed.
Therefore 'tis meet we render the Immortals
Gratitude unforgetting, since They gave us
Justice for that unconscionable rape,
And Ilios for one woman's sake lies sacked
By that grim monster, foaled of our Wooden Horse—
The steel-clad Argive host, that from its womb
Sprang, at the Pleiads' setting, like a lion,
Leaping across the battlements of Troy
To lap its surfeit of the blood of kings.
    So much I say in prelude to the Gods;

As for your loyalty, I too remember
What ye said once; accept it; and approve.
For few there are whose nature still can honour
A friend's good fortune, with no grudge of envy—
That spiteful poison, clinging round the heart,
Which lays on him that's once distempered with it
A double burden—pain for his own mischance
And groaning rancour at his rival's blessings.
I speak as one that knows; for I have looked
Long in that mirror where companionship
Shows its true feature.   Men I have found that seemed
To love me well—and yet mere shadow-shapes;
Odysseus only, though so loth to sail,
Once he had taken the yoke of war upon him,
Pulled with a will beside me—whether now
He be alive or perished.
Now touching this our city, and the Gods,
We will gather all our people to determine,
In full assembly.   There we must provide
How what is well may still continue so,
And what is sick and craves sharp medicine,
Wisdom may cure—with knife or cautery.
     But first to the palace, to the hearth of home!—
That I may greet the Gods who sent me forth
And brought me back once more.   May Victory,
Since She hath come to us, with *us* abide!

> *Clytemnestra with her women emerges from the palace.*

Clytemnestra. Men of this city—Elders of Argos—hear me!
For no false shame shall lock my lips from speaking
A true wife's love.   Time cures us in the end
Of such poor tonguefastness.   Too well my heart
Knows—ah, none needs to tell me—all I suffered
Through the long years while *he* lay under Troy—
The misery of a woman left at home,
Lonely, without her husband, listening
To curséd rumour on the heels of rumour,
One babbler first and then another after,
Bawling worse tidings than the one before him.
I tell you, had this man but half the wounds
That tales fast flowing home to Argos gave him,
His body is more riddled than a net.
Ay, had he died as often as men told,
Then, like a new, three-bodied Gēryon,

He might have claimed a triple coverlet
Of earth—one for each of his three bodies slain.
Thanks to such cursed tidings, time on time,
They have cut the throttling noose about my neck—
Saved me perforce, all desperate for death.

And that is why our son, pledge of our love,
Stands not to-day to greet thee at my side,
As *should* have been—Orestes!   Look not startled.
The boy is safe with our own loyal ally,
King Stróphius, in Phocis; oft he warned me
Of those twin dangers—death for thee at Troy,
And our unruly commons, here in Argos,
Rising to cast Good Counsel from her seat.
(For men, by nature, ever spurn the fallen.)
Thus stands the guileless truth.

But, as for me, the torrents of my tears
Have flowed to their last drop; and these poor eyes
Smart still with watching, weeping, through the midnight
Under the lamp that never lit thee home.
Even abed the tiny, darting wing
Of a crying gnat would wake me from my dreams,
That seemed to see thee suffer in my sleep
More than my sleep had time for.   But to-day,
With all my sorrows ended, light of heart,
I hail my husband—watch-dog of the fold,
The mainstay of my bark, the rooted column
That holds my roof to Heaven—dear as a child,
A father's only child, and sweet as land
To sailor that never looked to see it more,
[As radiant morning after night of storm,]
As well-spring to the wanderer in the waste.
[Ah, good to escape the grip of circumstance!]
If now my full heart heaps such praises on him,
Let Heaven not grudge it—we have borne so much
In bygone days.   But come, dear heart, descend—
Step from thy chariot—treading not, my King,
On common earth with the foot that trampled Troy.
Ho there, my handmaidens whose task it is
To strew with tapestries the ground he treads on!—
Quick now and lay him here a path of crimson—
That Justice, past all hope, may lead him home.
The rest my care that sleeps not, by God's help,
Shall see accomplished, as is well and fair.

The women lay crimson tapestries from Agamemnon's chariot to the palace-door.

Agamemnon. Daughter of Leda, guardian of my home,
Long is thy greeting.   Well it may be so,
For long my absence was.   Yet keep due measure
In praising me—from other lips than thine
Such praise should come.   Coax *me* with no soft speeches,
As if I were some woman; gape not *thou*
With grovelling acclamations at my feet,
Like some barbarian king's;
Nor strew my way with finery, to awaken
Envy—keep all such tributes for the Gods.
A perilous thing it were for me, a mortal,
To walk on woven splendours of the loom.
[As *man* thou mayst do me honour—not as God.]
Embroideries for foot-cloths!—think what fame
Would bruit of me!   God's greatest gift to man
Is still to keep his judgment.   Call none happy
Till to his grave he has gone down in peace.
Enough!—I have said how far I dare to go.

Clytemnestra. Yet of *one* thing tell me thy honest thought.

Agamemnon. Ask on; and thou shalt have the truth for answer.

Clytemnestra. In peril, might you not have vowed this thing?

Agamemnon. If some wise prophet had prescribed it so.

Clytemnestra. And what would Priam in triumph like yours have done?

Agamemnon. Ah, Priam might well have walked on tapestries!

Clytemnestra. Then heed no more the carping tongues of men.

Agamemnon. There is a force to fear in common talk.

Clytemnestra. Unenviable is he that wakes no envy.

Agamemnon. Love of debate but ill befits a woman.

Clytemnestra. Yet it can grace the great, sometimes to yield.

Agamemnon. And *if* I yield?—is this so much to thee?

Clytemnestra. Do!—freely yielding, thou art master still.

Agamemnon. Well, have your will!   Quick now, let some hand loosen
The sandals that do service to my feet;
And may no God from Heaven with jealous eyes
                    [*Two of the handmaidens loosen his sandals.*
Watch as I walk upon these crimson webs.
In truth, I feel it shame to waste our substance,
Trampling on costly stuffs much silver bought.
Enough of *this*!   [*He points to Cassandra.*]   Do thou but entertain
This stranger kindly.   Kindly, in return,
God looks on conquerors that are merciful.

To none the yoke of servitude comes easy;
And this my captive is the chosen flower
Of all we won, my army's gift to me.
Now will I pass, since so thy prayers constrain me,
My palace-doors with feet that tread on crimson.

Setting foot on the tapestries he passes towards the palace.

Clytemnestra. Is there not all the sea—and who shall drain it?—
To breed us purple inexhaustible,
Costly as silver, to dye our royal robes?
And by God's grace, O King, with such rare treasures
Our palace teems, nor knows what want may mean.
How much rich raiment I had gladly vowed
For feet to trample, had some oracle
Enjoined it, when I sought my lord's salvation!
For while its root stands safe, the sheltering vine
Shadows man's roof against the Dog-star's glare;
And *thy* home-coming is as warmth in winter;
Or as, in parching days when Zeus transmutes
The sour young grape to wine, a blessed coolness.
So joys thy home in its full master's presence.

[Agamemnon enters the palace.

Zeus of fulfilment, now my prayers fulfil!
Do Thou dispose whatever is Thy will.

[Clytemnestra follows.

Chorus. Why in my foreboding soul,   strophe I.
    With relentless hoverings,
    Does this terror master me?
    Seer-like, it sings,
Unbidden and unhired, its prophecy.
    Why can I not spurn it hence,
    Like a dream of riddling sense,
    So that hope assured might reign
    In my breast enthroned again?
Long years now, since the cast-off cables, whirling,
    Lashed aloft the Aulis sand,
And our fleet with sails unfurling
    Stood to sea for Ilios' land.

    Now these eyes of mine at last   antistrophe I.
    Home again have seen them sail;
    Yet my hidden thoughts alway,
    Self-prompted, wail
A dirge of Furies, where no harp-strings play.

From my soul fails utterly
Happy trust in days to be;
Ah, these are no empty thing—
Apprehensions eddying
Within the heart that waits just doom to follow.
   Yet I pray—whatever *seems*—
That my bodings prove but hollow,
   And but fantasies my dreams.

In Health too rude lies danger.   *str.* 2.
Her neighbour hath ever been
Sickness, that strives
To break the wall between.
And Fortune in full sail,
As she runs before the gale,
Comes oft to wreck on shoal unseen.
Yet may Caution haply save
Part, by prudent jettison,
Lest there perish in the wave
All the wealth a house hath won,
And the vessel find her grave,
Sunk beneath too full a freight.
Dearth, too, and death may find surcease at last,
If on the harvest-furrows Zeus shall cast
   His bounty, ere too late.

But once on earth there dribbles   *ant.* 2.
The dark blood of the slain,
What spell avails
To call it back again?
Yea, God's own bolt was sped
On the leech that raised the dead—
Lest Nature's law grow void and vain.
Strait the bounds that Destiny
Sets on Man—vain to beseech
God for a larger liberty;
Else my heart, outstripping speech,
Would have cried what things I see.
Now, my spirit broods apart,
Lamenting in the shadows of its gloom,
Hopeless to turn in time the coming doom;
   And a fire devours my heart.

            Clytemnestra returns.

Clytemnestra. Get thee indoors, thou too! I speak to *thee*,
  Cassandra!—seeing that Zeus Himself hath made thee,
  His anger laid aside, a sharer now
  In the worship of our home, at our own altar
  Taking thy place with many another slave.
  Down from the chariot!—and bow thy pride!
  Even Alcmēna's son of old, they say,
  Stooped to be sold and eat the bread of bondage.
  And yet if fate assigns so hard a lot,
  At least it is a blessed thing to serve
  Masters whose wealth is ancient.
  (For those that suddenly have reaped new riches
  Are ever harsh and narrow to their thralls.)
  So now thou knowest what manner of house is ours.
Leader. To *thee* it was she spoke—and clear enough.
  The net of Fate hath caught thee—best obey,
  If that be not too hard. Maybe it *is*.
Clytemnestra. Surely my words must win obedience from her,
  Unless she only speaks, like a twittering swallow,
  Some barbarous, unintelligible tongue.
Leader. Follow! She says the best thy fate affords thee.
  Rise up, then, from the chariot, and obey.
Clytemnestra. I cannot loiter longer here without.
  Already they stand, the sheep of sacrifice,
  Beside our central hearth, awaiting slaughter.
  And so, if thou wilt hear, no more delay!
  But if my words reach not thine understanding,
  Make with thy barbarous hand some silent sign.

Clytemnestra waits questioningly.

Leader. Belike the stranger needs an interpreter?—
  Her ways are like some wild thing's newly caught.
Clytemnestra. Ah, she is mad!—heeds but her own heart's folly,
  This captive from a newly taken city
  That learns not, even now, to bear the bridle,
  Till she have frothed away her frowardness
  In blood and foam. I will not waste on her
  More words, for her contempt!

Clytemnestra goes back into the palace.

Leader. But I—for I pity her—will not be angry.
  Come quit, unhappy one, this chariot,
  Bow to the yoke of new necessity.

Cassandra. Woe, woe, woe!   *strophe* 1.
 Apollo, Apollo!
Leader. What!—couple cries of 'Woe!' with Loxias' name!
 His nature is not made for men that mourn.

Cassandra. Woe, woe, woe!   *antistrophe* 1.
 Apollo, Apollo!
Leader. Again with ill-omened cries she calls on Him
 Who hath no fitting part in lamentation.

> *Leaving the chariot, Cassandra moves towards the palace-door,
> where she sees the conical stone symbol of Apollo of the Ways.*

Cassandra. Apollo, Apollo of the Ways,   *str.* 2.
 Whose name, for me, is Doom!
 By Thee I am doomed indeed!—a second time!
Leader. It seems she will foretell her ruin to come?
 Slave though she be, God's gift yet lives in her.

Cassandra. Apollo, Apollo of the Ways,   *ant.* 2.
 Whose name, for me, is Doom!
 Where hast Thou led me now?   What roof is this?
Leader. The house of the Atreidae.   Know it not?
 I tell thee thou shalt find it true enough.

Cassandra. Nay, a house god-hating!   A house that remembers   *str.* 3.
  Loppings of heads and carnage of kindred!
 A slaughter-house of men!   Floors blood-besprinkled!
Leader. Keen-scented as a hound this stranger seems.
 She trails the track of murder—till she finds!

Cassandra. I see the proofs!   Too plain before me!   *ant.* 3.
  I see yon children, that wail for their murder—
 Their roasted flesh on which their father fed.
Leader. We knew of thy renown in prophecy:
 But we have need of no diviners here!

Cassandra. Ah God!   What plot is this,   *str.* 4.
  What new disaster!
 A plot—within these walls—intolerable
  For loyal hearts!
  And yet no hand can heal;
  And help's afar.

Leader. *These* prophesyings pass my understanding,
　　Though well I knew the former—Argos shouts them!

Cassandra. Canst dare it, wretched woman!   *ant.* 4.
　　Laving thy bedfellow
　Within his bath, and then—how speak of it!
　　Soon, soon it comes!
　　Hand after hand stretches out
　　To reach the end.
Leader. Still I grasp nothing.　For I wander lost
　In riddlings of dim-sighted oracles.

Cassandra. Horror on horror!　What vision now?   *str.* 5.
　　A net of Hades?—nay,
　A snare that shares his bed, and turns to share
　　His murder!　O Strife insatiate,
　　Cry above Atreus' race thy triumph
　　For a sacrifice that stoning should avenge.
Leader. What fiend is this thou biddest cry exultant
　Over our house?　These are no words to cheer us!
Chorus. To my heart the blood rushes, as ghastly yellow
　　As theirs that fall by the spear in battle,
　　When darkens the light of their life's last sun.
　　Now doom is hard at hand.

Cassandra. But look, ah look!　Keep from the steer   *ant.* 5.
　　His mate—she grips him fast,
　Caught in a robe, and with her black-horned cunning
　　Strikes!　And now in the brimming water
　　He falls!　Ah the tale that I must tell—
　　The treachery of the slaughter in the bath!
Leader. Not mine to boast of any subtle skill
　In oracles.　But *this* has a look of evil!
Chorus. Yet when have oracles prophesied
　　Good?　It is still with menaces
　　That the wordy chants of soothsayers
　　Bow down our hearts in dread.

Cassandra. Alas my sorrow!　For *I* must mourn   *str.* 6.
　　Myself—with my *own* grief crown the cup!
　Why hast Thou brought here *my* unhappiness?
　For what indeed, except to die as well?
Chorus. Mad creature, and by God possessed,
　　Now of *thyself*

A song thou singest, for song too bitter!
As the brown nightingale cries 'Itys! Itys!'
And bewails without cease her own life that burgeons
With pain on pain.

Cassandra. Ah, happier died the sweet nightingale!   *ant.* 6.
    For a feathered shape the Gods gave *her*,
  And a blissful life; not shrieks of agony!
But me abides the twin-edged, sundering blade.
Chorus. Whence comes this God-filled vehemence,
    This vain lament?
    What stirs thee to shrill such a song of terror,
    Loud-wailing, inarticulate?
    What guides thy steps to prophecy
    So sinister?

Cassandra. Woe!   *str.* 7.
    Ah bridal of Paris, doom to all that loved him!
    Alas Scamander, stream of home!
    In other days by thy banks I grew,
    A hapless girl;
    But by Cōcȳtus now, and Acheron's wave,
    Soon must my chants of prophecy be sung.
Chorus. What hast thou said? Ah, all too clear!
    A babe might understand thee now.
    It tears me, with a stab like death;
    And pity for thy wild crying
    Shatters my very heart.

Cassandra. Woe!   *ant.* 7.
    Ah griefs of my country, laid in utter ruin!
    Alas, the hecatombs of sheep
    My father gave before Troy-gates,
    Yet all in vain
    To save his city from the doom at hand!
    And soon now on earth my own hot blood shall flow.
Chorus. Still to its old track keeps thy speech;
    Still some demon with heavy hand
    Thrusts thee onward to chant a strain
    Of death and of desolation—
    But the end lies hid from sight.

Cassandra. Look you, no longer shall my prophecy
    Peer like a bride new-wed betwixt her veils.
    Clear as a dawn-wind towards the rising sun,

Its breath shall blow; and like a wave before it
Into the light shall surge calamity
Far vaster yet.   I will teach no more in riddles.
But you I call to witness that, unerring,
I follow up a trail of ancient evil.
For round this roof there haunts, departing never,
A chorus that intones with one accord
A chant discordant—for its theme is grim.
There fills this house a rout of revellers,
Made bolder by long draughts of human blood,
No easy guests to speed upon their way,
The Erīnyes of the race.
Gathered about its doors, they hymn their hymn
Of the first crime that cursed it; each in turn
Spitting their hate of that adultery
Whereby a brother's bed cursed him that fouled it.
How now?   Have I aimed amiss?—or hit the mark?
Am *I* false prophet now, or vagrant babbler?
Swear, if thou canst, that thou hast never heard
These old ancestral sins of Atreus' house!

Leader. What help or remedy in any oaths,
     However loyally sworn?   Yet much I marvel
     That thou, a stranger of an alien tongue
     From overseas, canst hit upon the truth
     As if thine eyes had seen it.

Cassandra. The seer Apollo made that power mine.
Leader. Smitten with love for thee, although a God?
Cassandra. In times gone by I was ashamed to tell.
Leader. Ah yes, the heart grows proud in prosperous days!
Cassandra. Yet, in His grip, I felt what grace He breathed.
Leader. And came ye to that union lovers crave?
Cassandra. I promised Loxias—yet cheated Him.
Leader. Gifted already with His inspiration?
Cassandra. Yes, even then I told the doom of Troy.
Leader. How couldst thou, then, escape Apollo's anger?
Cassandra. After my sin, no man believed me more.
Leader. Yet *we* believe thy divinations true.
Cassandra. Ah horror, horror!
     Again the anguish of prophetic vision
     Troubles and drives me, with its ghastly prelude.
     Do you see?—there yonder—sitting by the palace,
     Those young shapes, like the phantoms of a dream?
     Children—I feel it—murdered by their kin!

Their hands are filled with flesh—with their *own* flesh,
Served for a banquet—there they stand revealed,
Lifting the piteous load of their own entrails,
Whereof their father ate!
In vengeance for these things, I say a plot
Is laid, alas, against the King returned
By one that stayed at home, a craven lion,
Tumbling his master's bed.
But he that led the ships, that conquered Troy,
Knows not what doom the lustful bitch that fawned
With smiling mood and long protracted welcome,
Like some insidious Ātē, now shall wreak,
In evil hour, upon him.
Such is her daring!—female not afraid
To slay her male! What monster's name shall fit her?
An amphisbaena? Some crag-haunting Scylla,
Mortal to sailors? A mother hellish-hearted,
Breathing a truceless war on closest kin?
All-daring, how she raised her cry of triumph,
Like men that see the tide of battle turn;
Yet seems so happy that her lord comes home!
Believe my words, or no—what matter now?
What comes, will come. Soon thine own eyes shall see it,
And thy pity call me but too true a seer.

Leader. Thyestes' banquet on his children's flesh!—
I recognize it, shuddering, aghast.
These things are very truth, no mere conjecture:
But in all else I wander wholly lost.

Cassandra. I say thou shalt see the death of Agamemnon.

Leader. Hush, hapless one!—no word so evil-omened!

Cassandra. It is no healing spirit guides my lips.

Leader. Not if they tell the truth! But God forbid!

Cassandra. To prayer *thy* thoughts are turned. But *theirs* to murder.

Leader. What man is it that brings such dire disaster?

Cassandra. Thou art far astray from what I prophesy.

Leader. I do not grasp *who* shall perform the plot.

Cassandra. Yet but too well I speak the speech of Hellas.

Leader. And so does Pytho's shrine. Yet speaks but dimly.

Cassandra. Aie!
How fierce a flame! It comes on me—it comes.
Oh, oh, oh!
Ah, Lycian Apollo! Woe is me!
This lioness with two feet, who gave her body,

In the noble lion's absence, to a wolf,
Will kill me, all-unhappy!   For me too
She mixes poison in her cup of wrath;
Yes, while she whets her sword to slay her husband,
Vows to repay my coming with my blood.
   Why longer keep these mockeries of myself—
This staff, these prophet's bands about my throat?
Now, if I die, yet *you* shall perish first!

[She tears them off.

Down, to perdition!   Go!—thus I requite ye.
Make in my place some other rich in ruin!
But see!—it is Apollo's self that strips me
Of all my prophet's emblems—empty splendour,
Wherein he has watched me made a laughing-stock
Of friends that were but foes—ay, vainly mocked,
Like some poor cheat that gathers gifts for Heaven—
Called 'wretched,' 'beggarly,' and 'god-forsaken'!
Thus hath the God of Prophecy made *me*
A prophetess—and led me but to death;
Brought me to find, not now my father's altar,
But a slaughterer's block, red with my own hot blood,
As victim in a funeral-sacrifice.
Yet Heaven shall leave us not all unatoned;
There shall rise up another to avenge us,
A son that wreaks his sire, and slays his mother.
He is an exile now, far from his country;
But come he shall, to set the coping stone
On the ruin of all his race.
The Gods have sworn it, with a solemn oath—
His fallen father's blood shall bring him home.
Why do I wail, then?   Why lament myself?
Since, after seeing what a fate befell
My country, I have also lived to know
God's judgment falls in turn on her destroyers,
I too will dare to go my way to die.
I greet this portal as the Gate of Death;
And all I pray for is a blow to the heart
That lets my life ebb forth without a struggle,
A speedy end to seal these eyes at last.

Leader.   O woman full of wisdom, full of tears,
How long thy lamentations!   If thou seest
Thy death so clear, how canst thou yet so calmly,
Like some God-goaded beast, draw near the altar?

Cassandra. I might delay death, strangers; not escape it.
Leader. Yet the last hours of life are prized the dearest.
Cassandra. My last is come.   Small gain in flinching from it.
Leader. Thou art indeed a brave heart, and enduring.
Cassandra. *That* is a praise the happy never hear.
Leader. There still remains some grace in dying well.
Cassandra. O father, father!   O my gallant brothers!

> *She makes towards the door, but recoils appalled.*

Leader. What is it now?   What terror turns thee back?
Cassandra. Faugh, faugh!
Leader. What brings that cry from thee?   Some thing abhorrent?
Cassandra. This house breathes stifling with the blood of slaughter.
Leader. Slaughter?   It is the victims at the hearth.
Cassandra. Nay, but the reek that rises from a tomb!
Leader. *That* is no eastern perfume for a palace!
Cassandra. Yet I will enter—there beneath its roof
  To wail a last dirge both for my own doom
  And Agamemnon's.   Now enough of life!
  Oh strangers,
  I do not cry out idly—like a bird
  Scared by an empty bush.   When I am fallen—
  And when, to atone my death, another dies,
  Woman for woman,
  And for this king miswived another man—
  Then bear me witness that I told you true.
  This is a stranger's dying prayer to ye.
Leader. Poor woman!—passing open-eyed to death!
Cassandra. *One* final word I have; *one* last lament—
  My own; *one* prayer to this bright sun I leave—
  May my lord's avengers make my murderers
  Pay for me too—poor slave so lightly slain.
  Ah human life!   Even its happiness
  Fades as a shadow—its unhappiness
  Grows a mere blur a wet sponge wipes away.
  And *this* to me is still more pitiful.

> *[She disappears through the gateway.*

Chorus. Never the hearts of men are sated
  With Fortune's favours; and no voice warns her
  From gates of the mighty, where point all fingers;
  To *her* none cries: 'Thou hast come *enough*!'
  Thus to our lord the Immortals granted
  To take Priam's city;

And honoured of Heaven he cometh home.
But if he must pay for the blood shed aforetime,
If now to the dead, that died of old,
His *own* death must atone,
What man dare boast, who hears his story,
That his own lot standeth sure?

Agamemnon (*within*). Ah, I am wounded—stricken to the death!
Leader. Hush! Who *is* it cries of wounding? *Who* is stricken to the heart?
Agamemnon. Ah God, ah God, again!—a second blow!
Leader. Loud the King cries out in anguish. All is done, I fear, past cure.
  Take we counsel, all together—is there any course that's sure?
First Elder. Then *my* advice is—raise the alarm in Argos
  And call her citizens before the palace.
Second Elder. Better that we ourselves break in at once
  And prove the crime, while yet their swords drip red.
Third Elder. Such is my counsel too. I vote for action!—
  Without delay!—No time for loitering!
Fourth Elder. All's clear enough—this deed looks like the prelude
  To setting up a tyranny in Argos.
Fifth Elder. Yes, for we dally.   *Their* hands do not sleep,
  And *their* feet spurn at any praise of Caution.
Sixth Elder. *I* do not see what course can meet our need.
  Theirs is the action—*theirs* the power to plan.
Seventh Elder. And *I* agree with him.   What potency
  Has talk of ours to raise the dead again?
Eighth Elder. What!—must we cling to life, and grovel helpless
  Before defilers of our royal house!
Ninth Elder. Intolerable!   Far better we should die.
  That were a milder doom than tyranny.
Tenth Elder. But shall we, then, divine the King is dead
  From the mere witness of the cries we heard?
Eleventh Elder. We need clear knowledge to debate these things;
  And far indeed from knowledge stands conjecture.
Twelfth Elder. *That* judgment I approve abundantly.
  We must make sure how it stands with Atreus' son.
  > *The palace opens and Clytemnestra is revealed standing between*
  > *the dead Agamemnon, who lies in his silver bath beneath an*
  > *embroidered robe, and the dead Cassandra.*
Clytemnestra. I *have* said many things were framed perforce
  To meet the moment's need—I will not blush,
  Now, to unsay them.   How else *could* I wreak
  My enmity on these my enemies,

Who passed for friends; and fence them in a net
Of doom, too high for any overleaping?
Mine was an ancient feud, long brooded on;
And justice, when it came, was long prepared.
But now 'tis done; and where I struck, I stand.
Mine the contrivance—I will not deny it—
That left him powerless to fight or flee.

She lifts the embroidered robe, stained now with blood.

Round him I flung, like a fishing-net escapeless,
These folds of fatal splendour; then I struck
Twice—and with twice-repeated cry of woe
His limbs gave way beneath him; where he fell,
A third time yet I hewed him, as in prayer
And sacrifice to the infernal Zeus,
Deliverer of the dead.
So on the earth he gasped his life away,
And from his lips burst forth a gush of blood,
That splashed me, like a shower of dark red rain;
And I rejoiced in it, as wheat grows glad
With heaven's moisture, when the ear is born.
   Elders of Argos, thus the matter stands.
I wish ye joy—such joy as ye can find;
But I—I glory in it.   Could glad libations
Be poured upon the body of the dead,
Then *I* might justly do it—more than justly.
So deep a bowl of curst calamity
He filled for all his house—and, home returning,
Hath drunk to the dregs himself!

Leader. Such boasts above thy husband's murdered body!
  We stand aghast at thy effrontery.

Clytemnestra. Ye would play upon me, as a witless woman;
  But *my* heart quails not—to your faces now
  I tell ye, heedless of your praise or blame,
  Here lies my husband, Agamemnon, dead
  By this right hand—that did a work of justice.
  So stands the matter.

Chorus. What baneful herb of the land,   *strophe.*
  What deadly draught from the swirling sea,
  Hath made thee, woman, so infatuate,
  To draw on thy curst head thy people's hate?
  Thou hast cut off—cast out.   So *thou* shalt be
  In Argos!   Loathed and banned!

Clytemnestra. Me you would doom to banishment from Argos?
  To the hatred and the curses of her people?
  Yet against *him* ye had not a word to utter
  Then, when (as ruthlessly as it had been
  Some *beast* that died, among the teeming thousands
  That filled his fleecy folds) he sacrificed
  His child, the dearest of my womb, to bind
  The gales that blew from Thrace!   Why did ye not
  Ban *him* for that foul crime?   But harsh ye are
  To judge what *I* have done.   And yet I warn you,
  If thus ye threaten, know that I am ready
  On equal terms to face you—and to bow,
  If force defeats me; but if God ordains,
  That things go otherwise, *ye* shall be schooled
  Sharply, though late, to learn due modesty.

Chorus. So boldly undismayed!   *antistrophe.*
  Such bluster!   Indeed, thy heart is grown
  Frenzied, with this most bloody happening here.
  Within thine eyes the stain of blood stands clear.
  Forsaken, friendless, thou shalt yet atone,
  And blow for blow be paid!

Clytemnestra. And, further, hear you now my solemn oath?—
  By Justice, that made perfect this revenge
  For my slain child; by Ātē and Erīnys,
  To whom I slew this man in sacrifice,
  My Hope treads not within the house of Fear,
  Long as I have, to kindle here my hearth,
  Aegisthus—loyal to his long love for me,
  The mighty shield wherein I put my trust.
  Dead lies this shamer of his wedded wife,
  Charmer of old priests' daughters under Troy;
  And dead with him this slave, this fortune-teller,
  This loyal paramour, the god-inspired,
  That shared his bed—ay, shared his galley's bench!
  Now they have paid their price—for here he lies,
  And here beside him, all her swan-song ended,
  His mistress, that has brought to me this day
  One relish more for the feast of my revenge.

Chorus. Would that quickly, with no pain,   *strophe* 1.
  Nor the sick man's weary bed,
  Fate might bring us, without end,

The last long sleep! Since *he* is dead,
Our lord, our guardian, our friend.
He toiled, he warred, for a woman's guilt:
By a woman's blow his blood lies spilt.

Ah Helen, how deadly a frenzy found thee!—
Through *thee* so many a life,
So many past telling, by Troy was slain!
With a triumph supreme this day hath crowned thee—
With blood past cleansing! Thou sower of strife
Within this house, for a husband's bane!

Clytemnestra. Do not, by sorrow overwrought,
   Make death your prayer.
Cast not your curses on Helen's head
As a murderess that, alone, hath shed
The blood of Greeks past count, and brought
   Griefs more than man may bear.

Chorus. Fiend, whose onfall crushes down   *antistrophe* 1.
   Both our royal Pĕlopidae,
From two ill women Thou hast Thy power!
(And the thought of it wrings the heart in me.)
Like a loathly raven in this hour,
Perched on our murdered lord, he sings
The hoarse chant of his triumphings.

Clytemnestra. Ah, *that* was a wiser thought of thine.
   To call on *Him*—
Yon thrice-gorged demon of Pĕlops' line,
Who breeds in our bowels this thirst to slay;
So that, ere one wound's healed away,
   A new sore rots the limb.

Chorus. Of a fiend indeed thy praise is,   *str.* 2.
   (Alas, an evil praise!)
Doom for this house he raises,
   With wrath no ruin allays.
Woe, woe! This comes of God's hand still,
   Who all contrives, and causes all.
What doom is accomplished without His will?
   What happens, but He bade it fall?

Alas and alas, my king, my king!
How weep thee dead?

What words for my long love's uttering?
With a spider's web about thee spread,
Thou liest gasping out thy breath,
Alas, alas!
Thine was a base, a bondman's death,
Thus by a treacherous wife betrayed,
Felled by a woman's whetted blade!

Clytemnestra. So sure that *mine* this deed hath been?
  Ye dream in vain
  That I am Agamemnon's Queen.
  Disguised as the wife of this man slain,
  Yon ancient grim Avenger made
  This death atone
  Grim Atreus' banquet; and repaid
  Child-lives with a victim grown.

Chorus. This murder's absolution—   *ant. 2.*
    What witness grants it thee?
  Who dare?   (Though his sire's pollution
    Could add its curse, maybe.)
  Mid kindred blood that freshly flows,
    The dark God of Slaughter strides amain;
  Round Him, wheresoe'er He goes,
    Chill of death, and young lives slain.

Alas and alas, my king, my king!
How weep thee dead?
What words for my long love's uttering?
With a spider's web about thee spread,
Thou liest gasping out thy breath,
Alas, alas!
Thine was a base, a bondman's death,
Thus by a treacherous wife betrayed,
Felled by a woman's whetted blade.

Clytemnestra. Why 'bondman's death'?   Not so to me!
  Why was it 'treacherous,' my design?
  Had *he* not dared by treachery
  To ruin his line?
  Iphigeneia, child of woe—
  He that begot her, laid her low,
  His child and mine.

Pain he gave: he has suffered pain.
(In Hades let him not grow proud!)
He that had slain
By the sword, to the sword hath bowed.

Chorus. My judgment gropes, blind to discern;   *str. 3.*
    Thought's grasp has lost its power.
In a tumbling house, where should man turn?
For this roof I dread—not now a shower—
Nay, a thunderstorm of blood outpoured.
On new whetstones Doom whetteth in this hour
    New judgments of the sword.

Ah earth, would thou hadst welcomed me,
Ere my lord had lain, for mine eyes to see,
In this bath with its silver wall!
Who shall lament him?   Make his grave?
Wilt thou, his murderess, show thy face
To wail the great deeds of the brave,
To do his spirit a graceless grace,
When *thy* sin brought his fall?
Who shall give now to the hero's dust
Last praise of all,
With tears of truth and trust?

Clytemnestra. Not *thy* concern!   It was by *me*
He fell, he died;
And mine to make his grave shall be,
No sorrowing household at its side.
Nay, there's a daughter for him to meet,
Where swift at the ferry swirls Acheron's tide.
Iphigeneia he shall not miss!
There *she* shall greet
Her sire, with clasp and kiss.

Chorus. Ah taunt and counter-taunt!   Our eyes   *ant. 3.*
    Peer for the truth in vain.
Yet spoiled is the spoiler, the slayer dies:
While Zeus remains, shall His law remain.
'The guilty pays'—He hath ordered so.
Yet from this house who lifts its curse of pain?
    Race welded fast to woe!

Clytemnestra. True oracle!   But now at ease
My heart would rest, might a pact be sworn

With this fiend of the House of Pleisthĕnes—
That we should accept what we have borne,
Though bitter; if only he give us grace
Henceforth, while he plagues some other race
With mutual butchery!
Rich I should count me with little store,
Could I but know this hearth set free
From madness and murder evermore.

Aegisthus enters with his bodyguard.

Aegisthus. Hail, kindly light of the day of retribution!
Now can I say that on the woes of earth,
As justicers of men, the Gods look down!
Since here before me lies—most happy sight—
This dead man, in the robe the Erīnyes wove him,
Atoning for his father's treachery.
For that same father, Atreus lord of Argos,
His sovereignty being challenged—am I plain?—
Drove his own brother (and my sire)—Thyestes,
Away from land and home to banishment.
Till, in the end returning, that poor exile
Thus far found mercy, that he did not stain
With his heart's blood the native earth of Argos
Himself—and yet from this man's godless father,
Atreus, found welcome far more keen than kind.
For Atreus, feigning a joyous festival
Of fattened victims, to Thyestes served
The flesh of his own sons!
The feet and the branching fingers he hid beneath,
The other parts were strewn above, and laid
Before my father, where he sat apart;
Who, all unguessing, took and ate those portions
No man might know—a feast (thou seest now)
Of ruin unredeemed for all our race!
Then, when he saw the unconscionable truth,
He fell back shrieking—vomiting that carnage,
And imprecated on the line of Pĕlops
Doom past endurance; praying that, as he spurned
That table headlong, so in just requital
Might topple all the House of Pleisthĕnes.
Thence (thou canst see it) this man's fall is come.
And just it was that *I* should spin the plot
To bring him death.

For Atreus drove me too to banishment
With my unhappy father—his third son,
A swaddled babe.   But when I grew to manhood,
Then Justice led me home, to lay my hand
Upon this man, although I stood without—
For mine was the framing of the fatal plan.
So, even if I died now, all were well,
Since I have seen him caught in the toils of Justice.

Leader.   I take no keep, Aegisthus, of men that triumph
On others' ruin.   To this man's wilful slaying
Thou hast confessed—yes, to the whole contrivance
Of this pitiable murder!   Then I tell thee,
When Justice comes, be sure thy head shall not
Escape the curses and the stones of Argos.

Aegisthus.   Such talk from thee, mere oarsman on the bench,
When 'tis the helmsman on the poop must rule!
Thine age shall find 'tis bitter, at thy years,
To be put to school again to learn discretion.
Old as thou art, there is no holy leech
Shall lesson thee so perfectly to wisdom
As prison-fetters, and the pinch of fasting.
Hast eyes, yet canst not see this?   Do not kick
Against the pricks; lest thy own foot should smart!

Leader.   Thou woman, thou!   These men came back from *battle*!—
And thou at home, fouling a husband's bed,
To plot such death for a mighty chief of war!

Aegisthus.   This insolence, too, may end in bitter crying.
Thy tongue indeed is Orpheus' opposite:
His voice led all things, ravished, after him,
But *thou,* with thy childish yappings to provoke me,
Shalt be led off thyself—and tamed and mastered!

Leader.   To think of *thee* as ruling us here in Argos!—
Coward that, contriving murder for his king,
Dared not lift hand to strike him!

Aegisthus.   The reason's plain—guile was the woman's part;
But I, from of old, an enemy suspected.
Yet now, with the dead king's treasure, I will shift
To rule your Argives.   He that disobeys
Shall be yoked with a yoke that's heavy—not for *him*
The life of some young trace-horse fat with barley!
Grim Hunger, dwelling in the House of Darkness,
Shall make him meek enough.

Leader.   Yet why, thou craven soul, couldst thou not kill him

Thyself?—why leave his wife to do the murder,
Defiling Argos and the Gods of Argos?
Ah, does Orestes somewhere see the sun,
That *he*, by fortune's favour, coming home
May bring remorseless vengeance on them both!

Aegisthus. Nay, if *such* thy words and actions, *I* must make thee understand.
Ho, good spearmen! Mark my orders! Here is action hard at hand.

Leader. Ho, my friends, now make ye ready! Grasp your sword-hilts, one and all.

Aegisthus. Grasped is *mine*, too. I am willing, if my death be come, to fall.

Leader. Ah! Of 'death' thy word was? Welcome! God fulfil that augury!

Clytemnestra. Nay, enough of wrong and violence, dearest of all men to me!
Ill on ill is done already—harvest we must reap in dread.
Ay, we *have* our fill of anguish. Hold!—before man's blood be shed.
Reverend elders, get you homeward, ere your rashness makes ye pay.
What this day has seen enacted, ye must bear as best ye may.
Happy *we*, if to our troubles we at last could cry: 'No more!'
Grim the fiend that yet pursues us, and his hoof hath trampled sore.
Thus I say (that am but woman), would ye hearken to my word.

Aegisthus. Yet that *these* should fling me insults!—tongues with idle folly stirred!
Utter threats like these against me, blindly tempting Providence!
Flouting him that is thy master! Lost thou art to sober sense.

Leader. Never shall true men of Argos cringe before a scoundrel's will.

Aegisthus. None the less my retribution shall hereafter reach thee still.

Leader. Not if doom shall guide Orestes safely to his home again.

Aegisthus. Well I know how men in exile feed on empty hopes, in vain.

Leader. Go thy ways! Feed fat thy surfeit—fouling Justice. Thine the power.

Aegisthus. Take my word, for this thy folly thou shalt pay, when comes my hour.

Leader. Swagger on, in thy assurance, like a cock his hen beside.

Clytemnestra. Never heed these hounds' vain yelping. Thou and I, with powers allied,
Masters of the House of Atreus, all its ways to good will guide.

> *Aegisthus and Clytemnestra enter the palace. The Chorus files out of the orchēstra.*

THE LIBATION-BEARERS AND THE EUMENIDES
(458 B.C.)

The boy
With his white breast and brow and clustering curls
Streaked with his mother's blood, but striving hard
To tell his story ere his reason goes.

Browning.

The Libation-bearers opens, after an interval of some seven years, with the coming of the avengers. The young Orestes, with his friend Pýlades from Phocis, stands in prayer at his murdered father's tomb. There they are met by his sister Electra and the Chorus of captive Trojan women; for Clytemnestra, alarmed (like Atossa in *The Persians*) by an evil dream, has sent her daughter to offer appeasing libations to the dead. But shall Electra obey? By the advice of the Chorus, she prays rather for her banished brother, for herself, for vengeance. Then she notices on the tomb a lock of his own hair just laid there by Orestes. The joyful recognition of brother and sister is followed by a third prayer and a long magical invocation rousing to vengeance the spirit of the murdered king. Then Orestes and Pýlades approach the palace, disguised as Phocian strangers; and the son tells his mother false tidings of his own death. The old nurse of Orestes (drawn with realistic touches that faintly foreshadow Juliet's nurse) is sent by Clytemnestra with a summons for Aegisthus to come, *with* his bodyguard, and question the strangers; but is persuaded by the Chorus to falsify the message and bid him come *without* his guards. The usurper walks into the trap; and his death-cry rings out from behind the scenes. A palace servant shouts warning that the dead are slaying the living; but Clytemnestra, with her old courage, calls for an axe to defend herself. Face to face with a mother pleading for her life, Orestes falters; but Pýlades (in his only utterance throughout the play) reminds him that Apollo commanded vengeance; and Orestes leads her in to die beside her lover. Then the palace-door opens; and again, as in *Agamemnon*, an avenger is seen standing above two victims. Blood has had blood. But, even in the hour of triumph, the curse works anew. The slaying of a mother is even more terrible than the slaying of a husband. Before the growing frenzy of Orestes' vision rise the Erinyes.

> Ye see them not. But I—I see them well.
> They hunt me—I must away.

And he flees to sanctuary at Delphi.

106

There *The Eumenides* opens, with a prologue spoken by Apollo's priestess. She then enters the shrine, but rushes out in horror—she has seen there a suppliant clinging to the altar, while round him sleeps a band of black and hideous beings. The temple opens to reveal the Erīnyes. (There is a story, perhaps legendary, that at the first performance their aspect so appalled the audience that women miscarried in the theatre.) But now Apollo himself stands forth to bid Orestes seek deliverance in Athens, whither Hermes shall lead him. No sooner are Hermes and Orestes gone, than the wraith of Clytemnestra, now more fiend than woman, with angry reproaches rouses the sleeping Erīnyes to pursue. They turn on Apollo, who denounces them as fiends, of a barbarism alien to Hellas:

> No place is my holy house for your defilement;
> But there where slaughter reigns, and 'justice' hews
> Heads off, and gouges eyes; where boyhood's flower
> Is maimed, unmanned; where men are stoned to death,
> Where limbs are lopped, where groan in lingering anguish
> Wretches impaled with stakes beneath their spine.
>
> (185–90.)

After fierce altercation the Erīnyes rush out to pursue their prey.

The scene changes to Athens. There on the Acropolis, after long wanderings through the world, Orestes clings to the image of Athena. But still the Erīnyes are hard at his heels; and gathering round they sing to their victim their gruesome Binding Song.

> Neither Apollo nor Athena's power
> Shall save thee now—forsaken thou shalt perish,
> With heart that has forgot what joy may mean,
> A bloodless shadow, rent by the powers of vengeance.
> No answer? Wilt thou spit away my words?
> O victim bred and dedicated mine,
> Thou shalt not die upon the altar—*living*,
> Thy flesh shall be our banquet! Listen now,
> While we intone the spell that binds thee ours.
>
> Come, link the dance, O sisterhood,
> For lo! the hour
> To tell in grisly chorus
> How among men we wield the power
> That Fate hath set before us.
> Just we deem our ways, and good.
> For he whose hands are clean and clear
> Hath never wrath of ours to fear,
> His days pass by unshaken;

But if such a slayer as hideth here
Our anger shall awaken,
In righteous witness to the dead
We rise, for the blood his hands have shed,
Till a life for a life is taken.

Hear us, O Mother Night.   Thou gavest birth   *strophe* 1.
To us that hound all sinners over earth,
And beneath it.   See us put to shame!
Lēto's son hath snatched away
Him that, hare-like, cowering lay.
Ours he is.   His hand did slay
His own mother.   Him we claim.

Over the victim that they bring
This is the chant the Erīnyes sing,
Heart-wildering, brain-shattering,
No such tune as harp-strings play.
Fettered soul, and senses fey,
Whoso hears it, wastes away.

Such is the office that eternal Fate   *antistrophe* 1.
Hath spun for *us*, with thread inviolate—
Evermore to hound implacably
Him whose wantonness shall dare
Slay his kindred—everywhere,
Till the tomb.   And even there
Scant shall be his liberty!

Over the victim that they bring
This is the chant the Erīnyes sing,
Heart-wildering, brain-shattering,
No such tunes as harp-strings play.
Fettered soul, and senses fey,
Whoso hears it, wastes away.

(299–346.)

But now appears Athena, and the Erīnyes accept her offer to arbitrate.
Orestes stands his trial before judges from her city, and is defended by
Apollo, who pleads that his Delphic oracle, in bidding Orestes avenge his
father, had uttered the will of Zeus Himself.   To the Erīnyes' sneer that,
after all, Zeus had dethroned and chained His own father, Apollo retorts
with perhaps finer eloquence than logic:

O loathsome monsters whom the Gods abhor,
Chains may be loosened and their smart be healed,
And many a means may bring deliverance.

But once the dust hath drunk the blood of man,
There is no rising back to life again.
My Heavenly Father hath Himself no cure;
Though all things else His hands turn upside down,
Just as He wills, without one labouring breath.

(644–51.)

He then proceeds to the quaint plea that the father is biologically the real parent, the mother only a seed-bed for the living seed. Athena, pointing out that she herself had a father, Zeus, but no mother, gives her voice for Orestes. When the votes are counted they prove equal; and he is therefore acquitted. In their rage the Erīnyes threaten havoc to Athens; but Athena gradually calms them and persuades them to take their places as honoured goddesses in the city's worship. Garbed in the crimson cloaks worn by resident aliens at the Panathenaea, they are led in solemn procession to make their home beneath the Acropolis.

As spectacle these two plays must have been vivid—the children of the dead Agamemnon beating on his grave, which acts its mute, sinister part in the drama, like the cold monument of Arthur, between Lancelot and Guenevere in Morris's *King Arthur's Tomb*; the wild incantation of the Chorus to rouse the murdered monarch in his sepulchre; the golden-haired Apollo confronting, bow in hand, the Gorgon-like Erīnyes; the solemn conclave on the Hill of Ares; the torchlight procession at the close.

Both plays are also full of historic significance—the battle between the old powers of darkness, whose terrors had been needed to restrain the savagery of primeval barbarians, and the new gods of the Greek sunlight; the clash between the blood-ties of primitive matriarchy and the newer sanctities of marriage; the growth of law to replace 'the ancient blinded vengeance' (though if this was so important for Aeschylus as some scholars have made it, he might well have put it more lucidly; actually the murder of Clytemnestra is justified—not clearly condemned as a futile, outworn thing). Those who wish can also see here, retrospectively, a conflict between the northern and Mediterranean elements in European history and religion; or can even modernize *The Eumenides* into a parable where the Erīnyes of guilt, lurking in the darkness of the less conscious mind, are calmed by the Goddess of Reason in the clear light of truth faced unafraid. With time, masterpieces can acquire new meanings that the masters themselves never dreamed.

Still, as drama, I cannot myself compare these two tragedies with *Agamemnon*. They have suffered more from time's corrosion. For us matricide has become a difficult theme—too exceptional and barbaric. Think if Hamlet had killed Gertrude! He would have killed the play. Even in the comparative savagery of our early fourteenth century, one cannot easily imagine the young Edward III (though *his* father had perished in Berkeley Castle far more cruelly than Agamemnon) murdering the guilty mother whom, instead, he honourably confined in Castle Rising.

Further, while *Agamemnon* has characters that grip, these sequels may seem at moments a little too like *Hamlet* without the Prince of Denmark. For Orestes remains a puppet, driven by Apollo with frightful threats to a crime that then brings him frightful threats from the Erīnyes; and the heavenly figures rather lack human interest, like the good angels in *Paradise Lost*. Apollo quibbles too much. Again, if Orestes did God's will, it seems harsh that he should be so long punished for it. And finally it remains a little absurd that the Erīnyes should have to be bribed—as if the police, furious at a defendant's acquittal, should then proceed to blackmail the judge. Zeus should have kept them in better order.

None the less this final close in peace and reconciliation makes no unfitting end to the life-work of that old fighter of Marathon, who was now to leave for ever the Athens he had so long glorified by word and deed, and find his last rest on the alien shores of Sicily.

FRAGMENTS OF LOST PLAYS (AND EPIGRAMS)

God

Zeus is the ether; Zeus, the earth, the sky;
Zeus is all things, and a mightier thing than all.

(*Hēliades*; Nauck, *Tragicorum Graecorum Fragmenta*, 1889, fr. 70.)

Death

Alone of Gods, Death takes no keep of gifts.
Libations touch him not; nor sacrifice.
He has no altar, and he hears no hymn,
And from his feet alone Prayer halts afar.

(*Niobe*; Nauck, fr. 161.)

Thĕtis Denounces Apollo for Slaying her Son, Achilles

Loud once he hymned my happy motherhood—
No sickness for my son, no early death!
'Blest above all, and dear to Gods in Heaven,'
He called me, in the paean of his praise.
And I believed that Phoebus' tongue told truth,
Divine with prescience of all things to be.
Yet he that sang, yea, he that feasted there,
That promised this—he, it is *he* has slain
My son, my son!

(Nauck, fr. 350.)

On the Dead in a Battle in Thessaly

Dark Death slew these men also, as staunchly they awaited
  The shock of spear, for their country and her fair hills white with sheep.
Dead—yet their memory dies not; although those limbs ill-fated
  Now are lying mantled with the dust of Ossa's steep.

(Loeb Aeschylus, ii, p. 520.)

His own Epitaph

This gravestone here holds hidden Euphórion's son below it,
  Aeschylus the Athenian, where the corn of Gela grows.
But, for his worth in battle, ask, if ye would know it,
  The Marathonian woodland, and the long-haired Mede that knows.

(p. 520.)

NOTES ON AESCHYLUS

THE PERSIANS

[Page 23] *There came a Hellene.* On the eve of the battle Themistocles sent his slave Sicinnus to Xerxes with this ingenious warning. It both lured the Persians to fight at Salamis and forced the wavering Greeks to do so; for it led the Persians to block their westward retreat. (See Heródotus, viii, 75.)

PROMETHEUS BOUND

[Page 33] Violence, in Greek (*Bia*), is feminine and must here have been a female figure.

[Page 35] *'Prometheus'* ... *'forethought.'* 'Prometheus' means 'provident,' 'forethoughtful,' 'far-sighted.'

[Page 35] Only after nearly a hundred lines does Prometheus speak. Aeschylus was famous for these tense silences of his characters—such as Atossa, Clytemnestra, Niobe, Achilles. Thus he made a dramatic virtue out of what had originally been (with only two actors available) a dramatic necessity.

[Page 36] It is disputed whether the Ocean-nymphs arrived in a large flying chariot or (perhaps more probably) on separate winged sea-horses. From the genealogy opposite it will be noted that Océanus is Prometheus' uncle, the Ocean-nymphs his cousins (and sisters-in-law).

[Page 38] *To annihilate The race at once—create, instead, a new.* Cf. Hēsiod, *Works and Days,* 109–201 (*Greek Poetry for Everyman,* pp. 198–200). Looking back over human history, one may wonder if Prometheus would not have done better to let Zeus have his way.

[Page 39] *Blind hopes.* In Hēsiod, Hope comes from Zeus, among the plagues in the jar of Pandora.

[Page 41] *Typhon.* A monster with a hundred dragon-heads, born by Earth to Tartarus. (Perhaps of Asiatic origin.)

[Page 42] *Streams of flame.* There was a violent eruption of Etna from 479 B.C. till, perhaps, 476. Cf. Pindar's description of it in *Pythian,* i (*Greek Poetry for Everyman,* pp. 265–6).

[Page 43] *Colchis.* A country on the S.E. coast of the Black Sea. 'Arabs' seem out of place here; but perhaps their first syllable helped Aeschylus to associate them with *Ar*menia.

[Page 43] *Maeōtis.* The Sea of Azov.

[Page 46] *Io.* Ínachus, an Argive river-god and king of Argos, was son of Océanus and so Prometheus' cousin. When his daughter Io, priestess of Hēra, was loved by Zeus, Hēra changed her rival into a white heifer,[1] and entrusted her to the rigorous custody of the sleepless, many-eyed Argus. Then Zeus sent Hermes to kill Argus; but Hēra retaliated by sending a gadfly to hunt Io in frenzy across the earth.

Aeschylus' account here of Io's wanderings shows more passion for geography

---

[1] This is the version of Aeschylus in *The Suppliants.* In another account Zeus himself transformed Io to hide her from Hēra.

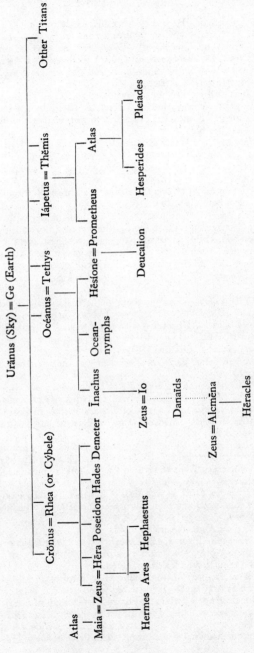

TITANS AND GODS

Uranus (Sky) = Ge (Earth)

Other Titans

Iápetus = Thémis

Atlas

Pleiades

Hesperides

Océanus = Tethys

Hēsíone = Prometheus

Deucalion

Ocean-nymphs

Īnachus

Zeus = Io

Danaïds

Zeus = Alcmēna

Hēracles

(In this trilogy Aeschylus identifies Thémis with Ge.)

Crŏnus = Rhea (or Cȳbele)

Poseidon Hades Demeter

Atlas

Maia = Zeus = Hēra

Hephaestus

Hermes Ares

than knowledge of it. Her route remains partly unintelligible—Argos—
Dōdōna (N.W. Greece)—Scythia—Prometheus' rock—N. of Black Sea—
Caucasus (clearly much misplaced)—Cimmerian Isthmus (Crimea)—Asia—
Ethiopia—Egypt. In *The Suppliants* (p. 21) Io followed a shorter itinerary,
which brought her to the Byzantine Bosporus, but not, as here, to the Cim-
merian Bosporus (Strait of Kertch).

In Egypt Zeus restored her human shape and she bore Épaphus, the ancestor
of the Danaïds, of Perseus, and of Hēracles. Later, Io (perhaps a moon-
goddess) was identified with Isis, who was in turn identified with the horned
Egyptian goddess Hathor.

Some readers may recall that Horace Walpole took exception to our play's
having for its 'leading lady' a cow!

[Page 48] *Lerna*. On the coast S. of Argos; in its swamp Hēracles slew
the Hydra.

[Page 49] *Cerchneia*. Perhaps the Argive Cenchreae on Mount Parthenius.
But again the geography is vague.

[Page 49] *Hybristes*. 'Insolent.' Variously identified with the Kuban,
flowing from Caucasus into the Black Sea, or with the Borysthenes (Dnieper).
It has also been conjectured, from the remark of a scholiast, that the true reading
is 'Araktes' (*arasso*, 'smite') and that Aeschylus meant the Caucasian (not the
Persian) Araxes. But all this is mapping fairyland.

[Page 50] *Themiscyra*. On S. coast of the Black Sea, between Sinōpe and
Trebizond.

[Page 50] *Salmydessus*. On W. coast of the Black Sea, 60 miles N.W. of
Constantinople. The vivid 'stepmother of ships' may have been suggested
by the local legend of King Phīneus, whose two sons by Cleopatra, daughter of
Boreas, the North Wind, were blinded by their *stepmother*, Eidóthea (cf. p. 152).

[Page 50] *Bosporus*. 'Ox-ford,' 'Cow-ford.'

[Page 51] *Strait that parts two continents*. The Cimmerian Bosporus
(Strait of Kertch).

[Page 51] *Phorcys*. Son of Nereus and Earth, and a plentiful begetter of
monsters—of the Three Grey Women and the Gorgons; of Scylla, the Sirens,
and the dragon of the Hesperides; and of Thoōsa, mother of Polyphemus.

[Page 51] *The Gorgons*. Medusa, slain by Perseus, and her two immortal
sisters, Stheno and Eurýale.

[Page 52] *Arimaspians*. A legendary northern people who fought for gold
with the griffins that guarded it. Cf. Milton, *P.L.*, ii, 943: 'As when a Gryfon
through the Wilderness With winged course ore Hill or moarie Dale, Pursues
the *Arimaspian*.'

[Page 52] *To prove I tell no idle tale*. This seems rather a clumsy pretext
for yet more geography; and mere retrospect comes as an anticlimax after the
previous prophecy.

[Page 52] *Gulf of Rhea*. Adriatic.

[Page 53] *Épaphus* (from *haphe*, 'touch') was identified by the Greeks
with the Egyptian Apis.

[Page 53] *Fifty maidens*. The Danaïds (p. 19).

[Page 54] *Wise . . . was he*. An allusion to Pittacus of Mitylene (c. 650–
570), one of the Seven Sages. Being asked whether it was better to wed a girl
of higher station or of one's own rank, Pittacus bade his questioner listen to some
small boys, who were whipping their tops with the cry: 'Keep to your own!'

[Page 54] *Yet Zeus, I say*. There is, I feel, a certain rudeness of workman-
ship in the fantastic inability of the strong, silent Prometheus to hold his tongue

about this vital secret. Such indifference to the risk of ever-increasing torments instils a certain incredulity about the torments being really so terrible. No doubt this is all part of the Titan's *hybris*; but the insolence of Clytemnestra seems better motivated.

[Page 55] *Adrasteia.* Nemesis, Retribution.

[Page 56] *Subterranean thunders.* Earthquakes.

[Page 57] *Some other God . . . Shall take thy doom.* Cheiron, the wise Centaur, wounded accidentally by one of Hēracles' poisoned arrows, sought an end to his agonies by giving up his immortality and descending to Hades in Prometheus' place.

[Page 58] *With him will I suffer.* This desperate defiance on the part of the Chorus is unparalleled in any later Greek tragedy.

AGAMEMNON

[Page 63] *Night.* The sun may not yet have risen when this first play of the trilogy began in the theatre.

[Page 65] *Clytemnestra enters.* Others (less convincingly, I think) postpone her entry till just before her first speech (p. 70); in which case the Chorus here addresses her in absence (cf. p. 249). If we recall the brooding silence of Aeschylus' Niobe through whole scenes, there seems nothing impossible in that of Clytemnestra, like a statue of Doom, through one long ode. At this moment she may turn her back on the Elders to direct her servants' rites.

THE HOUSE OF ARGOS

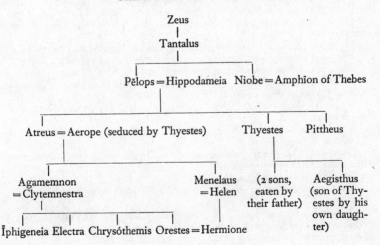

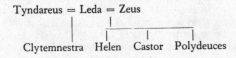

[Page 66] *She loathes the eagles' feast.* The anger of Artemis remains mysterious. (Clearly Agamemnon could not be held responsible for the brutalities of the eagles in his country.) The hare stands for Troy; the punishment of Troy was the express will of Zeus; why, then, did Artemis obstruct it, with an adverse wind?

In a lost epic, the *Cypria,* a motive *was* supplied; Agamemnon, hitting a stag near Aulis, rashly boasted that Artemis herself could not have aimed better (cf. Sophocles, *Electra,* 566 ff.). But there is nothing of that here.

However, it is as vain to ask too logically why such dire consequences should follow from the killing of a hare, as to ask why they should follow from the killing of Coleridge's albatross—in either case, the punishment is far crueller than the crime. (One may, of course, argue that the hare is simply symbolic.) What does seem clear is that Aeschylus was deeply shocked by the sacrifice of Īphigeneia.

[Page 67] *He that first was Lord . . . He that second came to birth.* Urănus (Sky), overthrown by his son Crŏnus; and Crŏnus, overthrown in turn by his son Zeus.

[Page 69] *Low trailed in the dust her saffron-dress.* Some take it that Īphigeneia threw her clothes on the ground and appeared stark naked; but this I find frankly incredible.

[Page 70] *Mother Night.* It has been suggested, perhaps rightly, that Clytemnestra uses this phrase because the mother in her remembers Īphigeneia's fate at Aulis.

[Page 70] *Hephaestus!* One of the most famous descriptions in Greek drama. Macaulay's vigorous imitation in *The Armada* has, I think, more merit than academic superciliousness has sometimes been willing to allow.

[Page 70] *Fishes leaping in their joy.* A pleasant touch; but the text is very dubious. The meaning may be simply that 'the force of the flame skimmed the sea.'

[Page 70] *Mācistus.* Now Kandēli; in Euboea, N.N.W. of Chalcis.

[Page 71] *Messāpion.* Now Ktypás; on the mainland opposite Chalcis.

[Page 71] *Asōpus* flows through the Boeotian Plain S. of Thebes.

[Page 71] *Gorgōpis' lake.* Perhaps the lake (now Vuliasméni) in the peninsula of Peraeum (Perachora).

[Page 71] *Aegiplanctus,* ('goat-wandered') is probably Mount Geraneia on the Isthmus.

[Page 71] *Arachnaeon.* A bare, grey, limestone peak (3,934 feet), 13 miles E. of Argos.

[Page 72] *Now if with reverence due . . .* Really, of course, Clytemnestra hopes the exact opposite; she is herself to tempt Agamemnon to *hybris* with her crimson vestments laid beneath his feet.

[Page 73] *Like basest bronze.* Bronze adulterated with lead is liable to blacken.

[Page 74] *The remembered faces.* It will be recalled that at this date (459–458) Athens was herself at war on half a dozen fronts (p. 4); many a remembered face must have been missing on the theatre benches this spring.

[Page 76] *Enters the Herald.* From Troy to Argos is 300 miles—two days and nights at 6 knots. Further there was a storm. But a choric ode in Greek drama, like the modern curtain, could cover an indeterminate lapse of time; though the interval is generally a good deal shorter than this.

Here, however, Verrall constructed one of his largest mares'-nests, on the theory that Clytemnestra was lying about the beacons—there was really only one beacon, on Mount Arachnaeon, as a private signal to the Queen from her lover Aegisthus, that her husband was approaching and the moment ripe. An exciting plot—had Aeschylus but written it!

What is really curious about the story of the ten years' siege of Troy is the apparent absence of communications between the besiegers and their homes. They never take any leave from the front; and there is not even news except for vague rumours. Clytemnestra knows something of Agamemnon's misbehaviour at Troy; but he seems to have only dark suspicions of his wife's intrigues.

Note how the Herald's tone veers strangely, but appropriately, between exultation and melancholy, triumph and foreboding,

[Page 76] *Pytho's King.* Apollo of Delphi, whose arrows brought pestilence on the Greeks in *Iliad*, i.

[Page 78] *Dip the tempered steel of war.* As she is soon to do in her husband's blood.

[Page 79] *A long disaster.* The lengthy story of the storm which follows seems rather episodic; though, of course, Agamemnon's murder was only made possible by his separation from his fleet and, in particular, from Menelaus.

[Page 79] *Two-headed goad . . . twin spears.* The two spears sometimes carried by Homeric warriors are compared to a charioteer's double-pronged goad, such as Laïus used to strike Oedipus (p. 191).

[Page 82] *From Weal, unending Woe.* Aeschylus is opposing the old idea of Heaven's jealousy—the belief which made Amāsis of Egypt, for example, renounce the friendship of Polýcrates of Samos, because 'I cannot remember hearing of any man of constant good fortune who in the end was not utterly destroyed.' (Heródotus, iii, 40–3, 125.)

[Page 83] *At the Pleiads' setting* could mean (1) 'early in November,' when they set before sunrise; (2) 'at dead of night.' Cf. Sappho's fragment (Diehl, *Anth. Lyr. Gr.*, i, p. 368):

> Moon's set, and Pleiads,
> Midnight goes by;
> The hours pass onward;
> Lonely I lie.

This last seems more likely. It does not matter here at what *season* Troy was sacked; and anyway, as it has just been sacked, Agamemnon's hearers know the season as well as he: but a *nocturnal* sack is yet more terrible than in daylight.

[Page 84] *Odysseus only, though so loth to sail.* Odysseus, newly married to Penelope, tried to evade the Trojan War by feigning madness. He ploughed with an ox and an ass yoked together, sowing salt; but the subtle Palamēdes exposed his real sanity by laying the infant Telemachus in the path of the plough. The fond father turned aside.

It remains strange, however, that Agamemnon should speak with this peevish disparagement of his other chieftains. In Homer they serve him loyally enough, even after his rash quarrel with Achilles. Perhaps it is to increase the general sense here of mistrust and treachery.

[Page 84] *What is sick.* It grows clearer that Agamemnon suspects his queen. Her only chance is to strike first. Contrast his coldness and her siren hypocrisy, after ten years of separation, with the happy reunion of Odysseus and Penelope in *Odyssey*, xxiii, 205–55. (*Greek Poetry for Everyman*, pp. 174–5.)

[Page 84] *Gēryon.* A three-bodied monster of the far west, killed by Hēracles; whose Tenth Labour was to fetch his famous red cattle.

[Page 85] *Stróphius.* Father of Orestes' friend Pýlades.

[Pages 85–6] The bracketed lines may be spurious.

[Page 86] *Trampling on costly stuffs.* The *hybris* lies (1) in the ostentation, (2) in the extravagance. Agamemnon seems torn between dread of what he is doing, a flattered desire to do it, and the serpent fascination exerted by Clytemnestra. He feebly tries to compromise by taking off his sandals; like Moses before the Burning Bush, or a Moslem in a mosque.

[Page 88] *The leech that raised the dead.* Asclēpius, son of Apollo and Corōnis, was struck by the thunderbolt of Zeus for restoring the dead to life. In revenge Apollo shot the Cyclōpes who had forged the bolt; and in expiation had to serve King Admētus for a year (p. 236).

[Page 89] *Alcmēna's son.* Hēracles, for slaying Īphitus (p. 164), had for three years to serve Omphăle, Queen of Lydia.

[Page 89] *The sheep of sacrifice.* Of course, with double meaning. The real sacrificial victim is Agamemnon.

[Page 90] *Woe, woe, woe! Apollo, Apollo!* With striking originality Aeschylus in this scene replaces the usual Messenger's Speech, relating what *has* happened, by a prophetess who sees what *is* happening, or about to happen, behind the blind walls of the palace.

[Page 90] *Whose name . . . is Doom.* A play on *Apollon* and *apollumi* ('I destroy').

[Page 90] *Yon children.* The young sons of Thyestes, on whose flesh Atreus feasted their father (p. 59).

[Page 91] *Ghastly yellow.* J. Symmons quotes (1824) Massinger, *Emperor of the East*, IV, 5: 'My blood within me turns, and through my veins, Parting with natural redness, I discern it Changed to a fatal yellow.' There, however, the emotion is not fear, but jealousy (cf. *Winter's Tale*, ii, 3, 106). But compare the modern slang use of 'yellow' for 'cowardly.'

[Page 92] *Itys.* Procne, daughter of Pandion, King of Athens, and wedded to the Thracian King Tēreus, found that her husband had ravished her sister Philomēla, then cut out her tongue. In revenge the two women fed Tēreus on the flesh of Itys, his son by Procne. Procne was changed into a nightingale, for ever wailing her child; Philomēla into a swallow; Tēreus into a hoopoe (cf. Swinburne, *Itylus*).

[Page 93] *No man believed me more.* Even the Gods could not take back their gifts, or undo the act of another god (cf. p. 278); but they could neutralize either by some further ordinance. A curious idea; but perhaps based on the realization that not even Omnipotence can make the past not have been.

[Page 94] *Amphisbaena.* A fabulous type of serpent, with a head at each end, enabling it to reverse.

[Page 94] *Scylla.* The six-headed monster, opposite the whirlpool Charybdis, who devoured six of Odysseus' comrades (*Odyssey*, xii, 223–59; *Greek Poetry for Everyman*, pp. 155–6).

[Page 96] *Ah human life . . . still more pitiful.* These lines have been transferred by some editors (mistakenly, I feel) to the Chorus. Cassandra seems to mean that the utter oblivion that swallows up even the memory of human suffering is more pitiful even than that suffering itself; which may, at the time, be redeemed by its tragic nobility and defiance. But the world forgets; the innocent blood cannot even cry from the ground; above it roll the grey floods of Lethe.

[Page 97] *Hush! Who is it cries of wounding?* As often at moments of excitement, the iambic is replaced by the trochaic tetrameter, which in earlier days had been the staple metre for tragic dialogue.

[Page 97] *Take we counsel*. These twelve speeches of the twelve Elders make the sort of passage that torments a translator. Do what one will, it remains a little ludicrous. Professor Platt omitted the lines from his version as absurd—otherwise, he said, he would have felt like Ham laying bare his father's nakedness. But this seems over-delicate. Professor Fraenkel, shocked by Platt's flippancy, defends Aeschylus: 'The complete inactivity of this body of loyal old men had to be accounted for.' But one can imagine it being accounted for rather better.

[Page 98] *And I rejoiced in it, as wheat grows glad*. I do not know any utterances in Greek tragedy so terrible as these speeches of Clytemnestra, with their exaltation of defiant and triumphant evil; even the daemonic Erīnyes are less real than this human inhumanity. Sophocles created no such woman as this; and beside her Euripides' Mēdēa turns pale.

[Page 99] *Old priests' daughters*. Literally, 'Chrȳsēīses.' Chrȳsēīs (whence our Cressida), daughter of old Chrȳses, priest of Apollo, was captured by the Achaeans and given to Agamemnon, who refused to restore her to her father. In punishment Apollo smote the Achaeans with plague; and the question of the girl's return caused the famous quarrel between Agamemnon and Achilles. (*Iliad*, i; *Greek Poetry for Everyman*, pp. 8–15.)

[Page 103] *Pleisthĕnes*. An obscure figure whose place among Agamemnon's ancestors is uncertain—perhaps between Pĕlops and Atreus.

FRAGMENTS AND EPIGRAMS

[Page 110] *Thĕtis*. Ironically enough, this fine fragment has been preserved by Plato's desire to have it suppressed. His tetchy puritanism was shocked (*Republic* 383B) by its suggestion that gods could deceive. Presumably Apollo sang his prophecy at the marriage-feast of Pĕleus and Thĕtis; Achilles' death is foretold by the dying Hector in *Iliad*, xxii, 358–60:

> Yet beware lest I bring the anger of Heaven upon thy head,
> That day when Phoebus Apollo and Paris strike thee dead,
> There in all thy glory before the Scaean Gate.

[Page 111] *Their memory dies not*. By Time's irony their memory has so completely died that the battle itself can no longer be identified. Some opening skirmish, in Thessaly, of the Persian invasion of 480 B.C.?

SOPHOCLES
(c. 496–c. 406 B.C.)

Les Grecs, amoureux du beau, ont des caractères simples, parce que la simplicité est beauté de lignes et noblesse d'attitudes. Les Anglais, amoureux du réel, ont des caractères complexes, parce que la vie est complexité. Les Français, amoureux des choses de raison, ont des caractères abstraits, parce qu'un caractère abstrait est une idée.

Faguet.

SOPHOCLES of Colōnus (on the outskirts of Athens) seemed to his contemporaries fortune's favourite. Handsome son of a rich father, he first appears to us leading a boyish chorus in the thanksgivings for Salamis (480); in 468, defeating Aeschylus, he was tragic victor, perhaps at his first attempt, when only twenty-eight (where Aeschylus had to wait for the prize till forty-one, Euripides till forty-four); and in some thirty-one tragic contests he was, by one account, twenty-four times first, and never below second (where Aeschylus won only thirteen victories and Euripides only five, one of them posthumous). He rose to be a Treasurer of the Athenian Empire; one of the ten Special Commissioners after the disaster at Syracuse; and, perhaps twice, one of the ten annual generals, though Pericles said he knew nothing of generalship, and Ion of Chios, a tragic poet of his day, describes him as a *bon viveur*, 'in public affairs neither clever nor energetic, but just an Athenian gentleman.' Even in extreme old age he kept his genius; even death was kind, in sparing him the sight of his country's surrender to Sparta (404). Dionysus himself, said the story, twice appeared in a dream to the Spartan commander and bade him give the old poet's body safe passage to its native Colōnus. Even after death, his pious spirit was honoured with shrine and sacrifice as 'Dexiōn,' 'the Welcomer,' in memory of the day when he had been chosen to welcome Asclēpius, the God of Healing, new-come to Athens across the Gulf from Epidaurus.

A public figure; yet, above all, an artist. It is hard to imagine him composing himself an epitaph like that of Aeschylus (p. 111). 'Gentle he was in this life,' says Aristophanes, 'gentle in the life beyond.' And Arnold's lines have become classic:

> But be his
> My special thanks, whose even-balanc'd soul,
> From first youth tested up to extreme old age,
> Business could not make dull, nor Passion wild:
> Who saw life steadily, and saw it whole:
> The mellow glory of the Attic stage;
> Singer of sweet Colonus, and its child.

This, I think, has much truth, as well as beauty. Though I doubt if Sophocles (unlike Arnold himself) was much burdened with 'business'; of his 'passions' there exist, right or wrong, other accounts less edifying; the praise of seeing life 'whole' should perhaps be kept for writers of wider range; and it may be questioned if Sophocles (or indeed any tragic writer) was really so 'mellow.' [1]

To judge him, we possess only seven plays out of over a hundred and twenty. But these show an artistry truly 'classic' in its conscious self-control. Aeschylus, he said, did right without knowing; Euripides drew men as they were, he himself as they ought to be drawn.[2] In short, the one was too romantic for Sophocles; the other too realist. His style (so far as we barbarians can judge) seems the man himself—graceful, yet subtle; careful, yet unstrained. It recalls the purity of Racine's French, without Racine's lack of vivid imagery.[3] It would not suit the lips of a Prometheus: but Sophocles did not deal in Titans. He is nearer to Mozart than to Beethoven. As a beginner, he said, he had tried the pomp of Aeschylus; then a 'sharp and artificial' manner of his own; finally, a style that he found 'best and most expressive of personality.'

For Aristotle (though one may not agree) the main thing in tragedy was plot; and, for him, Sophocles was *the* tragic poet. True, *The Women of Trāchis, Ajax,* and *Antigone* may seem to flag in interest towards the close. But the plot of *Oedipus the King* has roused endless, perhaps excessive, admiration. *Philoctētes,* too, is masterly; and far more credible. And the end of *Electra* remains a most ingenious piece of tragic irony.

The ordinary English reader, of course, is apt to complain: 'Very artistic, no doubt; but, like Racine, marmoreal—cold. Give me Chaucer, Shakespeare, Dickens—less art and more heart.' And the more intellectual reader is sometimes irritated by Sophocles' refusal to question, like Aeschylus and Euripides, the orthodoxy of his day. This feeling, indeed, has sometimes had paradoxical results. There are scholars who seem to argue: 'Great writers discuss the Universe. Sophocles is a great writer. Therefore Sophocles discusses the Universe.' And when (with rare exceptions like the rebellious close of *The Women of Trāchis*) Sophocles refuses to discuss the Universe except in the most traditional terms, they do it for

---

[1] Cf. pp. 122, 169, 220.

[2] The Greek (Aristotle, *Poetics,* ch. xxv) could equally well mean 'men as they should *be.*' But heroes like Ajax or Hēracles are hardly 'men as they should *be*'; still less Aegisthus or Menelaus. In any case Sophocles means that tragedy should seek a finer tone than mere realism.

It is in keeping with this interest in literary theory that Sophocles should also (we are told) have written a critical work, *On the Chorus,* and founded a literary club.

[3] It is significant of Racine's feeling for Sophocles that he preferred to adapt Euripides, precisely because he admired Euripides less. Louis Racine refuses to believe the story that his father had planned an *Oedipe,* 'puisqu'il a dit souvent, qu'il avait osé jouter contre Euripide, mais qu'il ne serait jamais assez hardi pour jouter contre Sophocle.' (Aeschylus— as one might expect from Racine's period and his temperament—interested him less.)

him and foist the result between his lines.   But criticism does not consist in
remaking a writer in one's own image.

It is not that Sophocles never thought about such things; but he kept his
thoughts within careful limits; he did not, like his two rivals, constantly
wrestle with them in public. 'The Gods,' he might have answered, 'are
all-mighty; Man, the shadow of a dream.   The Gods have given him unwritten laws; they have bid him be sober, self-controlled, just.   Are the
Gods themselves always just?   I do not know.   They judge us; not we
Them.   We cannot tell why the innocent suffer; at least we can see that
the guilty seldom escape.   He that endures undaunted may be justified at
last; though perhaps only, like Oedipus, on the edge of the grave; or, like
Ajax, beyond it.   But do not ask me to explain the world and justify the
Gods.   I am a poet—not a charlatan.'   The questionings of Job are met
in the end only with a magnificent Magnificat.   We are deafened, not
answered; entranced though, maybe, not satisfied.   Sophocles, I imagine,
was in attitude not altogether unlike the author of Job.   Only he turned
from questioning God, whom he did not know, to painting Man, whom he
knew.

This does not mean that he lacked convictions about life; but they were
few, simple, and implicit in his characters, rather than shouted from the
stage.   Just as Shakespeare, I feel, believed strongly in 'degree' and, still
more, in loyalty, so Sophocles saw the root of evil in arrogance, wilfulness,
and tyranny.   We may revolt at this Greek fondness for harping on the
need for perpetual moderation and self-restraint.   What platitudes!   Yet
we ourselves do not find them, whether platitudes or not, any easier to
practise.   Our world continues to be bedevilled by the antics of successful
demagogues, or the grimmer brutalities of dictators.   No doubt Sophocles
was more of a pure craftsman than his rivals, more concentrated on producing effective scenes and well-made plays.   But the poet who drew, in
the young Antigone and in the young Neoptolemus, the age-long conflict
of individual conscience and decency with the soulless monstrosities of the
State, was less indifferent to general ideas than some have supposed.   He
was no Ibsen bravely probing conventions of conduct; but his eyes were
fixed on what seemed to him 'the unwritten laws.'

Still, though interested above all in human beings, the artist in him
cared perhaps still more for plot than for character; for the whole than the
parts; for depicting the clash of two souls than for analysing a soul in itself.
He has left us no looming Clytemnestra, no self-tortured Phaedra.   And
though, like Shakespeare, he seemed to his fellows 'gentle,' he could also
be curiously ruthless.   'Like life,' they might both have answered.   When
Shakespeare has had his fun with Falstaff and his merry men (and women),
how relentlessly the poor puppets are flung aside to die, by grief or pox or
gallows!   And Sophocles is more relentless still; when Ajax and Heracles

and King Oedipus go their tragic ways with so little sign of regret, amid their prolonged outcries and lamentations, for the devoted women whose lives they have wrecked, one is left wondering. I confess I am repelled. It seems needlessly callous. Yet this same Sophocles has himself created the pathos of those very women; has dwelt again and again, still more tenderly, on the frail happiness of childhood, so unconscious of what life will be; has brooded as sadly as his fellow masters of style, Virgil and Tennyson, on 'the doubtful doom of humankind.' Strange blend of harsh and gentle. Perhaps in him, as in Socrates, Shakespeare, or Wordsworth, there lived an unusual violence of feeling beneath the external calm— an essential part of the man's energy, like the wild-briar stock at the root of the garden rose. One recalls his own Antigone's great utterance:

My nature is to share in love, not hate;

and how, all the same, it does not prevent her being at moments the harshest of young heroines. One recalls, too, his own Teiresias—a seer, yet fiercer at times than any true seer should be. By life Sophocles seemed, like Goethe, supremely favoured; yet about life he could be, like Goethe, at times supremely bitter. But it is by his more human side that he endures—and by a style where the words fit together like the marvellously cut masonry of those ancient city walls that, disdaining all aid of mortar, still crown many a Greek hillside with the flawless grace of simple stone.

AJAX

For my enemy is dead, the man divine as myself is dead.

Whitman.

Ajax, son of King Telamōn of Salamis, was the mightiest, after Achilles, of the Greek heroes before Troy. But when, after the slaying of Achilles by Apollo and Paris at the Scaean Gate, the divine arms once forged for the fallen hero by the god Hephaestus were awarded to Odysseus in preference to himself, Ajax in his fury planned to slaughter the Greek leaders. Athena, however, so crazed his wits that, like Don Quixote, he fell instead on the captured flocks and herds in the Greek camp.

At this point the play opens, before the hut of Ajax. (It is usually translated 'tent'; but the Greeks had curious ideas of comfort if they passed ten years before Troy in 'tents.') Odysseus enters, tracking by footprints the author of this massacre. Revealing herself, Athena confirms his suspicions of Ajax; and brings the madman to his doorway, gripping the blood-stained scourge with which he is about to flog the ram he mistakes in his frenzy for Odysseus. Then the goddess points out to Odysseus, before they go, the inevitable Greek moral:

> From such a sight as this, learn not to utter
> Proud word thyself against the Gods in Heaven;
> Nor swell in arrogance if hand of thine
> Prove weighty, or deep thy wealth, beyond another's.
> *One* day can sink, *one* day can raise again
> The scales of human fortune.
>
> (127–32.)

For Ajax in his pride had once bidden Athena go help the other Greeks— the line would never break where Ajax stood. That pride has found its fall.

Now appears a Chorus of Salaminian mariners of Ajax, dismayed by rumours about him. His mistress Tecmessa, captive daughter of the Phrygian king, reveals the truth—Ajax, after killing or torturing his dumb victims, has at last regained his senses. The interior opens and the hero is seen sitting in despair among butchered carcasses. Honour lost, he is resolved to die. Vainly Tecmessa pleads with him, for the sake of his parents, of their little son, of herself:

> Me too remember. Surely a man should keep
> Remembrance, where he *once* has found some joy.
>
> (520–1.)

Inflexible, Ajax orders her to bring their child; and the grim warrior softens for a moment into words full of Sophocles' recurrent tenderness for youth.

> Lift him now, lift him to me. *He* will feel
> No terror at this sight of blood and slaughter,
> If he is born indeed true son of mine.
> Like a young colt, betimes he must be trained
> In *my* stern ways, and moulded to my nature.
> My son, be luckier than thy father was,
> But like him else—thou canst not *then* be coward!
> Nay, even now I envy thee the blindness
> That hides our sorrows from thy innocence.
> The truest happiness is knowing nothing,
> Ere thou hast learnt what joy and anguish are.
> But when that day shall come, thou must teach my enemies
> What thou art worth, what father once begot thee;
> Yet now, meanwhile, be happy, little heart,
> Feed on light fancies, be thy mother's joy.
> No Greek, I know, will dare to put upon thee
> Insult or wrong—though *I* be far away.
>
> (545–61.)

After a lament by the Chorus, Ajax re-enters—seemingly with purpose
changed. He will 'bury' his sword, reverence the Gods, bow to the
Atreidae. After all—

> Even the strongest things, things full of terror,
> Must bow obedience—Winter's drifted snow
> Yields to the fruitful Summer, the endless round
> Of Night to the white-horsed splendour of the Morn;
> The wild blasts of the storm-wind leave to rest,
> At length, the moaning waves; and Sleep that conquers
> All, in the end unfetters what he bound.
> And how should *I*, then, not at last learn wisdom?
>
> (669–77.)

Meaning to mislead his hearers, so that he can die undisturbed, Ajax
has here misled some later critics. Why, they ask, this eloquent change of
mind? Surely it *must* be real? The answer seems simply that his mood,
indeed, *has* changed; but not his mind. He is calmer, and accepts necessity;
but it is only the calm of the doomed—the necessity of death. Sophocles,
a dramatic psychologist, but even more interested in drama than in psychology, merely wished here to increase his theatrical effect by a speech
full of the ambiguous ironies he loved, elating his other characters, and even
perhaps his audience, with false hopes before the final blow; as just before
the ruin of Oedipus the Chorus speculates exultantly what god can have
begotten him. Like Fate, the dramatist plays cat with mouse. So here,
after Ajax has gone out, the Chorus rejoices in his recovery, till a messenger brings word that his half-brother Teucer, now at hand, has been
warned by the prophet Calchas on no account to let Ajax stir forth to-day—
by to-morrow Athena's anger will have passed. Too late, Tecmessa and
the Chorus hurry in search.

The scene changes to the seashore. Ajax, planting upright in
Trojan earth the fatal sword that Hector once gave him, takes his
last leave of life:

> But thou, O Sun,[1] driving thy chariot
> Across high Heaven, when thine eyes behold
> The land that bore me, draw thy golden rein
> And tell the tidings of my ruin and death
> To my old father and unhappy mother.
> (Poor heart, when she shall hear it, well I know
> With what wild wailings she will fill our city!)
> But vain repining will not help me now—

[1] It should be remembered that in an open-air theatre such invocations would seem
far more vivid than on an electric-lighted stage.

Better the deed were done, without delay!
Come, Death!—ay, Death, turn now thine eyes upon me.
Yet—since with thee my converse shall be long
There in the grave—for this last time I call,
And nevermore, to *thee*, O Light of day,
To thee, O glittering chariot of the Sun.
Farewell, dear Light; farewell, my native land
Of sacred Salamis—and my father's hearth—
And glorious race of Athens, neighbours once;
And you, ye springs and rivers of this land,
Ye plains of Troy, a second home to me,
Farewell! This last time Ajax speaks to you—
The rest in Hades to the shades below.

(845–65.)

Hidden by some trees at the side, he falls upon his sword-point just before Tecmessa and the Chorus re-enter in quest of him. Tecmessa finds the body; Teucer joins her; then Menelaus hurries in to forbid the burial of this would-be assassin of the Achaean kings. With this matter of burial the last four hundred lines—nearly a third of the play—are concerned. The less unreasonable Agamemnon repeats his brother's ban; but is finally persuaded by the prudent Odysseus to relent.

No modern playwright could so risk anticlimax; and some readers, remembering the part played by interment in *Antigone* and *Oedipus at Colonus* also, might feel that Sophocles had the preoccupations of an undertaker rather than a poet. What a contrast with the condemned Socrates! 'How shall we bury you?' asks Crito. 'As you will—*if* you can catch me!'

But Socrates was far ahead of his age. This is one of the gulfs Time digs between period and period. For Athens, Ajax of Salamis was a national hero, almost a patron saint. One of their ten tribes was called after him 'Aiantis'; and quaintly enough, in memory of his rage at defeat, its chorus was never allowed to be placed last in a competition. Peisistrătus, Miltiades, Cĭmon, Alcibiades, Thucydides, claimed descent from Ajax; he was invoked in the perilous hours before Salamis, and a captured Phoenician galley dedicated to him after it; even in the second century A.D. his rites endured. And so for Athenians his last honours were of living interest; as in a Passion Play, the dramatic tension extended, after the fate of the hero, to the fate of his bodily remains.

All the same, the modern reader may be excused if he finds the wrangle with Menelaus rather squalid, and even Odysseus as chilling as some personified Prudence in a medieval Morality. Indeed from this somewhat bleak play I find my memory turns back to that grey ocean-shore in *The*

Odyssey where Odysseus meets for a moment the wraith of his old rival
and holds out the hand of reconciliation in vain:

'Nay then, dear lord, come hither—let us speak as friend to friend;
At last lay aside thine anger, thy pride that naught can bend.'
So I cried, but he answered not; and, silent thus,
He passed with the souls of the perished to the gloom of Erebus.[1]

That silence of Ajax, so admired two thousand years ago by 'Longinus,'
rings longer in my ears than all the wailing choruses of the play of Sophocles.
And Virgil remembered it, when he made his Dido lock her lips, with the
same speechless bitterness, against the false lover who met her phantom
upon the Plains of Mourning.

Antigone
(*c.* 442–441 B.C.)

And what is hate, O fierce and unforgiving,
And what shall hate achieve, when all is said?
A silly joke that cannot reach the living,
A spitting in the faces of the dead.

Stella Benson.

This play would be admirably clear—if only it had not been explained.[2]
After the defeat of The Seven who attacked Thebes, Creon, the new Theban
king, forbade the burial of the traitor Polyneices; whose sister Antigone,
preferring God's Law to Man's, disobeyed and was sent by Creon to her
death. For this, Creon was punished by Heaven with the suicides of his
own wife and son.

Hard to be simpler. No question that Creon was wrong—a man not
ill-meaning, but intoxicated with his new authority. A Greek audience
would soon place him, merely by the way he speaks. 'This fellow,' they
would say, 'talks like a *tyrant*' (a species of animal only too familiar to them,
as to us, alike from literature and life). Teiresias, the voice of Heaven,
condemns Creon as forcibly as Nathan condemned David. By that, even
the wavering Chorus are convinced. Creon himself is convinced—too
late, for now the judgment falls. Who indeed would not be convinced?

Not Hegel. For him, as already mentioned, life was divided against
itself by constant conflicts harmonized in higher and higher syntheses.
Thus Antigone and Creon are both partly right, partly wrong; they clash;

[1] *Odyssey*, xi, 561–4; *Greek Poetry for Everyman*, p. 153.
[2] Genealogical table, p. 227.

they suffer; but justice is done and there is no place for pity, that emotion of country cousins. Such is the true essence of tragedy. And since *Antigone* so neatly fitted his formula, it became for Hegel the grandest work of ancient or modern times. Sophocles might have been gratified by the praise: he would have been stupefied by the interpretation. Some, indeed, may feel that, with his Prussian State-worship, Hegel was himself a good deal too like Creon—except that no character of Sophocles could express himself in a style so execrable.[1]

But ingenuity did not end with Hegel. More modern critics have explained that Antigone says nothing of her lover Haemon, because she was really in love with her dead brother Polyneices. A little Freud is a dangerous thing. There is still time for other critics to discover that Antigone was also (in *Oedipus at Colōnus*) in love with her father; and Electra, no doubt, with her brother Orestes. One would have thought Greek tragedy already contained more than enough incest (a tedious theme, I think), without importing more. Nor is it clear why a dramatist who elsewhere treats the subject with brutal frankness should here veil it in innuendo too obscure for any audience. The question is not: 'Was Antigone in love with her brother?' (outside fiction, she does not exist), but: 'Did Sophocles mean his hearers to think so?' If so, he failed; and if he was so bad at conveying his meaning, it hardly matters what he meant.

Then there is the theory that Polyneices was really buried the first time, not by Antigone, but by Ismēne. But life is too brief for brooding on mares'-nests. Those who wish further details will find them in the late Professor Waldock's admirable little book on Sophocles, which contains more critical common sense than many volumes ten times its size.

This play keeps a special appeal because its central problem is still so deep and wide. It may be said, indeed, that we read too much into it— that Sophocles was merely depicting a simple clash between the laws of God and the laws of Man, not foreshadowing Hitler and Stalin. Yet we need not be too afraid of anachronism in seeing Antigone as an immortal

---

[1] It has been argued that Hegel did not mean that Creon was partly right, as well as Antigone; but merely that loyalty to the family and loyalty to the State are, in general, both important (a truism which hardly seems worth uttering). I find this hard to reconcile with Hegel's own words (*Ästhetik*, II, Abschn. ii, ch. 1; tr. F. P. B. Osmaston, 1920, ii, 215): 'Antigone, the woman, is pathetically possessed by the interest of the family; Kreon, the man, by the interest of the community.' But Teiresias does not see Creon as public-spirited; nor, I believe, did Sophocles. Such devotion to the commonweal does belong to the Theseus of *Oedipus at Colōnus*; but not to the Theban despot either of that play or of this. A century later Creon still figures as odious in the dying taunt of the self-poisoned Demosthenes to Archias the actor, who came on behalf of Antipater the Macedonian to arrest him on the isle of Calauria (322): 'Now, when you please, you can play Creon and fling me out unburied.' (Cf. Demosthenes' other allusion to Creon on p. 226.)

In fine, Hegel's view of tragedy would apply far better to the conflict between individual and Church in Shaw's *Saint Joan* (a play which, beside *Antigone*, seems to me far cleverer, but sometimes vulgar, sometimes cheap).

type.   Her 'unwritten laws' may often change; they may not be eternal, as she dreamed; but where is their home?   In the individual conscience. *That* endures.   And against it rises, again and again, the cold power of the State, whether single despot or compact majority, claiming as Caesar's the things that are God's.   In the Sparta of Sophocles' time, next the meeting-place of the magistrates was reared, with grim purpose, the Temple of Fear.   That too the ages have not destroyed.   To-day it casts its gloomy shadow far across the earth.   The challenge met by Antigone was essentially the same for Socrates, for Joan of Arc, for Charlotte Corday, and for our world to-day—the conflict of the Many and the One.

Dramatically, I think, the play weakens towards the close; it flags without Antigone; as *Ajax* without its hero, or *Hippolytus* without Phaedra. The cursings of Teiresias, and the description of Antigone's death and Haemon's despair, are indeed vivid, but less vivid; there is, as usual, too much lamenting; and it is hard to be much moved by Queen Eurydice's death—she was never really alive.

But though not Sophocles' most perfect play, it contains perhaps his greatest speech—Antigone's burning vindication of the unwritten laws.[1] And she remains, it may be, his most immortal character—hard, at times, and headstrong, like Cordelia, but heroic as few heroines have been; all the more because, between senile elders,[2] well-meaning sister, and domineering king, she stands so utterly and indomitably alone—'stern Daughter of the Voice of God.'   If the story is true that the Athenians made Sophocles a general for having written this work, it may not have been very prudent of them (though the generals had many duties *not* military); but it does great credit to their hearts.

[1] p. 141.
[2] Ordinarily in Greek tragedy where the main character is a heroine, the Chorus are women too.   But here, by forming his Chorus from old men of Thebes, Sophocles has heightened the lonely grandeur of Antigone.

ANTIGONE

ANTIGONE	EURYDICE, his Queen
ISMĒNE, her sister	TEIRESIAS
CREON, her uncle, King of Thebes	GUARD
HAEMON, his son, betrothed to Anti-	TWO MESSENGERS
gone	CHORUS OF THEBAN ELDERS

[Before the palace at Thebes.]

Antigone. Ismēne, my own sister, on us two
   That yet are living, does not Zeus let fall
   The burden of every sorrow ever sprung
   From Oedipus?   What is spared us?   There is nothing—
   No pain, no shame, no ruin, no dishonour—
   But I have seen it added to the ills
   We bear together.
   And now, what is this edict that men say
   The Lord of Thebes proclaims throughout the land?
   Has rumour reached you?   Or have *you* not heard
   How falls upon those we love the fate of foes?
Ismēne. To me, Antigone, of those we love
   No word at all has come—nor good, nor bitter—
   Since one day robbed us both of both our brothers,
   Slain by each other's hands.   But since there vanished
   The host of Argos, this past night, I know
   Nothing of happier news or worse disaster.
Antigone. I knew as much; and that is why I brought you
   Outside the palace-gates, to speak alone.
Ismēne. What *now*?   I can see your heart is brooding something.
Antigone. What, then, but this?—that, of our brothers, Creon
   Grants one an honoured grave, but leaves the other
   Unburied in his shame!   Yes, Éteocles
   He has laid in earth, honoured among the dead,
   With all observance of due right and custom—
   So runs the rumour—but has proclaimed to Thebes
   That none shall dare bestow on Polyneices,
   So miserably perished, either grave
   Or lamentation—*him* they must leave to lie
   Unwept, untombed, a rich and pleasant banquet
   To gladden the greedy eyes of birds of prey.

Such is the edict, as they say, proclaimed
By this good Creon unto thee and me
(Doubtless I too am counted)—and he comes
Hither, I learn, to make it clearly public
To all that have not heard; accounting it
No trivial matter—for the least transgressor
Death waits, by stoning, at the hands of Thebes.
So here you have the truth.   Soon yours to show
If you are noble as your birth—or born
Degenerate from your high ancestry!

Ismēne. And what then, stubborn heart, if this be true,
  Can *I* do more, to loose the knot or tighten?
Antigone. Think—will you dare to work and act with me?
Ismēne. In venturing what?   Where stands your purpose now?
Antigone. Will you help these hands take up our brother's body?
Ismēne. What!—plan to bury him!   Against the edict!
Antigone. I will do *my* part—yours too, if *you* will not—
  To bury our brother.   False I will *not* be found.
Ismēne. O reckless one, when Creon has forbidden!
Antigone. *He* has no right to keep me from my kindred.
Ismēne. Ah, sister!   Think, how first our father perished,
  Hated, dishonoured, driven by self-detection
  Of his own guilt, to stab his own two eyes;
  How she that was his mother, then his wife,
  Destroyed her life within that twisted noose;
  And then how both our brothers on one day
  With mutual blows of fratricidal hands
  Found for their misery one common end.
  And we two sisters, now, left all alone—
  Think how we too must die a grisly death,
  If we defy the law and break this edict
  Of Creon's sovereignty!
  Ah, yet remember we are only women,
  Not made to war with men.   And then, again,
  We are only subjects of the mightier,
  Bound to obey in this—or worse than this!
  Therefore, entreating Those beneath the earth
  To pardon me for what I do perforce,
  I shall bow before our rulers.   For indeed
  It is mere folly, striving past our powers.
Antigone. No mind have *I* to drive you.   Though you offered,
  I should find no pleasure, now, in help of yours!
  Play *you* what part may please you best.   But I

Will bury him.   If I die, it will be nobly.
Well loved, I shall sleep beside the man I loved,
For a crime that was my duty.   Let me please
The dead—their favour long outlasts the living;
For there I shall rest for ever.   As for you,
Prefer, if so you will, to leave dishonoured
Those laws the Gods have honoured.

Ismēne. I do them no dishonour.   But defy
The public voice of Thebes!—I have not strength.

Antigone. Take shelter in excuses!   *I* will go
And heap the earth upon my dearest brother.

Ismēne. Unhappy one!   Ah, how I tremble for thee!

Antigone. Fear not for *me*!   Mind your own course is safe.

Ismēne. At least breathe word to no one what you do.
Keep it a darkest secret.   So shall I.

Antigone. Ah no, denounce me!   Think what a grave disfavour
Your silence earns, not crying it to the world!

Ismēne. Ah, heart so hot, amid the chill of danger!

Antigone. To the dead my duty lies—sure, *they* approve.

Ismēne. If you succeed!   But you dream the impossible.

Antigone. Well, when my strength shall fail, I strive no more.

Ismēne. One should not seek the impossible at all.

Antigone. If you will use such words, I shall but hate you—
To *you* shall cling the just hate of the dead.
Leave me alone, in all my idle folly,
To meet this doom you dread so.   At the worst
I shall not die a death dishonourable.

Ismēne. Why then, go if you must—a fool to go,
Yet never doubt how loved by those that love you!

> *Antigone goes out to the left. Ismēne returns to the palace.*
> *There enters the Chorus of Theban Elders.*

strophe 1

Chorus. Sun of the dawn, so fair a morn on Thebes the seven-gated
There never rose before!
Hail, golden eye of day!—long waited,
Across the streams of Dirce thou glitterest once more!
And the host that out of Argos came, steel-clad, with shields of white,
Headlong thou drivest, with shaken rein, in ever faster flight.

Over our marches had swept the foe,
Like some white eagle, with wings of snow
And savage scream:
By Polyneices' hate possest,

So upon Thebes the Argive pressed,
With many an armoured rank agleam,
Many a tossing crest.

Hovering over our roofs he hung; round our ramparts seven-gated
   With greedy spears he came,
    Gaping for blood—yet he fled unsated,
Or ever his beak was reddened, or the Fire-god's pine-fed flame
Had gripped our city's crown of towers.   So fierce at his rear there rang
The rattle of steel; so grim to war our Theban dragon sprang.

For hateful to Zeus are the tongues of pride.
On the sweep of their army's torrent-tide,
With its glory of clashing gold, looked He;
The stormer stood on our topmost wall,
His goal within reach, on his lips the call
Of 'Victory!'—
But God let His lightning fall.

Hurled from his hold, there crashed on the bruising plain   *str.* 2.
That madman, torch in hand.   All, all in vain
Raged like a tempest-blast
The frenzy of his hate—
Baffled he lay at last;
And the heavy hand of Ares, our champion, hath cast
His fellows to their fate.

There came seven Argives to match their might
At our seven gates in single fight;
Yet all to the God of Victories
Left their arms forfeit—save *that* curst pair,
Whom *one* sire begot, *one* mother bare.
For, conquerors both, with their spear-points these
Won death for a spoil to share.

Thebes of the many chariots, since to thee   *ant.* 2.
With answering smile comes glorious Victory,
Forgotten now be war!
Come, and in joyous band
Round every temple-door
Gather with night-long dances, while Bacchus springs before
And shakes the Theban land.

Creon appears at the central door of the palace.

But yonder comes Menoeceus' son,
Whom these new wonders the Gods have done
Raise now to be our land's new king.
What is the course his counsels steer?
Why cried his heralds far and near
Our summoning?
Why meet we Elders here?

Creon. Our city, men of Thebes, the Gods that shook her
With heaviest seas, have raised erect again
On even keel.   But you I have summoned here,
Chosen from all the rest, as men I knew
Loyal always to the throne of Laïus;
And after—both when Oedipus instead
Guided our State, and when he too had perished—
Still firm upholders of this kingdom's heirs.
Now, since his sons with fratricidal guilt
By a twofold fate, both in a single day,
Have died as slain and slayer, I in turn
As next in right and kinship to the dead,
Possess their sceptre and their sovereignty.
Yet none can tell, until he has seen a man
Serve a full term of rule and lawgiving,
His judgment and his nature and his soul.
For him I hold—and have this many a year—
Basest of wretches, that wielding in a state
The power supreme, instead of cleaving fast
To what is counselled best, for fear of others
Keeps his lips sealed in silence.   And worthless he
That prizes any friend above his country!
Never could *I*—witness all-seeing Zeus!—
Sit dumb to watch while ruin drawing nearer
Imperilled the safety of my countrymen;
Nor take for friend of mine a man that hated
Our native land—well knowing that she alone
Preserves us all—only while *she* sails fair,
Can we aboard her make what friends we make.
Such are my rules to work the weal of Thebes.
And, true to these, I have set forth my edict
Thus, as concerns the sons of Oedipus.
Éteocles, who fell most bravely fighting
For this our country, shall be laid in earth

With all the honours done to the noblest dead.
But, for his brother, this same Polyneices,
This exile who returned from banishment
Eager to give to the consuming flame
His native city and the Gods of Thebes,
Eager to drink the blood of fellow Thebans
Or hale them into bondage—as for *him*,
It is proclaimed none give him tomb or tears—
Let him lie unwept, rank carrion for hounds
And birds of prey, a sight of ghastly shame.
Such my decision.   Never will I suffer
More honours for the evil than the just.
Honour I keep for those, both dead and living,
That bear true love to Thebes.

Chorus-leader. Son of Menoeceus, such then is your pleasure
   For the lover of his country, and the traitor?
   Yours is the power, past doubt, to frame your laws
   Alike for us that live and for the dead.
Creon. Then take good heed to guard my ordinance!
Leader. Lay *that* task, rather, upon younger shoulders.
Creon. To watch the dead, I *have* set guards already.
Leader. What further orders have you, then, for us?
Creon. To take no part with those that disobey me.
Leader. None's fool enough to fall in love with death.
Creon. Death is, indeed, the payment!   Yet too often
   Mere lust of gain has lured men's hopes to ruin.

                           [*A guard enters.*

Guard. My lord, I will not say that I am come
   Hotfoot with haste, or breathless with my speed.
   For often by the way I stopped to think
   And many a time I wheeled to the right-about.
   Indeed my heart had much advice to give me:
   'Why running, fool, so fast to punishment?
   Yet, wretch, what makes you loiter?   If King Creon
   Learns all from other lips, will *you* not smart?'
   So many meditations took much time,
   And my short journey stretched to a lengthy one.
   However—in the end—I *did* resolve
   To come.   And though my words be veriest nothing,
   They shall be said.   For firmly I hold to this—
   I can only suffer what is fated me.
Creon. What is it, then, that makes thee so despondent?
Guard. First I will speak upon my own account.

I did not do it—did not see who did.
There can be no just cause to punish *me*.

Creon. What pains to shield yourself! What fine precautions
In levelling at the matter! Clear enough,
You have strange news to tell.

Guard. Where danger lies, one well may stop to think.

Creon. Then out with it, and get you gone from here!

Guard. Well, this is it. Someone has newly buried
The body, and departed—scattering it
With thirsty dust, and doing the needful rites.

Creon. How! What man born could dare do such a thing!

Guard. I cannot say. There was no mark of pick,
No mattock's upcast earth. The ground lay dry
And hard—unbroken—with no track of wheels.
No sign of who had done it.
Soon as the day's first sentry showed it to us,
We stood astounded, all in blank dismay.
There lay the body hidden—buried, no!—
But lightly strewn with dust, as to avert
Pollution (and yet there was no trace of hound
Or wild beast coming near to tear the flesh).
Then curses buzzed among us thick and fast,
Sentry accusing sentry. In the end
We should have come to blows, with none to stop us;
For every man seemed guilty to the rest,
Each swore his innocence—and proof was none.
We all were ready to pass through the fire,
To handle red-hot iron, to swear by Heaven
We had not done it—did not know who planned
The deed, or put it into execution.
At last, when all our searching found no end,
One of us said a thing made all the rest
Look down with frightened faces—for we saw
No answer to his plan; and yet no safety,
Suppose we took it. For he urged we *must*
Tell the whole truth to you, without concealment.
So we resolved; then the lot fell on me—
Poor wretch!—to undertake this handsome service.
Unwilling I to come; unwilling you,
My lord, I know, to hear me. No man loves
The bringer of bad tidings.

Leader. Sire, my own mind misgives me this long while,
Asking: 'May this not be the hand of Heaven?'

Creon. Silence!—before your babble stirs my anger.
　　Take care of being found both old and foolish.
　　Intolerable!—to say the Gods could care
　　For preservation of this wretch's body!
　　Was it in honour of his *piety*,
　　Think you, that they interred him!—a man that came
　　To burn Their columned shrines, Their offerings,
　　This land They love—annihilate Their laws!
　　When have you seen Gods cherishing the wicked?
　　Never! This is the work of malcontents
　　Within this city, that misliked my edicts
　　And long have murmured, wagging their heads in secret,
　　With necks refractory to my righteous yoke.
　　They have suborned these sentries—well I know it!—
　　With bribery. On all the earth there grows not
　　One curse so vile as money—*this* destroys
　　Cities, and drives men exiled from their homes,
　　Perverting and debauching honest minds
　　To deeds of evil; breeding miscreants
　　Cunning in every kind of godlessness.
　　But those that sold themselves for such a service
　　Have made most sure of future retribution.
　　(*To the Guard.*) But thou, mark well — I take my oath
　　　　upon it,
　　As sure as Zeus enjoys my reverence—
　　Unless ye find and bring before my eyes
　　The perpetrator of this burial,
　　Not death alone shall meet your case—alive
　　Ye shall be hung up, first, till ye reveal
　　The guilty—and so are taught to look for gain
　　Henceforth with more discretion,
　　Not snatching profit from no matter whence.
　　I tell ye, more men find their own undoing
　　Than preservation, from such gains ill got.

Guard. May I say more? Or must I turn and go?

Creon. Still unaware how tiresome is your tongue!

Guard. Does it offend your ear, Sire, or your heart?

Creon. Why so precise about the seat of it?

Guard. I only vex your ears; your heartfelt anger
　　Must be for the man that did it.

Creon. God! What a babbler born you show yourself!

Guard. I talk, maybe; but I was *not* the doer.

Creon. Yes!—and a fool that sold his life for silver!

Guard. Oh!
  It is hard when men guess idly—and guess ill!
Creon. Fine talk of 'guessing'!—find me out the guilty,
  Or ye shall make confession, one and all,
  That the wages of corruption are disaster.
Guard. I pray he *may* be found—but found or no,
  As chance may order, *you* will never see me
  Come *here* a second time.
  For past all hope—beyond all expectation—
  I am got off.   And thanks to Heaven for that!

      He goes out; King Creon re-enters the palace.

Chorus. Many wonders hath the world,   *strophe* 1.
  But most wonderful of these,
  Man!—that steers with sails unfurled,
  By the wintry south winds hurled,
  Through the trough of toppling seas.
  Earth, of all Gods ancientest,
  Unwasting and unwearying,
  Yet feels his plough-teams tire her breast,
  As hither, thither, without rest
  They wheel with each new spring.

  Subtle he within the toils   *antistrophe* 1.
  Of his woven nets to snare
  Fishes of the deep beguiled,
  And the grim beasts of the wild,
  And the light-heart birds of air.
  Creatures of the waste and hill
  His contrivances constrain;
  Yoke on neck, beneath his will
  The tameless mountain-bull grows still,
  The horse with tossing mane.

  Language and wind-swift thought   *str.* 2.
  He hath devised, untaught,
  And that true temper which preserves a state;
  Roofs for the arrowy rain,
  The barbéd frost—his brain
  Invented all, forearmed for every turn of fate;
  Cures he hath made his own
  For many a dread disease:
  He shall find no remedies
  For Death alone!

His wit's invention teems *ant. 2.*
With a skill beyond all dreams,
That comes by turns to curse his life, and bless.
Who keeps the faith he swore
By God, and his country's law—
High stands his city: but who dares transgress,
From a fallen city flees.
Never may *I* give part
At my hearth, nor in my heart,
To such as these!

The Guard enters, with Antigone.

What wonder now have the high Gods done?
Can I gainsay what my own eyes see?
Oh past belief!—Antigone!
Unhappy one,
Child of unhappy Oedipus,
It cannot be!   Couldst *thou* transgress
The King's commands in wantonness,
That they bring thee captive thus!
Guard. Behold the guilty.   Here is she we sought—
Tombing the dead, we took her.   Where is Creon?
Leader. There—from the palace at your need he comes.
Creon (entering). How!   What has happened, to need my presence here?
Guard. Lord King, a man should never make a vow;
For later thoughts belie him.   I could have sworn,
Labouring in that late tempest of thy threats,
Long it would be, ere *I* came *here* again.
Yet—for there is no pleasure can compare
With luck that comes unlooked-for—here I am,
In breach of all my oaths, to bring this girl,
Caught paying her last honours to the dead.
This time we drew no lots—for *this* new windfall
Was clearly mine, no other's.   Take her, my lord,
Question her, as you will, and search her out.
But as for me, it's fair that I should find
A full and free release from all my troubles.
Creon. Where did you catch your prisoner?   How arrest her?
Guard. Burying him she was.   No more to tell.
Creon. Do you understand—and mean!—what you are saying?
Guard. I saw her giving burial to the body
Against your orders.   Is *that* plain enough?
Creon. How was she seen?   How taken in the act?

Guard. It fell like this.   Soon as we had returned,
  With your grim threats still ringing in our ears,
  We swept off all the dust upon the dead
  And left the oozing corpse once more stark naked;
  Then went and sat us down upon a hilltop,
  To windward, to avoid the stench of it;
  Girding at one another with rough threats
  Of what would happen, unless we kept good watch.
  But when we had sat there till the sun's bright circle
  Stood in the very zenith, and the heat
  Grew stifling, all at once the sky above
  Was troubled, and a headlong whirling wind
  Whipped up the dust-clouds far along the plain,
  Tearing its trees, and darkening the height of heaven.
  With eyes tight shut, a long while we endured
  This plague the Gods had sent; but when at last
  It cleared, we saw the girl—and heard her cry
  A sharp and bitter cry, like to a bird's
  That finds its nest left empty, nestlings gone.
  So she, at seeing the body bared again,
  Wailed out aloud, and called down angry curses
  Upon their heads that did it;
  Quickly she brought new handfuls of parched dust
  And from a fair bronze ewer, lifted high,
  Poured out threefold libation on the dead.
  Then headlong down we rushed, and seized upon her,
  Just as she stood there, wholly undismayed;
  And charged her both with what she now was doing
  And what was done before.   *She* made denial
  Of nothing.   And glad was I—yet sorry, too.
  Nothing so pleasant as escaping danger
  Oneself—and yet one hates to bring in trouble
  Those that one likes.   But still it is natural
  To care for such things less than my own neck.
Creon. You there—with face downcast upon the ground—
  Will you confess?   Or plead your innocence?
Antigone. I do confess.   I make denial of nothing.
Creon. You, fellow, get you gone—whither you will;
  You stand acquitted of this heavy charge.

                                          [*The Guard goes out.*

  And you!—no rambling answers!—yes or no!
  Was my edict, that forbade this, known to you?
Antigone. I knew.   Of course I knew.   It was made public.

Creon. And yet you dared, then, to defy the law?

Antigone. It was not God that gave me such commandments,
    Nor Justice, consort of the Lords of Death,
    That ever laid on men such laws as these.
    Nor did I hold that in your human edicts
    Lay power to override the laws of God,
    Unwritten yet unshaken—laws that live
    Not from to-day, nor yet from yesterday,
    But always—though none knows how first made known.
    I had no mind to answer to the Gods
    Transgressing *these,* for fear of any man.
    I knew my life was forfeit.   Well I knew,
    Without your proclamations.   If I die
    Before my day, why then, so much the better!
    Does death not come as blessing when, like mine,
    A life lies loaded with calamities?
    Therefore to meet this doom that waits for me
    Can grieve me nothing.   Had I left unburied
    My own born brother's body, grief indeed
    That would have been: but this!—I care not for it.
    And if my actions seem to you a fool's,
    Maybe it is a fool condemns my folly.

Leader. Harsh daughter of harsh father—clear enough!
    A spirit that never learnt to bow to storms.

Creon. But *I* would have you know the stubbornest spirits
    Are the most doomed to fall.   The stiffest iron,
    Heated to treble hardness in the furnace,
    Is soonest shattered into splintered shards.
    And I have learnt it needs but one small bridle
    To break the unruliest jade.   No place for pride
    In the slave before his master!
    Well schooled indeed in insolence was she,
    When first she dared to flout our public edicts:
    And now there follows this new insolence—
    She glories, laughing, in the thing she did!
    Now on my soul, *she* is a man, not I,
    If I let pass unpunished such presumption.
    I care not if she be my sister's child—
    Nay, were she closer in her kin to me
    Than any that bows to Zeus within my home—
    The worst of deaths shall not be spared to her!
    Nor to her sister—for I hold her also
    Guilty no less of planning this burial.

Go, call her too.   A moment since I saw her,
There in the palace, raving like one demented.
Often a traitor heart, that plots in darkness,
Will thus stand self-betrayed.
Yet I love those no better that, detected,
Strive none the less to glory in their guilt.

Antigone. Will it content you, now, to take and kill me?
Creon. Such is my will and purpose—that, no more.
Antigone. Why do you wait, then?   *I* can take no pleasure—
And God forbid I should!—in all your speeches;
Just as *my* words displease you in their turn.
And yet what act of mine could have won me honour
Greater than this—that I have laid to rest
My brother?   These, that stand here, would approve me,
All!—if their lips were not sealed fast for fear.
But rulers, among their blessings, have this too—
That *they* can talk, and act, at their good pleasure.
Creon. Alone of all in Thebes, you see it so.
Antigone. These see it, too.   But *their* tongues cringe before you.
Creon. More shame to you, that lack their loyalty!
Antigone. No 'shame' in doing my duty to my brother!
Creon. Was *he* not too your brother, whom this man killed?
Antigone. Yes, brother by one mother and one sire.
Creon. Why shame him then, by honouring his rival?
Antigone. Ah, that dead mouth will bear you no such witness.
Creon. It will!—if you honour the wicked like himself.
Antigone. It was his *brother* died there; not his slave!
Creon. But ravaging Thebes!   For which the other fought.
Antigone. I care not.   Death demands *His* laws be kept.
Creon. Not *one* law for the righteous and the evil!
Antigone. Who knows but in Hades *that* seems righteousness?
Creon. Love for an enemy?   No!   Not even dead!
Antigone. My nature is to share in love, not hate.
Creon. Ah, you must 'love'?—then get you to the grave
And love the dead!   But *me* no woman rules,
While life is mine!

                                             [*Ismēne is led in.*

Chorus. See where there comes from the gate of the palace
Ismēne, that weeps with a sister's love.
A cloud of grief on her brows leaves darkened
Her blood-flushed cheeks;
Tear-stained is that lovely face.
Creon. You too that, like a lurking adder coiled

Within my house, have sucked my blood in secret,
While unsuspectingly I nourished ye—
Two plagues, two overthrowers of my throne!
Out with it now, do you own complicity
In burying him?—or swear your ignorance?

Ismēne. I did the deed (if *she* will not deny me).
I too must bear my burden of the blame.

Antigone. Ah no! Justice forbids! *You* had no will
To help me then; nor I to accept your aid.

Ismēne. But *now* you are in trouble—my shame is gone,
And I would share your shipwreck.

Antigone. Those in the world beneath well know who did it.
I love not friends that only *talk* of friendship.

Ismēne. Ah sister, do not scorn me! Let me join
With you in dying and honouring the dead.

Antigone. Seek not to die with *me*. Claim *no* part now
In what you would not touch. *My* death's enough.

Ismēne. Ah, without *thee* what's left in life to love?

Antigone. Ask Creon that. It was *his* part you took.

Ismēne. Why torture me so? What use to you is that?

Antigone. Do I seem to mock you? Bitter mock for me!

Ismēne. Yet only say how can I help you now?

Antigone. Go, save yourself! *I* do not grudge you safety.

Ismēne. Ah misery! No hope to die together?

Antigone. Life was your choice, my sister: mine was death.

Ismēne. But only in despite of all my warnings.

Antigone. Some judged your way the wiser; and some, mine.

Ismēne. And yet we both are guilty—I as you.

Antigone. Take heart. You still are living—*my* soul died
Long since, to do this service to the dead.

Creon. I swear they both are mad. One from her birth—
And now the other too has lost her senses.

Ismēne. Even the reason Nature gives at birth
May fail, my lord, beneath the blows of sorrow.

Creon. Yours failed, at least, when you chose to share her guilt.

Ismēne. And yet, without her, what has life for *me*?

Creon. No more of 'her' and 'life'! Her life is done.

Ismēne. Can you put to death your own son's promised bride!

Creon. There are other women—other fields to plough.

Ismēne. But no such love as links those two together.

Creon. I want no evil wives for sons of mine.

Antigone. Ah dearest Haemon, how your father shames you!

Creon. Have done! Enough of you and of your marriage!

Leader. And yet how *can* you rob your son of her?
Creon. It is Death shall break this bridal; and not I.
Leader. Her death is then resolved on?—past reprieve?
Creon. It is fixed; for you and me. No more delays!
  Come, fellows, take them in. And see them kept
  Safe within doors, like women; not at large.
  For even the bold may run, seeing Death let fall
  Across their lives His shadow.

                    [Antigone and Ismēne are led away.

Chorus. Happy the life that tastes not lamentation!   *strophe* 1.
  But when with the curse of God a lineage shakes,
  From generation down to generation
  Comes no surcease of sorrow; so, when breaks
  The Thracian tempest and the dark surge wakes,
  Up from the deeps it whirls the sable sand,
While groan, in answer to the waves, the capes of the wind-vexed land.

  Lo, from of old the Labdacids are stricken—   *antistrophe* 1.
  On the sorrows of their dead new sorrows fall.
  Each generation sees the same curse quicken,
  Some God still ruins them, helpless. In the hall
  Of Oedipus *one* hope lit, last of all,
  One root yet living. Now, this too lies slain
By Hell's red dust, by a reckless tongue, by a Fury in the brain.

                                 str. 2.

Thy power, O Zeus, who can master? What pride of man's endeavour?
Sleep binds Thee not (that snares all else to rest),
Nor the tireless months of Heaven—Time leaves Thee ageless ever,
Throned in the dazzling glory of high Olympus' crest.
  But for Man, from long ago
  Abides through the years to be
  This law, immutably—
  All over-greatness brings its overthrow.

For Hope, that wanders ever, comes oft to Man as blessing; *ant.* 2.
Yet oft she cheats, till his giddy lusts are stirred.
Nearer she creeps, the deceiver, till he stumbles, all unguessing,
In the hot fires hid beneath him. Wise is the ancient word—
  That he whom God hath planned
  To ruin, in his blinded mood
  Sees evil things as good—
  And *then* the coming doom is hard at hand.

But yonder is Haemon, of thy sons
The last.   Does he come with spirit grieved
For his bride to be?—
For the doom that waits Antigone,
And the hope of his love deceived?

                                      [Haemon enters.

Creon. Soon we shall know; better than seers could tell us.
  My son, are you come now, raging against your father
  For my fixed and final doom of your betrothed?
  Or do I keep your love, in spite of all?
Haemon. Father, I still am yours.   Righteous the ways
  You set before me.   I will follow them.
  For me, there is no marriage I could prize
  Dearer than *your* good guidance.
Creon. Indeed, my son, this is your heart's best wisdom—
  To let your father's will stand ever first.
  This is the end for which men pray to get
  And rear beside their hearths obedient sons—
  That these may love the friends their fathers love
  And on their father's foes take fitting vengeance.
  For if a man's own children serve him not,
  What has he done but merely breed himself
  Troubles—and laughter for his enemies?
  Therefore let not your pleasure in a woman,
  My son, cast out your wisdom—knowing well
  An evil wife on the pillow at your side
  Soon chills the arms that clasp her.   What can wound
  Worse than to love the wicked?   So in loathing
  Give up the girl—she is our enemy.
  Let her go marry in the House of Death!
  For, having caught her in this flagrant treason—
  Her only, of all Thebes!—
  Never will *I* break faith to my own people,
  But kill her!—ay, however loud she clamours
  To Zeus, the God of Kinship.   Should I breed
  Those of my *own* blood thus to disobey,
  What can I hope from strangers!   It is the man
  Righteous at home, that in the commonweal
  Will show like justice also.
  No praise from *me* for froward law-breakers
  Or those that would browbeat authority;
  Whoever it is the city sets in power,
  Must be obeyed,

In matters great or little, right or wrong.
And he that so obeys, will prove, I warrant,
As good in ruling as in being ruled;
Or, when he stands amid the storm of spears,
Will keep his post, a true and trusty comrade.
For the worst of evils is indiscipline.
Cities it ruins, and leaves homes desolate,
And breaks in rout leagued armies of allies.
Where men succeed, it is obedience,
Above all else, that saves them.
So now, it is ours to uphold the cause of order,
Not let a woman put us all to shame.
Better, if need be, fall by the hands of men—
None could cry, then, that a woman worsted us.
Leader. All that you say, we judge most wisely said,
Unless old age deceives us.
Haemon. Father, it is the Gods alone that plant
Wisdom in man, the highest good he has.
I have no power—and Heaven forfend I should—
To question the rightness of the words you spoke.
And yet another's thought may have its weight.
For *your* sake, father, it is *my* part to watch
What things men say, or do, or find to blame;
For to your face no common man dare utter
Words that would find disfavour in your ear;
But *I* can hearken, hidden in the shadow,
How Thebes laments this girl:
'Never a woman that less deserved her doom,
Nor died so piteously for deed so noble;
Because she would not leave to birds of prey,
Or ravening hounds, the limbs unsepulchred
Of her brother fallen in the thick of carnage!
Is she not worthy, then, of golden praise?'
    Such the dim whispers creeping now through Thebes.
Nothing for me can be so precious, father,
As your prosperity.
For how can a son find nobler ornament
Than his father's happy fame?   Or sire than son's?
But let not one fixed humour sway in you,
To think *your* words, and yours alone, have truth.
Once a man deems his own the only wisdom—
That *his* speech and *his* spirit have no peer,
Such minds, laid open, show but emptiness.

It need not shame even the wise to supple
A will too stiff, and often stoop to learn.
See how the trees that grow beside some torrent,
By bending to it, keep their boughs unbroken,
While it sweeps away the stubborn—roots and all.
The mariner that will not slack his canvas
Strained by the tempest, only ends his voyage
With keel in air and thwarts rolled undermost.

    Cease then this anger—take a milder mood!
For if, young as I am, I may speak my thought,
Doubtless 'twere best that men were born all-wise,
But failing that—since things turn seldom so—
It is well to listen to good counsellors.

Leader. Sire, heed your son, if he has spoken in season;
    And *you*, too, heed your father.   Both speak well.

Creon. Is one of *my* years, then, to be schooled in wisdom
    By one of *his*!

Haemon. In nothing that is not right.   I *may* be young;
    But still—regard my actions, not my age.

Creon. Fine 'action' this!—to pay respect to rebels!

Haemon. I do not urge respect for evildoers.

Creon. Is not this girl infected, then, with evil!

Haemon. *That*, with one voice, the people of Thebes denies.

Creon. And shall my people, then, direct my rule?

Haemon. Can you not see such talk is all too young?

Creon. Who must be judge, but I, how Thebes is ruled?

Haemon. No city can be *one* man's appanage.

Creon. Who doubts that a sovereign is his city's master?

Haemon. Fine sovereign you, if Thebes were left dispeopled!

Creon. This fellow, it seems, would take the woman's part!

Haemon. If *you* are 'woman'!   My care is all for you.

Creon. How, villain!   Bandy law with your own father!

Haemon. Yes!—since I see you sin *against* the law.

Creon. A sin—is it?—to reverence my office!

Haemon. No 'reverence,' when you outrage Heaven's honours!

Creon. Soul of a scoundrel!—yielding to a girl!

Haemon. At least, you will not find me yield to baseness!

Creon. And yet each word you speak is for her sake.

Haemon. For yours as well—for mine—for the Gods below.

Creon. You shall not wed her!—never, while she lives!

Haemon. Then she will die; and will not die alone.

Creon. What, grown so bold!   Will you dare now to threaten!

Haemon. What 'threat' is there in combating ill judgment?

Creon. You shall rue the day your folly taught me wisdom.

Haemon. Were you not my father, I should call you indeed unwise.

Creon. No need for fawning!   Slave of a woman's will!

Haemon. Is your one wish to talk, and not be answered?

Creon. Can this be true!   Now, by this Heaven above,
  Be sure you shall not with impunity
  To all your blame add insults!
  Bring me that wretch—here she shall die at once
  Before her bridegroom's sight—yes, at his side!

Haemon. Not at my side—no, never dream of it!—
  Shall *she* meet death.   Nor shall you ever again
  Set eyes upon this face.   Rave at your pleasure
  Among your own friends—such as can endure it!

                           [He rushes out.

Leader. Your son is gone, my lord, in angry haste.
  A heart so young, in pain grows violent.

Creon. Let him go!—let him pursue his deeds, or dreams,
  Of more than mortal reach.   But those two women
  He shall not save.

Leader. Is it your purpose, sire, to kill them *both*?

Creon. Ah no; well said!   Not her that took no part.

Leader. And by what death, then, must the other die?

Creon. By some lone trackway where no footfall comes
  She shall be led, and tombed in a rocky cavern;
  And there beside her such small dole of food
  As serves for an expiation; lest we bring
  Upon all Thebes a curse.
  There let her pray to that one God she honours—
  Hades!   Let *Him* preserve her, if He will!
  Else she shall learn, although too late, how vain
  Labour it was to revere the Powers of Death.

                           [He goes out.
                             strophe.

Chorus. O Love in battle resistless!   O Love whose wild hands squander
    The wealth that years have gathered!   Thou watcher, sleepless still,
On the soft cheeks of maidens!   None 'scapes Thy feet that wander
    Alike the waves of ocean or the pastures of the hill—
Not short-lived men nor deathless Gods.   Thy touch drives mad the will.

Even the good—to evil, and ruin, Thou canst misguide them.   *antistrophe.*
    Strife betwixt son and father this day Thy hand has sown.
The Laws sit throned majestic—but Love sits there beside them;
    The lure of a girl's fair glances can leave them overthrown,
While conquering laughs the Queen of Love, the victory her own.

Leader. My tears burst forth in spite of me.
    Hardly can even I recall
    The Laws I serve, at sight of thee,
    Bound for that chamber that waits us all,
    Antigone!

strophe 1.

Antigone. This is my last long journey, O men of the land of my fathers.
    I look my last on the sunlight, never to see it more.
    Death gives to all their rest at last.   But me alive He gathers
        To Acheron's shore.
    I had no bridal-chanting; for *me* no revellers cried
    Before the bridal-chamber.   Nay, Death took *me* for bride.
Leader. Yet thus thou departest crowned with praise
    To that dark realm of the dead below;
    Thee no wasting sickness slays,
    No sword avenging.   Thy choice was so.
    Alone of mortals art thou to go
    Alive down Hades' ways.

antistrophe 1.

Antigone. That piteous tale I remember, that is told of Tantalus' daughter,
    The queen whom Phrygia gave us—how on Sípylus long ago
    The rock, like ivy, round her grew.   And still the wild storm-water,
        Still the snow
    Falls on her grief for ever.   Still from her brow to breast
    Hurry her tears.   So prisoned, God lays me too to rest.
Leader. A goddess she, of the race on high;
    And mortal we, of human birth.
    And yet, that thou didst live and die
    Like one divine, shall glorify
    Thee too beneath the earth.
Antigone. Ah, I am mocked!   Could ye not wait my going!—   *str.* 2.
    Thus, by the gods of our fathers, must ye taunt me to my face?
    Ah Thebes!   Ah wealthy sons of Thebes!   Ah streams fair-flowing
        Of Dirce!   O holy place
    Of charioted Thebes, bear witness to my doom!
        See how unpitied, friendless, I am led,
    By what harsh laws!—to my prison, my strange and living tomb,
    From earth a hapless exile; exile in Hades' gloom;
        Stranger alike to live and dead.
Leader. Ah child, thou wast too rash; thy feet
    Trespassed beyond the lofty seat
    Of Justice—and they fell!   Maybe,
    Thy father's guilt weighs yet on thee.

Antigone. Alas, ye have touched the bitterest of my story—   *ant.* 2.
  My father thrice-lamented, and all the sorrows shed
 On the lineage long-descended of Labdacus in its glory!
   Ah mother evil-wed!
 Ah for thy hapless slumber beside thy son, beside
  That father whence my ill-starred being grew!
 Outcast, unwed, accursèd, with *them* must I now abide.
 Thou also, O my brother—misfortune chose thy bride!
  Dead, thou hast slain me living, too.
Leader. God thou didst honour; we honour thee.
 Yet one that guards his power must see
 That power by no man disobeyed.
 Thy wilful heart left thee betrayed.
Antigone. Behold, I go, unwailed, unwed, unfriended,   *epode.*
 The way that waits before.
 Yon sacred light, wherewith high Heaven is splendid,
 Shall bless these eyes no more.
 None mourns my life that here is ended;
 None cares for what I bore.

Creon. Have ye not learnt, if song and lamentation
 Availed the dying, none would ever cease?
 Hence with the girl! Shut her, as I have ordered,
 In the cave that shall entomb her; and then go,
 Leaving her lonely in its solitude
 To die—or live there buried, if she will.
 Our hands at least are stainless of her blood.
 I do but ban her from this upper world.
Antigone. O tomb, O bridal-chamber, prison-house
 Deep-delved, sure-guarded ever, whither I
 Go gathered to my kin—that multitude
 Persephone hath numbered with her dead!
 Last of them all, of all most miserably,
 I too must follow, half my life unspent.
 And yet I trust to find a welcome there
 From *thy* love, O my father, and from thine,
 My mother, and from thine, brother beloved;
 Seeing that these very hands have bathed ye all,
 And laid ye out, and poured death's offerings
 Over your graves. And now that last sad service
 Done *thee*, my Polyneices, brings me *this*!
  Yet surely the wise will judge that I did well,

In honouring thee?   For never, had I been
A mother mourning for her children slain,
Or if my husband mouldered thus untombed—
Never would I have dared defy my country
To do this thing.
And if ye ask, in virtue of what law?—
This is my answer.   Husband I might have found
In place of him that died; or by another
Have borne a child instead of him I lost;
But since in Hades lie my sire and mother,
There can be no new brethren born to me.
Therefore it was, O brother whom I loved,
That I preferred thine honour; though Creon held me
Guilty of crime and mad audacity.
So now he brings me, captive of his hands,
Cut off from wedlock and from bridal-hymn,
From joy of marriage, and of motherhood,
Without a friend, alone in my despair,
To go down living to the vaults of death.
What law of God have I transgressed?   And yet
How can I look, alas, for help divine?
Whom can I cry to?   Since a pious deed
Is counted to me for impiety.
Ah, if this punishment earns Heaven's favour,
I will own that I have suffered for a crime;
But if the crime be others', no worse doom
I pray for them than this they have dealt to me.

Leader.   Still this tempest of her grief
    Beats on her heart, without relief.

Creon.   Have I not said: 'Take her and go?'
    Dear shall ye pay, for loitering so!

Antigone.   O bitter word!   Now, now I see
    Death drawing near.

Creon.   Hope nothing more!   Look not to me
    For comfort now, nor word of cheer.

Antigone.   O city of Thebes, Gods of my race,
    Dear earth of my sires, and mine,
   They lead me away, and I gain no grace!
   Ah, princes of this Theban land,
    Look on the last of your royal line;
   See what I suffer, and by whose hand,
    For honouring things divine.

                     [Antigone is led away.

Chorus. Thus did the loveliness of Danaë   *strophe* 1.
    From day to a brazen darkness pass of old,
  In living tomb imprisoned—though proud of birth was she,
    Though Zeus Himself, my child, in a shower of gold
  Had left His love to quicken in her keeping.
    So strange is fate; so grim the destined hour!
  Not wealth, nor war, nor mighty walls, nor black-hulled galleys, leaping
    Across the surges, baulk its power.

So too that Edōnian king of taunting tongue   *antistrophe* 1.
    Too swift to anger, the son of Dryas, lay
  Deep in his rocky dungeon by Dionysus flung,
    Till the rankness of his fury died away,
  And he knew the God he had assailed, blaspheming—
    Fool, that would rouse the piping Muses' ire;
  And quell the Maenads god-possessed; and quench the torches gleaming
    With Dionysus' holy fire!

And where, by the Dark-blue Rocks, a sea twofold   *str.* 2.
Upon the beach of Bosporus is rolled
    And savage Salmydessus meets the tide,
Before the Thracian God of War
The curst hands of a stepdame tore
    The eyes of Phīneus' sons—for vengeance cried
Those bleeding orbs to Heaven, robbed of light
By the piercing shuttles that had stabbed their sight,
    In the hand of their father's bitter bride.

Pining in prison, they wept their ruined life,   *ant.* 2.
Unhappy children of a hapless wife;
    Yet *she* had sprung from the old Erechtheïdae.
Daughter of Heaven, Boreas' child,
In caverns of the Thracian wild
    She grew, mid her father's tempests blowing free,
Swift as a colt to race o'er steep and fell;
And yet the ancient Fates on her as well
    Bore no less hard, Antigone!

The blind prophet Teiresias enters, led by a boy.

Teiresias. Princes of Thebes, here come we two together,
  One pair of eyes to steer us; since the blind
  Must follow still a leader.
Creon. How now?   What news then, old Teiresias?

Teiresias. That thou shalt hear.   Heed thou the prophet's voice.
Creon. Indeed!   I was never used to slight your wisdom.
Teiresias. On a straight course, thereby, thou hast steered this city.
Creon. I owe you much—and gladly own to it.
Teiresias. Mark me!   Once more thou art poised on a razor's edge.
Creon. What's this!   I blench to hear you.
Teiresias. Listen and learn, by the sure signs of my art.

 Of late in my ancient seat of augury
 I sat, where every bird was used to harbour;
 But now their notes were changed—I heard them screaming
 With rage and jargon unintelligible;
 And I could tell—so fierce the whir of wings—
 With murderous claws they tore at one another.
 At once, in fear, I essayed burnt sacrifice
 On altars fired to blazing.   Yet there rose
 Out of my offerings no brilliant flame—
 Over the ashes from the thigh-bones oozed
 Only a clammy sweat, that smoked and sputtered.
 The galls of the victims burst and splashed the air;
 The thighs, dissolving, lay revealed to view,
 Bared of the fat that hid them.
 And so, through this lad's eyes (for *he* guides *me*,
 As I in turn guide others), I found my rites
 All unavailing—dimmed my divination.

  But know that it is *thy* folly thus plagues Thebes!
 For now our public altars, one and all,
 Have been defiled by bird and hound with carrion
 From that ill-fallen son of Oedipus.
 Therefore the Gods accept from us no longer
 Prayer, sacrifice, or kindled offering;
 No bird's shrill cry brings us clear augury—
 They are gorged too full, with fat of human slaughter.
 And so, my son, consider.   For to err
 Is only the common lot of all mankind;
 But, error once committed, even then
 There *is* escape from folly and misfortune—
 Not for the man that stands inflexible—
 But for him that seeks a cure.
 It is stubbornness that earns the name of fool!
 Then yield thou to the dead.   Goad not the fallen.
 Is it valour to slay the slain a second time?
 My good will brings good counsel; happy he
 That learns from such good counsel to his gain!

Creon. Old man, like archers, you all make of me
  Your butt to shoot at.   Even divination
  Must serve your plots!   My sale, it seems, was settled
  Long since; and I am made a merchandise
  For trading soothsayers!   Go, seek your profits—
  Traffic, if so ye will, in India's gold
  Or Sardian electron; but this dead
  You shall not bury!
  Not though God's eagles bear his flesh in gobbets
  To the very throne of Zeus, not even so—
  Nay, not for fear of even such defilement,
  Will I grant to *him* a grave.   (Indeed I know
  There is no mortal can defile the Gods.)
  But even the cleverest, old Teiresias,
  Can stumble shamefully, when gain corrupts them
  To cloak in specious words some scheme of shame.
Teiresias. Ah me!
  Lives there one man that knows, and keeps in mind——
Creon. What now?   What stalest common-place comes next?
Teiresias.—how priceless, past all riches, wisdom is!
Creon. As lack of it, past doubt, is worst of ills.
Teiresias. Yet filled art *thou* with that infirmity.
Creon. I will not answer insults to—'the prophet'!
Teiresias. Insult enough, to call a prophet false!
Creon. Yes!   For all prophets dearly love their silver.
Teiresias. As all of tyrant stock love base advantage.
Creon. Do you know that you are speaking to your king!
Teiresias. *I* know.   *I* taught thee to deliver Thebes.
Creon. A clever seer!   But lacking honesty.
Teiresias. Thou wilt sting me to utter things I dare not speak.
Creon. Speak!—but take care you are not bribed to speak it.
Teiresias. Small chance, in what I now shall say of *thee*!
Creon. Be sure you will win no gains from *my* decision.
Teiresias. And *thou*—be surer yet, ere thou hast seen
  Many more circuits of the coursing sun,
  Thou shalt yield up a child of thy own loins
  Dead, in atonement for these other dead—
  Because thou hast lodged without pity in a tomb
  A living soul, thrust from the world above
  Down to that world below!—
  While, yet again, here above earth thou holdest
  A body belonging to the Powers beneath,
  Untombed, unhonoured, and unsanctified,

Although with such things of Death thou hast no part—
Nor have the Gods of Heaven, who in this
By thee are outraged!
Therefore on thee in retribution wait,
For thy destruction, the Erīnyes
Of Hades and of Heaven, bringing thee
Like doom for doom.
Now look, I pray you, if these words of mine
Are spoke for silver!   Quickly comes the hour
Shall fill thy house with wails of men and women.
Now too in hate against thee are aroused
The cities of those dead whose mangled bodies
Have had their last honours from wild beast or hound,
Or some winged fowl that bears their stench unhallowed
Back to the walls where lay their hearth and home.
Take—since thou hast provoked me—to thy heart
These arrows that my anger shoots against thee—
Arrows sure-aimed, whose barbs thou shalt *not* avoid.

     Come, boy, now lead me homeward, leaving *him*
To vent his spleen on younger men than I,
Till he learn to keep a tongue less turbulent,
And in his heart a wiser wit than now.

                         [Teiresias goes out

Leader. The seer is gone, my lord, with grim predictions.
   But this I know—never since first these locks
   Upon my head were bleached from black to white,
   Hath Teiresias failed to utter truth to Thebes.
Creon. I know it too.   Deeply my soul is troubled.
   For bitter, now, to yield.   Yet no less bitter
   By standing firm to wreck my pride in ruin.
Leader. Son of Menoeceus, this is an hour for prudence.
Creon. What must I do, then?   Speak, and I obey you.
Leader. Go, from her rocky cavern free the girl,
   And honour with a grave the unburied dead.
Creon. That is your judgment?—you would have me yield?
Leader. As quickly, sire, as may be.   Swift of foot,
   God's retributions overtake the guilty.
Creon. Ah, this is bitter!—but I quit my purpose.
   In vain to battle with Necessity.
Leader. Go, then, and see it done.   Trust not to others.
Creon. I will.   Without delay.   Come on, my servants—
   You that are here, call to the rest to follow—
   Take axes in your hands, and make all speed

To that spot you see before you!
And I—since now this new course must be taken—
Myself will loose her, as myself did bind.
Ah, I misdoubt 'tis better, till life's end,
Never to break the customs of the past.

[*Creon goes out with his servants.*

Chorus. Thou of the many names, Thou son and pride   *strophe* 1.
Of Sémele, the Thunderer's bride,
Thine is Icária far known,
And Eleusis' hill-girt plain is Thine,
Where pilgrims throng Demeter's shrine,
O Bacchus!   And Thou holdest as Thine own
Our Thebes, the home of Bacchanals,
Where glides beneath her city walls
Ismēnus' flow and, long ago, the Dragon's teeth were sown.

By the Twin Crags, by the fount of Castaly,   *antistrophe* 1.
Through smoke and flame the torches see
Thy face revealed before their blaze;
And from the cave Corycian spring
Thy nymphs of the mountain, revelling.
From Nysa's ivied hillside, from her bays
Where green the grape's thick clusters twine,
Thou comest, while a shout divine
Acclaimeth Thee, once more to see Thine own loved city's ways.

Surely to Thee, and Thy mother lightning-slain,   *str.* 2.
Thebes yet is dearest in your sight.
So now, when evil days constrain
Thy people, Lord, O aid our plight!
Hasten with feet of healing, across the moaning main,
Or over Parnassus' height!

Reveal Thyself, King born of Zeus most high!—   *ant.* 2.
Lord of the voices of the night!
Whom the stars follow across the sky,
With breath of flame, and dancing flight!
Come with Thy maddened Maenads, that on 'Lord Iacchus' cry,
A-dance till dawn grows bright!

[*A messenger enters.*

Messenger. O you whose homes are by these ancient walls
Of Cadmus and Amphīon,
There is no state of mortal life that I
Dare praise, or blame, as lasting.

For Fortune raises and Fortune sinks again
Men happy, and unhappy, evermore;
No seer can tell how long our lot abides.
Once Creon, in my eyes, seemed enviable.
He had freed all Cadmus' land from enemies;
He held its sceptre in sole sovereignty,
The prosperous father of a race of princes.
And now—all lost! For, once a man's forfeited
The joys of life, no more I count him living,
Merely a corpse that breathes.
Go, if you will, heap high your house with treasure
And live in the pomp of kingship—once you lose
The power to joy in them,
The rest I value less than a smoke-wreath's shadow.

Leader. What news? What *new* grief for our royal house?
Messenger. Some dead!—and some live guilty of their death!
Leader. Who is the murderer, say? And who the victim?
Messenger. Haemon is dead—his blood on no stranger's hand.
Leader. By the violence of his father? Or his own?
Messenger. Self-slain. In rage for the life his father took.
Leader. Ah prophet, how surely thou hast fulfilled thy word!
Messenger. So stands the truth. The rest needs *your* decision.
Leader. But look, there is coming from the palace-door
Our lord's unhappy Queen, Eurydice.
By chance? Or has she heard about her son?

[*Eurydice enters.*

Eurydice. Thebans, this moment as I left the palace,
Meaning to make my prayers to Our Lady Pallas,
I heard you. Hardly had I loosed the bolt,
Opening the door, when on my ears there broke
This ruin of those I love—and back in horror
I fell in my women's arms, and swooned away.
But tell me your news again. Ah, I shall hear it
With a heart well used to sorrow.
Messenger. I will speak, dear mistress, as one that saw it all,
Concealing nothing.
What use in soothing lies, that presently
Would prove me false? The best way still is truth.
Your husband took me with him, as a guide
To that far end of the plain where yet there lay
Unpitied, mangled by the teeth of hounds,
The body of Polyneices.
There, when we first had offered prayers to Pluto

And the Goddess of the Crossways, that their anger
Might now be softened, with a pure ablution
We washed the dead, and burned with new-plucked boughs
All that remained, and reared him a lofty barrow
Of his own Theban earth; then turned to enter
That stony cavern where Antigone
Was wed to Death.

But one of us heard, far off, a voice high-wailing
Beside that all-unhallowed bridal-bower,
And hurried back to tell it to our master.
And now, as the King drew near, there rang around
A sound confused of cries and lamentations,
And Creon groaned in anguish:
'Wretch that I am, is my foreboding true
And this the unhappiest road I ever trod?
It is my son's voice greets me. Quickly, men,
Run to the tomb—where its stones are wrenched away,
Slip through the gap, to the mouth of its inmost cell,
And see if the Gods deceive me, or indeed
I hear the voice of Haemon.'
Then, as our master bade in his misgiving,
We looked—and lo, at the grave-vault's farthest end,
With twisted strands of linen round her throat
We saw her hanging: and, beside her, Haemon—
Sunk forward with his arms around her waist,
Lamenting his love ill-fated, his father's crime,
And the doom of his dead bride.
But, seeing him, Creon with a bitter cry
Entered the tomb, and called in agony:
'Unhappy boy, what have you done? What folly
Drove you to this? Has sorrow made you mad?
Come out, my son! I beg you on my knees.'
But, with a savage glare in his wild eyes,
Saying not a word, the lad spat in his face;
Then by the hilt snatched out his sword—yet missed,
As his father turned and rushed from the vault before him.
Then the unhappy Haemon, full of rage
Against himself, pressed home, with all his weight,
The sword in his own side; and clasped the girl,
With a last effort, in his fainting arms,
While one swift jet of blood in his dying throes
Crimsoned his love's white cheek.
There he lies dead, in *her* dead arms, fulfilling

His ill-starred love, at least in the House of Death,
A witness to the world how lack of wisdom
Is worst of all the curses of mankind.

Eurydice goes back into the palace.

Leader. What can it mean? The Queen is gone again—
Vanished without one word of good or ill.

Messenger. I too am lost in wonder. But I hope,
Now she has heard these sorrows of her son,
She simply has withdrawn within the palace
To bid her women mourn this household grief;
Thinking it shame to wail before all Thebes.
She is a lady too discreet for folly.

Leader. I do not know. I do not less mistrust
Silence extreme than vain extremes of grief.

Messenger. I will enter the palace, then, and see for sure
Her passionate heart hides not some secret purpose.
For you say wisely—in excess of silence
Mischief may lurk.

                              [He goes in.

*Creon appears with his followers and the body of Haemon on a
bier.*

Leader. But see, King Creon himself approaches,
Bringing a witness all too clear,
Not of the blindness of another
(Dare we to say it?), but of his own.

Creon. Ah, folly of a mind demented,   *strophe* 1.
    Fatal pride!
See here before you the blood of kindred—
    A sire that slew, and a son that died.
Ah, blinded purpose that brought thy youth
    So young a death, my son, my son!
Mine was the fault,
    Not thine, that thy day is done.

Leader. Alas, how late you open eyes to justice!

Creon. I have learnt the bitter truth in my distress.   *str.* 2.
    The weight of God's hand struck, and maddened me
Down the hard pathway of the pitiless,
To ruin and trample my own happiness—
    Ah for the sorrows of mortality!

The Messenger reappears from the palace.

Messenger. Alas, my lord, I fear you are come like one
Whose hands and house alike are full of grief.

You bear one sorrow's burden; but more sorrow
Lies in your palace, waiting for your gaze.
Creon. On all my ills what worse ill follows now?
Messenger. Your wife has died—your dead son's own true mother.
    Unhappy heart!—she fell but a moment since.
Creon. Ah, harbour of Hades, past all appeasing,   *antistrophe* 1.
    Why breakest thou me!
Herald of ill, bringer of sorrow,
    What new word now of calamity?
Wilt thou murder me yet a second time,
    With tidings of still another slain—
Of my own wife's death!—
    Still crowning pain with pain!
Leader. Your eyes can see.   No more the palace hides it.

The doors open, showing the dead Eurydice.

Creon. For me, what now?   What fate is left in store?   *ant.* 2.
    Here is a second deed of horror done.
But now, it was my son that these hands bore;
And lo, another dead beside my door.
    Alas, poor mother!   Ah my son, my son!
Messenger. Here by the altar, stabbed with the whetted knife,
    She closed her eyes in darkness.   But first she wailed
That noble death of her lost Mégareus,
Then Haemon dead in turn; and last of all
Called ruin on *thee*, the murderer of thy sons.
Creon. Horror on horror!   Will *no* man press   *str.* 3.
A two-edged sword to the heart of me!—
    That am a thing of misery,
Sunken and drowned in hopelessness.
Messenger. Yes, so it was—she died denouncing thee
    For the fate of both her sons.
Creon. And how did she compass it—her fatal end?
Messenger. Soon as she learned her son's death loud-lamented,
    Her own hand plunged, straight to her heart, the knife.
Creon. Ah, never another mortal head   *str.* 4.
But mine must bear the guilt.   She died
Through me—through me she lies there dead.
This is the truth.   Come, servants, guide
My steps from hence.   Let me be brought
From all men's sight, that am less than naught.
Leader. You have said well—if anything be well

Amid such misery.   For of sorrow's roads
The shortest is the best.
Creon. Quick fall my fate!—the happiest one   *ant. 3.*
Left to me now.   Soon, soon, I pray,
Break now the dawn of my last day!
Let me not see another sun.
Leader. That is hereafter.   But ours are present duties.
For the future let Heaven care, whose care it is.
Creon. I did but pray for what sums all my longings.
Leader. Yet pray no further.   Men cannot avoid
Sorrow appointed them by Destiny.
Creon. Rash fool that I was, take me, begone!   *ant. 4.*
Ah son, ah wife, that I brought to die,
Not willing.   Which face shall I look upon?
On whom can I lean?   All goes awry
That my hands have touched.   On my head Despair
Has leapt, with a load too hard to bear.

Creon is led into the palace.

Leader. On wisdom, more than on all beside,
Stands happiness.   At holy things
Let no man mock.   For the lips of Pride
In the end must pay, for vaunts too great,
Great sufferings;
Till age grows wise—too late.

THE WOMEN OF TRĀCHIS[1]

*Oh murd'rous Coxcombe, what should such a Foole
Do with so good a wife?*

Shakespeare, *Othello.*

This most disconcerting of the dramas of Sophocles contains both his least attractive hero and his most touching heroine. A strange pair. Though they have been wed some twenty years we never see Hēracles and Dejaneira together in the play; nor is it very easy to imagine.[2] Hēracles, with his lion-skin, club, and poisoned arrows, battling with monstrous beasts, birds, serpents, and Centaurs, an endless wanderer about the earth, eating, drinking, making love on a gigantic scale, seems a more primitive figure than most heroes of Greek legend—a creature of peasant folklore rather than of heroic epic. Sophocles has not troubled much to polish him. Dejaneira, on the other hand, the princess of Calydon whom Hēracles won for bride in combat with the river-god Achelōus,[3] had been in older story an Amazonian character;[4] but Sophocles made her the gentlest of his women. It is a little as if Desdemona were married to Tamburlaine.

The play begins with Dejaneira waiting lonely in Trāchis, left fifteen months without news of her errant husband. Now at last her son Hyllus brings tidings that Hēracles is at war with Oechalia, in the neighbouring island of Euboea. But Dejaneira knows of oracles foretelling that in Euboea Hēracles is doomed to find either death or final happiness. Sharing her anxiety, Hyllus hastens away to seek his father. To the consolations of the Chorus of young Trachinian women Dejaneira replies with a typically Sophoclean passage on the happiness of youth, in contrast to the burdening cares of womanhood.

> For girlhood grows in its own place apart,
> Where neither heat of sun, nor rain, nor wind
> Can ever trouble that young springing life,

---

[1] The date is very uncertain. On stylistic grounds (F. R. Earp, *The Style of Sophocles*, 1944) it has been thought an early work.

[2] There are, I think, no happy marriages in fifth-century Attic drama—except perhaps in the fantastic *Helen.* (One can hardly count Alcestis happily married to a husband like Admētus.) There seems something unbalanced in this. Yet another example of the greater health and sanity of Homer's world.

[3] Cf. Bacchylides, v; *Greek Poetry for Everyman*, pp. 271–4.

[4] Her name means 'Slayer of Men'; compare the wild Atalanta whom her brother Meleager loved.

At ease and happy—till the maiden takes
The name of wife and, with it, in one night
Her share of life's long burden; worn with cares
Either for husband's or for children's sake.

(144–50.)

She herself is tormented because Hēracles, before departing, had told her that 'in fifteen months' he was destined to find either death or rest from his labours; and now the fifteen months are gone. But joyfully a man of Trāchis enters—Hēracles has successfully stormed Oechalia—his herald Līchas has just arrived with the captives. Līchas himself follows to confirm the glad news; yet Dejaneira is saddened by pity for the captive women —for one of them, above all, who stands there in noble silence. Who is she? Līchas does not know. But no sooner is Līchas gone than the man of Trāchis denounces him as a liar—only a moment since he was proclaiming in the ears of all Trāchis that this unknown girl is Íole, daughter of King Eurÿtus of Oechalia. And it was for love of her alone that Hēracles sacked her city. As Līchas re-enters, with noble dignity Dejaneira demands from him the truth.

Nay now, by Zeus that makes His lightnings flash
Down the high glens of Oeta, cheat me not
With words! Speak true! *I* am no evil woman,
Nor one so ignorant how the hearts of men
Were never made to love one thing for ever.
Those have but little wisdom who, like boxers,
Stand up to challenge Love with blow for blow—
Even the Gods He masters, when He will.
He has mastered *me*—why not another woman?
I should be mad if I reproached my lord
That he hath caught this sickness—
Mad, if I blamed this woman that is his,
For what does them no shame, no wrong to me.
Never! So now, if it was my husband schooled thee
To cheat me thus, *that* was a sorry lesson!
Or if thou wast self-taught to tell me lies,
Though kindly meant, it cannot come to good.
Out with the truth!—the whole! A liar's name
Is a deadly thing for any free-born man;
And dream no longer to escape detection—
You have spoken to too many. *They* will tell.
Or if you are afraid, 'tis an idle fear.
Not to be told—yes, *that* I *should* find bitter;

But what so dread in knowing? Of all men born,
Who has so often loved as Hēracles?
Yet of his loves not one has had from me
Harsh word or blame. Nor yet shall this girl now—
However hot her passion. No, with pity
I look upon her, seeing her loveliness
Has proved her life's calamity—poor maid,
By no wish of her own, she has condemned
Her native land to sack and slavery.
But all these things the wind of Fate must drive
Whither it will. Yet *this* I say to thee—
Cheat others, if thou wilt: lie not to me.

(436–69.)

Yes, Lĭchas owns, it is all true. He had lied to spare her. (Such
considerateness had not troubled Hēracles in importing a paramour into his
own home. But Hēracles is not much harassed by delicacy. He had first
treacherously pushed Íole's brother Íphitus off the rock of Tĭryns; then
butchered her father and destroyed her country to get her.) There follows
a choric ode on the terrible power of love, sadly recalling the far-off years
when Hēracles battled passionately, not for Íole, but for Dejaneira's own
young beauty.

Mighty, triumphant ever, the power of the Cyprian stands.   *str.*
Not now of the Gods above
I speak—how the Son of Crŏnus and the Shaker of the Lands
Have been beguiled by Love,
And Hades, Lord of Night.
Nay, who were the rivals, on either side,
That once, to win our queen as bride,
Rose up and rushed together, to the dust and blows of fight?

One, the might of a river, Achelōus with looming horn   *ant.*
Came down from Oeniădae,
A bull most grim; and to meet him the Zeus-sprung hero, born
In Bacchic Thebes, swung free
Club, spears, and bended bow.
There in their passion, face to face,
Those champions clashed. And the Queen of Grace
Stood arbitress between them, to judge how the fight should go.

Then thud of fist, and twang of string,   *epode.*
Thunder of great horns battering,

Climbing grip of wrestlers locked,
Deadly din of foreheads shocked—
From each deep chest broke groan on groan,
While high on the side of a far-seen hill,
Waiting her destined lord, sat still
That fair and delicate face, alone.

                                    (497–525.)

Dejaneira reappears.   She owns to the Chorus that her good resolutions
against jealousy have not proved so easy to keep.

Friends, while our messenger within the palace
Takes his farewell of the captive girls he brought,
I have stolen forth to you;
Partly to tell you what these hands have done,
Partly to mourn my troubles in your ears.
For now in my household—so I come to think—
I have taken aboard no maiden, but a mistress—
A freight that in the end will break my heart.
Now there are two of us, to wait in turn
The embraces of one bed!   Such recompense
For keeping safe his home these weary years
Has Hēracles—the loyal and good, I called him!—
Sent to me now!
Angry with *him* I cannot be, though often
He has fallen to such frailties; yet to *share*
My home, my husband, with her!—where is woman
That could endure it?
For well I see her youth draws near its flower,
While mine lies fading.   Hers is such a blossom
As men's eyes long to gather; while their steps
Turn from the bloom that withers.   So I fear
Soon tongues will tell that Hēracles is *lord*
To me, indeed, but this young rival's *husband*.

    Yet since, as I have said, it ill becomes
A woman that has sense, to yield to anger,
Listen, dear friends, how yet I hope to find
Balm for my pain.   Closed in an urn of bronze,
I have a gift was given me long ago
By a wild, primeval creature—still a girl
I took it from the lifeblood, as he died,
Of the shaggy-chested Nessus; who for hire
Would ferry men across deep-flowing Euēnus—

Not in a vessel, not with sail and oar,
But in his own strong arms.   Myself he took
Upon his shoulders, when my father gave me
As bride to Hēracles and first from home
I travelled with my lord.   But in mid-stream
The Centaur cast his wanton hands upon me.
Loudly I screamed—then swift the son of Zeus
Wheeled round and launched a feathered shaft, that hissed
Deep through his chest, to the lung; then that wild thing
Whispered, as life ebbed from him: 'Wilt thou listen,
Child of old Oeneus?   This much thou shalt gain,
As the last wayfarer I ever carried.
If with thy hands thou gatherest the blood
Clotting about my wound, where the shaft is steeped
In the black gall of Lerna's monstrous Hydra,
It shall serve thee for a charm to bind the heart
Of Hēracles—that never he shall look
With love on another woman more than thee.'
     And so, dear friends, mindful of those last words
(For I had kept that blood at home close guarded)
I have smeared this robe with it, just as he told me.
And now the work is done.
I would not learn, nor know, spells that were evil;
I loathe all women that would handle them;
But if love-philtres *could* charm Hēracles
And let me get the better of this girl . . . ?
So much I have contrived—unless ye think
I grow too rash.   If so, I will go no further.
Chorus-leader. If you have any ground of confidence
In this you do, we think it not ill-planned.

                                          (531–89.)

So Līchas bears off the fatal robe for Hēracles to wear on a day of thanksgiving.   The Chorus chants an ode of hopefulness; but soon Dejaneira
reappears, in dismay.   The tuft of wool she had used to smear the robe,
then thrown away in the sunlit courtyard, has crumbled into dust!   Can it
be that the Centaur was treacherous?   Her worst fears are confirmed by the
entrance of Hyllus in fury—her fatal robe is flaying Hēracles alive—in his
agony he has brained Līchas—now the dying hero is being borne home.
With her son's curses in her ears, Dejaneira goes mutely into the house.
Another chorus; and then her old nurse brings news that she has stabbed
herself.   Too late Hyllus realizes her innocence.

The tortured Hēracles is brought in—stupefied at first; then raging, swearing, begging to be put out of his anguish, thirsting to rend his false wife limb from limb. Hyllus succeeds in telling his father how she was fooled by the Centaur Nessus. In *that* name Hēracles sees at once the work of destiny—for an oracle had warned him he would die 'by the hand of the dead.' He orders his reluctant son to build a great pyre, where he shall be burned alive, on the summit of Mount Oeta; and to wed the unhappy Íole. And yet, even now, no word of pity for the faithful wife of twenty years. The play ends with a strangely Euripidean outcry against the cruelty of Heaven; but some readers' hearts cry out far more at the cruelty of Hēracles.

A curious play. What did Sophocles feel? For Professor Murray, Hēracles is an abysmal brute. But Sophocles can hardly have viewed so harshly a Hellenic hero, with whose divine appearance he closes his *Philoctētes*, and to whom, we are told, he himself privately raised a shrine, after Hēracles had visited him in a dream. Another modern critic has tried to redress the balance by condemning Dejaneira—what a wicked woman to use a philtre! But it does not much brighten the play to blacken its most lovable character. One questions whether Sophocles would have been very grateful. If we must guess, I should prefer to think that he was, once again, just trying to picture life, without comment—a life in which, often, men must work and women weep. Wives of heroes usually need heroism. Titanic creatures that storm through the world destroying monsters and cleansing the earth are apt to be imperfect domestic animals. To do good is one thing; to be it, another. The great doers may make the world possible to live in; but perhaps it is only the others—those who *are* good— that make life in it worth while. Human awe and gratitude glorify 'the great,' and forget the rest. And yet it has been said: 'All great men are bad.' In this exaggeration there remains at least enough truth for it to have been remembered. We may recall, too, the words of George Sand, who was not without experience: 'I am sick of great men . . . I should like to see them all in Plutarch. . . . There they do not make one suffer.'

OEDIPUS THE KING
(*c.* 430 B.C. ?)

Action is transitory—a step, a blow,
The motion of a muscle—this way or that—
'Tis done, and in the after-vacancy
We wonder at ourselves like men betrayed:
Suffering is permanent, obscure, and dark,
And shares the nature of infinity.

Wordsworth.

This is often thought the greatest of Greek dramas.[1] It is rather, for me, the most astonishing—a masterpiece of pure 'theatre.' Its characters are not very attractive, its theme repulsive, its plot incredible; yet, after two thousand years, it still grips. The psycho-analysts, of course, have their explanation; and that may help. But dramatic success would be simple if it sufficed to write plays about incest. There have been plenty. But Walpole's *Mysterious Mother,* for example, is stone dead; *Oedipus* lives. Why?

It rests on a primitive legend of popular fatalism. What would a decent man least like, and be least likely, to do? To kill his father and marry his mother. Well, answers this story, if it is fated, he will do it, struggle how he may. The Arab mind expressed the same philosophy in the tale of the merchant of Baghdad whose servant begged leave to flee to Samarra, because in the bazaar Death had met him and raised his hand as if to strike. When the slave had gone, his master went down to the bazaar, found Death still there, and asked why he had threatened the poor fugitive. Death answered that he had raised his hand, not in menace, but in surprise at seeing, here in Baghdad, one whom Allah had appointed him to take that very night in Samarra. To flee your fate is to rush to find it.

Handling a story far less neat, the skill of Sophocles lies precisely in bewitching his audience to overlook its flaws. What would have been the *rational* course for Oedipus?[2] If he had absolute faith in oracles, he could only resign himself; what must be, must. If his faith was less absolute, the safest remedy was immediate suicide; if that was too drastic, he could re-solve at all costs never to murder or marry; if he found those pleasures indispensable, he could at least resolve never to murder or marry anyone who could conceivably be even ten years older than himself. What, instead, does this wise man do? Only ten miles from the fatal oracle which

[1] The opinion, however, of Saint-Évremond (1616–1703) remains an amusing example of the relativity of taste: '*Qui pourrait traduire en français, dans toute sa force, l'Oedipe même, ce chef-d'œuvre des anciens? J'ose assurer que rien au monde ne nous paraîtrait plus barbare, plus funeste, plus opposé aux vrais sentiments qu'on doit avoir.*'

[2] Genealogical table, p. 227.

has just warned him, out of momentary pique he kills an unknown old gentleman (to say nothing of three servants) in a futile bicker about being jostled off the track. Then, having broken the heart of the Sphinx by reading her riddle, he allows the grateful Thebans to marry him to an equally unknown lady of unknown age. Doubtless Jocasta may have looked younger than she was; but we are further asked to believe that Oedipus lived happily with her for a dozen years or more, without a word said of his own past life, or of hers, or of her late husband's death.

Granted, all this falls, as Aristotle says, 'outside the play.' But even when the play has begun, this clever reader of Sphinxes' riddles fails to see obvious clues that are there (even after his wife has seen them), and sees fantastic conspiracies that are *not* there. We are further asked to accept a holy prophet who comes to Oedipus firmly resolved to lock the frightful truth in deepest silence, but is provoked by a most unholy irritability to bellow it in public. We are asked to accept holy gods that doom a man unborn to parricide and incest; then leave him to beget four innocent children; then kill off guiltless multitudes with a plague, merely to bring about the revelation of this guilt they have imposed upon their victim.[1]

How many competent dramatists would dare undertake such a plot? And what a dramatic hypnotist that, in spite of all, could bring it to success!

For Sophocles has not here, like Shakespeare sometimes, redeemed a fantastic plot by the human warmth of his characters. Jocasta, indeed, is moving; and the two herdsmen are vividly, though slightly, drawn. But Creon seems only a worthy stick; Teiresias, a cantankerous dervish; the Chorus, the usual band of melodious mediocrities; Oedipus himself (though some critics have admired him), a somewhat self-complacent, self-blinded, wildly suspicious and choleric person. His sneer at Jocasta (when she begs him to seek no further), that no doubt she is snobbishly afraid his birth will not prove sufficiently noble, though doubtless meant to heighten the impression of blind pride before its fall, seems itself needlessly ignoble. And when the truth breaks, he rouses in many of us less pity than repulsion by a frenzy that pursues Jocasta sword in hand (as if incest would be improved by matricide), then futilely digs out his own eyes. This last may, indeed, be truer to life than rationalists suppose—modern psychology has recorded a neurotic who destroyed his own eyes with pieces of glass, because he could no longer bear his own criminal impulses and wished to blot out a world grown intolerable.[2] But perhaps a more illuminating parallel is the frenzy of Philoctētes when, robbed of his bow, he shouts for

[1] On Oedipus Dr Johnson seems to show less than his usual acuteness. 'His obstinacy darkens the lustre of his other virtues, aggravates his impiety, and almost justifies his sufferings.' 'Our opinion of his piety is greatly invalidated by his contemptuous treatment of the wise, the benevolent, the sacred Tiresias.' (Preface to the translation of the play by T. Maurice in his *Poems and Miscellaneous Pieces*, 1780.)
[2] Fuller details in my *Literature and Psychology*, p. 26.

an axe so that he can hew off his own limbs rather than accompany his hated countrymen to Troy. The 'gentle' Sophocles certainly chose to create characters who are anything but gentle. And when, as the play closes, this lacerated Theban with bleeding, eyeless sockets is kept on the stage for over two hundred lines, elaborating with perverted ingenuity, even in front of his two young daughters, the complex combinations of kinship produced by incest, accustomed though one is to the Athenian passion for rhetoric and for theatrical weeping and gnashing of teeth, I cannot help thinking how much better Shakespeare contrived the end of Othello, that finer character with whom Iago has played the part that here the gods play with Oedipus.

As for critics who discover profundities of thought in this tragedy, they have not much to show but the final moral that no man should be called happy till safely dead. One doubts if a play could live long on this fossil chestnut. It might have been another matter if Sophocles had led up to the conclusion of universal forgiveness for all human sins and frailties because, in the words FitzGerald chose for his own epitaph, 'It is He that hath made us, and not we ourselves.' But not till a generation later, in the far more thoughtful *Oedipus at Colōnus*, did Sophocles stress the fundamental innocence of his hero, and strikingly turn this figure of outcast pollution into a guardian genius of the kindly land that sheltered him.

And yet it moves. How? Not by its ideas, not by its characters, not by plausibility of plot. But its great scenes grip. The first quality of drama is to be dramatic. And this quality the play has, supremely—thanks to the brilliance with which its action, cunningly delayed, yet never too much slowed, deviating now one way, now another, closes inevitably at last on its victim. In their suspense the audience are fascinated as if they watched some wanderer on a mountain blindly circling nearer and nearer to the precipice. He need not be a very attractive character—enough that he is a man. And to what is, in fact, the first detective play, the first 'thriller' in European literature, Sophocles has added his gift of style, his gift of tragic irony. *Oedipus the King* does not appear to me the highest kind of drama. Its influence-value seems slight. One feels that Plato must have as much disapproved its emotionalism as Aristotle admired its skill. But its pleasure-value has lasted. If it is not a play of the most admirable kind, of its kind it is an admirable play.[1]

---

[1] I realize (and so should my readers) that the above views are somewhat heretical; but I am comforted to find myself in agreement with a critic whose unfailing freedom from conventional cant has been my delight for many years—Professor H. W. Garrod: 'If anyone tells me that he does not know whether the *Oedipus* or *Hamlet* be the greater work of human imagination, frankly, I do not believe him, or I cease to respect him.' (*Scholarship*, 1946, p. 67.)

Yet, in fairness, I should like to end on a note less negative—with a distant echo of the voice of Racine. '*Je me souviens,*' says Valincourt, '*qu'étant un jour à Auteuil chez Despréaux avec M. Nicole et quelques autres amis d'un mérite distingué, nous mîmes Racine*

NOTE

The modern reader is apt to feel bewildered by the hysteria with which this play treats actions done in ignorance and innocence. After all, in Homer, though Epicaste (Jocasta) hangs herself on finding she has wed her son, Oedipus is spoken of as remaining King of Thebes, falling in battle, and being honoured with a great funeral feast. As not infrequently, Attic tragedy in contrast to Ionian epic shows an attitude less sane and less humane—something nearer to the primitive.

But this primitive horror at parricide and incest may itself be a relic of a painful advance in human ethics from a still more primitive stage when parricide and incest, far from being abnormal horrors, were normal custom.

Something of this savagery survives in the legend of Crŏnus castrating his father Urănus and seizing his power; in days when kingship descended through the female, more than one human Crŏnus may have killed his father to take his father's wife and crown (cf. Frazer, *Golden Bough*, IV, 193). In the *Internationale Zeitschrift für Psychoanalyse* for 1939 (XXIV, 434 ff.) Max Kohen thus explains a Sumerian seal found at Lagash in 1879, with a squatting female, a bearded man prostrate, and a younger man who seems to have killed him. The writer compares, from L. Frobenius' *Erythräa*, the customs of various African tribes; and also the historic parallel of Phraataces of Parthia, who *c.* A.D. 2 killed his father Phraates IV with the help of his mother, married her, and reigned with her.

Where such customs existed in primitive society, it may well have needed a violent upheaval to banish them, and the building up of a violent abhorrence to keep them banished. In the ancient Mediterranean such things were no doubt already remote; but less remote than for us, and less easy to view with rational detachment.[1]

---

sur l'Oedipe de Sophocle. Il nous le récita tout entier, le traduisant sur-le-champ: et il s'émut à un tel point, que tout ce que nous étions d'auditeurs, nous éprouvâmes tous les sentiments de terreur et de compassion, sur quoi roule cette tragédie. J'ai vu nos meilleurs acteurs sur le théâtre, j'ai entendu nos meilleures pièces: mais jamais rien n'approcha du trouble où me jeta ce récit: et au moment même que je vous écris, je m'imagine voir encore Racine avec son livre à la main, et nous tous consternés autour de lui.' (Pellisson et D'Olivet, *Histoire de l'Académie Française*, 1858 ed., ii, 335–6.)

[1] Two historical associations of the Oedipus legend are worth recalling. Nero had a passion for acting Oedipus (like Orestes) on the stage, as well as in real life. After his fall it was noted that, as his last part, he had played the Theban king, and that his last utterance then had been the words (from an unknown play):

> The father whose bride I shared ordains me now
> Most miserable death.
>
> (Suetonius, *Nero*, 46)

Again, at the end of 1718, the young Voltaire's *Oedipe* was acted with great success, before the Regent Orleans, while his daughter, the Duchesse de Berri, supposed to be her father's mistress, occupied with her ladies a large dais in the auditorium. (Michelet, *Histoire de France*, xvii, 158–62.)

OEDIPUS THE KING

OEDIPUS	A MESSENGER
JOCASTA, his mother and wife	A HERDSMAN, once servant of
CREON, her brother	King Laïus
TEIRESIAS	A SERVANT OF OEDIPUS
A PRIEST	CHORUS OF THEBAN ELDERS

[*Before the palace at Thebes. The Priest of Zeus enters with a band of suppliants—old men, youths, and children—who gather round the altars below the palace-steps. From the palace-door appears King Oedipus.*]

Oedipus. My children, in whose veins yet runs to-day
　　Old Cadmus' blood, how comes it that I see you
　　Sitting with branches wreathed in supplication;
　　While Thebes is filled now with the smoke of incense,
　　And hymns to the Healer blend with lamentations?
　　From your own lips, and not by bare report,
　　I thought it right to hear the truth, my children,
　　And so am come—
　　I, Oedipus, whose name fills all men's mouths.
　　(*To the priest.*) You there, old man, since it befits your years
　　To speak for these, say what it is that brings ye?
　　Some need? Some dread? Tell me!—as one most willing
　　To give you fullest aid. Hard heart were mine,
　　If I denied such suppliants my pity.
Priest. Oedipus, sovereign lord of this our land,
　　You see how every age is gathered here
　　About your altars—young things yet too weak
　　To fly far from the nest, and old men bowed
　　With weight of winters—priests (as I of Zeus)
　　And these our chosen youth. The rest of Thebes
　　Sits too, with suppliant garlands, in our markets,
　　Or by the prophetic ashes of Ismēnus,
　　Or the two shrines of Pallas.
　　For, as your eyes have seen, our ship of state
　　Labours beneath the tempest, powerless now
　　Out of the depths and surges of destruction
　　To lift again her head. Our land is stricken,
　　With fruits of the earth untimely withered; stricken

With dying herds in the pastures and, at home,
Abortive births of women.   There swoops besides
On Thebes, to harry her, that God who brings
The fire of fever—deadliest pestilence
Empties the House of Cadmus, and makes rich
With wailing and with weeping Hades' gloom.

    It is *not* because we dream you wield like power
With Gods, that beside your hearth we sit in prayer—
I and these children.   Yet, as the first of men,
We look to *you*; both in life's common cares
And in Heaven's visitations.
Only *your* coming rescued Cadmus' city
From paying her tribute to that savage songstress,
Though there was nothing *we* could tell or teach you,
To aid you *then*.   It was by some God's helping,
Men say—and think—you brought our lives salvation.
So now, thou greatest in the eyes of all,
Here at thy feet we beg thee, Oedipus,
Find us some help—whether it be by knowledge
Of utterance divine, or human wisdom.
It is the mind of deep experience—
That I have seen—whose counsels live and thrive.
Noblest of men, up now and save our Thebes!
Look to yourself!   Because so well you served her,
This land to-day salutes you as her saviour;
Then Heaven forbid we should recall your reign
As one that upraised us only to cast us down.
Therefore lift Thebes to safety once again
And, as you blessed us once with happy fortune,
Prove yourself such to-day!
If you would be true prince, as well as master,
Better a peopled than an empty land.
For towers and ships are nothing, lacking men
To fill them at your side.

Oedipus. My unhappy children, not unknown to me
The need that brings you here.   Too well I know it,
All that you suffer!   Yet among ye all
None suffers, at your suffering, deep as I.
For each of *you* feels grief for himself alone,
And for none else; but *my* soul groans aloud
Alike for Thebes, and you, and for myself.
So now ye do not rouse one sunk in slumber—
Many a tear, be sure, I have wept already,

Many a track my wandering thoughts have tried.
But all my searchings found one. cure alone,
And *that* I have set in action.   I have sent
Creon, Menoeceus' son, my own wife's brother,
To Apollo's shrine at Pytho, to inquire
What word or deed of mine could deliver Thebes.
And reckoning now the passage of the days
I am troubled for him; seeing that his absence
Prolongs itself, past need or likelihood.
But once he has come, then no true man am I,
If I fail in doing whatever the God reveals.

Priest. Most timely spoken!   For, yonder, men make signal
That Creon himself approaches.

Oedipus. O Lord Apollo, grant that he come indeed
With saving fortune, bright as the look he wears!

Priest. Good news he seems to bring us—he would not else
Come with his brows thus wreathed in berried laurel.

Oedipus. Soon we shall know.   He is in hearing now.
Son of Menoeceus, my own princely kinsman,
What answer have you brought us from Apollo?

Creon (*entering*). Good.   (For I hold that even hard conditions,
If they turn well, can still prove fortunate.)

Oedipus. What said the oracle?   Your words, as yet,
Leave me not over-bold, nor yet dismayed.

Creon. If you would have me utter all in public,
Here I will speak.   Or, if you will, within.

Oedipus. Speak before all.   Their sorrow weighs with me
More than my life itself.

Creon. Then let me tell the answer of the God.
The Lord Apollo plainly ordered us
To drive from Thebes a pollution that (it seems)
Is harboured here—not nurse it for our ruin.

Oedipus. What kind of taint is this?   How purified?

Creon. By exile—*or* by exacting blood for blood.
For that blood-guilt has brought this storm on Thebes.

Oedipus. And what man's murder does the God denounce?

Creon. My lord, the former ruler of this land,
Before your sovereignty, was Laïus.

Oedipus. So men have told me.   For I never saw him.

Creon. *Now* the God's clear command is violent justice
On those—whoever they were—that slew our King.

Oedipus. And where on the earth are *they*?   How shall be traced
This trail inscrutable of ancient murder?

Creon. Apollo said: 'In Thebes.'   Though things neglected
   May pass unpunished, seek and ye shall discover.

Oedipus. Was it here at home, or in the countryside,
   Or in a foreign land, that Laïus perished?

Creon. Bound on a sacred mission (so he said)
   He had quitted Thebes; and never came again.

Oedipus. But had he no companion on his journey?
   Was there no witness whose story might have helped us?

Creon. His followers perished with him—all but one,
   Who fled—and *he* could tell but one thing clearly.

Oedipus. And what was that?   One clue might lead to more;
   If only some slight beginning gave us hope.

Creon. Robbers, he said—not one man's strength alone,
   But a whole band—encountered them, and slew.

Oedipus. But how should any robber grow so daring—
   Unless suborned by silver sent from Thebes?

Creon. So we surmised.   But then, amid all our troubles,
   The blood of Laïus found no avenger.

Oedipus. What 'troubles,' when your own royal lord had fallen,
   Could so prevent your searching out the truth?

Creon. The subtle-singing Sphinx.   She turned our minds
   From hidden ills to the ills before our feet.

Oedipus. Then *I* must start afresh, and bring to the light
   These hidden things.   Most worthily has Phoebus
   (And worthily you too) thus taken thought
   For our dead King.
   And justly, therefore, you shall have my help
   To vindicate our country and Apollo.
   Not merely in loyalty to a man remote—
   For my own sake, too, I must dispel this curse;
   For the murderer of Laïus might be minded
   To aim in turn such violence at *me*.
   And so, avenging him, I serve myself.
   (*To the crowd.*) Quick, then, take up your boughs of supplication
   And rise, my children, from the altar-steps.
   And let one call the folk of Cadmus hither,
   With full assurance that I *will* do all.
   Either, so help us Phoebus, we will find
   Salvation—or our ruin.

Priest. Rise up, my children.   Freely the King has promised
   All that we came to ask.   Now may Apollo,
   That sent these oracles, Himself draw near,
   As Saviour and Healer of this pestilence!

Oedipus re-enters the palace; the suppliants disperse; and there enters the Chorus of Theban Elders.

strophe 1.

Chorus. Ah voice of Zeus sweet-spoken, what is Thy word they bring,
    From Pytho's shrine of gold
  To glorious Thebes?   I tremble—my heart throbs questioning:
    'Will this Thine edict hold,
  O Healer hymned in Delos, some new thing?
  Or comes, with the circling seasons, some old amends to pay?'
  O daughter of Hope the golden, O Voice eternal, say!

I cry, immortal Athena, daughter of Zeus, to Thee;   *antistrophe* 1.
    To Apollo, the Archer-king;
  To Artemis, our protectress, fair name of purity,
    Throned mid our market's ring.
  Shine out and from death redeem us, Saviours three!
  If ever, when Thebes was threatened, of old ye thrust away
  The fires of sorrow from her, come back to our aid this day!

Alas, no more can I count our woes.   *str.* 2.
For all our folk lies sickened; and never a mind that knows
Weapon to ward it.   No more the Earth
  With the glory of her gifts is blest;
  In vain women wail in the pangs of birth;
  And swifter than flames o'ermastering,
  Soul after soul, like a bird, takes wing
To the Dark God in the West.

In their deaths past number our city dies—   *ant.* 2.
From her dead on the earth unpitied, she sees new deaths arise.
Thronging the altar-steps of stone,
  Young wives, grey mothers, pray the while
  For grace from doom, with wail and moan:
  Mid hymns to the Healer there shrieks despair.
  Hear, golden daughter of Zeus, our prayer!—
On *us* let Thy succour smile!

This grim War-god that wastes us, not with the shields of war, *str.* 3.
Whose onset burns amid lost voices crying,
From Thebes ah, turn him backward, we implore;
  Let Thy wild winds whirl him flying
  To the far Atlantic's roar!

Fling him where crags of Thrace
Shelter no shipman's mast!
For now, if the night yield grace,
Yet comes the day to blast.
O Father Zeus, O Lord
Of the lightning's blazing sword,
Smite our destroyer with Thy bolts at last!

Lycēan King, to save us I would that *Thou* couldst stand,   *ant.* 3.
From golden bow Thy shafts resistless winging;
And Artemis, resplendent torch in hand,
Wherewith she rushes springing
Through the peaks of the Lycian land!
And, red-cheeked Bacchus, Thou
On whom the Bacchant cries,
With gold about Thy brow,
Lord of the Maenads, rise!
With joyous brand aflame,
From the town that shares Thy name
Ward off that God abhorred in all Gods' eyes!

Oedipus reappears from the palace.

Oedipus. So ye have prayed; in answer to that prayer,
If you will mind my words, and minister
To this your sickness, ye may find relief
And lightening of your burden.   Though a stranger,
Remote from this report, from the deed remote,
I yet must speak.   For if I searched alone,
Quickly my search must halt—no clue to follow.
Now therefore I, that only *since* this crime
Am counted as a Theban among Thebans,
To all the sons of Cadmus make this edict—
Whoever among you knows by what man's deed
Died Laïus, the son of Labdacus,
I order him to tell me all the truth.
And if he fears—still let him speak, assured
That so he shall clear himself.   For he shall suffer
No other molestation, but pass hence,
Unharmed, to banishment.
Or if there is any knows some foreigner
To be the slayer, let him speak it out.
I will pay his due reward; and he shall earn
Our thanks besides.

But if ye hold your peace, if any man,
In fear for friend or self, defy my order,
Then hear my retribution.
On him—no matter who—I lay the ban
Of Thebes, whose crown and sovereignty I hold—
That none shall shelter him, none speak to him,
None let him share in any prayer to Heaven,
In sacrifice, in sprinkled holy water.
All men shall thrust him from their doors, as being
Himself the pollution that now curses Thebes,
According to the Pythian oracle
Revealed me by Apollo.
Thus then I now take up the cause of God
And of Laïus so murdered.
And I pray that the guilty, whether that unknown
Did the deed unhelped, or had accomplices,
May wear away his wretched life with doom
As evil as himself.
Further I pray that if by hearth of mine,
With my own knowledge, he should find a home,
Then may the curse I have uttered fall on me!
And all that I have said, I charge ye do,
In *my* name, and Apollo's—in the name
Of Thebes, forsaken by the fruits of earth
And by the Gods in Heaven.
For though They had never sent this visitation,
Yet even so it was ill done to leave
This crime unpurged—when one of noblest worth,
A king, had died.   Ye should have searched the matter.
But since I hold the royalty that he held,
Since mine his bed, and mine the wife he loved
(Who might, had *he* been fortunate in issue,
Have linked us by the bond of common children),
Seeing that upon his head has leapt disaster,
I will battle in his cause, as if he were
My very father; and will spare no labour
To find whose hand it was that slew the heir
Of Labdacus, of Polydorus, and
Cadmus before him, and of old Agēnor.
And if any disobey me, may the Gods
Make their fields bear, henceforward, no more harvest,
Their wives no children—be it theirs to perish
By the doom that wastes us now—by dooms yet worse!

But you, the rest of Thebes, that loyally
Accept what I have said—may saving Justice
And all the Gods be with you evermore!

Chorus-leader. On pain of the curse, as you have asked me, sire,
I answer that I neither am the slayer,
Nor yet can point him out.   Indeed, Apollo
Should Himself have named whatever man it is.

Oedipus. True, that were just.   But there's none born on earth
That can compel the Gods against their will.

Leader. There *is* a course, which seems next-best to that—

Oedipus. Speak, though it were no more than third in worth.

Leader. I know one man alone
That shares most nearly Lord Apollo's vision—
The Lord Teiresias.   To one that searches
This matter, sire, *he* might give clearest answer.

Oedipus. In this as well I have not been negligent,
But sent, by Creon's counsel, men to bring him—
First one, and then a second.   Much I wonder
He is not here, long since.

Leader. The rest is only old and idle rumours.

Oedipus. What 'rumours'?   Say!   No tale but I would weigh it.

Leader. That the King was killed by certain travellers.

Oedipus. So I have heard.   But none sees him that saw it.

Leader. Unless the guilty knows not what fear is,
He *cannot* brave it out against such curses.

Oedipus. Who fears not evil deeds, will fear no words.

Leader. But here is one that *shall* bring him to justice.
Look, they lead hither the prophet in whose heart,
Alone of men, lives knowledge of the truth.

The blind Teiresias enters, led by a boy.

Oedipus. O thou whose soul grasps all—Teiresias!—
Alike the lore of Heaven and of Earth,
Things utterable and secret mysteries,
Blind though thou art, thou knowest well what sickness
Weighs now upon all Thebes—to thee alone,
Great sir, we look to save us and protect.
For now Apollo (in case my messengers
Have told thee nothing) to our question answers
That from this plague we cannot hope relief
Unless we learn who killed King Laïus
And punish blood with blood, or banishment.
Now therefore, if by voice of birds thou knowest,

Or any other path of divination,
Grudge not to heal both Thebes, thyself, and me—
Yes, heal this whole defilement from the dead!
For we are in thy hand. And man's best labour
Is to aid others, with all his means and power.

Teiresias. Alas, how fearful is wisdom that yet avails
The wise man nothing! Well enough I knew it—
And yet forgot! Or never I would have come.

Oedipus. What! Do you bring, then, such a heavy heart?

Teiresias. Let me go home! So doing, you will make
My load less hard to bear—less hard your own.

Oedipus. Such words are unbecoming!—and unkindly
To Thebes that bred you. Can you grudge us answer?

Teiresias. Yes. For I see you speak beside the purpose.
Better be silent; lest I too speak ill.

Oedipus. By Heaven, if thou hast knowledge, turn not from us—
We all beseech thee, suppliant on our knees!

Teiresias. Blind are ye all. No, never will I utter
My hidden sorrows (let me not call them *thine*).

Oedipus. What! Then you know, but will not tell!—determined
On treason against me, and ruin for Thebes!

Teiresias. I will not pain thee so, nor yet myself.
Why this vain questioning? I *will* not speak.

Oedipus. What, vilest of the vile!—will you utter nothing?
You would enrage a rock! Can you show yourself
So pitiless, so unpersuadable?

Teiresias. You blame my temper. But, reproaching me,
Are blind to that which dwells within yourself.

Oedipus. And who would *not* be angered by such words
As those you have spoken, in contempt of Thebes?

Teiresias. What comes *will* come, though wrapped by me in silence.

Oedipus. Then, if it comes, you well may utter it.

Teiresias. I will speak no further. Rage now, if you will,
With all the fiercest fury of your passion.

Oedipus. Now I'll spare nothing (you have so roused that 'passion')
Of all that I perceive. I think that thou
Thyself didst plot this crime, and execute it!—
Short of the very slaying. Hadst thou eyes,
I would have said thou wast sole murderer.

Teiresias. Indeed! And *I* tell *thee*—obey that edict
Thou hast thyself proclaimed! From this day forth
Speak no word more to these men, nor to me;
Being *thyself* this land's accurst defiler!

Oedipus. So shameless as to stir up talk like this!
   How do you dream to be safe from punishment?

Teiresias. I am safe already.   Mine is the strength of Truth.

Oedipus. Truth!   And who taught you this?   Not divination!

Teiresias. Who taught me?   Thou!—that hast made me speak, unwilling.

Oedipus. Made you speak *what?*   Repeat it!   I would be sure.

Teiresias. Not understand!   Or do you but seek to try me?

Oedipus. Say it once more.   Truly, I could not grasp it.

Teiresias. I say thou art that murderer whom thou seekest.

Oedipus. Again these horrors!   Ah, you shall be sorry!

Teiresias. Shall I say more, and make thee angrier yet?

Oedipus. Say what you please.   You will but waste your words.

Teiresias. Unknowing, thou hast had with thy next and dearest
   Dealings most foul—nor knowest now thy ruin.

Oedipus. Do you dream to repeat such things and not to pay!

Teiresias. Yes, if indeed the power of Truth abides.

Oedipus. For others, yes.   But what is Truth to thee,
   Whose eyes, and ears, and brain are darkened all?

Teiresias. Unhappy wretch!   These taunts you hurl at me
   Soon the whole world shall join to hurl at thee.

Oedipus. Creature of night unending, yours no power
   To injure me or any that sees the light.

Teiresias. Nay, not from *me* thy fall is doomed to come.
   Phoebus suffices.   *He* will fulfil it all.

Oedipus. Was this the plot of Creon, or your own?

Teiresias. It is not Creon ruins thee, but thyself.

Oedipus. Ah wealth and sovereignty and arts of power,
   Climbing amid ambition's rivalries,
   What a hoard of envy still ye hold within you!—
   If merely for the sake of this my greatness,
   Bestowed on me by Thebes, a gift unasked,
   The loyal Creon, my friend from long ago,
   By stealthy machinations undermines me,
   Setting upon me this insidious wizard—
   Gear-gathering hypocrite, blind in his art,
   With eyes for only gain!
   For, tell me now, *when* have you proved true seer?
   Why, when there came that chanting, monstrous hound,
   Had you *then* no answer to deliver Thebes?
   And yet her riddle was not to be read
   By the first-comer's wit—*that* was the time
   For powers prophetic.   But of *those* no sign

You gave us—neither by the voice of birds,
Nor taught by any God.   But then came I—
The ignorant Oedipus!—and closed her mouth
By force of intellect—no birds to help me!
And now you would depose me, with the hope
Of standing next in power by Creon's throne!
But you and he—that plotter!—yet may rue
Your purge of Thebes.   And but for your aged looks
You should have found sharp lesson for your folly.

Leader.   It seems to our judgment, sire, both you and he
Have said what you have said, too much in anger.
No hour for such things now—but to consider
How we may meet the commandment of Apollo.

Teiresias.   King thou mayst be; but mine be equal right
Of making equal answer.   *That* I keep.
I live to serve, not thee, but Loxias!—
I have no need of Creon for protector.
Thou hast mocked at me for blind: I say to thee
That *thou* hast eyes, yet seest not thy ruin—
Nor where thou dwellest—nor who shares thy home.
Knowst thou thy parents?   Thou hast been, unknowing,
A deadly enemy to thine own kin,
Both those on earth, and those whom Hades holds.
And forth from Thebes, one day, thou shalt be flung
By the dread-pursuing curse, with double scourge,
Of father and mother both!—and then thine eyes
That now see clear, shall gaze on gloom alone.
When that day comes, where shall thy cries not harbour,
What rock of all Cithaeron not re-echo,
Once thou hast learnt thy wedlock—and what shipwreck,
After fair voyage, has met thee there at home!
Blind, too, thou art to a thousand other ills,
That then shall abase thee level with thine offspring,
As low as in truth thou art.
Scatter thy filth, then, on the name of Creon
And on my prophecies!   For no man ever
Shall be stamped out more utterly than thou.

Oedipus.   Is this to be endured—such words from *him*!
Begone, to Hell!—out of my gates!—and quickly!
Back by the way you came!

Teiresias.   I never would have come, but at thy call.

Oedipus.   Could I know thou wouldst babble folly?   Or slow indeed
I should have been, to call thee to my gates.

Teiresias. Ay, such I am—to thee, indeed, a fool,
   Yet wise enough for the parents who begot thee.

Oedipus. My parents?   Stay!   Who *was* it gave me life?

Teiresias. This day shall bring thy birth—and thy destruction.

Oedipus. Always these riddles and obscurities!

Teiresias. And art thou not supreme at reading such?

Oedipus. Good!—mock the very gift that brought my greatness!

Teiresias. Yet that same happy fortune brought thy doom.

Oedipus. I care not, if at least I rescued Thebes.

Teiresias. Now I *will* go.   Come, boy, lead me away.

Oedipus. And quickly too!   Thou art insufferable
   Here; and thy going, good riddance.

Teiresias. Yes, go I will; but not till I have said
   That which I came for, fearless of thy frown.
   For *thou* canst not destroy me.
   I tell thee this—the man thou seekest for
   With threats and proclamations—Laïus' murderer,
   Is here.
   Passing as stranger and as alien,
   He yet shall prove true Theban.   But small joy
   That change shall bring him.   Blind, where once he saw,
   Beggared instead of wealthy, into exile
   He shall go forth, with a staff to grope his way.
   Then shall he be revealed as sire and brother
   To the children that he dwells with; son and husband
   To her that gave him birth; his father's slayer,
   Sharing that father's wife.
   Go in and think of it!   If thou shalt find me
   False, call me *then* a fool at prophecy!

        Teiresias is led out.   Oedipus re-enters the palace.

                       strophe 1.

Chorus. Whom now does the crag of Delphi with voice divine proclaim
   Guilty, with hands deep-reddened, of a crime too dark to name?
     Now, surely, he shall need
     Feet with a wilder speed
     Than tempest-footed steed.
   For on him now, armed with the lightning's flame,
   The Son of Zeus, Apollo, leaps to seize!—
     They, too, that never tire,
     The sure Erinyes.

                       antistrophe 1.

From snows of high Parnassus, like a beacon, burns revealed
The call of God, commanding to track the wretch concealed.

Through caves and wildwood trees,
Through mountain fastnesses,
Like a wild bull he flees.
Yet, as he shuns that voice from mid-earth's shrine,
Round him forlornly wandering
Flit still the words divine;
And still they live to sting!

But deep, how deep my trouble, when to the seer I hearken!   *str.* 2.
I approve not, I deny not, I find no word to say.
I flutter with forebodings.   The present, the future darken—
Too dim to see my way.
Never have *I* heard rumour tell, that the peace of our kings was broken
By feud with the heir of Corinth.   The fame of our lord is grown
Mighty in Thebes—can I wound it (and by what proof or token?)
To avenge a death unknown?

No human things lie hidden from Zeus and from Apollo;   *ant.* 2.
For Theirs indeed is wisdom.   Man passes man in wit—
Yet hath a prophet vision, that is truer?   Vain and hollow
Are all the proofs of it.
Till Oedipus be found at fault, I will not join to blame him.
When came that wingéd maiden, the wisdom of our lord
Shone forth, and Thebes was gladdened.   And therefore now to shame
him
My heart shall not accord.

                                        [*Creon enters.*

Creon. Men of this city, I hear King Oedipus
  Utters against me blackest accusations.
  Therefore I come, in anger.   If he thinks
  That *I* have harmed him in these present troubles,
  By word or deed disloyal, I care no longer
  For length of days—stained with such calumny!
  Not in myself alone such rumour wrongs me,
  But in what's dearest—seeing my name dishonoured
  In Thebes—dishonoured by my friends and you!
Leader. It well may be that violence of anger
  Made him so blame you—not deliberate judgment.
Creon. And was the charge that *I*, by schemes of mine,
  Prompted the prophet's lies?
Leader. Such things were said.   I know not their intent.
Creon. Could he, with steady glance, and steady temper,
  Utter against me such a charge as this!

Leader. I do not know.   I have no eyes to mark
   My sovereign's acts.   But see, here comes the King.

Oedipus reappears from the palace.

Oedipus. You there, what brings you?   Have you, then, indeed
   A forehead so unblushing, that you dare
   To cross my threshold—you that are clearly proven
   The assassin of your king—thief of my crown!
   Tell me in Heaven's name—did I, then, seem
   Coward, or fool, that you should lay this plot?
   Or did you think I should not see your treason
   Creeping against me?   Or, seeing, make no resistance?
   And was it not the project of a fool
   Thus, without friends or numbers at your back,
   To chase a crown—prize that is never won
   Except with wealth and numbers?
Creon. This you *must* grant me—fairly hear my answer
   To all your charges; when you have heard me, judge.
Oedipus. You're a glib speaker!   But bad listener I,
   For *you*—now proved my bitter adversary.
Creon. This *one* thing I would explain now—only hear me—
Oedipus. One thing I *will* not hear—that you are honest.
Creon. It shows small wisdom in you to suppose
   That you can gain by senseless stubbornness.
Oedipus. Nor very wise in *you*, if *you* suppose
   You can wrong your own kinsman with impunity.
Creon. I grant what you say is justice—only tell me
   What *is* this wrong complained of?
Oedipus. Did you, or did you not, urge me to send
   For that most reverend prophet?
Creon. Yes.   And I hold the same opinion still.
Oedipus. And how long is it now since Laïus—
Creon. Laïus did what?   I do not understand.
Oedipus.—was murderously attacked, and disappeared?
Creon. Many a long year *that* would be to reckon.
Oedipus. And was this prophet of yours then plying his craft?
Creon. As wise—as honoured—as he is to-day.
Oedipus. And did he ever, *then*, pronounce my name?
Creon. Never.   At least, when *I* was within hearing.
Oedipus. Did you inquire at all of Laïus' murder?
Creon. We did.   How should we not?   But could learn nothing.
Oedipus. Why did this 'wise' seer not tell *then* his story?
Creon. I know not.   I talk not of things beyond my grasp.

Oedipus. One thing you do know—well within 'your grasp.'
Creon. What? I will not deny it, if I know.
Oedipus. That never, unless he first had schemed with *you*,
  He would have dared name *me* as Laïus' murderer!
Creon. If he says so, *you* best know it. But I claim
  The right to question *you*, as you have *me*.
Oedipus. Ask on! You will not prove *me* murderer!
Creon. Now! Is my sister your own wedded wife?
Oedipus. *That*'s a truth past denying.
Creon. And do you both hold equal power in Thebes?
Oedipus. She never had a wish that I refused.
Creon. And am I not third partner with you both?
Oedipus. The very thing that blackens your treachery!
Creon. Never!—would *you* but stop, as I, to think.
  Ask yourself first—can you dream that any man
  Would sooner choose a crown, with all its fears,
  Than sleep at ease of nights, with no less power?
  I never could think it better to be king
  Than lead a life that's kingly—*no* man could,
  That's in his sober senses.
  For, as I am, all that my heart can wish for
  I have from *you*, untroubled. But were *I*
  Ruler myself, how much I must do distasteful!
  Why should I find a crown, then, pleasanter
  Than authority and power with never a care?
  I am not yet so blinded as to crave
  Vain honour's semblance, void of solid worth.
  To-day, all greet me; all men wish me well;
  All your petitioners pay court to *me*,
  In whom lies all their hope of good success.
  How should I quit this substance for that shadow?
  No balanced mind can sink to such sudden folly.
  I could neither fall in love with schemes so blind,
  Nor stoop to league myself with one that did.
  Would you have proof, go first to Pytho—ask
  If truly I reported Apollo's answer;
  Next, if you find that I have hatched a plot
  With this diviner, send me to my death—
  Not by your sentence only, but my own!
  But tax me not thus, with proofless, privy charges!
  What justice lies in recklessly mistaking
  True men for traitors, traitors for true men?
  As well, I think, a man might fling away

The life within him, dearest thing he holds,
As a good friend.
Well, you will learn the certain truth in time;
For time alone can show the honest man,
Though *one* day is enough to know a knave.

Leader. Wise words, my lord—to one that watches well
For fear to fall.   Quick wits are dangerous.

Oedipus. But when these stealthy planners move so quickly,
As quick must *I* be with my counter-plan.
I cannot wait inactive—or his scheme
Finds its fulfilment, and my cause is lost.

Creon. What is your will, then?   Banish me from Thebes?

Oedipus. Indeed not!   Death—not exile—is my will—

Creon. Can nothing shake you?   Can no proofs convince?

Oedipus.—so that men learn, by you, what envy brings.

Creon. Your judgment's blinded!   *Oedipus.* Not in my own affairs.

Creon. But think of *mine*, then!   *Oedipus.* No.   You are a scoundrel.

Creon. Yet, if you *are* so blind—   *Oedipus.* I still must rule!

Creon. But not *mis*rule.   *Oedipus.* Misrule!   Ah Thebes, my country!

Creon. Thebes is *my* country too.   Not only yours.

Leader. Cease, my good lords.   I see, from the palace comes,
In happy hour, Jocasta.   Let her help
Bring reconciliation to your quarrel.

[*Jocasta enters.*

Jocasta. Misguided men, what rouses you to wage
Such senseless war of words?
Have you no shame!—when Thebes herself lies sick,
Stirring up private brawls!   In, in, my lord!
Go, Creon!—home!   And do not, both of you,
Swell a mere nothing to a great disaster.

Creon. Sister, your husband Oedipus thinks fitting
To take his choice which outrage he shall do me—
Banish me from my home, or kill me here!

Oedipus. Yes, it is true.   For I caught him vilely plotting
A vile attack, good wife, upon my person.

Creon. May no good come to me—may I die accursed,
If ever I did these things you charge me with!

Jocasta. In Heaven's name, believe him, Oedipus!
Pay that regard to his most solemn oath;
And to myself; and to thine Elders here.

Leader. Change heart and mind and hearken,   *strophe* 1.
I beg of thee, O King.

Oedipus. What is the grace ye seek of me?

Leader. Regard this man, that was never fool,
   Pledged now by a mighty oath.

Oedipus. Dost thou know thy will?   *Leader.* I know it.   *Oedipus.* Speak
                                                                   it, then.

Leader. When thy friend hath called on the Gods to witness,
   Leave him not shamed, on a charge obscure.

Oedipus. Of this be sure—in seeking this, ye seek
   Exile from Thebes for *me,* or else my death.

Leader. By Him that leadeth the host of Heaven,   *str.* 2.
   The Sun, may I die as a wretch forsaken
   By friends, by Gods, if that thought were mine!
   But my soul is wrung for this land so wasted,
   To think that to all the ills it has suffered,
   From this your dissension, new ills shall cleave.

Oedipus. Then let him go!—though it should seal my death
   Or my dishonoured banishment from Thebes!
   Your prayer it is—so pitiful—that moves me;
   No pleas of his.   On *him,* wherever he comes,
   My hate shall follow.

Creon. As surly in yielding as you are violent,
   When passion sweeps you onward!   To themselves
   Such natures—as is just—prove bitterest.

Oedipus. Leave me and go!   *Creon.* I *will* go; having found
   In *you* but blindness, though *these* know me upright.

Leader. Wilt thou not hasten, lady,   *antistrophe* 1.
      To lead our lord within?

Jocasta. First I would learn what has happened here.

Leader. Mere blind suspicion, of rumour bred,
      And the sting of an unjust charge.

Jocasta. So both provoked it?   *Leader.* Yea.   *Jocasta.* And what the subject?
   Leader. Enough, enough!—when our land so labours.
      I pray, where it ended, let it rest.

Oedipus (to the Leader). You see!   To this you come now, in your prudence,
   Because you sought to dull and blunt my anger.

Leader. Sire, I have said it, and not once only: *ant.* 2.
   I should have shown me a fool insensate,
   Blinded with folly, to leave thee betrayed—
   Pilot that rescued my own loved country,
   Tossing madly beneath the tempest;
   And well mayest save her now again!

Jocasta. For Heaven's sake, my lord, tell *me* as well
     What made you so to steel your heart in anger?

Oedipus. I will.   (For *you* I honour more than these.)
     By Creon's fault.   Such plots he has laid against me.

Jocasta. Say clearly, whence your quarrel?   Why you blame him?

Oedipus. He calls me guilty of King Laïus' murder!

Jocasta. Did he claim to know it?   Or had others told him?

Oedipus. He set a knave prophet on me.   But good care
     He took to keep his own tongue clear of trouble.

Jocasta. Listen to me.   Acquit yourself of blame,
     And learn that no man born has any portion
     In arts prophetic.   Here's my proof—and brief.
     There came an oracle—I will not say
     From Apollo's self, but from his ministers—
     That warned King Laïus his doom would fall
     From his own child, whom *I* should bear to him.
     Now Laïus—so the story goes—was murdered
     By foreign robbers, where three trackways meet.
     As for the child, it had not seen the light
     Three days, before with ankles pinned together
     King Laïus gave it to the hands of others,
     To cast on the trackless hills.
     Therefore Apollo neither brought to pass
     That he should slay his father, nor that Laïus
     Should find that death he dreaded, from his son.
     So surely did those prophets fix the future!
     Regard them not.   Whatever Apollo seeks
     Or claims, with ease He will Himself reveal it.

Oedipus. Wife, at your words what wild and wandering thoughts
     Come over me!—what tumult in my soul!

Jocasta. What ails thee to make such answer?

Oedipus. I seemed to hear you say that Laïus
     Was murdered at a place 'where three tracks met'?

Jocasta. So ran the rumour—and is current still.

Oedipus. And where is the spot at which the crime was done?

Jocasta. Phocis the land is called; those cross-roads lie
     Where meet the tracks from Delphi and Daulia.

Oedipus. And how long time is passed since these things happened?

Jocasta. It was told in Thebes a little while before
     In all men's eyes you were enthroned as king.

Oedipus. O Zeus, what hast Thou planned to do to me?

Jocasta. Why take it, Oedipus, so much to heart?

Oedipus. Do not ask me yet.   But say what Laïus
  Was like in body.   What was his time of life?

Jocasta. He was tall—with hair just showing a touch of silver.
  In build, indeed, not much unlike to *you.*

Oedipus. Ah misery!   It seems as if, unknowing,
  A moment since, I grimly cursed *myself!*

Jocasta. What's this!   My lord!—I shrink to look at you.

Oedipus. Grimly my heart misgives—had yon blind seer
  Eyes?   Tell me one thing more—to make all clearer.

Jocasta. I tremble.   But ask on—and I will say.

Oedipus. Did he travel in little state; or like a king,
  With a great troop of spearmen?

Jocasta. They were five men in all—one was a herald.
  And in a single wain rode Laïus.

Oedipus. Ah, all grows plain!   Who was it, wife, that brought you
  The news of this, to Thebes?

Jocasta. A servant of this house—escaped alone.

Oedipus. Does the man chance to be in the palace now?

Jocasta. Ah no.   When home he came again, and found
  You on the throne of Thebes, and Laïus dead,
  Touching my hand as suppliant, he begged me
  To send him to the fields—to our sheep-pastures,
  As far as might be from the sight of Thebes.
  And so I sent him.   Indeed the man had earned
  (Granted he's but a slave) some greater favour.

Oedipus. Then can you have him quickly summoned here?

Jocasta. It *can* be done.   But why do you give this order?

Oedipus. I fear, good wife, I have spoken far too much;
  And therefore I would see him.

Jocasta. Then he shall come.   But surely I too may learn
  What is this load upon your mind, my lord?

Oedipus. Be sure you shall—since I am fallen so far
  In apprehension.   Whom should I rather tell
  Than thee, in such a crisis of my fortunes?
      My father, then, was Polybus of Corinth;
  My mother, Merope—of Dorian blood.
  And I was counted first of the men of Corinth,
  Until a chance befell, worthy of wonder,
  And yet not worth the heat it raised in me.
  For at a banquet, as the wine went round,
  One overwarm with drinking scoffed at me
  As not my sire's true son.

That weighed on me—yet, for the day, though hardly,
I curbed myself; then on the morrow went
And questioned both my parents.   Fierce their anger
Against the man that had insulted me;
And glad was I to see it.   None the less,
The thing still rankled.   Rumours crept abroad.
And so, unknown to my father and my mother,
I turned my steps to Pytho.   Thence Apollo
Sent me away, my question disregarded,
Yet with a prophecy of other things
Most dread, most grievous, and most miserable—
That I should sleep in my mother's bed, and bring
Before men's sight a brood intolerable,
And be murderer of the father that begot me.
When I heard *that*, I fled to banishment
(Enough, to measure by the distant stars
Where Corinth lay)—seeking some place where never
My eyes should see those evil oracles
Fulfilled in infamy.
Now on my road I reached that very spot,
Where you say the King was murdered.
I will tell you true, Jocasta.   As I came,
Journeying onward, near those three crossways,
There met with me a herald and behind him,
In a wagon drawn by colts, just such a man
As you have told.   The herald there in front
And the old man, his master, had a mind
To thrust me off the track; but when their driver
Pushed me aside, I struck him angrily.
At sight of that, the greybeard in his wagon
Waited until I passed him, then delivered
A blow of his two-forked goad full on my head.
But he paid in full—and over.   In a flash
A buffet from the staff in my right hand
Had rolled him from his car, upon his back.
And so I slew them all.
                                But if this stranger
Had any link with your King Laïus,
What man on earth so miserable as I?
What man could live more loathed in the sight of Heaven
Than I whom none, stranger or citizen,
May speak to, or give welcome at his hearth?—
Nay, all from their doors must hound me.   And myself,

No other, called these curses on myself!
With these hands too, that slew him, I befoul
The bed of him that's slain!   Am I not vile?—
Unclean to all the world?—if banished now
From Thebes, I dare not, even in banishment,
See my own kindred, tread my native soil,
On pain of wedding her that once hath borne me,
And murdering my father—Polybus,
Who got me and who bred me?   Would not one
That judged my fate, say rightly that it came
From a power that knows not pity?
Forbid, forbid, pure majesty of Heaven,
That I should see that day—from mortal eyes
Let me be hid, before I see my life
Smirched with the shame of such calamity.

Leader. Lord, at these things we shudder.   Yet until
   You have heard from that eye-witness, cling to hope.
Oedipus. Of hope, indeed, now this alone is left me—
   To wait the herdsman's coming.
Jocasta. And when he does appear, what would you of him?
Oedipus. This.   If the story that he brings be found
   The same as thine, I have escaped disaster.
Jocasta. What was there in my words so full of weight?
Oedipus. He told, you said, that Laïus met his death
   By '*robbers.*'   Now, if he again affirms,
   It *was* a number, *I* am not the slayer.
   One man could not be taken for a troop.
   But, if he speaks of one lone wayfarer,
   Then plainly the scale of guilt descends on *me*.
Jocasta. Such *was*, indeed, his story—be sure of that.
   Impossible he should retract it now!
   For all the city heard—not only I.
   And even should he quit his former story,
   At least, my lord, he will not show the doom
   Of Laïus fulfilled—since Loxias
   Foretold that he must die by a son of *mine*.
   Yet that poor infant never brought him death,
   But perished first itself.
   Therefore henceforward let me never turn
   My glance aside to the right hand or the left
   For any soothsayer.
Oedipus. Well judged.   But none the less send one to bring
   That hind before me here—do not neglect it!

Jocasta. I will send without delay.   Let us go in.
   There is nothing I would do against your wish!
                    They pass into the palace.

Chorus.   Oh let a life be mine   *strophe* 1.
   In word and deed both reverent and pure—
   True to those Laws whose feet, for ever sure,
      Tread still the heights divine!
   For Heaven alone begot them, to endure—
      Not our mortality
      Had power to bid them be;
   On *them* Oblivion's slumber hath no hold;
   Yea, God is great in them, and grows not old.

   But the Tyrant has his birth   *antistrophe* 1.
   From Insolence, puffed up with vain excess
   Of wealth undue, that cannot come to bless.
      He scales the heights of earth,
   Only to fall where the pit gapes bottomless
      And no foot climbs again.
      Yet let not God restrain
   True men who wrestle but to serve the State.
   Yea, God alone shall guide and guard my fate!

   But the wanton in act or word, who set aside   *str.* 2.
      Justice, and reverence not
      Shrines where the Gods abide—
      Accursed be their lot,
      And punished be their pride!
   They that touch things unclean, and seize,
      Eager for evil gain,
      Upon unsullied sanctities,
   How dare they hope the Gods will yet refrain
      The angry bolts they fling?
   If wickedness be honoured, then in vain
      Our dance, our worshipping!

   No more to Olympia, or to Abae's fane,   *ant.* 2.
      Or the sacred Navel-stone
      Of Earth, will I turn again,
      Until God's word be shown
      True, in all eyes made plain.
   O Zeus, with Thine Almighty power,
      If such indeed be Thine,
      Mark, O Eternal, in this hour

How pass to scorn those prophecies divine
   Of Laïus foretold.
No more through earth Apollo's glories shine;
   Fast fades the faith of old.

Jocasta (*returning from the palace*). Nobles of Thebes, the thought has
   come to me
   That I should seek the temples of the Gods,
   Bearing these suppliant boughs, these gifts of incense.
   Too wildly my husband's heart is whirled away
   By a hundred apprehensions—cannot judge,
   As a wise man should, things present by things past;
   But now is swayed in turn by each new speaker
   Whose tongue is full of terrors.
   Therefore, since all I counsel profits nothing,
   To Thee, Lycēan Apollo, now I come
   (For nearest Thou, to aid us) offering
   These supplications, that Thou mayest grant us
   Redemption from defilement.
   For now we all are shaken, as men that see
   The pilot of their vessel panic-struck.

                             [*A messenger enters.*

Messenger. Can ye tell me, strangers,
   Where stands the palace of King Oedipus?
   Or better—if ye know—where is the King?

Leader. Here it is, stranger—and our lord's within.
   This is his Queen, the mother of his children.

Messenger. God keep her happy, in a happy home,
   As his blest wife and consort!

Jocasta. God bless you likewise, stranger—you deserve it,
   Whose tongue is so fair-spoken.   Say what brings you—
   What news you have to tell?

Messenger. Good tidings, lady, both for home and husband.

Jocasta. And what are *they*?   Who sent you?

Messenger. I come from Corinth.   What I have to tell,
   Sure, will bring gladness—maybe, sorrow too.

Jocasta. What is it, then?—this good so blent with ill?

Messenger. The men of the Isthmian land (so it was said there)
   Will choose your lord their king.

Jocasta. How!   Is old Polybus no more their ruler?

Messenger. No more.   For now Death holds him in the tomb.

Jocasta. What?   He is *dead*?—the sire of Oedipus?

Messenger. Let me die myself, if I do not speak the truth.

Jocasta (*to one of her attendants*). Go, girl, and tell your master this at once.
Oracles of the Gods, where are ye now!
This was the man whom Oedipus so feared
To kill, that he fled to exile. Now he's dead—
By the mere hand of chance, not by his son.

Oedipus (*entering*). What is it, wife? Jocasta, dearest heart,
Why have you called me?

Jocasta. Hark to this man; and, hearing, think what now
Becomes of Apollo's solemn oracles.

Oedipus. Who *is* he, then? And what has he to tell me?

Jocasta. He comes from Corinth, bringing news your father,
Polybus, lives no longer. He is dead.

Oedipus. What, stranger! From your own lips let me hear it.

Messenger. If you would have me, first, confirm my message,
Take it for certain he is dead and gone.

Oedipus. How! By a plot? Or visited by sickness?

Messenger. A little tilt of the scale brings old men rest.

Oedipus. Poor soul! It was by sickness, then, he died?

Messenger. Yes, coupled with the long tale of his years.

Oedipus. How strange! Why then, good wife, should any man
Henceforth regard the Pythian hearth prophetic,
Or birds that scream from Heaven?—by whom we knew
I was doomed to kill my father! There he lies,
Dead, with the earth to hide him; and here am I
That have not lifted weapon—unless perhaps
It was longing for *me* that killed him? So, indeed,
I *should* have brought his death. No matter!—now
Polybus lies in Hades, and thither *with* him
Has swept these prophecies concerning me—
Mere things of naught!

Jocasta. Did I not say, long since, it would be so?

Oedipus. You did. But *I* was blinded by my terrors.

Jocasta. Then give these matters never another thought.

Oedipus. How should I not still dread to wive my mother?

Jocasta. What use is fear, when all man's days are ruled
By Luck; and there is nothing he can know
With sure foreknowledge?
Best to take life at random, as one may.
Cease from your fears of wedding her that bore you.
In dreams, likewise, many a man ere now
Lay with his mother. But he lives easiest
Who takes no thought for all such fantasies.

Oedipus. All this would be most excellently said,

Were not my mother living.   Since she lives,
Well though you speak, I cannot choose but shudder.

Jocasta. Yet your father's death is still a great light to cheer you.

Oedipus. Great; that I know.   But *I* fear her that's living.

Messenger. Who is this woman causes you such dread?

Oedipus. Merope, stranger, wife of Polybus.

Messenger. And what is there in *her* that leaves you troubled?

Oedipus. Old sir, a most dread oracle from God.

Messenger. May it be spoken?   Or must no man know?

Oedipus. Surely!   The voice of Loxias foretold me
I should lie beside my mother, and these hands
Should shed my father's blood.
Therefore, these many years, I left my home
In Corinth far behind me.   Well I prospered:
Yet parents' faces are the best to see.

Messenger. And was your exile just for fear of that?

Oedipus. For dread of her, old man, and my father's blood.

Messenger. Why, then, my lord (since I am come to serve you),
Should I not rid you of all your fears at once?

Oedipus. You would earn, be sure, such thanks as you deserve.

Messenger. My greatest hope, I own, in coming here,
Was your good will when you return to Corinth.

Oedipus. Never will *I* go where my parents are!

Messenger. It is clear, my son, that you know not what you do—

Oedipus. What do you mean, old man?   In God's name, speak!

Messenger.—if this is all that holds you from your home.

Oedipus. Yes—terror that Phoebus' word may yet come true.

Messenger. Lest you sin against your parents?

Oedipus. Yes, *that*, old sir!   That horror never leaves me.

Messenger. Do you know that all these fears of yours are idle?

Oedipus. How?   When they *are* my parents; I, their son?

Messenger. But Polybus was not your kin at all!

Oedipus. What's this you say!   Did he not give me life?

Messenger. As much as I that stand here—and no more.

Oedipus. A stranger as close in blood as my own father!

Messenger. Nor he, nor I begot you.

Oedipus. Why did he give me, then, the name of son?

Messenger. From *my* hands, once, he had you—as a gift.

Oedipus. From another's hands!—how could he love me so?

Messenger. His heart was moved by his long childlessness.

Oedipus. Had you bought this child you gave?—or was I *yours*?

Messenger. I had found you in Cithaeron's forest glens.

Oedipus. What errand took you *there*?

Messenger. Watching my sheep among the mountain pastures.

Oedipus. So *you* were a shepherd then, a vagrant hireling?

Messenger. Hireling—and yet your saviour, son, that day.

Oedipus. What was the plight, then, that you saved me from?

Messenger. You had better ask your ankles witness that.

Oedipus. Ah why remind me of old unhappiness?

Messenger. Yes, I unbound your feet, close-pinned together.

Oedipus. So basely dishonoured from my swaddling-bands!

Messenger. From that mischance your very name was given.

Oedipus. God! By my father? By my mother? Say!

Messenger. I know not. *He* knows more, from whom I had you.

Oedipus. You had me from another? You did not find me?

Messenger. No, I received you from another shepherd.

Oedipus. Who *was* he? Can you say?

Messenger. I think they called him 'one of Laïus' men.'

Oedipus. That Laïus who was once the King of Thebes?

Messenger. Ay, to be sure. *He* was this herdsman's master.

Oedipus. And is the man alive, for me to see him?

Messenger. You that live *here* can better say than I.

Oedipus. Is there any man among you here, that knows
    This shepherd whom he speaks of?—
    Has seen him in the country? Or in Thebes?
    Answer! High time these things should stand revealed.

Leader. I think the man must be the very same
    As you sent for from the fields. But this our lady,
    Jocasta here, might know as well as any.

Oedipus. Good wife, you remember him we summoned here
    A moment since—is that the man he means?

Jocasta. What matter whom he means? Give it no thought.
    Waste no remembrance on this idle chatter.

Oedipus. Impossible!—now I have found these traces,
    I will not stay till I reveal my birth.

Jocasta. In Heaven's name, if you care for your own life,
    Inquire no further. My own pain's enough.

Oedipus. Courage! Were *I* thrice bondman—born of women
    Enslaved three generations—it shames not *thee.*

Jocasta. And yet I beg you! Hear me! Do not do it!

Oedipus. I will not hear of leaving *this* uncertain.

Jocasta. Yet for your sake I speak—for your own good.

Oedipus. This talk of 'my own good'—I am tired of it!

Jocasta. May you never know, unhappy, who you are!

Oedipus. Go someone, bring that shepherd here before me.
    Leave her to glory in *her* rich ancestors!

Jocasta. Ah wretched, wretched! I have no other name
   To give thee now—no other evermore.   [*She rushes out.*
Leader. Why has the Queen rushed from us, Oedipus,
   So wild with sorrow? Ah, my heart misgives me,
   Out of that silence will some tempest break?
Oedipus. Let break what will! I will persist to know
   What seed I sprang from, howsoever little.
   But she, maybe (she is haughty, for a woman),
   Blushes before the baseness of my birth.
   Yet I, who count myself the child of Fortune,
   That kindly giver, shall not be dishonoured:
   She is my mother. And her months, my kinsmen,
   Have made me grow, now lesser, and now great.
   Being such by birth, I will not change my nature,
   Nor fear to search the secret of my race.

strophe.

Chorus. If mine be the gift of a prophet, and truth in the words I sing,
      Then, by yon Heaven's height,
      Cithaeron, thou shalt hear to-morrow night,
   As the full moon's splendour rises, thine own name proudly ring.
      For Oedipus shall hail thy hill:
   'Mother and nurse'; while gay we dance, for the peak that hath pleased
      our king.
   Ah glorious Apollo, be such indeed Thy will!

antistrophe.

   Was a long-lived Nymph thy mother, by Pan embraced, my son,
      As He roved the hills above?
      Or did some Oread bear thee, won in love
   By Loxias (who wanders where the upland pastures run)
      Or the Lord of Cyllene's wild?
   Or did one of His old-time playmates, the Nymphs of Helicon,
   Gladden the mountain Bacchus with *thee,* his new-found child?

The herdsman is brought in.

Oedipus. That shepherd, elders, whom we sought so long
   (If I may guess, who never saw his face),
   Is coming now. For in his length of years
   He matches this Corinthian. And besides
   I recognize my servants leading him.
   But you, perhaps, that have seen the man before,
   May better judge than I.
Leader. To be sure, I know him. Laïus had no servant
   (For a poor shepherd) trustier than he.

Oedipus. You first, Corinthian stranger.   Is this man
    The one you spoke of?   *Messenger.* Ay, the man before you.
Oedipus. And you, old fellow, face me now and answer
    All that I ask.   Did you serve King Laïus?
Herdsman. Ay!   As no bondsman bought—his own house bred me.
Oedipus. And what was the work you did?   Your way of life?
Herdsman. The most part of my life I kept his sheep.
Oedipus. And which were the pastures that you haunted most?
Herdsman. There was Cithaeron.   There were places round.
Oedipus. Can you remember meeting there this man?
Herdsman. Meet him doing what?   What man is it you mean?
Oedipus. The one that's here.   You remember dealings with him?
Herdsman. Not that I can recall it—out of hand.
Messenger. No wonder, sire.   But though he does not know me,
    I'll soon remind him.   Well I know he knows
    Those times that we ranged together round Cithaeron,
    He with two flocks; and I, close by, with one—
    Three full half-years, from spring to Arcturus' rising.
    When winter came, I would move down again
    To my own steading, and he to Laïus'.
    Am I talking truth or not?
Herdsman. 'Tis true enough; though a great while ago.
Messenger. Now say, can you remember giving me
    A child, to rear it as my fosterling?
Herdsman. What's this!   What makes thee ask me such a question?
Messenger. Because, good friend, here stands that very child.
Herdsman. A plague upon thee!   Canst not hold thy tongue?
Oedipus. Come now, old fellow, no rebuking him!
    Your own words need rebuke, far more than his.
Herdsman. Ah best of masters, how am *I* to blame?
Oedipus. Not answering what he asks.   About the child.
Herdsman. He talks in ignorance—mere trouble wasted!
Oedipus. Not speak to please me!   You shall speak for pain!
Herdsman. Do not—in God's name—do an old man harm!
Oedipus. Quick!   Will not someone bind his hands behind him?
Herdsman. Poor wretch that I am, for what?   What would you learn?
Oedipus. Did *you* give *him* this child he asks about?
Herdsman. I did.   And would God I had died that very day!
Oedipus. You shall come to that, unless you speak the truth.
Herdsman. And if I tell it, to a ruin far worse!
Oedipus. The fellow still seems trying to delay.
Herdsman. No, sire—I said long since, I gave the child.
Oedipus. Whence had it come?   From *your* home—or another's?

Herdsman. It was not mine—another gave it me.

Oedipus. What man in Thebes? From whose house had it come?

Herdsman. Master, for Heaven's sake, ask me no more!

Oedipus. If I must ask again, you die for it!

Herdsman. It was a child, then, from the House of Laïus.

Oedipus. A slave? Or born of the king's own royal race?

Herdsman. Ah, now I am near to speak that fearful thing!

Oedipus. And I to hear it. Yet it must be heard.

Herdsman. The child was called the king's. But all the truth
　　Could best be spoken by thy wife within.

Oedipus. Was it she that gave the child?　*Herdsman.* Herself, O King.

Oedipus. And for what purpose?　*Herdsman.* That I should destroy it.

Oedipus. Her *child*, wretched woman!　*Herdsman.* In dread of ills foretold.

Oedipus. And what were *they*?　*Herdsman.* That he should slay his father.

Oedipus. Why did you give it, then, to this old man?

Herdsman. In pity, master. I thought that he would take it
　　Far off to the country whence he came; but he
　　Saved it—for grief untold. For if thou *art*
　　The man he says—thou wast born indeed to sorrow!

Oedipus. Oh, oh! Now all's accomplished—all is clear.
　　Light of this day, let me look my last on thee!
　　Since now I stand revealed—curst in my birth,
　　Curst in my wedlock, curst in the blood I shed.

　　　　　He rushes into the palace. Herdsman and Messenger go out.

Chorus. Ah mortal generations,   *strophe* 1.
　　What things of naught your lives were born to be!
　　　　What man among your nations
　　　　Can find felicity?
　　　　Its shadow—that is all,
　　　　So swift to fade and fall!
　　　　Watching how *thy* days ran,
　　Sad Oedipus, I see it—and 'blest' henceforth I call
　　　　No child of man.

　　　　His skill once, like a master,   *antistrophe* 1.
　　Hit full the mark—won bliss without a flaw.
　　　　Yon singer of disaster,
　　　　Maid's face and crooked claw,
　　　　He slew. In our darkest hour
　　　　For Thebes he rose a tower.
　　　　So, from that day, we owned
　　Him for our lord and ruler—yea, here in Thebes the great
　　　　He sat enthroned.

But *now*—what man was heard of, more accurst?—   *str.* 2.
   With savage sorrows doomed to dwell,
Life's happiest transformed to worst!
     Ah thou whose fame men tell,
     Great Oedipus, when fate
     Harboured thy love, as well,
In that same bed where lay thy sire of late,
How could that field where once thy father ploughed,
Endure thee too so long, yet never cry aloud?

Despite thee, Time all-seeing hath tracked thy life   *ant.* 2.
   And judged thee; wed, yet wedded not,
In bonds where a mother turned to wife!
     Ah thou whom Laïus got,
     Would God, would God, mine eyes
     Had never seen thy lot!
Wail thee I must; as men wail one that lies
Dead on his bier.   For truly *thy* hand gave
Life to us once; but now—a darkness like the grave!

A servant of Oedipus appears from the palace.

Servant. Ever most honoured nobles of this land,
   What must ye hear!—what must ye see!—what sorrow
   Must load your hearts now, if like loyal kinsmen
   Ye care still for the House of Labdacus!
   Not all the waves of Phasis or of Ister
   Could cleanse, I think, this house of all the horrors
   It hides within, or soon shall bring to light—
   Deeds, not unwilled, but wilful!   Worst to bear
   Are griefs we see to be of our own choosing.
Leader. Anguish enough in what we knew already;
   What more to tell?
Servant. This, first, is soonest uttered, soonest heard—
   The royal Jocasta's dead.
Leader.   Poor Queen!   And how?
Servant. By her own hand.   Ye have been spared the worst,
   Ye have not seen it.   Yet hear now from *me*,
   So far as my memory serves, what she has suffered.
   When she had passed, in her agony of passion,
   Within the palace-hall,
   She ran, with both hands rending at her hair,
   Straight for her marriage-chamber, and flung to

Its doors behind her, shrieking out the name
Of 'Laïus,' that died those years ago—
Calling to memory that night long since,
When he got the son by whom he was to die,
Leaving herself to bear unhallowed children
To his own child; bemoaning that bed ill-starred
Where she had twofold issue—by her husband
Bearing a husband, sons by her own son.
But, after, how she died, I cannot say;
For on us, shouting, now burst Oedipus
And drew our eyes away from her misery
To watch him dashing madly to and fro,
Calling to us the while to bring a sword—
Where should he find that wife who was no wife,
That mother who had borne a double brood—
Himself and then his children?
    Then, though no man that stood there gave him aid,
Some unseen power yet led him in his frenzy;
For as if his steps were guided, with a cry
Most terrible, he sprang at the double doors,
And forced the bending bolts from out their staples,
And burst within the room.   But there we saw,
Hanged by the neck, in a twisted halter swinging,
The body of the Queen.
At sight of that, a fearful groan broke from him—
He loosed the cord and laid upon the floor
Her piteous body.   Then a grisly thing!
He tore from her dress the brooches of beaten gold,
That had adorned her—raised them high in air
And plunged them in his eyes to the very socket,
Crying: 'No more shall ye behold the horrors
I have suffered and have done.   Henceforth be darkened,
Eyes that saw whom ye should not—failed in knowledge
Of those I had longed to know!'
    And crying out that curse, with hands uplifted
Again and yet again he stabbed his eyes;
And as he struck, out of the wounded sockets
There streamed across his face, no tardy trickle,
But blood dark-gushing like a pelting storm.
So on these two, from what they did, hath burst
Calamity—alike for wife and husband.
All their old happiness in bygone years
Was happiness indeed—yet turns to-day

To lamentation, ruin, death, dishonour!
No grief that can be named, but it is theirs.

Leader. And has his wretchedness found respite now?

Servant. He shouts to unbar the palace-gates—lay bare
Before all Thebes the murderer of his father,
His mother's—word unspeakable, unholy!—
As one resolved to fling himself to exile,
Not make his house accurst with all the curses
Himself called down from Heaven.   Yet he lacks
The strength to do it, or a guide to lead him,
Stricken beyond endurance.
Yourself shall see it.   Look, the palace-doors
Are opening—now behold a spectacle
That even loathing must find pitiful.

The blinded Oedipus is led forth by attendants.

Leader. Oh horror too hateful for human sight,
Most hideous that these eyes of mine
Have looked on ever!   Unhappy wretch,
What madness took thee?   What power of evil
Sprang with a leap beyond all limits
On thy doomed life?
Alas, alas!
To look on thee—I cannot bear it,
Though longing to question, longing to hear thee,
Longing to see.
Thou art too horrible!

Oedipus. Oh bitterness!
Whither now do my feet go stumbling?
Whither flutter the words I speak?
O Fate, how far thou hast sprung!

Leader. Yea, to an end too dire for eye or ear.

Oedipus. Oh cloud of blackness,   *strophe* 1.
    Curse irresistible, horror unspeakable,
    Blown on the wind of my fate!
Woe!   Woe again!—the stab of double anguish—
The points that pierce, the pangs of memory.

Leader. Poor sufferer, small wonder if at once
Thine is a twofold pain, of flesh and spirit.

Oedipus. O friend that I loved,   *antistrophe* 1.
    Thou, at the least, hast not left me forsaken;
    For the blind thou carest still.

Ay me, I know thee clearly at my side,
I hear thy voice, though darkness now is mine.
Leader. Man of dread deeds, how couldst thou, then, endure
　To quench thy vision? Urged by what unseen power?
Oedipus. It was Apollo, my friends, Apollo,   *str.* 2.
　That made me suffer this misery;
　But my eyes were stricken by myself alone.
　What need had I to see,
　For whom life kept no sight of sweetness more?
Leader. As thou sayest, so it was.
Oedipus. What now can I look on,
　What can I love, my friends? Whose greeting
　Can give me gladness now?
　Take me away, then, swiftly, swiftly—
　Take me away—a thing of perdition,
　A thing accursed, of all men living
　By Heaven most abhorred!
Leader. Unhappy in thy fate; unhappy, too,
　In thy clear vision—would God I had never seen thee!
Oedipus. Curst be whoever it was delivered   *ant.* 2.
　My feet on the hills from their cruel fetters,
　Saved me and gave that thankless gift of life!
　Would I had died, and spared
　That agony of my loved ones, and my own!
Leader. As thou sayest, would it were!
Oedipus. Then had I never
　　Slain my own father—been called the husband
　　Of her that gave me birth.
　　Now, shamed in my parents, of God forsaken,
　　I have shared in the bed that saw me begotten.
　　If there be sorrow surpassing all sorrows,
　　Fate now hath made it mine.
Leader. Yet I cannot count well done what thou hast done—
　Better for thee than blindness had been death.
Oedipus. Ah cease advising me!—tell me not now
　That what I did was not the best to do.
　For, had I sight, I know not with what eyes
　I could have faced, there in the House of Death,
　My father, my hapless mother—having sinned
　Such sins against them as no strangling halter
　Could ever expiate.
　Yes, and my children—born as they were born,

Were *they* so lovely a sight to look upon?
Far let them be for ever from these eyes!
Nor would I see this city, nor her towers,
Her holy carven Gods—from all these things
I that was born of the noblest blood in Thebes
Have now cut off my wretched self, commanding
All men to ban that godless one whom God
Has shown defiled—the seed of Laïus!
Could I, that have revealed such guilt my own,
Look in the face of Thebans?
Never!   Could I but know some means to quench
The fount of hearing, too, within these ears,
I had not spared to shut quite from the world
This flesh of misery—blind—hearing nothing.
Well lives the soul that's fenced away from sorrow.
Alas, Cithaeron, why didst thou give me shelter?—
Not slay me that first night, that I had never
Shown forth to men the mystery of my birth?
Ah Polybus!   Ah Corinth!—ancient home
Of those miscalled my fathers, what a thing
Was *I* for you to breed!   A fair outside;
Within, all festering!   Behold me now
The cursed offspring of a cursed race.
Ah three tracks winding through that hidden glen,
Where led my own path, narrowing through the wood,
To those crossways that drank from my father's veins
His blood—that was my own—from my own hands!
Do you still remember what ye saw me do?
And what I did thereafter, here in Thebes?
Ah fatal wedlock, that once gave me life
And, from that life thou gavest, reared new seed,
Mingling before the world all ties of kinship,
Father, child, brother—bride and wife and mother—
Every defilement that man's race can know!
But foul it is, even to speak of things
So foul to do!   Now, in the name of Heaven,
Hide me somewhere beyond the bounds of Thebes—
Or kill me—or fling me in the gulfs of sea,
Beyond your sight for ever!
Come, grant my prayer—do not disdain to touch
My wretchedness.   Nor fear it.   Such my sorrows,
The load of them can light on none but me.
Leader. See now, to meet your need, with act or counsel,

Here Creon comes.   For he alone is left,
In place of you, as guardian of Thebes.
Oedipus. Alas, and what can *I* say now to him?
Why should he give me hearing, who am proved
To have dealt him mere injustice?
Creon (entering). I am not come to mock you, Oedipus,
Nor to reproach you with your former harshness.
(*To the attendants of Oedipus.*) But *you*—if you feel no shame before the
gaze
Of human eyes—at least let reverence
For yon all-nurturing splendour of the sun
Forbid you to leave exposed, in nakedness,
A pollution so unclean that its mere presence
Is more than earth, or daylight can endure,
Or the pure rain of Heaven.
Take him within the palace—and take him quickly.
For piety demands his kin alone
Should see and hear these ills that curse their kinsman.
Oedipus. By Heaven, since now you have belied my fears
And come in noblest spirit to me most vile,
Hear me.   I speak for *your* sake, not my own.
Creon. And what, then, would you ask for?
Oedipus. Cast me from Thebes, with all the speed ye may—
Far from the speech, far from the sight of man.
Creon. Be sure I would have done so; but I wished
First to consult Apollo.
Oedipus. But Apollo has revealed His will already—
Bids ye destroy me, wretch and parricide.
Creon. Such *was* His word.   Yet in this plight of Thebes
Better that we make sure what *is* our duty.
Oedipus. Question the God about one vile as I!
Creon. Yes, even you will hardly doubt Him now.
Oedipus. But Creon, I adjure you and beseech you,
Give such last rites as you yourself find fitting
To her that lies within.   She is your kin;
And yours the duty.
But as for me, let none condemn this city,
My father's Thebes, to bear my living presence—
Leave me among the mountains, where Cithaeron
Is linked with my name for ever.   There it was
My parents, when they lived, assigned my grave;
There let me die, according to their will
That sought to doom me then—yet well I see

No sickness, no mischance, had power upon me;
Who could never have escaped, had I not been
Reserved for some doom portentous.
But let my own fate drive to what end it will!
Yet my children, Creon?—I ask not that my sons
Should cause you care. (As men, they cannot lack,
Wherever their feet may come, for livelihood.)
But my two unhappy daughters, who once shared
My table, next beside me—ever took
Their share of all I tasted—care for *them*!
Now, above all, let me lay my hands upon them
And weep my heart out. Grant it me, noble prince,
Most noble from thy birth!
For if I could but feel them with my hands,
They would seem mine again; as when I saw.
What now! [*Attendants lead in the young girls, Antigone and Ismēne.*
Ah God, do I not hear my darlings weeping?
Has Creon been so pitiful—to send
The best loved of my children? Can it be?

Creon. It is. I saw to this. For well I knew
What joy, as in old days, it would give you now.

Oedipus. May Heaven reward you! Yes, for bringing them,
May a kindlier power watch over you than me!
Children, where are you? Come now, ah come nearer,
Come to these hands of mine—a brother's hands;
That now have left the light of your father's eyes
Thus, as you see, in darkness. For all unseeing,
And all unknowing, I became your father
By her that gave me life. For you no less
I weep, though I cannot see—too well foreseeing
The bitter future men will make you live.
How can ye come to gatherings in Thebes,
Or festivals, and not turn homeward weeping,
With grief instead of gladness? And when you ripen
To years of wedlock, where's the man shall dare
To wed your shame, my daughters—shame that falls
As ruinous on your children as on mine?
For indeed what curse is spared us?
Your father slew his father, sowed.new life
In her whence he had sprung, begetting you
In the same womb that bore him. Such reproach
Will be hurled at you, poor children—who shall wed ye?
None!—ye must wither in barren maidenhood.

Ah son of Menoeceus, you alone are left
Their father; since we, their parents, both are lost.
Let them not wander beggared and unmarried,
Nor leave them curst as I—they *are* your kin.
Pity them, seeing their youth deserted so—
Except for thee!　Promise me, noble heart,
With thy hand upon it.　Much advice, my children,
I would have given, could you understand it;
But, being so young, I would have you pray but this—
Always to live where measure is, and find
A happier fortune than your father did.

Creon. Now enough of tears and weeping!　Get thee back within thy hall.

Oedipus. Yield I must, however bitter.　*Creon.* Measure still is best in all.

Oedipus. Yet I *would* make one condition.　*Creon.* Say it—that I may decide.

Oedipus. Send me forth from Thebes to exile.　*Creon.* Ask not *me.*　The God must guide.

Oedipus. Yet the Gods hold me most hateful.　*Creon.* Then thou soon shalt have thy will.

Oedipus. So you promise?　*Creon.* *Any* promise, once I give it, I fulfil.

Oedipus. Then, at last, lead me away.　*Creon.* Let go thy children.　Pass the door.

Oedipus. Ah, not these—take *them* not from me!　*Creon.* Nay, you must play king no more.
Once in all things you were master.　But it has not lasted thus.

　　　　Creon, Oedipus, attendants, and children move towards the palace.

Leader. Dwellers here in Thebes our city, fix your eyes on Oedipus.
Once he guessed the famous riddle, once our land knew none so great—
Which among the sons of Cadmus envied not his high estate?
Now behold how deep above him there hath rolled the surge of doom.
So with every child of mortal.　Till man lies within his tomb,
Never dare to call him 'happy'—wait until your eyes shall see
That beyond life's bourne he travels, touched by no calamity.

ELECTRA
(c. 418–410)

Now fall the height of Heaven in headlong ruin above me,
Where it hangs its brazen menace above the heads of men,
If I give not love and helping to all the hearts that love me,
And to all that hate I give not havoc and hate again!

Theognis.

We possess plays by all three dramatists on Orestes' murder of his mother. For Aeschylus, the moralist, it became a theme of crime and punishment; for Euripides, the intellectual humanist, a lesson of the utter foulness of brutal vendetta and lying gods. Sophocles, more detached, chose to make it, not a problem-play, but a picture of vivid characters in vivid action—like, not *Hamlet*, but the original story of *Hamlet*; or like that other picture of a successful palace-conspiracy, Racine's *Athalie*. He uses all his skill to create suspense, surprise, sudden reversals of situation, subtle elaborations of irony; and to portray a heroic girl—like Antigone, loyal at all costs to father and brother. The play is not *Orestes*, but *Electra*. Unfortunately, unlike Antigone, Electra is vehement not only with love, but with hate. At times she herself feels warped; but less, I think, than some critics have wished to believe.

The play begins with the entrance of three travellers before the palace at Mycenae—the young Orestes; his old tutor, who once carried him as a child to safety in Phocis; and his friend Pýlades. Orestes now gives his orders for the 'righteous bloodshed' Apollo has commanded. First the old tutor will announce in the palace that Orestes has perished in a chariot-race. Then Orestes and Pýlades will follow, with seemingly independent confirmation—the very funeral-urn supposed to hold the dead prince's ashes. The three go out; and their place is taken by the faithful Electra, dreaming always of her brother's return, but now almost in despair. The friendly Chorus, fifteen women of Mycenae, urge her to resignation. Then her gentler sister, Chrysóthemis, enters with offerings which Clytemnestra, dismayed by a dream, is sending to Agamemnon's tomb. Electra persuades her sister at least to pray instead for Orestes and vengeance.

Next, a bitter altercation between Electra and Clytemnestra herself, who vainly tries to defend her crime against her contemptuous daughter. But now a new turn of fortune—the old tutor appears with an elaborate story of the chariot-race where Orestes died. Clytemnestra, shocked for a moment, grows exultant; Electra is overwhelmed.

Then the dramatist brings a new change of mood. Chrysóthemis
returns excited from the tomb—she has found it honoured with a tress of
hair, offerings, and flowers. By Orestes? But Electra breaks the bitter
truth—he is dead! And in her despair, like Antigone, she urges her sister
to join her in doing their duty alone. Girls though they are, let *them* kill
Aegisthus.[1] Chrysóthemis is afraid? Then Electra will do it alone.
And now the disguised Orestes and Pýlades bring in the funeral-urn, over
which Electra pours out her heart in the most famous speech in the play.
(The well-known actor Polus, we are told, when playing this part, once
used an urn with the real ashes of his own newly dead son—a curious, but
hardly, I feel, very admirable source of inspiration.)

As in *Ajax* and *Oedipus* Sophocles introduced a scene of radiant hope
just before the final darkness falls, so here he blackens the despair just before
the sunrise of new hope.

> O last memorial of my best beloved,
> All that is left me of Orestes now!
> Ah, what a different homecoming is this
> From the brave hopes with which I sent thee forth!
> I sent thee forth, my brother, bright with promise:
> Now thou art naught—frail dust within these hands.
> Would I had died before the day I stole thee
> In secret from thy murderers, and conveyed
> Far off to safety in a foreign land!—
> For then thou too hadst perished on that day
> And found thy portion in thy father's tomb!
> But now an evil doom hath ended thee,
> A stranger and an exile far from home,
> Far from thy sister's side!
> These loving hands bathed not thy poor cold limbs
> In last sad service, nor from the funeral flame
> Lifted thy ashes, as a sister should.
> Nay, strangers mourned thee, brother—thou comest home
> Light dust and little, in a little urn.
> Woe for the care wherewith I cherished thee,
> And all in vain!—labour of many days,
> That yet I loved—for thou wast never dearer
> To thine own mother than thou wast to me.
> There was none nursed thee in our house but I,
> To thee I was ever 'sister.'

[1] Note that Electra does not say a word of killing Clytemnestra, though it would be
easier and though she encourages Orestes to it. Presumably Sophocles here too did
not wish to stress too much the matricide.

But now, with this thy death, a single day
Has ended all—thou hast torn *all* from me,
Like a whirlwind in its passing, at one sweep.
Dead is our father; dead am I to thee;
Thyself art gone to death—my enemies
Laugh, and our mother, with no mother's heart,
Grows frenzied with rejoicing.   Oft in secret
Thou didst send word that *one* day thou wouldst come
To punish her; but now thy evil genius,
And mine, has killed our hope and brought thee *thus*,
In place of all I loved—
A strengthless phantom and a pinch of dust.
Oh transformation all too pitiful!
Woe, woe, woe!
This bitter homecoming has broke my heart,
Broken my heart, my brother.
Let me come join thee in thy narrow room,
And dwell beside thee in the House of Death,
Dust with thy dust for ever.   All thy life
We shared alike in all things—let me die
And come as thy companion to the tomb!
For I see that sorrow does not vex the dead.

(1126–70.)

Now Orestes reveals himself; the old tutor warningly interrupts the
ecstasies of brother and sister reunited; and the drama rushes to its close.
The slayers enter the palace.   We hear the shrieks of Clytemnestra for
mercy, answered from without by her ruthless young daughter:

Thou didst not spare thy son!—nor yet his father! . . .
Strike her, if thou hast strength, a second time!

(1411–15.)

For Sophocles, however, the climax, very significantly, is not the matricide; he lavishes his most pointed tragic irony on the more difficult killing
of Aegisthus, who now enters in his turn.

Aegisthus. Which of you knows where are these Phocian strangers,
Arrived, they say, with tidings of Orestes
Dead in the wreckage of his chariot.
(*To Electra.*) Thee I ask, thee!—yes, thee, so insolent
In days gone by.   This touches *thee* most nearly,
I well believe; and most *thou* knowest of it.
Electra. Indeed I know.   Could I take so little part
In the fortunes of my nearest and my dearest?

Aegisthus. Where are these strangers, then? Out with it quickly!

Electra. Within. They have touched their hostess to the heart.

Aegisthus. Then it is *true*? They bring news of his death?

Electra. Not only news. They have brought himself as well.

Aegisthus. Orestes' self, for my own eyes to see?

Electra. Ay, he is here. And yet a grisly sight.

Aegisthus. For once thou bringst me joy! 'Tis little like thee.

Electra. I wish thee joy—if joy it brings indeed.

Aegisthus. Silence, I say! Throw wide our palace-doors
For Argos and Mycenae to behold;
So that if any lived on idle hopes
Of this Orestes, they may see him dead,
And bow them to my curb, and court no more
My righteous wrath, perforce to teach them wisdom.

Electra. I do my part. For time has taught *me* wisdom.
I take my stand now with the mightier.

> *The palace opens, revealing the disguised Orestes and Pýlades
> beside Clytemnestra's shrouded body on a bier. Aegisthus goes
> up to it.*

Aegisthus. O Zeus, I see a doom that hath not fallen
Save by Thy jealous hand. Yet if there be
Offence in this I say, be all unsaid.
Lift back the face-cloth from the face that I,
For kinship's sake, may pay my due of mourning.

Orestes. Lift it thyself. It is for thee, not me,
To see what lies there, and to call it dear.

Aegisthus. Thou sayest well. I will. (*To Electra.*) But, quickly, go,
Call Clytemnestra, if she is within.

Orestes. She is beside thee. Seek her nowhere else.

Aegisthus (*lifting the face-cloth*). God, what is this!

Orestes. Afraid? Is that face so strange?

Aegisthus. Ah, bitter! What men are these? Into whose net
Have I now fallen?

Orestes. Still so slow to see
That those thou miscallest dead, are yet alive?

Aegisthus. Alas, I read thy meaning. This can be
None other speaking than Orestes' self.

Orestes. So wise a seer, and yet so long deceived!

Aegisthus. O wretched, I am ruined! Yet suffer me
But one word more.

Electra. By Heaven, no, my brother!
Suffer him not to spin out time with words.
For when man's life is caught in misery,

What profit in a brief respite from death?
Slay him at once!—and cast him, slain, to find
Such burial as he should, in ravening mouths,
Out of my sight.   This only can atone
For all my many years of wretchedness.
           Orestes leads Aegisthus within the palace to his doom.

                                                    (1442–90.)

It remains curious that Sophocles, who so stressed the horror of marrying a mother, even in ignorance, should take so calmly the deliberate murdering of one; even though Clytemnestra was herself an adulteress and murderess, whom her son, saved from her in childhood, could not know by sight. Some of Sophocles' critics are horrified; perhaps with a touch of exaggeration. After all, our ancestors admired Abraham for preparing to murder his own child, likewise at God's command; Rome respected stern fathers, like the elder Brutus, who executed their own sons, commanded only by an iron sense of duty; even to-day, it is said, there is honoured with a tomb in the Kremlin wall a village-boy who denounced his own father and was murdered for it by understandably outraged relatives.   All these are hateful; but all cold-blooded taking of life is hateful; does a physical blood-tie make it so much worse?   I suppose Sophocles might have answered: 'I took the fierce old saga as I found it, and tried to make it live.   The story says it was God's will.   I was not writing a thesis, but a play.'

All the same there remains about *Electra*, I feel, a certain insensitiveness which jars.   But this is not mended by arguing, like some critics, that Sophocles meant us to take Orestes as an unpleasant youth, the old tutor as a hoary corrupter, Electra as a girl wrecked by hatred, and the murder as a ghastly crime.   They do it from genuine admiration for their author; but truth is more than Sophocles.   If he meant all this, why on earth did he not say so?   It would have been so easy.   Why did he take for his climax, not the awful matricide, but the killing of Aegisthus?   Any Greek audience must have felt itself expected to sympathize, as in Aeschylus, with Orestes and Electra, and to regard the end as we regard the end of *Macbeth*—with a sense of guilt punished and of justice done.

Electra is an exciting, well-made play, for the stage rather than the study. And of well-made plays it is usually unwise to demand too many other qualities.

PHILOCTĒTES
(409 B.C.)

Feare not my truth; the morrall of my wit
Is plaine and true, ther's all the reach of it.

Shakespeare, *Troilus and Cressida.*

When, by his own command, Hēracles was burnt on the summit of Oeta, the young Philoctētes lighted his pyre and was rewarded with the hero's bow and arrows.   Years after, sailing against Troy, Philoctētes was bitten by a serpent on an islet; the wound grew noisome and the Greeks abandoned him on Lemnos.   But ten years later the captured Hélenus, son of Priam, revealed that Troy could not be taken without Philoctētes and his bow. 'The stone that the builders rejected . . .'   How was the deserted and embittered warrior to be appeased and brought to Troy?

The subject had been handled some seventy or eighty years before by Aeschylus and some twenty years before by Euripides (431).   Euripides by introducing a counter-embassy of Trojans had gratified his passion for debate; now Sophocles, aged eighty-seven, more wisely chose to place the conflict in the generous heart of a youth—Neoptolemus, the frank son of the frank Achilles.[1]

In the play, Neoptolemus and Odysseus enter before the cave of the absent Philoctētes.   Odysseus explains that he himself would be attacked at sight by Philoctētes, as the hated enemy who once marooned him here; therefore the victim must be trapped by Neoptolemus, whom he has never seen.   Reluctantly the young hero lends himself to the deceptions of statecraft.   He succeeds only too well in winning Philoctētes' heart, tricking him, and securing the divine bow; but then the agonies of his dupe move him so unbearably that, despite the rage and threats of Odysseus, he freely gives back the bow and prepares to take Philoctētes home to Mālis, since he will not hear of helping the hated Greeks against Troy.   Only the divine intervention of Hēracles bends his purpose.   So at last Philoctētes sets sail for Troy, with a final farewell to the cavern of his ten years' solitude.[2]

> Farewell, my cave, henceforth for ever,
>   That watched with me long nights awake!
> Farewell, ye Nymphs of mead and river,
>   Ye deep-voiced waves that used to break

[1] Cf. the words of Achilles (*Iliad*, ix, 312–13):
> For I hold that man as hateful as the very gates of Hell,
> Who says one thing, while another in his heart lies hidden well.

[2] Cf. the farewell of Ajax to Troy (p. 126).   La Harpe (1739–1803), adapting the play, chooses precisely this passage to omit, as an irrelevant embellishment.   Such a pedantic 'princess of parallelograms' did the Muse of French classical tragedy become, with her eternal motto: '*Le plan, toujours le plan, l'inflexible unité.*'

About my headland!—where at will
Of southern tempests from the sea
Spray drenched my hair, while Hermes' Hill
Answered for ever, echoing shrill,
The storm-gusts of my agony.

(1453–60.)

The modern reader may regret this conversion by a god in a machine; and wish that Philoctētes had freely changed his own mind, generously yielding to the generosity of Neoptolemus, even if he would sooner have died than be forced by Odysseus.[1] But doubtless to a Greek in the theatre this divine epiphany (which after all *could* be regarded as a symbol of Philoctētes' own thoughts) seemed more dramatic than if the hero had imitated the stage miser who 'leans against a wall and grows generous.'

Other plays of Sophocles contain more memorable scenes and speeches; one may regret the way in which the Attic stage so often turned Homer's heroic Odysseus, as Circe had failed to do, into an ignobler creature; but no extant work of the old dramatist has so genial a subject as this triumph of youthful chivalry over the cynical disillusion of Machiavellian middle-age; of individual decency over the impersonal beastliness of statecraft.

OEDIPUS AT COLŌNUS
(produced 401 B.C.)

Nothing is here for tears, nothing to wail
Or knock the breast, no weakness, no contempt,
Dispraise, or blame, nothing but well and fair,
And what may quiet us in a death so noble.

Milton.

This is the rather grim 'Nunc Dimittis' of a poet of some ninety years.[2] (Though we cannot be certain this was his last work, it seems likely enough.)

Perhaps twenty years have passed since Oedipus blinded himself at Thebes. Now, outcast like Lear, he is wandering alone with an Antigone as devoted as Cordelia. Crossing the marches of Attica, they rest near Colōnus (a mile N.N.W. of Athens, with a noble view of the Acropolis) in

---

[1] Cf. Ellida in Ibsen's *Lady from the Sea.*
[2] Cf. Corneille of his own old age in 1676:
    Tel Sophocle à cent ans charmait encore Athènes ;
    Tel bouillonnait encor son vieux sang dans ses veines.

a grove of the Eumenides.   The Chorus, Elders of Colōnus, insist on their
withdrawal from this holy ground and, when they learn in horror who the
old stranger is, from Attica as well.   Oedipus appeals to the traditional
hospitality of Athens and to the judgment of King Theseus.   While
Theseus is being summoned, Antigone's sister Ismēne brings news from
Thebes that their countrymen have been warned by oracles that it is vital
for them to possess the grave of Oedipus; and so King Creon will soon be
here to seize him.   Theseus enters and Oedipus reveals this anxiety of the
Thebans to secure his person, for fear of future defeat in Attica.   But,
Theseus objects, there is no enmity between Thebes and Athens.   Oedipus
answers with a famous piece of political wisdom, still as true, unhappily,
as when first written:

> Dear son of Aegeus, to the Gods alone
> There comes not near for ever Age nor Death;
> But all things else all-mastering Time confounds.
> The strength of the fields grows faint, the body's strength,
> And old trust dies, and new distrust is born,
> And the same breath of friendship blows not long
> 'Twixt man and man, nor yet 'twixt land and land:
> But, be it soon or in slow lapse of years,
> Things loved grow bitter, then beloved again.
> Though now 'twixt Thebes and thee all be fair weather,
> Yet infinite is Time, and infinite
> The days and nights his passage brings to birth,
> Wherein they may dissever with the spear,
> On slight occasion, this pledged harmony;
> Upon that day my buried dust that sleeps
> Cold in the grave, shall drink their steaming carnage,
> If Zeus be Zeus still, Phoebus still His prophet.

(607–23.)

So Theseus grants asylum; and in one of the most celebrated of Greek
odes the Chorus sing the glories of Colōnus and of Athens.   So, for a last
time, the old poet can praise his birthplace of ninety summers before and
the land he must soon leave for ever.

> Of noblest steeds this land is mother,   *strophe* 1.
>   Stranger, where thy foot abides;
> All the earth knows no such other
>   Home as white Colōnus hides.
> Here the nightingale loves singing,
>   In the green of holy glades,

Mid their wine-dark ivy clinging
  And their myriad-berried shades.
Here no gust of tempest blows,
  Here there burn no scorching suns;
Through His deep, untrodden close,
Dancing, Dionysus goes
  With the Nymphs that nursed Him once.

Here narcissus, dewed with morning,   *antistrophe* 1.
  Clusters ever, fair and free,
As in days of old adorning
  Demeter and Persephone.
Gold the crocus springs where, ever,
  Founts unfailing feed the stream
Of Cēphīsus' wandering river,
  And his stainless waters gleam
With their daily bounty rolled
  Wide across the bosomed land;
Here the Muses from of old
Dance, and far the reins of gold
  Flash from Aphrodite's hand.

And here is a marvel Asia hath not known,   *str.* 2.
Whose like not all the island of Dorian Pĕlops rears;
  A growth invincible, self-grown,
  The dread of hostile spears,
  Which in our land springs gloriously—
  The grey, child-nurturing olive tree!
  Never the blade of a foeman's sword,
Be he old or young, shall blast it; for sleepless, night and day,
  Thereon the Mŏrian Zeus keeps ward,
  And Pallas Athena's eyes of grey.

This praise hath Athens too, immortally,   *ant.* 2.
This other gift God-given, that crowns her land with fame;
  Her pride in steeds, young steeds and the sea,
  O Son of Crŏnus, from Thee they came!
  Thy hand, Poseidon, first did fit
  In the charger's champing mouth the bit
  Upon these roads around our home;
And Thou hast given to Athens her glory of oars that beat,
  Following swiftly across the foam
  The dance of the fifty Nēreïds' feet.

                    (668–719.)

Now Creon enters with his guards and tries, first, treacherous persuasions, then open force.   He has already carried off Ismēne, then Antigone, and would seize Oedipus himself, did not Theseus arrive to the
rescue of the old man and his daughters.   After Oedipus has poured out his
gratitude, Theseus tells him that a stranger, his kinsman, begs to speak with
him.   At once Oedipus guesses it to be his son Polyneices; and only reluctantly, at Antigone's prayer, consents to see him.   There follows
another famous chorus inspired by the sorrows of Oedipus—and of
humanity.   Some critics, quailing at its bleak pessimism, have refused to
hear in it the voice of Sophocles himself.   We cannot know.   But if he
did not put it here to vent his own feelings, it is not easy to see why he put
it here at all, in the mouths of dwellers in happy Colōnus.   It may express
only a mood; but, I suspect, a mood genuinely felt.   Sophocles had enjoyed
a lucky life; but the luckiest men are not always the happiest.   And even
those whose prime was happiest may feel most bitterly the deepening
shadows of old age and death.

> He that craves in life a span   *strophe.*
> Past the common lot of man
> Sets his heart, past questioning,
> On a vain and empty thing;
> Whoso lives beyond his share
> Slowly sees the creeping years
> Leave no trace of gladness there,
> Turning all his joys that were
> Into things more close to tears;
> Till One alone is left to heed his call—
> One no bride-song gladdeneth,
> Nor yet dance, nor music—Death,
> That brings an end of all.

> Never to be born is best;   *antistrophe.*
> Next to that, far happiest
> He that hastens from his birth,
> Fast as may be, back to earth.
> Soon as, with its follies light,
> On its way our Youth is past,
> Then, of sorrows infinite,
> What is spared us?—tongues that bite,
> Faction, battle, slaughter!—last,
> There comes Old Age, the strengthless, the accurst,
> Age that knows not love, nor friend,
> On whose solitude attend
> Griefs of *all* griefs the worst.

Such is this old man's lot, not mine alone.[1]   *epode.*
As on some northward-facing shore are thrown
Wild surges of the winter sea,
So upon *him*, with rage
That nothing can assuage,
Ruin breaks relentlessly:
Sorrows from the sunset west,
From the sunrise, beat his breast;
From the south spring sorrows forth,
From the black peaks of the north.

(1211–47.)

Polyneices enters. He is marching with Argive allies against his usurping brother Éteocles in Thebes—will not his father give his blessing? Instead, this brings from Oedipus perhaps the most terrible cursing in all Greek tragedy.

Therefore God's eye looks on thee—and *shall* look
More grimly yet, if indeed thy armies march
On Thebes. Think not to take it—thou shalt fall,
Thou and thy brother, stained with each other's blood.
Such Curses I sent against ye long ago;
And now anew I call them to my help,
That ye may learn a father must be honoured,
And not insulted—blind though he be, who got
Such sons as you! (My daughters sinned not so.)
Therefore my Curses have a mightier power
Than all thy prayers, thy dreams of royalty,
If truly Justice, from old times revealed,
Sits, by the right of immemorial law,
Next Zeus enthroned.
Hence then, begone, accurséd and unfathered,
Vilest of villains!—take these execrations
I call upon thy head—that thou shalt neither
Master thy native Thebes, nor yet return
To hollow Argos; but with fratricide
Slay and be slain by him that drove thee forth.
That is my curse. And I call on Tartarus
To house thee in its grim all-fathering gloom;
I call the Erinyes that haunt this grove;
Ares I call, that set betwixt ye both

[1] A slightly curious phrase, if the poet is *not* speaking in some degree for himself.

This fell dissension. Now thou hast heard me. Go!
Tell to all Thebes and thine own loyal allies—
Such are the honours Oedipus divides
Betwixt his sons!

(1370–96.)

It is deadly dangerous, as Shakespearian criticism has shown, to find autobiography in drama. Various ancient writers tell that the last days of Sophocles were embittered by conflict with his son, Iophon. For the poet had another, illegitimate son, who in his turn begot a child called, likewise, Sophocles—his grandfather's favourite. The jealous Iophon is supposed to have brought his father into court as senile; to which the old man replied by reading the above-quoted ode on Colōnus and was acquitted with applause. Afterwards, however, he forgave his son. All this may be invented; but, if so, it was a very clever invention.

Whatever the truth, one is once more amazed by the bitterness latent in this 'gentle' poet. Lear is not more savage to Regan and Goneril; and Polyneices, though erring, is no Goneril or Regan. He goes out from his father's presence to die in accord with his sense of honour, however mistaken; and Sophocles, after making Oedipus so ruthless, puts no less tenderness into Antigone's parting with her doomed brother.

But now thunder rolls. The terrible old man realizes that the hour of his passing has come. The story of that passing is one of the finest things in Sophocles.[1]

Chorus-leader. Is he dead, that man of sorrows?
Messenger.   Dead indeed!
  All his long days upon this earth are done.
Leader. How came it? By Heaven's hand? And did his griefs
  Find quiet end?
Messenger. Quiet—and most wonderful.
  Thyself thou sawest how from hence he went,
  No longer led by hands he loved, but striding
  Alone before us on the way he chose;
  Till, by the threshold of that sheer descent
  With brazen steps deep-founded in the earth,
  On one of the many paths that there divide,
  At length he paused, where a basin hewn in rock
  Commemorates the friendship sealed for ever
  By Theseus once and King Peiríthoüs.
  Between that basin, the Thorician Crag,
  The hollow pear-tree, and the stone-built tomb,

[1] Specially praised by 'Longinus,' *On the Sublime* (ch. xv).

He sat him down, and loosed his rags from off him,
And called to his daughters to bring him running water
For ablution and libation.
Then to the hill of Our Lady of Green Things,
Demeter, near in sight, the maidens hurried
And drew the water, and bathed their father's limbs,
And clad him new, as custom has ordained.
But when the old man had done his will, and they
Obeyed his utmost bidding,
Then suddenly the Zeus of the Underworld
Thundered—to hear it both the maidens trembled,
And clinging close about their father's knees
They wept and beat their breasts with cries of sorrow
Nothing could comfort.   But old Oedipus,
Hearing that burst of sudden bitter grief,
Clasped them and said: 'My children, from this day
Ye have no father.   Now my life is done.
Ye shall not toil to tend me any more.
How hard it was for you, I know, dear daughters;
Yet that one word of "love" repaid it all.
No man could give you deeper love than mine.
And now without me
You both must pass the remnant of your days.'

   So the father and his children, close-embraced,
Wailed out their sorrow—then, as their sobbing died
And silence fell upon their lamentation,
There pealed a sudden voice that cried his name,
Stiffening the hair upon our heads with terror,
As again and yet again God's summons rang:
'Oedipus, Oedipus, why wait we still?
Thou lingerest overlong.'

   Then, hearing how God called him, the old man bade
Theseus draw near, and said: 'Friend of my heart,
Now to my children give thy hand—my daughters,
Give the King yours.   By that time-honoured pledge
Promise that thou wilt never willingly
Leave them forsaken—but perform for them
Whatever in thy judgment seems the best.'

   So, like his noble self, with no weak tears,
King Theseus swore to do his guest this service;
Then quickly, laying on his daughters there
His sightless hands, again spoke Oedipus:
'Now, children, with the strength of noble hearts,

Hence ye must go, nor seek to look upon
Sights that ye may not, or hear forbidden things.
Begone!—and quickly!   'Tis the right alone
Of Theseus to behold these mysteries.'
    Then all of us obeyed as he commanded
And weeping uncontrollably we went,
Following his daughters.   In a little while
We turned again to look behind us—lo!
That man was vanished!
Only the King stood there with hands that covered
His face and hid his eyes, as from a sight
Of terror too appalling to behold.
For one brief moment, then, we saw him bow
In worship both of Earth and sacred Heaven.
But by what end passed Oedipus, no man
On earth can utter—save the King alone;
For in that instant no fierce lightning-flash
From skyward struck him down; no storm-wind seized him,
Swooping from seaward—either some messenger
Of Heaven took him, or the infernal floor
Of Earth gaped wide to give him painless welcome.
For without pang of sickness, without wail,
He passed—by the strangest passing man hath known.

                                              (1583–1665.)

Those who still read the Old Testament may recall the end upon Mount
Nebo of that Moses whom God Himself buried 'in a valley in the land of
Moab, over against Beth-peor: but no man knoweth of his sepulchre unto
this day.'   And of the extraordinary old poet who wrote this we may feel,
in the words of the same chapter of *Deuteronomy* (xxxiv): 'His eye was
not dim, nor his natural force abated.'

The play would better have closed here with the 'peace and consolation'
of *Samson Agonistes*, that still grimmer picture of a blinded hero's end.
Unfortunately Antigone and Ismēne protract their lamentations to an
unconscionable length, which a modern producer might be wise to
shorten.

The two plays on Oedipus offer a striking contrast—the one so deft in
the steely precision with which it advances to its end; the other far looser in
structure, full of delays that do not so much heighten suspense as postpone
the close, yet richer in pure poetry, more individual in its character of
Oedipus, more moving in its meditations on mortality.

But *Oedipus at Colōnus* should perhaps also warn us how little, in some
ways, we can really understand the past.   Sometimes scholars forget this

—sometimes because they want to forget it.   These dead of over two thousand years can seem so close in thought or sympathy; yet at moments a
gulf opens between them and us.   Here Oedipus is no Christian saint,
recompensed for earthly anguish by heavenly bliss.   He is merely to become
a dimly and grimly brooding presence, in a grave that will be pleasantly
watered with the blood of his own invading countrymen.   The Greek,
still in some ways strangely primitive, might honour as 'hero' one not
specially heroic—enough that he was specially potent or awesome (or
simply specially handsome).[1]   As Mr D. W. Lucas points out, had the
hated Thebans secured their old king's body, it would have been as effective
a mascot on *their* side.   To us, such an after-existence might seem bleak
amends for all the woes of Oedipus—remoter than the stark old Scandi-
navians' dreams of singing and feasting, like Gunnar or Thorstein Cod-biter,
in their lonely howes above the Iceland sea.   But for Sophocles, apparently,
it was enough.   Partly, no doubt, it is the ancient craving for fame, for
mere remembrance, after death.   But we cannot really comprehend.   Like
Socrates, let us own our ignorance.   That confession of his, at least, is a
point where ancient and modern minds can meet.

NOTE

In 1907 there were found, at Oxyrhyncus in the Nile valley, papyrus
fragments of a satyric play by Sophocles—*The Trackers* (*Ichneutae*).
They comprise some four hundred lines (often mutilated)—perhaps half
the drama; which deals, less happily than the Homeric Hymn to Hermes,
with the infant god's theft of Apollo's cattle and his invention of the lyre
from a tortoise-shell.   Its humour does not seem to me of a level to leave
one heart-broken for the loss of the rest.

FRAGMENTS OF LOST PLAYS

Love

My children, Love is more than Love alone,
For Love hath also many another name.
Ay, Love is Death; Love is a force eternal;
'Tis passion's heady wine, 'tis wailing anguish,

[1] Philippus of Crotona was worshipped after death at Egesta, because he was so
beautiful; and compare the curious cases of the athletes Cleomēdes and Theógenes
(F. L. and Prudence Lucas, *From Olympus to the Styx*, 2nd ed., 1949, p. 301).

'Tis frenzy at its starkest.   Love hath all—
Strong purpose, utter peace, wild violence.
It melts its way into the hearts of all
That breathe on earth—what does not yield to Love?
It moves the plunging fishes of the deep,
Seizes the four-foot creatures of the land,
Flutters its wings among the birds of air:
Nor beasts nor men escape, nor Gods in Heaven.
With Love what God that wrestled hath not found
A triple overthrow?   If I dare say it—
And why may I *not* say what is the truth?—
Love masters Zeus Himself.
Love needs no spear, no sword-blade, to confound
The wisest plans alike of God and man.

(Nauck, fr. 855.)

Like children that beneath a frosty heaven
Snatch in their eagerness at icicles
(First they are ravished with this latest toy;
Yet soon they find it hurts their hands to hold
That icy thing; and yet how hard to drop it!)—
Even such are lovers too, when what they love
Tears them betwixt 'I would not' and 'I would.'

(*The Lovers of Achilles*, fr. 153.)

Enforced Marriage

[*Procne, princess of Athens, laments her marriage to the barbarous Thracian king Tēreus.*]

But, exiled, I am nothing.   Ah, how often
I have seen what things of naught, in our life's lot,
We women are!   Young, in our father's house
We lead, I think, the happiest lives on earth,
Still blissful in our childish innocence;
But when we come to youth and understanding,
They put us up for sale and cast us out,
Far from our fathers and our fathers' Gods,
To hands of strangers, or barbarians,
To homes of all unhappiness, or shame:
One bride-night seals our union—and thenceforth
We must accept our fate, and say 'tis well.

(*Tēreus*, fr. 524.)

War

For War is blind, O women, blind and eyeless,
And like a rooting swine snouts up all evils.

(Fr. 754.)

The Poplar

                    Like the towering poplar—
Though all things else lie still, some breath of air
Still sways her head and lifts its feathery lightness.

(*Aegeus*, fr. 22.)

World's End

Beyond the sea, to the utmost bounds of earth,
The springs of Night, the portals of the Heavens,
The immemorial garden of the Sun.

(Fr. 870.)

Home

Ah, what more perfect happiness than this?—
Safe back from sea, to lie with drowsy senses
And hear the rain-drops on the roof of home.

(Fr. 579.)

NOTES ON SOPHOCLES

ANTIGONE

[Page 131] *No mind . . . to drive you.* One senses a touch of satisfaction in the lonely heart of Antigone, that Ismēne will not help and she herself must act alone.

[Page 132] *Dirce* and *Ismēnus* were two small northward flowing streams, west and east of Thebes respectively.

[Page 133] *The stormer.* Cápaneus, one of the Seven Champions attacking Thebes, boasted he would take it despite the lightning of Zeus himself. It struck him as he surmounted the wall; and his wife Evadne threw herself into his funeral flames.

[Page 134] *Creon appears.* The opening speech of this 'Pillar of Society,' with its pontifical platitudes and its self-satisfaction about an essentially impious edict, already bodes the worst.

In his speech *On the Embassy* (343) Demosthenes taunts Aeschines with having played Creon in his acting days ('for it is the privilege of third-rate actors to play *tyrants*'); but he quotes these 'excellent lines' of 'the wise Sophocles' (from 'Yet none can tell' to 'what friends we make') as the flat opposite of Aeschines' own political conduct.

[Page 135] (*A guard enters.*) This guard is one of the best of the few comic characters in Greek tragedy. His speech here inevitably recalls the perplexities of Launcelot Gobbo in *The Merchant of Venice*, ii, 2.

[Page 137] *The work of malcontents.* Creon suffers as fantastically from conspiracy-mania, the moment he is crossed, as Oedipus in the next play, where Creon himself becomes the suspect. It suggests how uneasily the heads of Greek rulers lay beneath 'the sword of Damocles.'

[Page 138] *It is hard when men guess idly. . . .* To modern ears, the guard is strangely impudent. Greek kings are not hedged with divinity, like Shakespeare's; and their subjects are free-spoken, like Shakespeare's Fools.

[Page 141] *It was not God that gave me such commandments.* For some, this is the finest speech in Sophocles—and as typical of him as Clytemnestra's magnificent declamation (p. 84) is of Aeschylus.

[Page 143] *I did the deed.* The new courage with which the gentle Ismēne rises to the crisis (like Īphigeneia at Aulis, p. 344) is a human touch. But even now she has to beg leave of the masterful Antigone; only to be again rejected by that 'harsh daughter of harsh father.'

[Page 143] *Ah dearest Haemon.* The manuscripts give this line to Ismēne; but, apart from general appropriateness, '*your* marriage' in the next line supports giving it to Antigone. Such mistakes are not uncommon—the manuscripts give the line after this ('And yet how *can* you . . . ?') to Ismēne.

[Page 145] *Obedient sons.* Again the intolerable Creon proses like a more sinister Polonius.

[Page 146] *Father, it is the Gods alone.* Haemon's pathetic attempt to reason tactfully with this elderly child in tantrums contrasts with the vacillating acquiescence of the Chorus, whose complete spinelessness brings out all the more the desperate loneliness of Antigone.

THE HOUSE OF THEBES

Agēnor, King of Phoenicia

Aphrodite = Ares

Harmonia = Cadmus

Europa = Zeus

Minos
(House of Crete)

Sémele = Zeus

Dionysus

Autónoë = Aristaeus

Actaeon

Īno = Áthamas

Polydorus

Labdacus

Laïus

Oedipus

Jocasta

Dragon's Tooth

Echion = Agāve

Pentheus

Oclasus

Menoeceus

Creon

Menoeceus
or
Mégareus

Haemon

Polyneices

Éteocles

Antigone

Ismēne

[Page 146] *Is she not worthy, then, of golden praise?* I see no reason to doubt that such is the view of Sophocles himself—that here at least, for him, 'the voice of the people is the voice of God.'

[Page 148] *To kill them both.* Nothing better illustrates the blind frenzy of wounded vanity in this man whom Hegel thought 'possessed . . . by the interest of the community,' than his failure even to remember how many victims he proposes to execute. Next he plunges into a mixture of vain superstition and arrogant blasphemy.

[Page 149] *Tantalus' daughter.* Niobe (genealogical table, p. 115). Her father reigned on Mount Sípylus in Lydia; she herself wedded Amphīon, King of Thebes, to whom she bore six, or seven, sons and as many daughters. But she boasted of her superiority in this to Lēto, mother only of the twins, Apollo and Artemis; who thereupon slew Niobe's children with their arrows before her face. In her grief Niobe was changed into an ever-weeping rock on Sípylus. (Cf. *Iliad*, xxiv, 602 ff.; *Greek Poetry for Everyman*, p. 77.)

[Page 150] *Misfortune chose thy bride.* Before the fatal march against Thebes Polyneices had wedded Argeia, daughter of the Argive king, Adrastus.

[Pages 150–1] *Yet surely the wise . . . living to the vaults of death.* It has been much disputed whether these lines can be genuine. They seem based on a passage of Sophocles' friend Heródotus (iii, 119), telling how Dareius, King of Persia, sentenced to death for conspiracy a certain Intaphernes, together with his kinsmen, but granted to the prayers of Intaphernes' wife a pardon for whichever one she should choose. She then chose her brother; as being, unlike husband or children, irreplaceable.

For Antigone to use this primitive argument is inconsistent with her appeal to the eternal laws of reverence for the dead. On the other side it is argued that inconsistency is human; that Antigone is a character who feels rather than argues; and that here, unnerved and confused (like Joan of Arc at moments in her trial), she catches at straws.

In his *Rhetoric* (iii, 16) Aristotle quotes two lines of this passage as genuine. Most modern readers will wish it away; but it seems best to suspend judgment.

[Page 152] *Danaë.* Acrisius, King of Argos, grandson of the Danaïd Hypermnestra (p. 21), was warned by an oracle that he would be slain by the son of his daughter, Danaë. To prevent her having a child, he shut her in a brazen tower (perhaps a memory of the bee-hive tombs of Argolis, with bronze ornamentation on their walls); but Zeus came to her in a shower of gold. She bore Perseus, was set adrift with the infant by her father, and was washed ashore on Seríphos in the Cyclades. Growing up there, Perseus slew the Gorgon, rescued Andromeda, and then, at an athletic contest, accidentally killed his grandfather with a discus.

[Page 152] *Son of Dryas.* Lycurgus, King of the Edōnes in Thrace, opposed Dionysus, went mad, and was imprisoned by his subjects in a cave, before being torn by horses, or eaten by panthers.

[Page 152] *By the Dark-blue Rocks.* For Cleopatra and her sons, see p. 114. Cleopatra's mother was Oreithyia, daughter of Erechtheus, King of Athens; this princess, wandering beyond the River Ilissus, was carried off by Boreas, the North Wind.

The Dark-blue Rocks, or Symplēgades, at the entrance to the Black Sea, crushed between them all ships attempting to pass, until Argo succeeded; then they became fixed. (See J. R. Bacon, *Voyage of the Argonauts*, 79–80.)

[Page 152] *Teiresias.* One of the most famous of ancient seers. He was blinded for having seen Athena bathing, but recompensed by her with the gift of prophecy (see Callimachus, *Hymns*, v; *Greek Poetry for Everyman*, pp. 300–1; and *Odyssey*, xi, 90–151; *Greek Poetry for Everyman*, pp. 146–8). Teiresias will return—no better tempered—in *Oedipus the King*; and—mellower —in *The Bacchae*.

[Page 154] *Electron.* An alloy of gold and silver. There were gold deposits on Mount Tmōlus, and in the Pactōlus, flowing from it past Sardis.

[Page 154] *No mortal can defile the Gods.* Creon, after ranting like a medieval Herod, is suddenly frightened by his own blasphemy.

[Page 156] *Icária.* A centre of Dionysiac worship in Attica (p. 6). But the manuscript reading 'Italia' may be right.

[Page 156] *Dragon's teeth.* Cadmus (p. 227), coming from Phoenicia to Greece in quest of his sister Europa, who had been carried off by Zeus, founded Thebes; killed a dragon at the spring of Ares; and sowed its teeth, from which (as in the Jason-story) there sprang armed men. Cadmus set them fighting each other and only five were left; from whom descended the Theban nobility of the *Spartoi* or 'Sown Men,' including Creon himself.

[Page 156] *The Twin Crags.* The Phaedriad rocks (2,000 feet) overhanging Delphi; the stream of Castalia falls from them; and in the uplands of Parnassus above them, 7 miles N.E. of Delphi, lies the Corycian Cave.

[Page 156] *Amphīon*, son of Zeus and Antíope, built the walls of Thebes by playing his lyre.

> Did not Amphion's lyre the deaf stones call,
> When they came dancing to the Theban wall?
>
> Campion.

[Page 157] *Eurydice enters.* There seem hardly any rules that genius cannot defy. But one of the hardest to override is the dramatic rule that audiences refuse to feel deeply about a character who appears late in a play. It certainly applies here to the fate of Eurydice. Agāve in *The Bacchae* is perhaps a partial exception; but of her we have at least heard a good deal before she appears.

[Page 158] *Goddess of the Crossways.* Hecate.

[Page 160] *Mégareus*, or Menoeceus, son of Creon, had sacrificed himself to save Thebes when attacked by the Seven (p. 304).

THE WOMEN OF TRĀCHIS

[Page 163] *What does them no shame, no wrong to me.* Dejaneira is making, like a true Greek, desperate efforts to be reasonable; but she 'protests too much,' and the reaction is to follow.

OEDIPUS THE KING

Genealogical table, p. 227.

[Page 172] *I, Oedipus . . . all men's mouths.* A first sinister note. Such pride is dangerous; and his name is soon to be still more 'in men's mouths,' as a byword of horror.

[Page 172] *Prophetic ashes of Ismēnus.* At the temple of Apollo Ismēnus, beside the River Ismēnus, the future was divined by the flames of burnt-offerings.

[Page 172] *Our land is stricken.* For folk-beliefs that incest can cause plague see Frazer, *Golden Bough*, ii, 115.

[Page 173] *Savage Songstress.*   The Sphinx, sitting on a mountain near Thebes, devoured all who could not answer her riddle—what is it that has now four feet, now two, now three, and whose voice is weakest when it has most feet?   When Oedipus gave the answer 'Man,' she hurled herself from her rock; and he was raised to the throne by a grateful Thebes.

[Page 173] *Not unknown to me.*   If Oedipus knew (as he must) about the plague, the reader may ask why he pretended not to, so that the plague had to be described to him at length.   There is of course Puff's answer in Sheridan's *The Critic*: 'The less inducement he has to tell all this, the more, I think, you ought to be obliged to him.'   Probably the ordinary audience does not notice the difficulty; which Sophocles could easily have avoided, had he wished, by putting the description in the mouth of Oedipus.   But if dramatic audiences do overlook points so patent, what is the use of expecting them to notice the tenuous subtleties sometimes excogitated by literary critics?

[Page 173] *Each of you feels grief for himself alone.*   A somewhat egotistic assumption by Oedipus that everyone in Thebes but himself is egotistic.

[Page 174] *Pytho.*   Delphi.

[Page 175] *Robbers, he said.*   Why did the man lie?   The audience has no time to think.   Presumably to excuse himself.   But Sophocles is curiously inconsistent about the announcement of Laïus' murder in Thebes.   Here Creon implies that the sole survivor reached Thebes before Oedipus; but Jocasta (p. 190) says that he found Oedipus already on the throne.   Attempts to remove the discrepancy are unconvincing.

[Page 175] *Suborned by silver.*   The conspiracy-mania of Greek rulers (cf. p. 226), which is soon to make Oedipus suspect both Creon and Teiresias.

[Page 176] *Healer hymned in Delos.*   Apollo.

[Page 176] *Artemis . . . fair name.*   With reference to a Boeotian cult of Artemis Eucleia, 'Our Lady of Fair Fame.'

[Page 176] *War-god.*   Ares was a destroyer in general, not only in war.

[Page 177] *Lycēan . . . Lycian.*   *Lykeios,* as an epithet of Apollo and Artemis, may be connected with *lykos,* 'wolf': but both deities were also associated with Lўcia in S. Asia Minor.

[Page 177] *Town that shares Thy name.*   This seems merely to mean that Thebes is often given the epithet 'Bacchic.'

[Page 177] *Stranger . . . from the deed remote.*   One example among many of the tragic irony with which this play is packed.   Cf. 'mine his bed,' 'bond of common children,' 'as if he were My very father' (p. 178).

[Page 179] *Teiresias.*   See p. 228.

[Page 180] *Never I would have come.*   The behaviour of Teiresias is odd. His prophetic power must work fitfully; or he would have foreseen the uselessness of coming.   One can imagine his inspiration—or, we might say, telepathic faculty—awaking as he enters Oedipus' presence.   But the irritability which so easily breaks down his reticence remains a little grotesque.   Seldom was holy man less holy.

[Page 181] *Chanting, monstrous hound.*   The Sphinx.

[Page 183] *Not till I have said That which I came for.*   Some readers may find that this last speech is excessive, as letting the cat too far out of the bag. One would expect Oedipus to be more struck than he is by the coincidence of so many odd facts: (1) Apollo foretold his parricide and incest; (2) Teiresias now accuses him—quite independently, it seems—of precisely those two rare crimes; (3) he is unsure of his parentage; (4) he has killed at least four men unknown.

[Page 185] *Clearly proven.* Even allowing for his excitability, Oedipus has truly extraordinary ideas of 'clear proof.' This squabble with Creon seems to me rather foolish and tedious, unnecessary to the plot, and degrading to the characters—far inferior in fact to Shakespeare's quarrel of Brutus and Cassius, which throws vivid light on both men.

[Page 186] *No man could, That's in his sober senses.* Creon is not a subtle pleader. He begs the question that he *is* in his sober senses. And he knows little of human nature if he imagines that a good position cures men of ambition for a still better one. (Cf. Hippolytus' similar plea, p. 271.)

[Page 187] *Quick wits are dangerous.* One of the essential themes of this play.

[Page 189] *I will not say From Apollo's self.* A piece of lip-reverence which the free-thinking Jocasta soon drops. One has a sense that the pious Sophocles thought her a distinctly impious character.

[Page 189] *Those cross-roads.* A still desolate spot (though somewhat marred, since I first saw it, by the making of a modern road), roughly half-way between Delphi and Lebadeia, with the 8,000-foot Parnassus to N.W. and the range of Helicon to S.E.

[Page 191] *And so I slew them all.* Even allowing for a rough age, one may find a little breath-taking the offhand brevity with which Oedipus relates this slaughter.

[Page 193] *Abae's fane.* A temple and oracle of Apollo in Boeotia, N.W. of Lake Cōpāïs.

[Page 193] *Navel-stone Of Earth.* Delphi, supposed to be earth's centre; as Zeus found by letting two eagles fly simultaneously from extreme east and west. They met at Delphi. The site was important as early as 1600 B.C.: and excavation has revealed several navel-stones, including one as old as 600.

[Page 195] *How! By a plot?* Again this obsession with conspiracies.

[Page 195] *In dreams ... Lay with his mother.* For example, Hippias dreamed this when invading his motherland, Attica, with the Persian army defeated at Marathon (Heródotus, vi, 107).

[Page 196] *Rid you of all your fears.* He is to do exactly the reverse. Aristotle (*Poetics*, ch. xi) gives this episode as an example of *peripeteia*, that tragic irony by which human blindness produces exactly the opposite result to what it intended.

[Page 197] *Feet, close-pinned together.* 'Oedipus' means 'swollen-foot.' The original idea of this mutilation may have been to prevent the child's ghost from walking.

[Page 198] *Yet I, who count myself the child of Fortune.* A line applied to himself by Sulla (138–78 B.C.), the dictator of Rome.

[Page 201] *Phasis.* A river flowing, S. of Caucasus, into the S.E. corner of the Black Sea.

[Page 201] *Ister.* Danube.

[Page 202] *By her husband Bearing a husband.* Whenever he gets started on the intricacies of incest, Sophocles seems to lose his head and become as silly-clever as Seneca. I find it hard to imagine any woman of any period sinking to such puerile ingenuities while preparing to hang herself.

[Page 204] *For, had I sight ... House of Death.* There seems something curiously primitive in this conviction of Oedipus that, having blinded himself living, he will still be blind among the dead.

[Page 205] *To quench The fount of hearing.* If Oedipus really had this insane desire, it might have occurred to him that he need only pierce his eardrums.

[Page 205] *Alas, Cithaeron.*   Cf. Marcus Aurelius, *Meditations*, xi, 6 (preaching resignation): 'Though Oedipus may cry "Alas, Cithaeron!", he still must bear his load.'

[Page 207] *Has Creon been so pitiful?*   From being too arrogant, Oedipus seems to become too abject.

[Page 207] *Come to these hands of mine—a brother's hands,* etc.   Another example of the relativity of taste.   Sophocles clearly thought it pathetic for an incestuous father to address his young daughters with this string of epigrams; some modern readers will find it odious.   The grim facts were facts; but why play with them like a cat with a chestnut?   One wonders if the subject did not possess for Sophocles a certain perverse fascination.

OEDIPUS AT COLŌNUS

[Page 220] *Peiríthoüs,* son of Ixíon, helped his friend Theseus to carry off the girl Helen from Sparta; and in return was helped by him in an attempt to carry off Queen Persephone from Hades.   Peiríthoüs perished and Theseus was chained living in the Netherworld, till rescued by Hēracles (p. 286).

FRAGMENTS OF LOST PLAYS

[Page 225] *World's End.*   This seems a description of the happy land of the Hyperboreans, to which Boreas carried off Oreithyia, princess of Athens.   The garden of the Sun is apparently the Garden of the Hesperides, sometimes located in the north, though usually in the west.

EURIPIDES
(*c.* 485–406 B.C.)

EURIPIDES gives the impression of a man battling through his long life against wind and tide, where Sophocles had both in his favour. But this was hardly chance; as so often, the destiny of each seems to have lain largely in his own character. Euripides was driven by a compulsion to criticize and denounce the powers both of this world and of the other; often in generous defence of their helpless victims—women and children, poor men and slaves and aliens. It would not be strange if this rebelliousness of Euripides went back in part (like Ibsen's) to an unhappy childhood, and the harmony of Sophocles to a happy one, such as his poetry loves regretfully to describe.[1] Even in art, Euripides shows a tendency to criticize his elder, Aeschylus, which anticipates the conflict of the two poets in Aristophanes' *Frogs*.

Whatever the cause, Euripides is not only the first European writer to dwell on the inward conflicts of a divided mind, like Phaedra's or Mēdēa's (where Sophocles gives us rather the conflict of contrasted characters like Antigone and Ismēne, Electra and Chrysóthemis, Odysseus and Ajax[2]); his own mind, too, seems often divided against itself. Was he feminist or misogynist, philanthropist or misanthrope? The likeliest answer seems: 'Both.' (So Milton found it hard to live either with women or without them.) Again, different passages of Euripides argue with equal vehemence that one should have children, and that one should not. Which did he really feel? Again, probably both. It is not enough to answer that a dramatist merely expresses the views of his characters, not his own: it is not by accident that a writer chooses certain themes to harp on. He already betrays himself by what he selects. Because of this inner complexity Euripides, though uneven as a dramatist, becomes more intriguing as a character than his two rivals.

Further, through much of his work there runs a deeper contradiction. He had to dramatize legends that might attract him as a poet, yet irritate him as a thinker. Sceptics like Marlowe or Swinburne, Flaubert or Anatole France, may be drawn at times to religious themes like *Dr Faustus* or *The Masque of Queen Bersabe, La Tentation de Saint Antoine* or *Thaïs*; but that is very different from being forced to write on nothing else. Sometimes Euripides can surrender himself and suspend his scepticism (though

---

[1] Cf. pp. 162, 224.
[2] His Neoptolemus in *Philoctētes* seems exceptional; there is also a certain conflict between love and jealousy in Dejaneira.

not without touches of irony), as in *Hippolytus* or *The Bacchae*; sometimes, as in *Ion* or *Electra*, he seems deliberately to burst the old bottle of traditional faith with the corrosive of his rationalism, like Voltaire exposing the biblical brutalities of Samuel towards Agag in *Saul*; often he wavers between both attitudes. In consequence, his work shows stresses and tensions unknown to his two predecessors.

In youth he is said to have trained as an athlete (compare the tirade against athletes on p. 346); then as a painter. But literature was his destiny —indeed he was to be the first really literary writer, the first study-poet. The tradition portrays a lonely, sombre, bearded figure; aloof from most men, though drawn to thinkers like Anaxágoras, Protágoras, Pródicus, and Socrates; brooding in his library or, day-long, in his cavern beside the moaning seas of Salamis. Unlike Sophocles, he seems to have taken little part in public life, except for one embassy to Syracuse. He may have served in war; but no record remains.

Out of perhaps ninety-two plays we possess nineteen (if we count the doubtful *Rhēsus*). His earliest extant work, the tragi-comic *Alcestis* of 438, portrayed an egoist and his redemption by one of Euripides' many noble women. *Mēdēa* (431) pictured on the contrary a heroine turned into a devil by man's falsity and cruelty (a theme repeated in *Hecuba*); characteristically Euripides made his heroine a 'barbarian' and her betrayer a Greek. With *Hippolytus* (428), one of his masterpieces, he again challenged convention—this time by depicting with sympathy a woman's struggle against her own guilty passion. Presumably within this period (432–22) fell his prosecution for impiety by Cleon.

For a time the outbreak of the Peloponnesian War (431) turned the poet's aggressiveness against the invaders of his country (*Hēracleidae* and *Suppliants*) and the reactionary brutality of Sparta (*Andrómache*); but, like Anatole France in 1914–18, he grew disillusioned by the savagery of war and his answer to the Athenian massacre at Mēlos (416) was the harrowing *Trojan Women* of 415.

Hēracles, of uncertain date (424–423?), reads at times almost like a retort to Sophocles' *Oedipus the King*. In frenzy Hēracles has butchered wife and children; but, whereas Oedipus blinded himself and sought exile, the wise Athenian Theseus consoles Hēracles with the commonsense truth that no man can be stained with guilt by deeds done in ignorance, and welcomes him to Athens.

But Euripides was not only rationalist and realist; like Shakespeare and Ibsen, Balzac and Flaubert, he was at the same time a romantic. *Iphigeneia among the Taurians* is an exciting adventure-play of an escape from the Crimea; *Ion* is an equally picturesque tale of a mother happily saved from murdering her own lost son. But here the rebel in Euripides was again able to attack orthodox religion, in his heroine's impeachment of the Delphic

Apollo. *Electra* (*c.* 413) is a similar attack on the folly of vendetta, though blessed by Apollo's oracle. A sequel, *Orestes* (408), is a realistic melodrama, where most of the characters are either bad or mad.

In 408–407 Euripides left his unsympathetic Athens for the court of Archelaus in half-barbarous Macedon. There the old man of near eighty, under the stimulus of new and wild surroundings,[1] produced a final masterpiece, *The Bacchae*—a recognition, by this lifelong rationalist, of the terrible power of the irrational, of fanaticism, of the impulsive levels of the mind. To be controlled, these must be allowed their share in life. It is not rational to try to be too rational. Dionysus repaid this admission by inspiring perhaps the poet's finest play.[2]

The year 406 brought death to Euripides in his Macedonian exile; torn to pieces like his own Pentheus, said the legend, by the king's hounds. Already he was a power in the Greek world outside Athens. Syracusans had released Athenian prisoners who could recite him; later, Dionysius, despot of Syracuse, himself a tragic poet though a poor one, appears to have bought for a large sum the lyre and writing-tablet of Euripides and offered them to the Muses; in 404 an air from *Electra*, it is said, helped to save Athens herself from destruction by her conquerors.[3] In the centuries that followed he far out-topped the rivals who had once overshadowed him. He had championed slave and stranger; the new cosmopolitan world left by Alexander repaid the debt.

But, just as his own mind was divided, so are ours divided about *him*: he loved debates too well, and he has himself become the subject of them. There is a risk in writing problem-plays: the play may die with the problem (unless the problem itself is eternal). All that Euripides said about Apollo or vendetta was true; but it has become truism. Further, like many 'intellectuals,' he was sometimes too clever and lacked wisdom—the wisdom of balance, of intuition, of artistic tact. And sometimes, instead of being too intellectual, he swung to the opposite extreme and became lachrymose. Just as he was given to dressing characters in realistic rags, he could at times tear a passion to tatters.

Liberals and humanists have tended to overpraise him—a natural piece of ancestor-worship. The parallel with Ibsen is obvious; but, as a dramatist, I feel the old Norwegian had a keener brain, a subtler technique, a sterner Scandinavian self-control.

---

[1] One is reminded of Wordsworth finding new inspiration, after the blood of Paris and the dust of Godwin, among the valleys of the Quantocks and of Westmorland; or of Michael Angelo at eighty discovering Nature among the hills at Spoleto: 'The better part of my heart is still there, for truly in the woods alone is peace.'

[2] So Goethe thought it. Cf. Macaulay: '*The Bacchae* is a most glorious play . . . as a piece of language, it is hardly equalled in the world.' (Which seems going, as was Macaulay's way, a little far.)

[3] p. 300.

But perhaps Euripides would have been content to pay the price of being, sometimes, a less good poet, in order to become a better propagandist. Immortality, he might have said, is not everything. His influence went to make the world gentler, more human, more cosmopolitan. After all, it was Euripides, if the story is true, not Sophocles, nor the grave of Œedipus, that saved Athens from Theban hatred in 404. He remains one of the first writers to transcend the bounds of country and become a good citizen of the world.

ALCESTIS
(438 B.C.)

Methought I saw my late espousèd saint
Brought to me like Alcestis from the grave,
Whom Jove's great son to her glad husband gave,
Rescued from death by force, though pale and faint.

Milton.

Asclēpius, son of Apollo and the faithless Corōnis,[1] grew so skilful a leech that he raised the dead. This would never do; so Zeus slew him with a thunderbolt. The angry Apollo replied by shooting the Cyclōpes who had forged the bolt; and was punished by having to keep for a year the sheep of Admētus, King of Phĕrae in Thessaly. Grateful for this master's kindness, Apollo obtained for Admētus, when the Fates had doomed him, a reprieve on condition that another should die in his stead. Only his wife Alcestis was willing to make the sacrifice.

The play opens on the fatal day. After a prologue by Apollo and a bitter altercation between him and Death, a servant describes to the Chorus of Elders of Phĕrae the scenes of despair within the palace. Then the dying queen is carried forth, and Admētus begins to realize that he has saved his life only by making it not worth living. Hardly has Alcestis expired than the jolly Hēracles arrives. Admētus, honouring hospitality, hides his own loss to welcome his old friend; and the admiring Chorus recall the bygone happy days when a god himself had been their master's shepherd.[2]

Forth leapt the spotted lynxes, delighted by his playing,
To join the flock around him; from glens of Othrys straying,
Trooped lions with tawny mane.

[1] Cf. Chaucer, *Maunciple's Tale*.
[2] Cf. Meredith, *Phoebus with Admetus*.

Yea, as Thy lyre, Apollo,
        Rang out its merry strain,
The dappled fawn from the pine-wood shadow
On airy hoofs across the meadow
        Came dancing in Thy train.

                                              (579–87.)

By his self-effacing courtesy Admētus has taken a step towards redemption. But first comes his bitterest humiliation—a squalid bandying
of home-truths, above his dead wife's body, with the old father who had
refused to die for him. Meanwhile the unsuspecting Hēracles has begun
to bellow drunken catches and mock at the gloomy face of the servant who
waits upon him.

        Why, if my judgment is worth anything,
        Your solemn folk, that scowl with knitted brows,
        Make life not life, but mere calamity.

                                              (800–2.)

The servant, unable to bear it longer, breaks the brutal truth; and the
sobered hero stalks out to wrest Alcestis from Death himself. He returns
to Admētus, whose despair has only deepened, leading a veiled and silent
figure. Will the king take charge of this woman that Hēracles has just
won as prize in the neighbouring games? Reluctantly Admētus consents.
Then comes, perhaps, the most pleasing moment in the play.

Hēracles. Courage! Stretch out your hand and touch my stranger.
Admētus. I do—yet as if I severed a Gorgon's head.
Hēracles. Have you good hold?
Admētus.   I have.
Hēracles.   Then keep it now!—
        And you shall own, one day, the son of Zeus
        Was a true friend.

                                              (1117–20.)

Alcestis herself never speaks again. This may have been originally for a
technical reason—that the play employed only two speaking actors. But
no words could have befitted this figure returned from the mystery of the
grave so well as silence. As with Lazarus:

        The rest remaineth unreveal'd;
        He told it not; or something seal'd
        The lips of that Evangelist.

Alcestis, replacing the usual satyric drama as fourth piece of a tetralogy, shows more comedy and a lighter touch than ordinary tragedies. It is Euripides' *Egoist;* and those who, like Browning, have wished for a nobler hero, might as well have tried to improve Meredith's work by turning Sir Willoughby Patterne into a Sir Philip Sidney. Not a great play; but a pleasant one, and historically important; for it points forward to our own romantic drama—in particular, to *The Winter's Tale* with its long-suffering Hermione.

The Hēracleidae (Children of Hēracles)
(*c.* 430–427 B.C.)

After the death of Hēracles, Eurystheus, King of Argos, who had burdened the hero's life with Labours, proceeded to persecute his old mother Alcmēna and his children. Now they have taken refuge in Attica, and an Argive herald tries to seize them, as Creon with Oedipus in Sophocles. Like Theseus there, so here Theseus' son and successor Dēmophon comes to the rescue. War ensues; and when a virgin-sacrifice is demanded for victory, Macária, daughter of Hēracles, offers herself—one of Euripides' army of maiden-martyrs. The best lines in the play are her disconsolate protest against the idea of another life hereafter—this one is more than enough.

> I have not failed you—for my race I died.
> *That* comfort for my childless maidenhood
> Alone is left me—*if* there is life in Hades.
> But I pray there may be none! For if the dead
> Must find, there too, more sorrows to endure,
> Ah whither should we turn? For death, at least,
> Has seemed the one sure medicine of grief.

> (589–96.)

The invading Argives of Eurystheus are then defeated, he himself captured, and sent to death by the pitiless old Alcmēna. A rather thin patriotic play.

MĒDĒA
(431 B.C.)

Gin my seven sons were seven young rats
  Running on the castle wa',
And I were a great grey cat mysel,
  I soon wad worry them a'.

                    Lord Thomas and Fair Annie.

Greek legend knows no more romantic figure than the young Jason who was reared by the wise Centaur in the glens of Pēlion; and came down across the wild Anaurus to claim his kingdom of Iolcus from his usurping uncle, Pélias; and was tricked by the tyrant to sail with his heroic comrades in Argo and win the Golden Fleece from King Aeētes; and succeeded because the king's daughter, Mēdēa, loved him and lent her magic aid.[1]   But on love followed crime; she murdered her young brother and cast his limbs into the sea, to delay her father's pursuit; she horribly avenged Jason on Pélias by duping the old usurper's daughters to kill him.   For that atrocity she and Jason had to flee from Iolcus to Corinth; and there Jason's self-seeking heart turned to the young beauty of the daughter of King Creon.

Here the play begins.   After a famous prologue by her nurse, Mēdēa, sentenced to instant banishment, pours out to the Chorus of Corinthian women her sense of the wrongs of womanhood.

> Men say we lead a sheltered life at home,
> While *they* must battle in the press of spears.
> Fools!—I had rather stand in the battle-line
> Thrice, than once bear a child.

                              (248–51.)

Then the self-important old Creon enters and she wheedles from him a day's respite from banishment—enough for her revenge.   There follows one of the finest lyrics of this often feminist play.

> Backward the waves of the sacred streams are driven—
>   All things lie confounded, Justice overborne.
> Men are turned to traitors and their solemn pledges, given
>   In Heaven's sight, forsworn.
> 'Tis time earth's songs were altered, to sing of Woman's fame—
> Ay, honour shall be rendered, at last, to Woman's name;
>   No more the ancient slanders shall hold us up to scorn.

[1] Cf. Pindar, *Pythian*, iv, and Apollonius Rhodius, *Argonautica* (*Greek Poetry for Everyman*, pp. 264, 320–6).

And *they* shall be silenced, the bards of old that chide us,
  Harping still their stories of false wives that fell.
Well for Men that Phoebus, the Lord of Song, denied us
    The poet's godlike spell!
Else *we* had sung our answer, and loud our lips had rolled
To men a chant of challenge. For Time, from years of old,
  Many a tale of the dealings 'twixt us and Man could tell.

(410–30.)

But now Euripides the poet yields place to Euripides the advocate, in a drably realist wrangle between Mēdēa and a Jason more egoistic even than Admētus, which ends in her scornful defiance. Next, Aegeus, King of Athens, arrives, on his way home from Delphi; and from him Mēdēa gains a promise of protection. Her retreat thus secured, she reveals to the Chorus her scheme of revenge—poison for Jason's bride, the sword for her two children by him. The horrified women of Corinth ask how such guilt shall find shelter in holy Athens.

Happy of old is the race of Erechtheïdae,
  Sprung from the blessed Gods in the days that were.
Never that land most holy has bowed to an enemy;
  Nurtured on glorious knowledge, bathed in translucent air,
They walk on their gracious ways; and the tale yet lingers,
How Harmony golden-tressed by the Nine Sweet Singers,
    The Muses, was cradled there.

And where the streams of fair Cēphīsus flow,
  Ever, they say, the Cyprian holds her place,
Drawing their living waters, and breathing soft and low
  Her balmy winds on Athens; o'ershadowing her face,
Fresh roses scent her tresses; by her sending,
Her Loves sit throned with Wisdom, ever lending
    The life of man new grace.

(824–45.)

This praise of Athens, with its foreshadowing of Plato, has itself earned enthusiastic praise. Yet dare I own that I feel in it, also, a touch of preciousness, as sometimes in Plato himself—a breath of that over-idealism which tends to prefer dream-beauties to the stern nakedness of truth? I distrust the Ivory Gate, like the Ivory Tower. This beautiful Athens was at that moment entering on those years of folly and brutality which were to fill the cold, calm pages of Thucydides, and goad Euripides himself to the extreme of sorrow and anger.

After Mēdēa has duped Jason by a seeming submission, she sends by her children's hands the poisoned robe and crown for the bride; then wrestles in agony with herself, whether or no to murder the children. The Chorus question whether it is worth having children at all. Their ode is perhaps worth quoting as an example of the strange blend of prose and poetry in Euripides. It *has* feeling—but not inspiration; its generalities read, in parts, too like a versified essay.

> Oft have I pondered
>   On words where truth was hard to find;
> Oft through disputations wandered
>   Hard to weigh for a woman's mind.
>
> Yet some of the wisdom of the Muses
>   Women as well can make their own;
> Some among *us* Their wisdom chooses—
> Who tries many women, not all refuses;
>   To women too are the Muses known.
>
> Therefore I say: whom none calls father—
>   The childless hearts—are the happiest ones;
> These are the fortunate, these, far rather
>   Than sires of sons.
>
> Through life they pass without discerning
>   If sons in the end be joy or care,
> Blest in their ignorance, never learning
>   The griefs that others bear.
>
> But those that have boys by their hearths upspringing—
>   Ah, lovely their growth!—and yet I see
> That ever the sires for their sons' upbringing
>   Live disquieted endlessly—
>
> Toiling ever to leave behind them
>   Wealth for their heirs; unknowing still
> What they shall find them,
>   For whom they labour—good or ill?
>
> And last of all, one crowning sorrow
>   For every home yet lurks in wait:
> Their sons may lack not for the morrow,
>   And their boyhood grow to man's estate,

The years may prove them noble-hearted—
    Yet, if God's will shall so befall,
Death comes—and the young life fades, departed
      To Hades' hall.

Sorrows enough beyond relieving
    We know: why must God also make
This bitterest of all man's grieving,
      For children's sake?

                        (1081–1115.)

A messenger bursts in—the princess and her old father have perished, as horribly as Hēracles by the poisoned robe of Dejaneira. Mēdēa then butchers her little sons; and as Jason batters too late at the doors, she appears above the roof in a dragon-chariot. With hideous taunts she refuses him even the dead bodies and predicts his own death, with one particularly horrible sneer at his laments of loneliness:

    You have yet to feel it.   Wait till you are *old*!

Then she soars away towards Athens. And so to the summing-up of the Chorus:

    In the treasure of Zeus lies many a lot.
      The Gods ordain what none foreknows.
    What men deemed sure, ensueth not;
      And what none dreamed of, They dispose.
      Such now this story's close.[1]

                        (1415–9.)

The play's influence has been vast. Through Antiquity artists vied in depicting its scenes.[2] When Alexander the Great's mother Olympias, likewise discarded for a rival, plotted the murder of his father Philip (336 B.C.), Alexander himself is said to have been sounded beforehand and to have given approval with a quoted line from *Mēdēa*. Brutus quoted another before stabbing himself after Philippi (42 B.C.). Cicero was reading the play in his litter when waylaid by Antony's cut-throats (43 B.C.). Even in A.D. 217 the Emperor Caracalla, the last time he dined with Dio Cassius before his assassination, with a kind of premonition cited the closing stanza of the Chorus (see above). Virgil learnt something from Mēdēa for his Dido; Ovid helped to transmit the heroine of Euripides through the dusk of the Middle Ages, to take her incongruous place among Chaucer's *Good Women*. Seneca, Corneille, Grillparzer, and many another redramatized

---

[1] A similar stanza ends *Alcestis, Andrómache, Helen,* and *The Bacchae.*
[2] See D. L. Page's admirable *Mēdēa* (1938), pp. lvii–lxviii.

the story.   Even to-day *Mēdēa* has been judged 'perhaps the finest work of Euripides.'

Others may feel about the play something brassy and theatrical.   It lacks that unity of tone which, essentially, Shakespeare keeps in his Roman plays, despite anachronisms, thanks to Plutarch and his own genius; and which, deliberately, Shaw's historical plays fail to keep.   It is easy, and sometimes fashionable, to assume that our forefathers differed from us only in their clothes.   But it is false.   Caesar was *not* like a twentieth-century Fabian; the Argonauts were *not* like fifth-century bourgeois.   One can understand why Aristophanes loathed attempts to make them so.

But one can also sympathize with the quandary of Euripides.   Part of him wanted to write modern plays: religious convention forced him, unlike Menander in comedy, to use ancient subjects.   If Ibsen had been forced to write *Hedda Gabler* in verse, date her in the period of King Harold Fairhair, and remove her from the stage mounted on a lindworm, his work would have suffered.

But, in addition, Euripides was both realist and romantic.   No harm in being one or other by turns, like Flaubert; but it is dangerous to attempt both in the same work.   Here Euripides has tarnished the golden legend of the Golden Fleece, yet has not, I think, created a satisfying modern play. *Mēdēa* falls between two ages.

Further trouble, I feel, arises from an effort to overstress the agony and barbarity.   In another more rational version of the story, Mēdēa's children were killed by the Corinthians, in revenge for their murdered king and princess.   But Euripides was set on Mēdēa's ghastly infanticide—indeed there is reason to think he invented it.   No doubt it gives scope for anguished mental conflict.   No doubt human beings are capable of anything, even of murdering their children to annoy their husbands.   But this becomes a little monstrous for realist drama.   Why not take her children away with her?   I do not really care about their being butchered, because I feel they are butchered for my benefit.   Ungrateful perhaps.   But authors should be careful of too deliberately wringing their hearers' hearts; nothing grows tougher than a heart too deliberately wrung.

Fortunately in our next play Euripides was to avoid these pitfalls.

HIPPOLYTUS
(428 B.C.)

Love is long-suffering, brave,
Sweet, prompt, precious as a jewel;
But O, too, Love is cruel,
Cruel as the grave.

Hardy.

Late in life, Theseus [1] wedded the young Phaedra, daughter of Minos, King of Crete, and sister of that Ariadne he had forsaken on Naxos long ago, after she saved him from the Minotaur. But he already had a natural son by Hippolyta, Queen of the Amazons. The tragedy came when this Hippolytus touched the heart and senses of the young Queen of Athens.

Here, as in *Mēdēa*, but far more finely, Euripides has studied a divided soul. And Phaedra's conflict is still real to us—the struggle of duty and honour against devouring desire. Indeed, with this play the Goddess of Love, who opens it, begins also that long reign of hers in the theatre, which has grown at times too tyrannous.

Our play is not Euripides' first version. In its earlier form, now lost, Phaedra was a wanton, like Sthéneboea (p. 11), making open advances to Hippolytus, till he veiled his face for shame. (Some idea of this first *Hippolytus* may be gained from the Latin *Phaedra* written by Nero's minister, Seneca—a piece, like all his plays, full of clever, but detestable decadence.) But this first draft shocked Athens, as well as Hippolytus. Revising it, Euripides changed his heroine to a guilt-tormented woman who, instead of wooing Hippolytus, speaks to him not one word. This reticence, like that of Alcestis returned from the grave, gains an impressiveness of its own. And by her inward struggle Phaedra becomes as superior in interest to her predecessor as, on a larger scale, Shakespeare's self-questioning Hamlet to *his* original.

Racine in his *Phèdre*, unwilling to forgo the drama of a love-scene between hero and heroine, followed Seneca, not Euripides; but in other respects he only amplified the Greek in making Phèdre an anguished soul, overwhelmed by irresistible temptation, like the Christian from whom God has withheld the gift of grace. Here Arnauld could recognize the signs of Racine's coming conversion, the indelible influence of a boyhood passed in the religious shades of Port-Royal. Unfortunately Racine, while developing Phèdre, was driven by the fashions of his day to spoil Hippolyte, by turning a *farouche* young recluse into a sighing gallant, *style Louis Quatorze*.

[1] Genealogical table, p. 353.

Like Seneca and Racine, Euripides might well have called his play after his heroine. He has drawn better characters; but never a character better. Her nurse, too, lives with a coarse but devoted vitality that yet does not clash too crudely, as Euripides' realist characters sometimes do, with the play's romance. Unfortunately Phaedra does not find any adequate counterpart in the noble prig Hippolytus; still less in the irritable old Theseus. Therefore the play languishes after her death, till it revives for a moment as Artemis bids farewell to the dying Hippolytus.

Apart from this, it is one of Euripides' best plots. The issue is still living; and Phaedra's revenge from beyond the grave, though horrible, is not unconvincing. And whereas the prologues of Euripides are often as dry as half-animated theatre-programmes, and his epiloguing deities often too like pantomime magicians, here the Aphrodite of the opening and the Artemis of the close, balanced as harmoniously as sculptured figures at the ends of a temple-pediment, stand for eternal realities—the two sides of Nature; the lush Nature that cares for fecundity, not for chastity; and the colder Nature of the lonely hills and 'winds austere and pure.' If both are amoral, that too is true. No Greek play expresses better the Greek sense of the importance of measure, balance, and restraint. With too little passion, life becomes a kind of death; with too much, it can become Hell.

Further, if Euripides was never a saner thinker, he was never a finer poet than here in some of the lyrics—the romantic longings of his tortured Phaedra, or the flight of his Chorus from the nightmare before them into dreams of the legendary past, of the legendary ends of the earth.

Wisdom, it is said, keeps school out of doors. Euripides often felt, not unlike Wordsworth, the contrast between the honest countryman and the sophisticated chatterer from the town. In a curious way that contrast sometimes applies to different sides of himself. Here and in *The Bacchae* he can lift his heart at moments to Nature and the hills—to Artemis or Dionysus. And his genius seems stimulated almost out of recognition.

It is typical too that *Hippolytus*, as we have it, is a second attempt. Ages ago 'Longinus' (first century A.D.) noted that Euripides was a laborious, not an effortless, genius; like a lion needing to lash itself with its tail. I doubt if Euripides was much like a lion; but it remains true that, where Aeschylus gives a sense of intuitive inspiration and Sophocles of happy balance between creation and self-criticism, Euripides, like our own age, seems to suffer often from a critical excess that cramps spontaneity and leads alternately to repression and to exaggeration. But, if he needed to hammer, sometimes he hammered well. Had only *Hippolytus* and *The Bacchae* survived, we should not know his versatility; his influence would have been far less; but he would hardly have seemed a smaller poet—very possibly a greater.

HIPPOLYTUS

APHRODITE	HER NURSE
ARTEMIS	OLD HUNTSMAN
THESEUS, King of Athens	SERVANT OF HIPPOLYTUS
HIPPOLYTUS, his natural son by	CHORUS OF HUNTSMEN
the Queen of the Amazons	CHORUS OF WOMEN OF TROEZĒN
PHAEDRA, daughter of Minos and	ATTENDANTS
wife of Theseus	

[*The palace of Troezēn. Before it, on opposite sides, images of Aphrodite and of Artemis. Above it appears Aphrodite herself.*]

Aphrodite. Great upon earth and high in Heaven endures
　　My power, nor dim my glory, that am called
　　The Cyprian Queen.　To all that live and look
　　Upon the sunlight, 'twixt the Pontic surge
　　To eastward and, to west, the Atlantic Gates,
　　Favour I give if they revere my greatness,
　　But, if they flout me—ruin!
　　For thus is the nature even of the Gods—
　　To be well pleased with honour from mankind.
　　And soon, that my words are truth, my deeds shall show.
　　　For Theseus' son by the Queen of Amazons,
　　Hippolytus, by the blameless Pittheus bred
　　Here in Troezēn, alone throughout the land
　　Dares to call *me* of all Gods evillest!—
　　And spurns at love and shuns the touch of wedlock.
　　Instead, as greatest of all Gods, he honours
　　Apollo's sister, Zeus-born Artemis;
　　And dedicated to that fellowship
　　Higher than human, he follows his Maiden Queen,
　　With his swift hounds, through the green woods for ever,
　　Clearing the land of beasts.
　　For *that* I care not.　What is *that* to me?
　　But, for his sin against myself, this day
　　I will smite Hippolytus.　Long since pursued
　　My purpose was; and little's left to do.
　　　For once from Pittheus' hall Hippolytus came
　　To the land of King Pandīon, there to see
　　The Holy Mysteries, as initiate.
　　And there, by my own devising, his father's wife,

246

The noble Phaedra, saw him; and her heart
Was gripped by passion's anguish.
So even then, in the days before she came
Here to Troezēn,
She raised a shrine beside the Rock of Pallas
To me, the Cyprian, looking towards this land,
Because her love was far.   For *his* sake there
She made that shrine, henceforth to bear his name.
But now—since Theseus, to escape pollution
From the blood of Pallas' sons, has bowed himself
To a year of banishment from Cĕcrops' land,
And brought her hither with him—his poor Queen,
Goaded by passion, sighs and wastes to death,
In silence.   None of all her household knows.
Yet not in silence shall her passion end.
I will open Theseus' eyes, and the truth be known,
So that he kills this son of his I hate,
By his own prayer; according to the promise
Vouchsafed him once by the sea's lord, Poseidon—
That whatsoever boons Theseus should ask,
Three times the God would grant them.

   And Phaedra, noble princess as she is,
Must perish too.   *Her* griefs I cannot weigh
Against such vengeance on my enemies
As sates my soul.
But here I see, from the sweat of the chase returning,
This Theseus' son, Hippolytus—I go.
Thick at his heels a rout of servitors
Come bawling out their hymns to Artemis;
But little he knows that already the Gate of Hades
Gapes; and, above him, stands the last sun he sees.

> *Aphrodite disappears and Hippolytus enters with his huntsmen.*
> *They pass Aphrodite's image without doing it reverence.*

Hippolytus. Praise, as ye come, on Her heavenly throne,
   Praise to the Zeus-born Artemis!—
   To Her that loves us as Her own!
Huntsmen. Hail, O Queen revered, adored,
      Maid most fair!—
   Daughter of Creation's Lord,
   Child of Zeus, that Lēto bare!
   Beside Thy Father in Heaven's height,
   Where His walls gleam golden-bright,
      Thy dwelling is.

Fairest, fairest Thou of all
Maids that tread Olympus' hall,
   Hail, Artemis!
       Hippolytus brings a wreath to the image of Artemis.
Hippolytus. To Thee I bring this garland, mistress mine,
  Twined from the flowers of an untrodden field,
  Where never shepherd dares to feed his flock,
  Nor scythe of mower came.   The bee alone
  Wings in the spring across that virgin meadow,
  Which Purity herself keeps watered green.
  And none may pluck its flowers—no evil heart—
  But those alone whose inbred, unschooled nature
  Still loves, in all life's ways, self-mastery.
  Mistress beloved, take Thou, from a hand revering,
  This garland to enclasp Thy locks of gold.
  To me alone of men Thou grantest this—
  To be beside Thee and to talk with Thee,
  Hearing Thy voice, although Thy face be hid.
  As in the beginning of my race of life,
  So be it to the end!
Huntsman. My lord—for the name of 'master' fits alone
  The Gods—may I proffer you a word of counsel?
Hippolytus. Why, surely!   Else, I should show but little wisdom.
Huntsman. Know you a rule that governs all men's hearts?
Hippolytus. Not I!   What means your question?
Huntsman. This!—to resent unfriendliness and pride.
Hippolytus. Rightly.   What pride is not insufferable?
Huntsman. Far different from the grace of courteous lips?
Hippolytus. Most true—a precious thing, of little cost.
Huntsman. Think you the like may hold true of the Gods?
Hippolytus. Yes.   If our human ways resemble theirs.
Huntsman. Yet there is *one* dread Goddess *you* ignore.
Hippolytus. Whom then!   Take care now, lest your tongue should trip!
Huntsman. She stands here at your gate—the Cyprian!
Hippolytus. From far I honour *her*.   My hands are pure.
Huntsman. Yet dread is She, and honoured in the world.
Hippolytus. I love not Gods whose powers are of the night.
Huntsman. *All* Gods, my son, should have due reverence.
Hippolytus. Yet men, like Gods, love better some than others.
Huntsman. May happiness be yours!—and wit to find it!
Hippolytus. Go now, my men!—indoors and take your meal!
  After the hunt a well-filled table's welcome.
  And see my horses groomed—when I have eaten,

I will yoke them to my car for exercise.
As for your Cyprian—fare she well, for me!

> *He goes out.   The old Huntsman turns to the image of Aphrodite.*

Huntsman. But *I*—for not for *us* to imitate
The young and thoughtless—humbly as fits a slave,
O Cyprian Queen, before Thy image here
Bow down in prayer.   Thou shouldst be merciful,
If any in the headstrong heat of youth,
Speaks idly of Thy name.   Seem not to hear him.
Surely the Gods should be more wise than men.

> *He too goes out.   There enters the Chorus of Women of Troezen.*
>
> *strophe* 1.

A Woman of the Chorus. From Ocean's hidden deeps, men say, uprushing,
　　A water subterrene
Fills, from the rock-face gushing,
　　Our pitchers in Troezēn:
And there by that waterside
　　I met with a friend I knew—
　　Mantles of purple hue
She dipped in the stream, and dried
On rocks where the sun beat warm.　'Twas she
First told me our Queen's calamity—

That in her palace now, by sickness faded,　　　　　*antistrophe* 1.
　　She wastes upon her bed;
With soft veils overshaded,
　　Dark lies her golden head.
Now the third day she lives
　　With lips divine sealed fast—
　　Through them not once hath passed
The bread Earth's Mother gives.
Suffering and still, she hasteneth
Towards that grim harbour whose name is Death.

Another. Has a God then, lady, possessed thee?—　　　　*str.* 2.
　　Is it Pan, or Hecate?
Has the Mountain Mother oppressed thee,
　　Or the dread Corybants, maybe?
Another. Or hast thou angered Dictynna,
　　　　The Huntress-queen, not keeping
　　Her rites, and her dues denied?
For far She can follow the sinner,
　　By water, by land, overleaping
　　　　The swirl of the eddying tide.

Another. Or thy lord, the long-descended   *ant. 2.*
    Prince of Erechtheus' line—
Has *he* by stealth offended,
    As he crept to a bed not thine?
Another. Or comes there some seafarer
    From a Cretan haven sailing,
      To hospitable Troezēn?—
Of bitter news the bearer,
    That in sorrow unavailing
      Chains to her couch the Queen?

Another. Yet frail is woman; hard to guide,   *epode.*
    Her nature's jarring elements;
Hers, for her sorrow, still abide
Labouring womb and craving sense.
Such travail-storms ere now oppressed
Me too—but on Her that easeth birth,
Queen of the Bow, I cried distrest.
She heard—and for ever I hymn Her worth,
Where She walks among the Blest.

Chorus-leader. But see—the Queen comes from her room.
Out of the palace her old nurse brings her—
Her own brow dark with a deepened gloom.
Ah, would to God some tongue could say
What evil wrings her,
That her beauty wastes away!

        Phaedra is led in by the Nurse. Her women follow.
Nurse. Ah, sickness!—the sorrows that life must see!
What now can I do? Or leave undone?
Here is your bed where you wished to be—
Outside, where Heaven arches free,
And shines the sun.

Hither you needs must come! In vain.
You will only long for your room again.
Nothing can please your fickleness.
You crave what you lack; what you possess,
But brings you pain.

        The attendants help their mistress to a couch.
Still worse to nurse the sick than bear
The sickness! A nurse has double grief—
Arms that ache and a heart of care.
Yet life brings sorrow for all to share,
And for labour no relief.

And if, after life, aught better abides,
Mists enfold it and darkness hides.
Vainly we yearn for some thing unknown,
Behind the grave we glimpse its gleam;
Yet hidden is life beyond our own,
And mystery over the tomb is thrown,
And we drift on tales of dream.

Phaedra. Raise up my body. Lift my head,
My women. Take these hands still fair—
The strength that knit my limbs is fled.
Unbind my coif—it aches to wear;
And over my shoulders loose my hair.

Nurse. Take courage, child!—not fretfully
Toss to and fro!
Nothing can ease this pain for thee
But a brave heart's tranquillity.
All born must suffer so.

Phaedra. Ah for some cool spring in a meadow!—
To drink clear waters plunging past!
There underneath the poplar-shadow,
In the long grass to lie at last!

Nurse. What means this moan,
My daughter? With so wild a tone
Cry not mad words in ears unknown.

Phaedra. Take me up, to the hills, to the hunting-grounds,
To the high pine-woods—with hunting-hounds
Athirst for slaughter, let me follow
The dappled deer!
Ah God, to shout the huntsman's hollo,
Gripping a lance of Thessaly!—
To feel my yellow hair toss free,
To fling my spear!

Nurse. But, child, what folly blinds thy brain!
What has the hunt to do with thee?
Why crave for torrents of the hills?
This green slope by our palace spills
Clear streams to drink, and drink again.

Phaedra. O Lady of Limne by the sea—
Tracks where the hammering horse-hoofs gleam!
To be there, with a wild Enétian team!—
And break them to my mastery!

Nurse. How swiftly thy folly changes fashion!
But now, thy fancy turned thy feet

To hunt the hills—now is thy passion
  For steeds, on the sands where no waves beat!
Wise indeed were the seer could say
What spirit drives thy heart astray
  And robs thee of thy senses, sweet.

Phaedra. What have I done? Ah, misery!
  Where have I wandered in my mind?
  Crazed, fallen, by God's hand struck blind!
  O dear nurse, veil again my head.
I blush for the words that broke from me.
  Cover my face, and the tears I shed,
  And the shame that bows my forehead low.
The sane have too much suffering;
  Yet madness—'tis a fearful thing.
  Better to die, and not to know!

Nurse. I veil thy head, then—would the earth
  Hid mine, at rest!
Of all life's lessons, from my birth,
  None true as this—that happiest
Are they that never love too deep
And give their hearts to none to keep!
  Better the passion that passes by,
Lightly come and lightly fled.
  Too bitter the burden, when *one* must try
  To bear the griefs of two; as I,
For this dear head.
The loyalty that loves unchanging ever,
  Brings life, they tell, small happiness;
Sick grows the soul with its endeavour;
  I praise, past all that seeks excess,
        The middle way—
And the wise will witness what I say.

Leader. Old dame, the faithful nurse, these many years,
  Of our unhappy Queen, we see her sorrow,
  But what it is that ails her—*that* lies hidden.
  May we not know?—not hear it from your lips?
Nurse. All questionings are vain—she will not tell.
Leader. Not even how her trouble first began?
Nurse. It is all the same. She will not speak a word.
Leader. How faint she lies there, in her faded beauty!
Nurse. How should she not? Three days she has tasted nothing.
Leader. Is she distracted? Or resolved on death?
Nurse. On death—at least, this fast she keeps grows deadly.

Leader. Strange! But her husband?—can he leave her so?

Nurse. Ah, but she hides it—will not own she suffers.

Leader. Can he not *see* the whole truth in her face?

Nurse. No.   For it happens he has left Troezēn.

Leader. Can you not wring it from her, by compulsion,
   Find what it is that ails her—clouds her mind?

Nurse. I have tried all; and tried it all in vain.

   Yet I will *not* give over, *not* lose heart.

   Come, you shall see yourself if I am true

   To my mistress in her trouble.

      Listen, dear daughter.   Let us both forget

   What we have said—but be not so forbidding!

   Smooth out that brow of gloom, and change your thoughts.

   And I—if before I too much shared your sadness,

   Now I will turn to try a wiser way.

   Come!—if your sickness is a secret one,

   These women here will help to bring you through it.

   But if a man may hear it, then speak out,

   And we will tell the truth to your physicians.

                              [*Phaedra does not answer.*

      Ah God, still silent!   Silence is wrong, my child!

   If what I say is false, point out my error;

   If it is true—why, then accept the truth.

      Oh speak!   Look in my face!   Ah bitterness!

   See, women of Troezēn, we lose our labour,

   And gain no ground at all.   My former pleadings

   Left her unmoved; and still she will not listen.

      Yet hear me now—to this too, if you can,

   Be deafer than the sea!   If thus you die

   Abandoning your children, *they* will forfeit

   All birthright from their father—yes!   I swear it

   By that bold-riding Queen of the Amazons

   Whose son shall be their master—well you know him!—

   That bastard with a soul of true-born honour,

   Hippolytus—

Phaedra.   My God!

Nurse.   So *that* can touch you?

Phaedra. Nurse, thy words kill me.   Now, by Heaven above,
   Never again breathe *that* man's name to me!

Nurse. You see the danger!—yet, with open eyes,
   Will neither save yourself, nor help your children!

Phaedra. I love them.   This storm that sinks me blows not *thence.*

Nurse. There is no blood-stain, child, upon your hands?

Phaedra. My hands are clean: the stain is on my heart.

Nurse. Is there some enemy has done you wrong?

Phaedra. One I love ruins me.   Neither of us willed it.

Nurse. Is Theseus guilty of some fault against you?

Phaedra. Never may *he* have fault to find with *me*!

Nurse. Why then, what fear makes you resolved to die?

Phaedra. Leave me to err!   I err not against *thee*.

Nurse. Leave you!   I *will* not.   It is I that am left—forsaken!

She kneels before Phaedra.

Phaedra. What!   Will you force me!—clinging to my hand!

Nurse. And to thy knees!   I will not let thee go.

Phaedra. Bitter, poor nurse, you would find the truth—too bitter!

Nurse. What bitterer pain to bear than losing thee?

Phaedra. You will be my ruin!   I do this for my honour.

Nurse. Yet what I ask is good—can you refuse?

Phaedra. I am struggling to pluck honour out of shame.

Nurse. Speak then—your fame shall only stand the fairer.

Phaedra. In God's name leave me now—let go my hand.

Nurse. No!   You deny me the trust that is my due.

Phaedra (slowly). I give it then.   I am shamed to grudge your prayer.

Nurse (rising). I say no more.   *Your* tongue must speak the rest.

Phaedra. Ah mother!   What a passion once was thine!

Nurse. What do you mean, my child?   The Bull of Crete!

Phaedra. You too, poor sister—bride of Dionysus!

Nurse. What ails you, child?   These tales that blot your race!

Phaedra. And now I am the third to be undone.

Nurse. This grows too horrible!   What follows next?

Phaedra. Thence falls an ancient curse on all our blood.

Nurse. But still this leaves my questioning unanswered.

Phaedra. Ah!

Would God that *you* could say this thing, not I!

Nurse. *I* have no prophet's gift, to read such riddles.

Phaedra. Ah, what is this strange thing that men call 'love'?

Nurse. The sweetest thing in life; yet bitter too.

Phaedra. But mine, I fear, must be its bitterness.

Nurse. What are you saying, child?   In love!   With whom?

Phaedra. The Queen of Amazons—she had a son. . . .

Nurse. Hippolytus!

Phaedra.   *Thou* namest him, not I.

Nurse. Child!   What comes *now*?   Your words are death to me.

O friends!—unbearable!—I *cannot* bear
Life any longer!   Light of day, I curse thee—

I curse thee, Sun in Heaven.   Let me go,
And hurl me headlong, and be quit of life,
Laid with the dead.   Farewell!   This is the end.
For now I know that even honest women,
Fight how they may, can still grow passionate
With love of evil.   Ah, Love is no Goddess,
But a thing more powerful than any God,
Destroying her, and me, and all her race.

One of the Chorus. Marked you the Queen!
    Ah, when have been
    Words of such anguish spoken?

Another. For me, dear Lady, better death
    Than what thy madness suffereth!

Another. Poor heart, by its sorrows broken!

Another. Ah pain, that is man's daily bread!

Another. Lost!—thou art lost!—such horrors to disclose!

Another. What shall this long day bring thee, ere it goes?

Another. Sure, for this house some doom of dread.

Another. Too clear, poor child of Crete, to what dark end
    This curse of the Cyprian must at last descend.

Phaedra. Ah women of Troezēn, that have your dwelling
    Here at this outer gate of Pĕlops' land,
    Oft in the night's long watches I have pondered
    What cause it is brings human lives to ruin.
    I cannot think it is defect of reason
    Leaves us undone.   For many have discernment.
    To me the truth seems other.
    We well know what is good; we understand,
    Yet will not face the struggle—some are idle,
    Some sacrifice their honour for the sake
    Of pleasure—life can bring so much of pleasure—
    Long hours of talk; and idleness, sweet poison.
    [And our own sense of pride.   Two kinds there are
    Of pride—one not dishonourable; but one—
    False, and a household curse.   If men judged rightly,
    They could not use one word to name them both.]
        Now since I hold this certain, no enchantment
    Could have the potency to overturn
    My sure conviction.   So, in my present trouble,
    I reasoned thus:
    When first Love wounded me, I asked myself
    How best I might endure.   In the beginning
    My choice was silence, and to hide my hurt.

For how could I trust my tongue? Our tongues are glib
To school the hearts of others with advice,
And yet most deadly for our own undoing.
Next, I resolved that I would bear my madness
Nobly, and crush it out by self-control.
Lastly, when both these remedies proved vain
Against Love's violence, I vowed to die.
And this—past all denial!—is the best.
I would not see obscured my better actions;
But few be the eyes that see me sink dishonoured!
I knew that all I did now—all I suffered—
Would bring me shame; knew, too, I was a woman,
And so a thing men hate. Accurst the wife
Who first dared to defile her marriage-bed
With a seducer! Such iniquity
First took its rise with women of noble blood;
For once the high-born turn them to foul ways,
Quickly the base will find them fair enough.
Curst, too, be all those modest-spoken wives
That yet in secret dare all shamelessness!
How can they bear, O sea-born Cyprian Queen,

She turns to the image of Aphrodite.

To look unblenching in their husbands' eyes?
Nor shudder at the darkness their accomplice,
Nor fear the very walls will cry aloud?
      Dear friends, *this* is the cause that brings my death—
That never I may shame before the world
My husband, and my children.   Let them live
In glorious Athens with free hearts, frank faces,
And honour unblemished from their mother's side.
For a father's guilt, or mother's, makes a man,
Stout-hearted though he be, creep like a slave.
Well it is said, that naught stands up to life
But a spirit that is just and honourable;
For Time, one day, confronts the base with all
His baseness; as a girl sees her young beauty
Clear in her mirror.   God keep *that* from me!
Leader. O Heaven, how lovely, always, goodness is—
    A flower whose fruit is honour!
Nurse. Ah mistress mine, how you did frighten me
    At first with your misfortune!
    But now I see, I was poor-spirited,

And second thoughts are wiser.   This your passion
Is nothing so unheard of, nor past reason.
It is Aphrodite's anger falls upon you.
You are in love?   What wonder?   Many are.
Because you are in love, why talk of death?
Fine end for all the lovers in the world—
And all that shall love hereafter—just to die!
Love's Goddess is too hard for human strength,
When She puts forth Her power.   Gently She comes
To those that bow to Her; but when She finds
A heart presumptuous and arrogant,
Why, then—what would you?—then She tramples it.
Her path is through the Heavens; Her feet are set
Upon the surging seas; all springs from Her.
For still She sows love's seed, still quickens passion
From which we children of this earth are born.
They that have turned the scrolls of ancient lore,
Conversing with the Muses, know full well
How Zeus once fell in love with Sémele,
And how fair-glittering Dawn once snatched to Heaven
Her darling Céphalus.   Yet those they loved
Abide in Heaven still—*they* do not flee
From their immortal lovers—well content,
Methinks, with what befell them.
Will *you*, then, still be stubborn?   Ah, if you
Will not accept these laws that rule our nature,
Your father should have sealed some covenant,
Before he got you—made a pre-condition
Your life should bow to other Gods than ours.
How many, think you, most sagacious husbands
See well that their marriage ails, but shut their eyes!
How many fathers stand accessary
To the passions of their children!   Worldly wisdom
Warns us to let unhandsome things lie hid.
Vain to be *too* elaborate in life.
Even the beam that bears the roof aloft
Cannot lie wholly straight.   What hope, for you,
To swim from such deep waters safe to shore?
You are but human—rest you well content
If the goodness in your heart outweighs the evil.

   And so, dear daughter, cease this black despair,
Cease from this pride of heart—for pride it is
To think you can be stronger than the Gods.

Have the courage of your passion.   For a God
Hath willed it so.   And since your soul is sick,
Deal wisely with the sickness.
There are, for such things, magic words and charms
And we will find some sovereign remedy.
Ay, truly men would be hard put to it,
Without us women to find out a way.

Leader. Phaedra, in this thy grief thy nurse's tongue
Speaks the more shrewdly—but *thou* hast still my praise.
And yet my praise must be less pleasant hearing,
And colder comfort, than her counsel is.

Phaedra. Ah, this it is brings ruin on human homes
And prosperous cities—too fine-sounding phrases.
Men need, not speeches pleasant to the ear,
But what will lead them on the path of honour.

Nurse. What lofty talk!   It is not specious words
You need—it is the *man*!   We must see clear
At once, by speaking out the truth about you.
If it was not your *life* that hung imperilled,
If *you* were a woman mistress of herself,
So far I would not lead you, for the sake
Of passion, or of pleasure.
But now—to save you needs a crowning effort;
And who shall blame me?

Phaedra. O monstrous words!   Will you not hold your tongue!
Have done with uttering such foulnesses.

Nurse. Foul they may be: foul means will serve you now
Far more than fair.
Better the act that saves you—if it can—
Than some fine name to deck you when you die.

Phaedra. No more, by Heaven!   You speak too cleverly
Such words of shame!   I have subdued my soul
To bear my love; but with your specious tempting
I shall be sunk in the very sin I hate.

Nurse. If that's your mind, your heart should not have sinned;
But since it *has*, now hear.   Not much to grant me!
There in the house I have—now I remember—
Philtres with power to charm all love asleep.
And these shall cure you, if you have the courage;
Nor touch your honour; nor derange your mind.

Phaedra. This drug of yours—is it a salve or potion?

Nurse. I know not, child.   You need a cure; not questions.

Phaedra. I fear this air of over-subtlety.

Nurse. You would fear anything! Afraid of what?
Phaedra. That you may breathe some word to Theseus' son.
Nurse. Let me alone, child. I will manage all.

          She turns to the image of Aphrodite.

Only do Thou, O sea-born Cyprian Queen,
Grant me Thy help. What else I have in mind—
Enough to speak of *that* to friends within.

                                  [She goes into the palace.

Chorus. Ah Eros, Eros, whose hand distils   strophe 1.
   Into our eyes the grace that fills
   With sweetness hearts Thou wouldst assail,
   Come not with Evil on Thy trail,
     Come not too wild!
   There is no star so blasting, fire so hot,
   As are the shafts that Love hath shot,
     The Thunderer's child.

In vain by Phoebus' Pythian shrine   *antistrophe* 1.
Hellas heaps high her slaughtered kine,
And by Alphēus' stream in vain,
While Eros, all earth's suzerain,
   We worship not—
Guard of sweet Aphrodite's bridal door,
Whose onset racks with ruin and war
   Our mortal lot!

Thus by the Cyprian's will   *str.* 2.
   Was given, virgin still
And innocent, as bride to Hēracles,
   Oechalia's daughter torn
   From her father's house, forlorn
As maddened Maenad, or shy Nymph that flees.
Mid smoke and blood, that from men slain
   Ran streaming red,
With battle-cries to sound her bridal strain,
   Poor maid, she wed!

   What Cypris' coming brings,   *ant.* 2.
    You too, O Dirce's springs,
And, hallowed towers of Thebes, too well you know—
   How with thunder and lightning's flame
   To Sémele Love came,
Mother of twice-born Bacchus, and laid her low;

The bride at last of Doom was she,
  With death for dower.
Fierce through the world flies Love, as flies a bee
  From flower to flower.

                  Voices within.   *Phaedra goes to the door and listens.*
Phaedra. Hush!   O my friends, now I am lost indeed!
Leader. What terror shakes you, Phaedra?   What's within?
Phaedra. Wait!—let me catch their voices.
Leader. I say no more.   This prelude's grim enough!
Phaedra. Oh, oh, oh!
  O misery of my fate!
Leader.   What means your cry?   What voice is there?
    Tell me, good lady!
    What are these words that bring despair?
Phaedra. Ah, I am ruined!   Come hither to the door!
  Listen to that wild outcry there within!
Leader.   Nay, *thou* art nearer.   It is for thee
    To catch their speech.
    What is this new calamity?
Phaedra. The son of that bold-riding Amazon,
  Hippolytus, heaps curses on my woman.
Leader.   I hear a shouting—yet cannot hear
    What words they are
    That break through the doors upon thine ear.
Phaedra. Ah, clear enough!   'Accursed go-between,'
  He calls her—'traitress to her master's bed.'
Leader.   Alas, dear heart!   Betrayed and sold!
    What counsel now?
    'Tis ruin for thee—thy secret's told!
Phaedra.   Oh, oh!
Leader.   Betrayed by her that you loved of old!
Phaedra. She has destroyed me, telling my misfortune.
  Her love sought healing—but it brings me shame.
Leader. And now what will you do, in this despair?
Phaedra. Only one way I know.   One cure alone
  For what has come upon me—quickest death!

                 Hippolytus rushes forth through the door, followed by the Nurse.
Hippolytus. O Mother Earth!   O all-revealing Sun!
  What have I heard—what things unutterable!
Nurse. Be quiet, my son!   Your shouting will be heard.
Hippolytus. Too hideous what I heard, to keep it quiet!
Nurse. By this right hand, by this fair arm I beg you——

                              [*She clings to him.*

Hippolytus. Keep off your hand.   Dare not to touch my garment.
Nurse. I *beseech* you!—by your knees!   Do not destroy me!
Hippolytus. What frightens you?   You *say* you have done no wrong!
Nurse. Son, what I said is not for common ears.
Hippolytus. What's well is but the better, told abroad.
Nurse. Dear son, do not dishonour your sworn word.
Hippolytus. My tongue it was, but not my heart, that swore.
Nurse. What will you do, son?   Ruin those that love you?
Hippolytus. Faugh!   Never evil heart had love of mine.
Nurse. Forgive, my son!   All frailty is but human.
Hippolytus. Ah God, why hast Thou set beneath the sun
   This curse of man, this counterfeit called 'woman'?
   If Thy will *was* to multiply mankind,
   It should have been by other means than that!
   Better if men made offering in Thy temples—
   Gold, iron, or massy bronze—and bought thereby
   Offspring to match its value.   Then their homes
   Could have been free from women's tyranny.
   The curse they are is clear enough by this—
   That the very fathers who begot and bred them,
   Must give rich dowries to be rid of them.
   Then wretched men take home these pests—rejoicing,
   Wasting their wealth, their happiness, to deck
   With finery and fairest of adornment
   These foulest idols!
   The lightest lot is his that keeps at home
   Some futile fool, some nothing of a wife;
   But the clever ones I loathe—may hearth of mine
   Never be cursed with a woman that thinks too much!
   It is in nimble brains the Cyprian breeds
   Readiest mischief; while a stupid woman
   Is saved from such follies by mere want of wit.
   But never wives should have she-servants' visits—
   Better it were they lived with dumb, brute beasts
   And never a soul to talk or listen to.
   For these adulteresses hatch at home
   Plots that their women carry forth abroad;
   As thou, base wretch, hast come to me to traffic
   With the inviolate bed of my own father.
   Faugh!   Let me find some stainless running water
   To wash my ears of it!
   How couldst thou dream that I would stoop to listen,
   Who feel myself polluted but to hear it!

Be thankful, woman, that my scruples save thee!
Hadst thou not trapped me unawares with oaths,
Nothing should have withheld me from revealing
All to my father.　As it is, so long
As *he* is from Troezēn, I quit this palace.
I *will* keep silence.　But the day I come,
Returning with King Theseus, I shall watch
How you and your mistress dare to meet his eyes—
Then I shall know, and taste, your brazenness.
Curse you!　No, never can I utter all
My loathing of women!—not though I be blamed
For harping on one theme eternally;
For *they* no less repeat their infamy.
Let *them* learn modesty, or be it mine
To cry their shame for ever.

Ignoring the silent Phaedra, he goes out.

Phaedra. Ah, desolate
　Is woman's fate!
　What now can I do, or say,
　To loose this noose of doom drawn tight—
　My punishment?　O Earth, O Light,
　Where flee away?
　Such suffering grows too hard to hide.
　What God, what man, will help me now, my friends?
　Lend me his hand, or gather to my side?
　Evil I did—and thus it ends!
　Past all escape comes ruin on me.
　When knew a woman such agony?
Leader. Alas, it is finished.　All your nurse's arts
　Are gone to wreck, dear mistress.　Evil hour!
Phaedra (*turning on her Nurse*).　Accursed wretch!　The ruin of those
　　　　　　　　　　that loved you!
　What have you done to me!　May Zeus my grandsire
　With his lightning blast thee to annihilation!
　Did I not bid you—yes, I guessed your purpose—
　Say not a word of what has stained my name?
　But *you* must talk!　Gone now my hope of dying
　With honour!　I must find some new defence.
　For now this man, whetted to sharpest anger,
　Will denounce me to his father for your fault—
　Denounce all my misfortune to old Pittheus—
　Fill the whole world with foulest accusations!

A curse upon you and all meddling friends
That force their ignoble help on the unwilling!

Nurse. Mistress, you well may chide my ill success.
It stings you to the heart; and blinds your judgment.
But even to this I have—if you will but listen—
An answer still.   I nursed you and I love you.
I tried to heal your pain.   But failed to reach
What I had hoped for.   If I had, ah then
How wise you would have called me!   Wisdom's credit
Hangs merely on the luck that crowns the issue.

Phaedra. Ha, this is fair, you think?—and should content me?
You cut me to the heart—then bandy words!

Nurse. We talk too much.   True, I have played the wanton;
Yet even now, my child, there is chance of safety.

Phaedra. Have done!   Your first advice to me was evil;
Vile your attempt.   Begone!   Think of yourself.
And I will set my own affairs to rights.
                                              [*The Nurse creeps out.*

But grant me, noble daughters of Troezēn,
This my one prayer—
To hide all you have heard, in secrecy.

Leader. I swear by Artemis, dread child of Zeus,
Never to bring your sorrows to the light.

Phaedra. Thanks to you all.   One way alone I find,
In this disaster, that will give my children
An honourable life, and help myself,
As things have fallen now.
I will not shame the royal race of Crete,
Nor blush before the face of my own husband,
For one life's sake.

Leader. Some plan of evil irretrievable—?

Phaedra. Yes.   Death!   But how?—*that* must be *my* decision.

Leader. Ah, say not so!

Phaedra.   Yes, friends!   From you at least
Let me have *good* advice.
Since the Cyprian destroys me, I this day
Will take my leave of life—yes, She shall triumph,
And I fall victim to love's cruelty.
And yet, dead though I am, I will be deadly
To one that lives.
So he shall learn not to look down in pride
Upon my ruin.   He *had* part in my sickness—
He too shall learn the need for modesty!
                                              [*She enters the palace.*

Chorus. God, to some trackless mountain-hollow   *strophe* 1.
    Would I had wings to fly!—
Wings, where the wild birds flock, to follow
    Across the western sky,
To where Erídanus' waters
    Sweep down to Adria's wave,
And the Sun-god's sorrowing daughters
    Bewail their brother's grave,
While gleaming through that purple deep
Amber fall the tears they weep!

Or where, while apples round them redden,   *antistrophe* 1.
    Chant the Hesperides,
And the Sea-god guards, to ships forbidden,
    His purple waste of seas!
For there, in Atlas' keeping,
    Lies Heaven's sacred bound,
There springs divine rise leaping
    By walls where Zeus hath found
Peace, and the kindly Earth doth bless
The Gods' immortal happiness.

Ah white-winged ship of Crete,   *str.* 2.
That over the surges' beat
Through wastes of sea conveyed
My Queen, from out the home of happy years,
A happy bride—and yet the bride of tears!
Curst was that keel, the day from Crete she weighed
To fly like some dark bird of bane
Towards glorious Athens and the strand
Of Mūnychus; curst, when her sailors made
Her fast again,
And trod the Attic land!

For now, by a love perverse   *ant.* 2.
And Aphrodite's curse,
Beneath her misery
Our Queen lies broken.   Soon shall a rope be cast
From the beams of her bridal-chamber, and made fast
About the throat that was so white to see.
Bowed by her shame, by Love opprest,
She has chosen still the better part;
Honoured at least she leaves her memory.
And lays to rest
That ache within her heart.

Cries are heard within the palace.

A Woman's Voice (*within*). Help, help!
　　Come quickly, hasten!—here within the palace!
　　Our mistress—the Queen of Theseus—she is hanged!

One of the Chorus. Ah, all is over!　Round her neck the noose,
　　Dead is our royal lady.

The Voice (*within*). Will you not hurry!　Quick, a two-edged knife,
　　To cut away the cord!

Another of the Chorus. Ah friends, what shall we do?　Enter the palace?—
　　Loose from the Queen this knot that strangles her?

Another. What use?　Has she not her young men-servants there?
　　And life is perilous for meddling hands.

The Voice (*within*). Straighten the limbs of the unhappy dead—
　　This bitter thing that keeps house for our Lord!

Another. Poor woman!　Life is over.　I can hear—
　　As a dead body, now, they straighten her.

　　　　　　　　King Theseus enters with his followers; his head garlanded, for
　　　　　　　　he is returning from a pilgrimage to some shrine.

Theseus. What means this clamour, women?—can you tell me?—
　　There in the palace?　Loud with grief I hear
　　My servants' voices.　And the doors are closed,
　　That should stand wide with welcome to a pilgrim
　　Come from the House of God.
　　Has anything befallen Pittheus' age?
　　Far gone in years he is; yet a bitter blow
　　It would be, still, to know our house had lost him.

Leader. Theseus, what now has happened touches not
　　The old.　It is yours to mourn for death in youth.

Theseus. God!　Has a child of mine been robbed of life?

Leader. *They* live.　Their mother's dead.　Most bitterly.

Theseus. What!　My wife gone!　How did she come to die?

Leader. Within a hanging rope she noosed her neck.

Theseus. Some cold despair of life?　Or some disaster?

Leader. We know no more.　Only this moment, Theseus,
　　I reached your threshold here—to share your grief.

Theseus. Oh, misery!　Unhappiest of pilgrims,
　　What serves me now this garland round my head?

　　　　　　　　　　　　　　　　　　　　　　　　[*He tears it off.*

　　Undo the bolts, men, fling the doors wide open!
　　Bring to my eyes this sight of bitterness—
　　My wife!—that, dying, leaves me, too, destroyed!

　　　　　　　　The palace-door opens, revealing Phaedra on her bier with
　　　　　　　　mourning women round her.

One of the Chorus. What hast thou suffered, what hast done,
    Sad, suffering heart!—
A deed to wreck the royal line of our land!
Another. To an evil end so rashly run!
    Poor wrestler, overthrown thou art
      By thine own hand.
    Who *was* it darkened from thy days the sun?
Theseus. Ah burden of sorrow!   Ah Troezēn!   *strophe.*
      No grief like this my life hath seen!

How hard on this house, O Fate, thy foot hath trod!
O brand burnt deep by some Avenging God!

    Ruin of my life!—no life for me,
    Before whom spreads a boundless sea

Of sorrows, wave on wave, for evermore;
I drown in it, far off from sight of shore!

    Wife that I loved, what word shall guess
    This secret of thy dim distress?

Slipped from my hands, as some bird fluttereth,
Thou hast plunged headlong down the Gulfs of Death.

    Alas my sorrow!   This sure is sent
    By the high Gods upon my head
    As punishment
    For sins forgot of my fathers dead.
Leader. Lord, thou art not alone in suffering so;
Many a husband weeps a true wife dead.
Theseus.   Out of the light, out of the light   *antistrophe.*
      Would God I were laid, in the House of Night,

Since I am left without thee, sweet, alone!
Death thou hast dealt me!—bitterer than thine own!

    Ah but to know—what was it woke
    This thought of death in thy heart that broke?

Can *no* man tell me?   Are ye useless all,
Servants of mine that crowd this royal hall?

    Alas, my lost one!   Oh despair
    Too deep for words, too black to bear,

Darkening my home!   Now all my life lies ended;
Orphaned, my children; and my hearth unfriended

Thou hast left them alone now—left them forgot!
Ah best and dearest, the like of thee
The sun sees not,
Nor all night's starry eyes can see.

One of the Chorus. Unhappy king, with tears my eyes are blind
To watch thy fate,
And all thy house left desolate.
Yet I shudder to think what waits behind.

Theseus. But look!
What can it mean, this tablet hanging here
From her dear hand? Maybe, it can tell us more?
Or, rather, has she left some last request,
Poor Queen, about our children; or my marrying
Some other after her?
Fear not, poor heart! There lives no other woman
Shall share the home of Theseus, or his bed.

                                 [He lifts the tablet.

How smiles on me the old familiar seal
From the gold ring of her that's gone for ever!
Now to unwind the threads that wrap the wax,
And see what it will tell me.

                                   [He reads.

Another Woman. Alas and alas, how ill on ill is hurled!
Disaster on disaster Heaven brings!
After such misery
Life loses worth for me.

Another. Lost and undone—no longer of this world—
I count the race of our ancestral kings.

Leader. God, if it may be, hearken to my prayer—
Wreck not this house! For now, as a prophet marks
Some boding bird, I see the signs of doom.

Theseus. Horror on horror! Unendurable!
Unspeakable! What wretchedness is mine!

Leader. What is it? Say, my lord—if I may hear?

Theseus. It cries out things unutterable—it cries,
This tablet. How escape such agony!
These characters traced here before my eyes
Wail out a dirge to me.

Leader. Ah *there* speaks what a prelude to disaster!

Theseus. It sticks at the gates of speech, this word
Of horror. Yet it *shall* be heard!
Hear, all Troezēn!

Hippolytus has dared by force befoul
My bed!—defied the dreadful eye of God!
But Thou, Poseidon!—Father!—that hast promised
Fulfilment to three prayers that I should pray,
Hear this one now!
Destroy my son!—yea, let him not outlive
This day!—if indeed Thy gift was not a dream.

Leader. In Heaven's name, my lord!—call back your prayer!
The future shall yet confute you.   Trust my word!

Theseus. Impossible!   To exile, too, I doom him.
One fate, or other, surely shall strike him down.
Either Poseidon, hearkening to my curse,
Shall thrust him dead to Hades;
Or else, a homeless exile from Troezēn,
He shall drag a bitter life through alien lands.

Leader. But look!   Your son himself—Hippolytus!
Timely he comes.   Ah, Theseus, lay aside
This fatal anger—think of your royal line.

Hippolytus (entering). Father, I heard your voice—raised loud in sorrow—
And hurried here.   Tell me—for I know nothing—
What is your grief?

He sees the dead Phaedra.

Ha, what is this!   My father!   Your own Queen,
Dead!   But how strange!   One that I only left
A moment since—that looked upon the sunlight
So short a while ago!
What happened to her, then?   What brought her death?
I beg you, father!—tell me!
Silence?   What use is it to grieve in silence?
The human heart, that longs to know all truth,
Even when truth is bitter craves it still;
And, father, *you* are wrong to hide your sorrows
From those that are your friends—and more than friends.

Theseus. O race of men
So often erring, yet no wiser still!
What use are all the thousand arts you teach—
All your devices and discoveries,
When this one thing
You neither know nor ever tried to know—
How to plant sense within the brain of fools!

Hippolytus. It would be a master of his art, indeed,
That could compel a fool to quit his folly!

But this is no time for subtleties, my father.
I fear this grief has left you overwrought.
Theseus. Would God that men had but some certain sign
To put to proof the hearts of those they love,
And know which was the loyal, and which the traitor!—
Ay, would we all had *two* tones in our speech—
One for true dealing, and the other merely
To serve occasion; so the lying tongue
Might stand revealed beside the tones of truth,
And we no more be duped!
Hippolytus. What!—has some friend been breathing in your ear
Slanders of *me*!—tainting my guiltless honour!
This thing grows ghastly.   Yes, aghast they leave me,
Your words that ramble from a brain distracted.
Theseus. Ah heart of man—what lengths will it not go to?
What limits to its wanton shamelessness?
For if it swells with each new generation,
If in extravagance of villainy
The sons outdo the fathers, to this earth
Heaven must add some other world to hold
Its ruffians and scoundrels.
Behold this man that, born a son of mine,
Defiled my bed!—now by my dead wife's word
Convicted, past all doubt, of infamy!
Look in my face, since you have sunk indeed
To this pollution.   Meet your father's eye!
Is it *you* that are no ordinary man,
But walk with Gods!   Yes, *you*, the self-controlled,
The pure of heart!   Ask not that *I* believe
Your boastings; or be fool enough to think
The Gods so blind as *that*!
Go, swell your pride, purchase a peddling glory
By meals kept pure from flesh!   Cry 'Lord' to Orpheus!
Pursue your pious vapours—hold in honour
The holy books of Bacchus!
Now you are caught!   And I bid the world beware
Of you and all your like—schemers of vileness,
That with fine phrases hunt your private ends.
My Queen is dead—do you hope her death shall save you?
Scoundrel!   It shall but brand your guilt the deeper.
What oaths, what pleadings, in your own defence
Can weigh against *her* witness?
Will you say she hated you?—that bastard sons

Can find no favour with a wedded wife?
Truly she held life cheap, if just for spite
She sacrificed the dearest thing men have!
Will you plead that men are no such fools of passion,
But 'tis inbred in women? Yet I know
Young men that are as little to be trusted,
Whenever the Cyprian troubles youth's hot blood.
Their very manhood makes them but the bolder.
So now—but why should I bandy words with you,
When the dead bears this clearest testimony?
Begone from this land, at once!—to banishment!
Dare not to tread the earth of god-built Athens,
Nor any frontier subject to my sword.
For if I let you triumph, this outrage done,
Not even the witness of the Isthmian Sïnis
Can leave men sure I did not boast but idly
His overthrow; and those sea-bordering rocks
Of Scïron will in vain proclaim aloud
That *I* bring death to villains.

Leader. How from this day dare I call any man
'Happy'?—for now our noblest are brought low.

Hippolytus. Father, this gathered fury in your soul
Is terrible. Your charge may lend itself
To lofty-sounding phrases; yet, laid bare,
It shows but ugly. All unskilled am I
To speak before a crowd. I could plead better
In presence of a few—as young as I.
But men whom the wise hold cheap—so fate has willed it—
Are cleverer at haranguing multitudes.
Yet since this ill has chanced, I must perforce
Give my tongue rein. First for this first indictment
You sprang upon me—hoping I should be crushed
And struck too dumb to answer. Look you there
Upon this sun above, this earth beneath us—
No living man they know, say what you will,
More pure of heart than I. For I have learnt,
First, reverence for Heaven: next, to choose
For friends of mine, not men with a love of evil,
But hearts too honourable to tempt to wrong,
Or by base services repay their comrades.
Nor am I, father, one that mocks his fellows,
But loyal in their absence as their sight;
And, above all, untouched by that one sin

Of which you would convict me. To this day
My flesh is virgin. Nothing I know of love—
Except by talk and seeing pictures of it.
And little zest have I for even that,
Being maiden still in spirit.
Little, maybe, you care for my restraint;
Yet show, at least, what was there here to tempt me?
Could I find no woman's body in the world
Lovely as hers? Could *I* hope to inherit
Your house by wedding *her?*—your Queen and heiress!
I should have been mere fool—no, downright mad.
The sweetness of a throne? Who cares for that,
Whose soul is upright—though it *can* corrupt
Minds that are dazzled by mere sovereignty.
Far rather *I* would choose to stand the first
In our Greek games; but hold a second rank
In my own city—and so live at ease,
Friend to its noblest. *There*'s a life of action,
Yet free of danger—happier than a king's.
You have my answer—save for one thing more:
Had I some witness to my own true nature,
Were *she* but living still to plead against,
The facts themselves would *make* you see the guilty.
But now—by Zeus and by this Earth beneath us,
I swear I never touched your marriage-bed—
Nor could have wished it—no, not dreamed of it!
Were I so villainous, then let me perish,
Nameless and fameless, homeless, cityless—
A banished outlaw wandering through the world!
And, even dead, let sea and land alike
Reject my carrion!
But as for *her*—if fear drove her to death,
I do not know. And more I must not say.
Honour she had not; yet she died with honour:
But I that have it, kept it all in vain!

Leader. You have made full answer to your accusation.
　　Weighty indeed, this oath you have sworn by Heaven.
Theseus. Now is he not a wizard!—a magician!—
　　That dreams mere smooth assurance must prevail
　　On *me*—the parent he has left dishonoured!
Hippolytus. *You* give me, father, no less cause for wonder.
　　If *you* were a son of mine, and *I* your father,
　　And *I* believed you had dared to touch my wife,

You would have paid your crime with more than exile.
I should have killed you.

Theseus. Well said, well said!   Yet not so *you* shall die!—
Not by the penalty thus self-invoked
(For speedy death is kindest for the wretched);
But as a beggared outcast from your home.

Hippolytus. Ha, what's your will?—not even wait till Time
Can witness to the truth!   Banished at once!

Theseus. Yes, if I could, beyond the Pontic Sea,
Beyond the bounds of Atlas!—I so hate you.

Hippolytus. Not put to proof my oath—my sworn denial!
Consult no prophet!   Cast me out untried!

Theseus. This tablet here needs no diviner's arts,
It stands your sure accuser.   What care I
For all the fowls that fly above my head?

Hippolytus. Ah God, can I not at last unseal my lips?—
Since, honouring Thee, I only find my ruin?
But no!   I should break in vain the oath I swore—
Not even *that* would touch this heart I plead with.

Theseus. Heavens, you choke me with your sanctimony!
Go!   Go, I say!   Out of your father's kingdom!

Hippolytus. Where shall I turn my wretched steps?   What stranger
Can I beg to give me shelter?—charged with *this*!

Theseus. Find one who loves to welcome as his guests
Seducers that defile the hearth they share.

Hippolytus. Ah *that* cuts to the heart!   Yes, I could weep
To seem to men so vile.   And you believe it!

Theseus. *Then* was the time to weep and fear the future,
When first you dared to shame your father's wife.

Hippolytus. Ah walls of home, could *you* but cry aloud
In witness whether I am vile or no!

Theseus. Wisely you call to witness speechless things.
But *without* tongue the facts denounce you guilty.

Hippolytus. Ah, were I *you,* judging my son before me,
How I should weep for what that son endures!

Theseus. Always self-worship!   *That* you have learnt far better
Than the honour due to those that gave you life!

Hippolytus. Ah my poor mother!   Ah my bitter birth!
God save all those I love from bastardy!

Theseus. Out with him, men!   Have you not heard my sentence,
Pronouncing, long ago, his banishment!

Hippolytus. Let them touch me if they dare!—they shall repent it.
Do it yourself, if you have heart enough.

Theseus. I will, if still you disregard my orders.
   Your exile stirs in me no touch of pity.
Hippolytus. No hope, it seems, to move you.   Ah my sorrow,
   To know the truth, and yet not how to tell it!

> *Theseus goes out with his guards. The palace closes on the*
> *dead Queen. Hippolytus pauses before the image of Artemis.*

Daughter of Lēto, Goddess best-beloved,
My comrade in the chase, comrade in life,
I must be banished, then, from glorious Athens.
Farewell, dear land and city of Erechtheus!
Farewell, Troezēn!—most happy of all homes
For years of youth!   I take my last sight of you,
The last of all farewells.
Youths of Troezēn, friends of my boyhood, come,
Bid me good-bye.   And cheer me on my way.
You will not ever find another friend
More honourable—though not so thinks my father!

                                           [He goes out with his friends.

Chorus. The load on my heart grows lighter, when I trust in the care of
                     Heaven;   *strophe* 1.
   Yet that hid hope in some all-guiding Mind
Falters, to see how mortals have suffered still, and striven—
How upon change there follows change, and all man's days are driven
   Down wandering ways and blind.

                                           antistrophe 1.
This is the lot I long for, would the Gods but heed my crying—
   A fortune kind; a soul from sorrows free;
A judgment not too narrow, nor counterfeit and lying;
An easy heart, with chance and change from day to day complying;
   And friends to be glad with me.

                                           str. 2.
But I see what I had not dreamed of—the peace of my soul is vanished.
   For now to foreign lands afar
There wanders forth, alone and banished,
   Of Athens, and Greece, the brightest star,
     A son by his angry sire denied.
Ah sands of Troezēn, with your ripples playing!
Woods of the hills where he wandered, slaying
Beasts of the wild with his swift hounds baying,
     At dread Dictynna's side!

Never again shall the beaches of Limne echo ringing   *ant.* 2.
   With thy Enétian coursers' flight;

Hushed now thy harp, hushed is thy singing
 That waked through watches of the night
  Thy father's hall. For Lēto's child,
No hands with garlands now shall cover
Those bowers She haunts when hunting's over;
No jealous maids crave now for lover
  This wanderer far exiled.

A Maiden. And mine must be, for thy sorrow,
 A destiny of pain.
Ah my unhappy mother,
 You gave me life in vain!
I rage at the Gods! Fair Graces,
 That join true hearts in one,
Why was it that you tore him
Away from the land that bore him?
 What evil had he done?

Leader. But look! A servant of Hippolytus
Comes hurrying, with a face all wrapped in gloom.

          [The messenger enters.

Messenger. Speak, women!—if you know it, tell me where
To find King Theseus, sovereign of Troezēn?
Within the palace?   *[Theseus comes forth.*

Leader. See, from its door he comes himself to meet you.

Messenger. Theseus, I have a heavy tale to utter,
Alike for you and for all those that dwell
In the walls of Athens and Troezēnē's marches.

Theseus. What is it now? Has some disaster fallen
On our two neighbour-cities?

Messenger. Hippolytus—'tis almost truth to say—
Is dead! For by a hair yet hangs his life.

Theseus. Who killed him? Had he made some enemy,
Whose wife he violated—like his father's?

Messenger. He was destroyed by his own chariot-team,
And by the curses that your own lips cried
To the God of Sea, your sire, against your son.

Theseus. Ah Heaven! Ah Poseidon, then indeed
Thou art my Father, thus to hear my prayers!
How did he perish? Tell me how the blow
Of Justice felled this shamer of my blood.

Messenger. Down by the beach with its great rollers breaking
We all were combing out our horses' manes,

In tears. For word had reached us that our master,
Hippolytus, was forced to quit Troezēn,
Sentenced by you to bitter banishment.
Soon came the prince himself, tears in his voice,
Like ours; and with him followed to the shore
An endless stream of friends and young companions.
Awhile he wept; then, mastering his sorrow,
'Why this despair?' he said. 'I must obey.
Men, put the horses to my chariot.
Troezēn henceforward is no home for me.'
      Then every one of us sprang quick to work
And, sooner than tongue could tell it, to our master
We brought his mares all harnessed.
From off the chariot-rail he caught the reins
And standing there, with sandalled feet well braced,
Lifted his hands to Heaven, crying: 'Zeus,
Let me die, if I am guilty!
Oh grant that my father find how he has wronged me,
Before my death—or at least when life is done.'
      With that he gripped the goad and struck his team;
And we that served him followed, crowding close
About his car and by the horses' heads,
Along the road to Argos and Epidaurus.
But when we came where, in the desert lands
Beyond Troezēn's frontier, the coast falls shelving
Towards the Sarōnic Gulf—just then we caught
A sullen roar like subterranean thunder—
Grisly to hear. The horses raised their heads
And pricked their ears. And we in consternation,
Wondering from whence it came, looked towards the breakers;
And lo! to Heaven towered a wave prodigious,
So high it masked from sight the Rocks of Scīron
And hid the Isthmus, hid Asclēpius' crag.
Swirling aloft and spewing jets of spray,
It rolled in shoreward, where the chariot stood;
And as it broke, in one great crash of foam,
Out of its midst there rose a monstrous bull,
That lifted up its voice till all the land
Re-echoed with a shudder—as we looked,
It seemed too horrible for eyes to bear.
At sight of it, our master's team went wild
With terror. But he, well skilled in handling horses,
Gripped hard the reins and leaning all his weight

Backward, like rower heaving at his oar,
Tugged; yet his coursers, taking in their teeth
The forged iron bits, swept him away, unheeding
Alike his guiding hand, and their own harness,
And the chariot behind them.   If he tried
To rein them towards the softer ground, the bull
Headed them off and each time turned them back
In madder frenzy still; but when, in panic,
They swerved to the rocks again, the monster followed
And drew, in silence, nearer, ever nearer,
Until he forced one wheel against a crag
And flung our master headlong—all was chaos—
Naves, linchpins, hurled to Heaven; but the driver,
Caught miserably within the tangling reins,
Was dragged—his dear head pounding on the boulders,
His flesh ripped from him—fearful came his cries:
'Stand!—do not tear me—you that I bred myself!
Woe for my father's curse!   Will no one save me?—
Innocent as I am!'   But we, though eager,
Lagged far away behind; till—God knows how!—
He slipped from the reins that held him, hardly breathing.
But fatal bull and horses disappeared
Amid the hidden places of the hills.

  Sire, I am only a servant in your house,
But nothing on earth shall ever make me think
This son of yours was guilty of dishonour—
Not though I saw the total race of women
Hanged!—nor all Ida's pine-woods felled for tablets
Of accusation!   For I *know* him noble.
Leader. Alas!   Now falls a new calamity.
None can escape his fate and the destined hour.
Theseus. At first, my hate for him that has suffered this
Made your words welcome.   Yet, in respect for Heaven,
Even for *him*—for still he is my son—
I take his doom with neither joy nor sorrow.
Messenger. But now?   Shall we bring him, this unfortunate?—
Or what's your pleasure?
Decide, my lord.   And yet, would you only hear me,
You will *not* be harsh to your unhappy son.
Theseus. Bring him!—this man who swore he had not shamed
My bed!—that my eyes may see him, and my mouth
Confute him with the judgment of the Gods.

                                        [*The Messenger goes.*

Chorus. The hearts of men, the hearts of Gods that yield not,
      O Cyprian, own Thy sway!
    Beside Thee, swift on glancing pinions
       That circle round His prey,
   Love soars across the lands—across
       The thundering ocean-spray.

    Swooping on wings of gleaming gold,
       He maddens, and soothes, with His sorcery
   Creatures alike of hill and wold,
       Of earth and sea.
   All life beneath the blaze of sun—
   And men! They are subdued, each one,
      O Cyprian, to Thee!
       Above the palace appears the Goddess Artemis; though to the
       mortals on the stage she remains invisible.

Artemis. Son of King Aegeus, so proudly descended,
    Give ear to my voice!
    Lo, I am Artemis, daughter of Lēto.
    Thrice-miserable Theseus, in folly exulting
    Over this son thou hast foully slain—
    Believing the lies of a wife that told thee
    Things all unproven—thou proven fool,
    Go now and hide in the darkness of Hades
    Thy guilty head!
    Or soar aloft like a bird to Heaven,
    Away from this sorrow that snares thy feet!
    For never again among men of honour
    Shall place be found for *thee*.

Listen now, Theseus. Hear thy tale of ruin.
True, I can help thee nothing; only grieve thee.
Yet I am come to show thy son's true heart,
That *he* may die in honour,
And Phaedra's frenzy—that yet, in certain sort,
Was noble. Though passion seized her for thy son,
To it her heart was goaded by that Goddess
Most loathed of us whose joy is maidenhood.
And though she strove to overpower by reason
The Cyprian's violence, despite her will
She was worsted by the cunning of her nurse;
Who told thy son what ailed her, under oath
Of secrecy. But, being honourable,

Hippolytus was deaf to all her prayers;
And yet too godfearing to break his pledge,
For all thy fury.   But meanwhile thy Queen,
Dreading discovery, forged her own false tale
And by that treachery destroyed thy son.
And yet thou couldst believe her!

Theseus. Oh misery!

Artemis. Does it bite thee to the heart?   But, Theseus, wait
   To hear what follows—and to mourn yet more!
   Rememberest thou those three sure prayers thy father
   Promised to grant thee?   One, ignoble fool,
   Thou hast misused to strike—no enemy—
   But thine own son!
   Thy sire, Poseidon, in His wisdom, duly
   Performed what He had promised.   Thine the guilt,
   In *His* eyes, as in mine.   So mad thy haste,
   That would not wait for proof, nor prophet's word—
   Searched not the matter—left not the truth for Time
   To bring to light—but launched upon thy son
   This curse that killed him!

Theseus. Ah Lady, let me die!

Artemis.   Heinous thy sin;
   Yet, for thee too, not unforgivable.
   Thus was the will of Cypris.   Thus She wreaked
   Her anger.   And in Heaven this is law—
   No God may thwart another God's resolve;
   We must let it take its course.
   Be sure, had I not feared the wrath of Zeus,
   Never could *I* have sunk so low in shame
   As to let perish him that I loved the best
   Of all on earth.   Yet pardoned is thy folly,
   First, that it knew not what it did—and then
   Phaedra, by death escaping from all question,
   Left thee deceived.
   So now on thee there falls this heaviest sorrow.
   Yet *my* heart too must mourn.   For good men's deaths
   Can bring the Gods no gladness: but the wicked
   Our wrath consumes—their children and their homes.

Leader. Look, he draws near us, this son of sorrow.
      Torn now, and mangled, is that young body,
      That golden head.   Ah house of destruction,
      What double disaster the hand of Heaven
      Has wrought upon thy roof!

The injured Hippolytus enters, leaning on the shoulders of two attendants.

Hippolytus. Oh, oh!

Wretch that I am, thus torn and tortured
By the unjust doom of an unjust father!
This is the end.
It shoots through my head, this stabbing anguish,
The spasms shudder across my brain,
Stop, let me rest!—for my limbs give way.
Oh, oh!
Accursed team!—with my hands I fed you,
With death and destruction ye have repaid.
Ah, by the Gods, good fellows, gently,
Where on my wounds your hands take hold!
Who is there standing upon my right?
Carry me carefully—draw me on evenly—
Curst and destroyed by my father's fault!
Ah Zeus, ah Zeus, hast Thou eyes to see?
I, the godfearing, the stainless in honour,
Who lived more purely than all beside,
Go down to the pit that gapes before me,
A broken creature.   In righteousness
Towards all men I laboured—
And all for naught!
Ah, ah!
Again it pierces, the pain, the pain!
Let go!—for my anguish,
O Death, come as Healer!
Kill me now, kill me!   I long for the stab
Of two-edged steel,
To cleave me and lay me, at last, to my rest.
Oh fatal prayer that my father prayed!
Sin of my sires, from ages forgotten—
Why has it fallen
Thus on the guiltless years of my youth?
Ah, what can I utter?
How to escape from this merciless torture?
Oh that the doom, in darkness enfolded,
Of sunless Hades might give me sleep!

Artemis. Unhappy one!   Bowed to what misery!
And ruined, too, by thy own noble heart!

Hippolytus. Ah!
What fragrant breath divine!   Through all my pain

I breathe it—and this load of flesh grows lightened.
Is this the deathless Artemis beside me?

Artemis. She *is*, poor heart—the Goddess thou lovest best.

Hippolytus. Seest Thou, Mistress, my calamity?

Artemis. I see.   Yet eyes immortal may not weep.

Hippolytus. None now shall serve Thee; none shall lead Thy hunt—

Artemis. Too true.   But I love thee—even in thy death.

Hippolytus.—none guard Thy images; nor watch Thy steeds.

Artemis. So willed, in her wickedness, the Cyprian.

Hippolytus. Ah?   Now I know what Power it was destroyed me!

Artemis. Stung by thy scorn.   Hating thy purity.

Hippolytus. So *Her* sole hand has brought three lives to ruin!

Artemis. Thee, and thy father, and thy father's queen.

Hippolytus. My father's grief—*that* too I sorrow for.

Artemis. Yes, he was blinded by a power divine.

Hippolytus. Ah my poor father!   What unhappiness!

Theseus. Son, I am broken.   Life has lost its joy.

Hippolytus. Both so deceived!—but you I pity more.

Theseus. Would I could die, my son!—die in your stead!

Hippolytus. A bitter gift your sire Poseidon gave!

Theseus. Ah, that my lips had never breathed of it!

Hippolytus. What matter now?   Your anger could have killed me.

Theseus. Too true!   Such madness Heaven sent upon me.

Hippolytus. Ah!
If only human lips could curse the Gods!

Artemis. Let be!   Though thy soul descend to nether darkness,
Not unavenged shall be the Cyprian's anger
That dared to strike thee down—so pure of heart,
So reverent of the Gods!
This hand of mine with its unerring arrows
Shall smite in retribution that one man
She in Her turn holds dearest.
But *thou* poor suffering heart—in recompense
For all thou hast endured, I promise thee
Honour supreme in this Troezēnian land.
For, in thy name its brides, long years hereafter,
Shall shear their tresses ere the wedding-morn
And pay thee solemn tribute of their tears.
Thou shalt be a theme eternal for the songs
Of maiden lips; and Phaedra's love for thee
Shall perish never from the mouths of men.
    Now, ancient Aegeus' child, take up thy son
And clasp him in thy arms.   Thou hast destroyed him,

Not knowing what thou didst.   When Heaven wills it,
Man needs must err.   And thou, Hippolytus,
Hate not thy father.   For thy doom ordained
This end for thee.   Farewell!   It is not lawful
That I should look on death, nor let these eyes
Be sullied with a mortal's agony.
And well I see that thou art near thy hour.

                            [Artemis disappears.

Hippolytus. Farewell to Thee, O happy Maiden Queen.
Lightly Thou leavest our long companionship!
But at Thy bidding I forgive my father—
Never these ears were deaf to word of Thine.
Ah, fast the night falls now across my eyes.
Clasp me, my father!   Stay me in your arms!
Theseus. My son, my son!   What will you do to me?
Hippolytus. My end is come.   I see Death's gates before me.
Theseus. Will you leave me?—with this stain upon my hands?
Hippolytus. Ah no!   For I acquit you of my death.
Theseus. Truly!   Release me from all guilt of blood?
Hippolytus. So witness Artemis, the Archer-queen!
Theseus. My dearest son, how generous to your father!
Hippolytus. Pray that your *true*-born sons may be the same.
Theseus. Ah noble and upright heart!
Hippolytus. Farewell, you too, my father—a long farewell!
Theseus. My son, do not forsake me!   Still endure!
Hippolytus. To the end I have endured.   It is finished now.
    Quick, father!—lay the clothes above my face!
Theseus. Ah glorious land of Pallas and of Athens,
   What a son is lost to you!   Wretch that I am!
   Long, Cypris, long till I forget Thy curse!
        He follows the body of Hippolytus into the palace.
Chorus. Sudden and strange this sorrow came
      On all Troezēn.
Many a tear this death shall claim;
Long must memory mourn the name
      Of greatness that has been.

(*c.* 430–419 B.C.—possibly 427–425)

When Troy fell, Neoptolemus, son of Achilles, carried off Andrómache, Hector's widow, to his home in Thessaly, where she bore him a son. Now he has gone to Delphi to make his peace with Apollo, from whom he had impiously dared demand satisfaction for the god's slaying of his father Achilles at the Scaean Gate. In his absence Andrómache has been driven to take sanctuary at the shrine of the sea-goddess Thĕtis, mother of Achilles. For Neoptolemus has also a wife—Hermione, daughter of Menelaus and Helen; and this childless wife hates the slave-mistress who has borne her husband a son, as bitterly as, in the house of Abraham, Sarah hated Hagar. Menelaus himself has come from Sparta to his daughter's help; has got hold of Andrómache's child; and by threatening to murder it he now forces her to leave sanctuary. As soon as the mother has surrendered to save her baby son, he treacherously announces that the child's fate must rest with Hermione. Here Euripides puts into Andrómache's mouth all the bitterness of Athenian hate for Sparta—that frenzied hate between Greek cities which in the end was to ruin them all and leave the future to the nation-states of Macedon and Rome; as, thanks to Europe's follies, it lies to-day with the super-states of the U.S.A. and the U.S.S.R.

> Race most abhorred by all humanity,
> Dwellers in Sparta, counsellors of fraud
> And lords of lying, plotters of ill on ill,
> Tortuous, twisted spirits of corruption,
> What foul injustice are your triumphs in Hellas!

(445–9.)

But now the old Pēleus, Achilles' father, enters indignantly, rescues mother and child, and flutters the (somewhat absurdly) timid Menelaus home to Sparta. It is Hermione's turn to be in agonies of apprehension— what will her husband do to punish her when he returns? But now there arrives her cousin and former lover, Orestes, who still cares for her. Clutching at her chance, she begs him to take her home to her father. He reveals that he has already instigated the Delphians to murder his rival Neoptolemus. Hardly have Orestes and Hermione departed, than a messenger describes how that treacherous plot has succeeded and Neoptolemus fallen, after prodigies of valour, at the Delphic shrine. The speech ends with an angry gibe at the pro-Spartan Apollo.

> Thus hath the Lord that gives men oracles,
> This judge of righteousness for all the earth,
> Dealt with Achilles' son, that came to Him
> Only to make amends!   The God remembered,
> Like some bad man, only his ancient grudge.
> And where, then, lies his wisdom?
>
> (1161–5.)

As the aged Pēleus weeps over his dead grandson's body, the divine Thĕtis, bride of his youth, reveals herself with words of comfort and a promise to take him back to her in the depths of the sea.

As so often, Euripides is torn between romance and realism, ancient and modern.   Lyrics about Centaurs jostle oddly with Machiavellian Spartans; this realistic portrait of a spoilt, petulant heiress, trying to browbeat a slave-mistress, harmonizes but ill with the romantic vision of Thĕtis rising from the sea.   Racine, rehandling the subject in *Andromaque*, while still tied to verse and royal personages, was at least able to turn more from mythology to psychology, and to picture the primitive fierceness of human passions, even beneath the silks and satins of Versailles.   Though his Oreste was played by an actor of nearly seventy, so prodigiously fat that his belly had to be supported by an iron girth, Racine's play gained at once a success it has never lost.   For not only is his construction admirable; his work lives by that still more precious excellence of the best drama—living characters. The possibilities that Euripides had only glimpsed, Racine realized.

HECUBA
(*c.* 424 B.C.)

> *Green earth forgets,*
> *The gay young generations mask her grief;*
> *Where bled her children, hangs the loaded sheaf.*
> *Forgetful is green earth; the Gods alone*
> *Remember everlastingly: they strike*
> *Remorselessly, and ever like for like.*
> *By their great memories the Gods are known.*   Meredith.

When Troy drew near its fall, Priam and Hecuba sent their youngest son Polydōrus for safety to a friendly Thracian chief, Polymestor.   But when the city was taken, this barbarian thought it safe to murder the boy for his gold.   The play opens on the Thracian shore of the Hellespont with the ghost of Polydōrus describing his death and how he has revealed it to his mother in her dreams.   Entering, the captive Hecuba learns that the Greeks have decided to sacrifice her daughter Polýxena on the grave of Achilles.

Despite the old Queen's pleadings, the cold Odysseus leads the girl away to
her heroic death. (Polýxena is a noble character. But Euripides repeats
this theme too often. One begins to suspect that he is out to draw tears;
and virgins should not be used as onions.) A servant fetching sea-water to
bathe Polýxena's body finds the dead Polydōrus. Hecuba is convinced,
as she recalls her dream, of the guilt of Polymestor; and from an old woman
broken by sorrows she quickens to a frenzied Oriental, mad like Mēdēa for
revenge. Agamemnon, though not unfriendly (as Cassandra's lover), is
afraid to grant her justice; but he will not prevent her taking it. So she
invites Polymestor and his two sons to the camp. At this point the Chorus
of Trojan women sings the most beautiful lyric of the play—a remembrance,
amid the blood and brutality, of their last night of happiness.

Ah Troy beloved, henceforth   *strophe* 1.
No more among maiden cities stands thy name;
So dense a cloud of conquerors hides thy shame,
    Sacked by the spears of wrath.
The diadem of towers that was thy fame
    Is torn away, the brand
Of burning blackens all thy beauty o'er!—
    Poor, suffering land,
Where *I* shall tread no more.

One midnight brought our fall—   *antistrophe* 1.
That hour when feasts are done, and sleep is shed
Soft on men's eyes; at rest my husband's head,
    After our festival
Of dance and song, lay in our bridal-bed—
    High on the wall his spear.
For now we saw the Argives sailed again,
    That many a year
Trampled the Trojan Plain.

Before my mirror's gleaming   *str.* 2.
    Depths of lucid gold,
I stood, with tresses streaming,
    To braid them fold on fold,
Before I slept. But then a roar
Shook Ilios—the voice of war!
And up the streets of Troy at bay
    A great shout passed:
'When, sons of Hellas—when shall dawn the day
    That low ye lay
Tall Troy, and turn home at last?'

From the bed of our love upleaping,   *ant. 2.*
    In my shift, like a Dorian maid,
To Artemis' holy keeping
    I fled—but ah, no aid
Her altar gave my agony.
Our conquerors dragged me to the sea,
I saw where cold before me lay
    My husband slain;
I saw, as their galleys homeward clove the spray,
    Fade far away
My land—and swooned with pain;

Crying my curse on Helen, child of Leda,   *epode.*
And her shepherd-prince of Ida,
    Paris, the abhorred.
    'Twas *she* cast me abroad,
    A slave; my country fell
That *she* might wed—ah, wedding made in vain,
    Nay, rather matched in Hell!
Never may ship bear *her* across the foam!—
    Never again
Come Helen safely home!

(905–52.)

Polymestor, duly arriving, is lured into the captives' quarters and his eyes put out, while his two children are butchered. When Agamemnon refuses redress, the furious Thracian predicts to Hecuba that she will be changed into a hound; to Agamemnon, that both he and Cassandra will be murdered by Clytemnestra. For his pains Agamemnon orders the blinded wretch to be thrown on a desert island; then conquerors and captives prepare to sail for Hellas.

Hecuba, like *Mēdēa,* pictures the frightful revenge taken by a tortured soul—in either case a barbarian and a woman. Whether Euripides was as shocked as some modern critics by the odious murder of Polymestor's children, and meant Hecuba's transformation into a hound to be a symbol of her inhuman degradation, is far from clear. If this *was* his intention, Euripides could easily have said so, through his characters or his Chorus. No one could call him a laconic writer. To me he here gives the impression not so much of a moralist pointing a lesson as of a melodramatist making the most of a lurid *crime passionnel.*

At Byzantium this play, with *Orestes* and *The Phoenician Women,* was, oddly enough, a favourite for use in schools. At the Renaissance its popularity became amazing. In particular the vengeance-seeking ghost of Polydōrus, helped by two crude imitations in the tragedies of Nero's

minister Seneca, peopled the Renaissance stage with armies of gibbering
offspring—grotesquely culminating, in Gay's *The What d'ye call it,* with
the ghost of an unborn child! Some modern readers, on the other hand,
may feel that this drama shows nothing they did not know about human
barbarity and meanness; and does not show a great deal else.

HĒRACLES

(*c.* 424–423 B.C. ?)

This rather frigid play (often known as *Hēracles Mad*) tells how, when
the hero had gone down to Hades to fetch the hound Cerberus, Lўcus, the
tyrant of Thebes, attempted to murder his wife Mégara, his children, and his
old father Amphitryon.   In the nick of time Hēracles returns and kills the
tyrant; but Hēra, Queen of Heaven, ever jealous of her bastard stepson,
sends Madness with her snaky hair against him, so that in frenzy he murders
wife and sons.   When the fit is over, Hēracles, like Ajax in Sophocles, sees
no course left but suicide.   But Theseus, King of Athens, whom Hēracles
had rescued from Hades, gradually persuades him that acts done in ignorance
should not crush him with guilt; then this loyal friend leads him away to
find a new home at Athens.

Two passages stand out.   In one, Hēracles protests eloquently against
stories of the Gods' wickedness (a little incongruously, when his ruin has
just come from the wickedness of Hēra; but Euripides felt too deeply to
repress what is really his own comment):

> I cannot think Gods do adultery,
> Nay, I have ever scorned, and ever shall,
> To dream a God can bind a God with chains,
> Or one be born by fate another's master.
> For God, if God indeed, has need of nothing.
> These are but poets' old unhappy tales.

(1341–6.)

The other passage is a beautiful, though not very relevant, lyric on old age,
chanted by the Chorus of Theban Elders; but here too one catches the
voice of the poet himself, who may now have been about sixty.

> Ah Youth, still loved delight!   *strophe* 1.
>   Old age upon me lies
> Heavy as Etna's height;
> It bows my head, and the light
>   Darkens before my eyes.

What profit, though I lorded
   O'er all the East as king?
Or golden treasures hoarded?—
   Youth is a fairer thing.
In the house of wealth still Youth is best
And lovely is Youth to the neediest.

But Age I hate.   For tears it brings
   And death.   Would God that it were swept
   To drown in Ocean—that it leapt
Far off through Heaven on whirling wings;
   So that its feet might never find
   Cities and homes of humankind!

Ah if the Gods saw plain,   *antistrophe* 1.
   If They were wise towards earth,
For the good They would ordain
To have their youth again—
   And *that* should stamp their worth;

While, from the tomb returning,
   Once more their race they ran,
The base should perish, earning
   Only a single span;
And so had all men understood
Which were the evil, which the good,

As clearly as eyes of seamen trace
   The hosts of Heaven through cloudy night.
   But now no sign to mortal sight
God gives, to sever good from base;
   And the circling seasons, onward rolled,
   Only heap higher the rich man's gold.

Yet the Muses alike and the Graces   *str.* 2.
   Shall still abide with me.
Let me die ere I lose the faces
   Of that sweet company!
Still to my head let garlands cling,
Still shall the aged poet sing
      Of Memory.

                                 (637–79.)

The Suppliant Women
(*c.* 422 B.C.)

A propagandist war-play, like *The Hēracleidae.* After the fall of The
Seven before Thebes, their leader, King Adrastus of Argos, and their
mothers, who form the Chorus, appeal to Theseus of Athens to win for the
dead that burial which Thebes refuses them (as in 424 she had refused it,
for a time, to the Athenian dead of Dēlium). Theseus, at first reluctant,
is won over by his mother Aethra's passionate appeal to the age-long honour
of Athens, as champion of right and justice.

> My son, when men cast scorn upon thy Athens,
> Saying that she hath no wisdom, canst thou see
> The flame that flashes from her eyes in answer?
> It is from toil and danger she grows great.
> Let other cities keep their wise inaction—
> Dim are their deeds and dim grows all their vision.
> But *thou*, my son, wilt *thou* not rise to aid
> Dead men dishonoured, women left to weep,
> That cry to thee for succour?

> > (321–7.)

(It is bitterly ironic that within the next few years this same Athens was to
perpetrate the massacres of Sciōne and Mēlos.) Now enters a Theban
herald to demand the expulsion of Adrastus and the neutrality of Athens.
Here Euripides inserts a debate on liberty and despotism, quite misplaced,
yet interesting as a picture of what Athens still meant to idealists like
Euripides (though he already sees the dangers of democracy), before her
war-madness had brought disillusion and disgust.

Herald. Who is the lord of Athens?
  To whom must I deliver here the message
  Of Creon, now master of the folk of Cadmus,
  Since by his brother Polyneices' hand
  King Éteocles has fallen in the field
  For our seven-gated city?
Theseus. Stranger, thy speech has found a false beginning,
  Asking in Athens: 'Who is lord?' She bows
  To the rule of no single master. She is free!
  Our commons rule by turn through the circling years,
  Granting the rich no privilege—the poor
  In *our* law's eye stand equal.

Herald. Here, in the game of policy thou yieldest
  To Thebes the first advantage.   For my country
  Does 'bow to a single master'—not a mob!
  We have no windy demagogues that puff
  With flatteries our State this way and that,
  Each to his own advantage—honeyed talkers,
  To-day delightful, fatal in the end;
  That then evade the penalties of failure
  By further calumnies of other men.
  How should a multitude that cannot weigh
  The speeches that it hears, direct a city?
  Ripe counsel is a surer, safer guide
  Than a people's rash decisions.   Can poor peasants,
  Even although they be not boors, find leisure
  From all their labours, for the commonweal?
  And what a plague for all a country's noblest,
  When some mean fellow, that climbed up from nothing,
  Rises to fame by a tongue that dupes the crowd!
Theseus. A clever herald, and an eloquent
  In talking from the purpose!   But since thou *hast*
  Challenged us to debate, why, sirrah, listen—
  'Twas thou began, not I.
  Nothing so deadly to a state as despots.
  For first of all it means there are no laws
  Common to all—but one, that wields the law
  In his own hands, is master.   So right dies.
  But where the law stands written, rich and weak
  Alike have justice—poor men can accuse
  The prosperous, charge for charge; and humble folk
  With right upon their side, defeat the mighty.
  For *this* is Liberty—when the herald cries:
  'Who has good counsel for the common weal,
  Now let him speak.'   Then he that wills to speak,
  Has honour: he that wills not, holds his peace.
  What rule more fair than this?
  And where the people governs, it takes pleasure
  To see the city rich in growing youth;
  But despots dread it—so they kill the best
  And wisest (as they judge), to keep their power.
  How should a country grow to greatness thus,
  When some hand plucks and docks what's young and stirring,
  Like the tall ears in some spring field of corn?

                                        (399-449.)

All this has little relevance to the events of the play, already as remote in date from Euripides as King Stephen's reign from us; but it is only too relevant to our modern world.

The rest of the tragedy lacks interest. The pious Theseus defeats Thebes, brings back the dead, and buries them. Their spectacular obsequies are melodramatically heightened by one of the widows, Evadne, hurling herself (before the audience!) on to the blazing pyre of her husband, Cápaneus; and by the divine apparition of Athena, who bids Theseus exact from Adrastus an oath of the eternal friendship of Argos for Athens (as if such oaths had value) and predicts that the sons of the fallen will one day take Thebes.

A piece with much spectacle, some ideas, but little genuine drama.

Ion
(c. 420–411 B.C., ? 418–417)

Creūsa, daughter of King Erechtheus of Athens,[1] was violated by Apollo and bore a son, whom she exposed. Hermes carried him to Delphi, where the boy Ion grew up in his father's shrine. Now King Xuthus, husband of Creūsa and successor of Erechtheus, has come with her to Apollo's oracle, to ask how they may have a child.

There is charm in the opening scene (after a wordy prologue by Hermes) as the young acolyte,[2] happy in his pious duties, sweeps the temple in the light of dawn, and half fondly scares with his bow the defiling birds (an opportunity, we learn from an ancient critic, for graceful miming by the actor).

> Look!—towards the altar with wings a-beat
>   Another swooping low!—
> A swan. Be off, with your scarlet feet!
> Or your song—though Apollo's is not more sweet—
>   Shall not save you from my bow.
> Fly! Far away!
>   Stoop to the wave of the Delian mere.
> Or blood shall end, if you disobey,
>   That melody calling clear.

(161–9.)

Preceded by the Chorus of her maidens, Creūsa enters. An instinctive sympathy awakes between mother and son; and she tells him how 'a friend' of hers, once violated by Apollo, is still longing to learn what became of her lost child. Ion is shocked. Could Apollo do such things? At least, he feels, the God is unlikely to answer such a question. Then Xuthus arrives,

---

[1] Genealogical table, p. 353.
[2] Compare the Joas of Racine's *Athalie*.

goes into the shrine, and reappearing falls on the neck of the amazed Ion.
The God has said the first man he met would be his son. Xuthus must
have begotten Ion on some Delphic Maenad, one drunken night long ago.
Ion remains distrustful—will he be happy, as here, in a jealous Athens?
And what will Creūsa say to an unknown stepson? Xuthus brushes his
doubts aside, warning the Chorus to keep silence for the present, on pain of
death. None the less when their loved mistress returns, they break the
bitter news. She is to grow old in barrenness, while a foreign upstart in-
herits the throne of Erechtheus. Then, in the face of Delphi, Creūsa
lifts up her voice and curses Apollo.

> To thee I cry, to thee, the singer,
> 　Lord of the lyre with seven strings!
> Though so sweet beneath thy finger
> 　The lifeless horn awakes and sings,
> O Lēto's child, before this sun
> I will cry the shame that thou hast done!
>
> One day as in my garment's fold
> 　Yellow flower on flower I pressed,
> 　A golden garland at my breast,
> You came—with your hair of gleaming gold.
> By *your* hands these white wrists were haled
> 　Into that cave beneath the hill.
> 'Mother, O mother' my sorrow wailed—
> 　But you, a god, dared wreak
> 　Your force upon the weak
> 　　And work the Cyprian's will!
>
> My child of grief I bore you;
> 　And lest my mother learn, in dread
> I took the babe and laid it sleeping
> On that same bitter bed of weeping
> 　Where you had marred my maidenhead.
> Ah birds of prey have borne away
> 　My child, hard heart, and thine.
> Yet your lips can chant, your hands can play
> 　　Their hymns divine!
>
> Ah I accuse thee, son of Lēto,
> 　There on thy golden throne!
> Hear thou my accusation,
> On thy seat of divination
> 　Beside earth's navel-stone!

Shame on thee, faithless lover!
  What had my lord, then, done,
That now to *him* thou hast given
  Beside his hearth a son?
My child, and thine, by the fowls of Heaven
From his swaddling-bands was torn and riven!
  You cared not—heartless one!

For that thy Delos shall abhor thee—
  Loathe thee thy laurels, planted nigh
That whispering palm, where Lēto bore thee
  As son of Zeus most high!

                                    (881–922.)

An old retainer prompts her to revenge. Burn Delphi? She is afraid. Kill Xuthus? No, he has been good to her. Kill the boy? Yes, she can provide the old servant with poison—the Gorgon's blood once bestowed by Pallas on the royal race of Erichthónius. Let him put it in Ion's cup at the thanksgiving feast. After the interval of a choric ode, a slave brings news that the murder has failed. (He wastes time grotesquely on an elaborate description of the festival-tent, before coming to the urgent truth.)

                         Then a herald,
Rising full height, summoned to join the banquet
Whoever wished, among the men of Delphi.
So, wreath on head, they filled that great pavilion
And feasted to the full.   This pleasure ended,
Into the midst of all an old man came
And moved much laughter in the banqueters,
So busy was he—with self-appointed zeal
Pouring from pitchers water for their hands,
Burning the gum of myrrh, and taking charge
Of all the golden goblets.   But when the hour
Came for the flutes and the common mixing-bowl,
'Away,' cried he, 'with these small cups!—and bring
Bigger, the sooner to rejoice their souls.'
New turmoil then, as on the board were set
Beakers of gold and silver.   But the greybeard
Took and filled full a goblet of the choicest,
As honouring his young master.   Yet within
He dropped a potent poison, which they say
Our mistress gave him, to end the young lad's days.
But no man guessed.   Then, as the new-found heir

Lifted, among his guests, the God's libation,
Some servant there let slip a word ill-omened.
The lad, long temple-reared by noble prophets,
Marked well the presage, and gave word to fill
Another mixing-bowl, while on the earth
He poured his wine, and bade the others pour it.
Then all fell silent.   In the sacred bowl
We mingled water with the Byblian vintage;
But, as we laboured, into the tent came flying
A merry flight of doves—for in the House
Of Loxias they live by none molested—
And thirstily, where lay the drink outpoured,
They dipped their beaks and sipped with glossy necks.
Unharmed, the others swallowed the sacred wine;
But one, that had settled next our new-found prince,
Soon as she tasted, writhed her wingéd body
In wild convulsions, screaming in her pain
Sounds inarticulate, while all the feasters
Sat wondering at her trouble; till she fell,
Gasping her last, with scarlet legs relaxed.
Then the young heir by God revealed flung out
Bared arms across the table, with the cry:
'Who, then, has schemed my death?   Speak out, old man!
You did this busy service—from *your* hand
I took the cup!'   And seizing his aged arm
He searched the slave to find the venom on him.
So caught, the greybeard owned, reluctantly,
The poisoning plotted, and Creūsa's rashness.
Then from the tent the lad, Apollo's chosen,
Rushed, with his guests about him, to the presence
Of those that rule in Delphi; standing there,
'Most hallowed Earth,' he cried, 'Erechtheus' daughter,
The stranger woman, seeks my death with poison!'
So then the Pythian lords, by many voices,
Condemned my mistress to be flung to death,
Sheer from the Delphic crags, as planning murder
For the God's servant in His holy precinct.
Now all the city hunts her, unhappy woman,
Brought hither by an errand as unhappy.

(1166–1226.)

Creūsa takes refuge at the altar from the angry Ion.   But the Pythian
priestess enters, bidding him be merciful and producing the basket in which

he was found as a child.   Creüsa recognizes the tokens within it—mother and son fall into each other's arms.   Yet can Apollo really be his father? Ion would question the oracle point-blank.   But now from Heaven appears Athena, to confirm the truth.   Let Xuthus be left in happy ignorance. Ion will have a glorious posterity, as ancestor of the Ionian race.

A strange drama.   One god reveals how another god, having violated a girl, proposes to plant his offspring on an unsuspecting pilgrim.   The divine plan miscarries—Creüsa finds out the truth at Delphi; not, as intended, later in Athens.   And at the end Athena has to put the best case she can for her brother Apollo, who turns out to be not only bad lover, but also bad prophet.   All's well that ends well?   Apollo has had the pleasure of one more seduction; Xuthus will (perhaps) remain a happy dupe; and if Creüsa has suffered nearly twenty years for a son who was alive after all, that cannot be helped.

Strange deities!   So, doubtless, Euripides meant his intelligent hearers to feel.   At moments—when Ion is shocked, when Creüsa curses Apollo— he shows his hand.   But only at moments.   If he wished to make the thoughtful think, he wished to keep the many excited and entertained. Had the characters been, not divine or legendary, but Athenian bourgeois, this play with its largely invented plot, violated girl, exposed infant, long-lost heir recognized through trinkets, and happy ending, might almost be a work of the New Comedy a century later.

Historically, then, the piece is important; as drama, for all its naïveties and incongruities, it remains still interesting, sometimes moving, sometimes real poetry.   Indeed it might be performed less rarely than it is.

THE TROJAN WOMEN
(415 B.C.)

When a piled town was litten like a candle
To show one man his way to bed again.

Gordon Bottomley.

This is Euripides' fiercest denunciation of war.   In the previous year Athens had massacred the islanders of Mēlos and sold their women and children into slavery, because, being of Laconian blood, they wished to remain neutral.   The piece is not so much a drama as a series of scenes, bitter as sketches by Goya, illustrating the miseries of victory.   The old Queen Hecuba sees her daughter and daughter-in-law made slave-concubines of their captors, another daughter sacrificed on the grave of Achilles, her little grandson hurled from the Trojan wall.   Only the guilty Helen, it appears, will escape the fate of those she ruined.

The opening is unusually grandiose for Euripides.   While the white-haired Hecuba lies prone in the dust of the Greek camp, above appear the the powers that play with human life; as Virgil's Aeneas saw them revealed for a moment above the flames of Troy, as Hardy saw them above the Europe of Napoleon.

Poseidon. Up from the salt sea-depths of the Aegean,
     Where the white feet of Nēreïds interweave
     Their lovely dances, I, Poseidon, come.
     For since that day when Phoebus and myself
     Reared plummet-straight about this hill of Troy
     Her towers of stone, my heart has never lost
     Its ancient love of Ilios, that to-day
     Lies overthrown and sacked by Argive arms,
     Belching her smoke to Heaven; since Epeius,
     The Phocian from Parnassus, by the guile
     Of Pallas, built and brought within these ramparts
     That fatal Horse, big with its brood of spears.
     Waste lie the holy places, and the temples
     Drip yet with slaughter, and King Priam's self
     Hath fallen on the very altar-steps
     Of the guardian God of Home.
     And now the Achaeans carry to their galleys
     The spoils of Phrygia, her wealth of gold,
     And the victor host of Hellas only waits
     For a fair wind astern to bear them, joyful
     After ten springs, to wife and child again. . . .
          Athena enters, armed with helm and spear.

Athena. May I, forgetting ancient enmity,
     Address that mighty God whom Heaven honours
     As my Father's closest kin?
Poseidon. Speak, Queen Athena, for the heart must own
     The spell of kinship and old days together.
Athena. Great sir, all honour to thy gentleness.
     I touch a matter that concerns us both.
Poseidon. New tidings hast thou brought from some Immortal?
     From Zeus, or some spirit of the unseen world?
Athena. Nay, it concerns this Troy whose dust we tread.
     I come to seek thy power to league with mine.
Poseidon. What, is thine ancient hatred turned to pity
     For these fire-scarred foundations?

Athena. Answer me first my question.   Wilt thou join
    Counsel with me and match thy will with mine?
Poseidon. I will.   But, tell me, what is now thy purpose?
    Does it relate to Trojans or Achaeans?
Athena. It is to cheer the Trojans whom I hated,
    And give the Achaeans a bitter home-coming.
Poseidon. Why leap so suddenly from mood to mood,
    Too violent in thy random loves and hates?
Athena. Knowest thou not the outrage they have done
    To me and to my altars?
Poseidon. Cassandra raped by Ajax?   Yes, I know.
Athena. And yet the Achaeans have left him still unpunished,
    Even unblamed!
Poseidon. Although it was *thy* arm that gave them Troy!
Athena. Therefore, with *thy* help, they shall feel my anger.
Poseidon. Thou hast thine asking.   Tell me thy resolve.
Athena. They would fare home—but evil they shall fare!
Poseidon. Here before Troy?   Or on the Aegean surges?
Athena. When they have set their sails from Ilios.
    Then Zeus shall send intolerable rain,
    And hail, and winds that whistle through the gloom;
    And to my hand He promises His lightning
    To smite and set aflame the fleet of Argos.
    But be it thine to fill the Aegean Channel
    With towering surf and eddies wildly whirled.
    Till their dead choke the Hollows of Euboea.
    So for the future shall the Achaeans learn
    To reverence my altars and the Gods.
Poseidon. So be it.   I grant thy will.   'Tis said and done.
    The Aegean shall be troubled.
    Scyros and Lemnos and the reefs of Delos
    And Mýconos' beaches and Caphēreus' headland
    Shall be heaped high with bodies of the drowned.
    Go!—to Olympus!—take the levin-bolt
    From Zeus thy father and then lie in wait,
    Until the Achaean fleet puts proud to sea.
    Ah, fool is he that puts tall towns to sack,
    Plunders their temples and the holy tombs
    Of them that rest—then fares himself to die!

                                        (1–22, 48–97.)

The gods disappear; Hecuba and the Chorus of captive women lament;
Talthybius the Herald announces their fates—Cassandra to be the prize

of Agamemnon; Andrómache of Achilles' son Neoptolemus; Hecuba
herself of Odysseus.   After chanting a frenzied marriage-song, Cassandra
foretells the vengeance of Clytemnestra on Agamemnon—and on herself.
But at least Troy too will have been avenged.   Andrómache, with the little
Astyanax, rides in on a wagon glittering with Trojan spoils—only to bring
news of the sacrifice of Polýxena on Achilles' tomb.   Hecuba bids her bow
to her new lord—she may at least save her child.   But horror follows
horror—reluctantly Talthybius reappears to take the child to die, flung
from the Trojan rampart.   Then enters Menelaus in search of the accursed
Helen.   She shall be executed; but not yet—only when they reach Sparta.
For a moment the broken-hearted Hecuba forgets her agony in savage
exultation.

> Sustainer of the earth, o'er earth enthroned,
> Whoe'er Thou art, so dim to our conjecture—
> Zeus, or the Law of Nature, or Man's own Mind,
> I cry to Thee!—who on Thy noiseless path
> Leadest all human things the way of Justice.

>   (884–8.)

Bitterest irony of all.   For the audience knew that Helen was to live
happy again at Sparta and become herself a goddess.   Coaxingly Helen
pleads she was the helpless victim of destiny, from the hour when Aphrodite
promised her to Paris, in return for the fatal apple.   Hecuba retorts, with
all the caustic rationalism of Euripides:

> I cannot think that Hēra and virgin Pallas
> Could ever fall to such a pitch of folly—
> That Hēra would barter to barbarians
> Her Argos; or Pallas make her Athens slave
> To Phrygia!   If indeed they ever came
> To Ida for some childish trial of beauty!
> For why should Hēra so crave loveliness?
> Could she hope to find some lordlier love than Zeus?
> Did Pallas court some marriage, then, in Heaven?—
> She that abhors the bridal-bed, and prayed
> Her sire for maidenhood!   Ah do not gloze
> Your fault by casting follies on the Gods,
> Lest fools alone should heed you!
> At my son's side to Menelaus' hall,
> You dared to say (a thing for endless laughter!)
> The Cyprian came.   Sitting at ease in Heaven,
> Had she not power to waft you through the skies
> To Ilios?—and all Amyclae with you!

My son was of a beauty past compare
And your own heart at sight of him became
'Cypris.'   For all the wantonness men do,
They call it 'Aphrodite'—'the Foam-born Queen'—
And well the froth of folly fits her name!
You saw my son in his barbaric splendour,
Glittering with gold—and all your soul grew lust.

                                                            (971–92.)

The shattered body of the little Astyanax is borne in and laid for burial—by his mother's parting wish—in the dead Hector's shield.   Amid the keening of her women, the old Hecuba catches at a desperate faith that somehow, after all, defeat may be nobler than conquest.

                              Had not God
        Turned upside-down the happiness of Troy,
        We should have lain forgot, instead of giving
        Songs to the poets of the after-time.

                                                            (1242–5.)

Then comes the final order for the Greek army to fire the fallen city. While flames leap from the ruins behind them, the captives are driven down to embark.

ELECTRA
(413 B.C.)

Aeschylus had treated the matricide of Clytemnestra as a religious moralist, Sophocles as a pure dramatist; Euripides comes to it with the just indignation of a critical humanist.   It was a monstrous crime; the poetry that idealizes it is monstrous; the religion that could instigate it is monstrous also.   *Écrasez l'infâme.*

The Electra of Euripides has been married off, out of mischief's way, to an honest peasant (though of good family) who has refrained from consummating the marriage.   When Orestes and Pýlades arrive, Electra gives her unknown brother a passionate message for Orestes, spurring him to revenge.   Then an old shepherd recognizes him by a scar; and the two youths go off to murder Aegisthus, who has his neck cloven from behind at a sacrifice he has invited them to share.   This somewhat ugly feat is followed by an uglier.   Pretending childbirth, Electra lures her mother to her cottage.   That shallow, tired, but not unaffectionate woman walks trustfully into the trap and is duly butchered, crying for mercy.   Then the murderers themselves are overwhelmed by a revulsion of remorse, that hardly needs the appearance from Heaven of Castor and Polydeuces to point the pitiful moral and condemn, with some embarrassment, the folly of Apollo in commanding it.   Orestes is told that he must flee before the Furies, till assoiled at last in Athens; brother and sister, only a moment since reunited, must part again in tears.

Electra herself is a realistic study of a young woman poisoned by loneliness, childlessness, and obsession with vendetta.   She might have shone in a Resistance movement; she might have made a fanatical young Communist; she presents a vivid picture of the way a narrow personality, not without heroism, can feel itself called to save the world, and lose its soul in the process.   It is as if an Antigone, by some hateful perversion, had grown too like Creon.   With this play it is still worth reading Mérimée's clever adaptation of it to Corsican vendetta—*Colomba*.

Good rationalist propaganda; but not pleasant drama.   Its motto might be Lucretius'—

> To so much misery can Religion lead.

Yet one may ask if Athenian religion was really so pernicious.   By medieval standards it was tolerant.   It drove Anaxágoras and perhaps Protágoras from Athens; it was to help the condemnation of Socrates; Euripides himself had been indicted for impiety.   In Arcadia human sacrifice may have continued till the second century A.D.   But Arcadia was remote and primitive; Socrates could easily have escaped, had he not courted execution; and Euripides himself was allowed to go on for decades being persistently impious in the very theatre of Dionysus.   .

Perhaps Athenian religion caused follies rather than crimes.   Prophets and soothsayers encouraged the mad venture against Sicily; hysteria over the mutilation of the Hermae helped to ruin it; and that ruin was completed when on August 27th of this year 413 the moon was eclipsed and the pious Nicias ensured his own destruction by deciding to delay retreat till the next full moon.

Nor is it clear that Euripides had much to give the ordinary Athenian in place of the faith he criticized.   Many human beings seem definitely to need a religion; as they are human, the religion is unlikely to be perfect; and both Socrates and Euripides, in exposing the fallacies of others, may themselves have been guilty of the serious fallacy of supposing men more rational than they are.   Both thinkers may sometimes have sown dragon's teeth.   Still, that is a risk the revolutionary writer must face; though few have faced it as frankly as Walt Whitman: 'Nor will my poems do good only, they will do just as much evil, perhaps more.'   And it is dubious if the general course of declining paganism would have differed much had neither Socrates nor Euripides ever been born.

And yet, though *Electra* is not one of Euripides' best plays, a fragment from it may, by a strange chance, have saved Athens herself from total ruin.   Nine years later, in 404, the city fell before the Spartan league; but, says the story, as its leaders debated whether to raze Athens from the earth and enslave her people, as she had enslaved others, they were touched to sudden pity by the voice of a man of Phocis casually chanting a choral passage from *Electra*, about the heroine's desolate home.[1]   Two thousand years later Milton remembered this, when the army of King Charles stood before London:

> Lift not thy spear against the Muses' Bowre,
>   The great *Emathian* Conqueror bid spare
>   The house of *Pindarus*, when Temple and Towre
> Went to the ground: And the repeated air
>   Of sad *Electra's* Poet had the power
>   To save th' *Athenian* Walls from ruine bare.

ÏPHIGENEIA AMONG THE TAURIANS
(*c.* 414–409 B.C.)

Here Euripides allows himself, like Aristophanes in *The Birds,* like Shakespeare in *The Tempest,* to relax into a happier mood of romanticism. Far away on the shores of the Crimea it was perhaps possible to forget for a' moment the darkening horizons of the war at home.   Escape is one of the gifts of poetry—not a fault, as puritans have pretended; unless it is abused. It can serve like that gift of anodyne 'nepenthe,' which Helen in her beauty brought to Telemachus.

For the earlier story of Ïphigeneia's sacrifice at Aulis see p. 344.   Now, for close on twenty years she has been priestess of Artemis among the Taurians, condemned to sacrifice any strangers that might arrive—a lonely woman nearing forty, torn between bitter memories of her own sacrifice and longings for her far-off home.   She has just had a dream that seems to imply Orestes' death; but in fact he and Pýlades have lately landed in the Crimea.   Still haunted by some of the Erinyes, who had refused to be appeased at Athens (p. 109), he had been bidden by Delphi to bring the image of Artemis from the Black Sea.   Captured by the Taurians, the two youths are led before Ïphigeneia and the Chorus of captive Greek women. After questioning the unknown Orestes for news of her family, she offers to

---

[1] A large part of the effect may, of course, have lain in the music which was composed for his words by Euripides, and is lost to us now.

spare his life if he will take a letter to her kin in Argos. Nobly he insists that Pýlades, not himself, shall be set free to bear it. Iphigeneia reads aloud her letter, unconsciously revealing who she is. It is written to Orestes; and Pýlades simply hands it to the comrade at his side. A neat recognition—one of the best in all Greek drama. It now remained for the dramatist to contrive an exciting escape from the savages. Iphigeneia persuades their king, Thoas, that she must purify the holy image and the two captives in the sea; for she has found one of them to be a matricide (an adroit use of truth itself for deception). There the comrades force a way with their fists through the Taurian guards to Orestes' ship. This lively episode has shocked some critical persons by its duplicity. No doubt it was very low of Odysseus, likewise, to deceive the poor simple Polyphemus. But I own that I cannot breathe at such moral altitudes. True, in Goethe's adaptation, *Iphigenie auf Tauris,* the heroine finally flings aside deception; but then Goethe had made Thoas a far more civilized character than he is in Euripides.

The Greek poet, however, wanted his usual deity in a machine; nor did he wish to leave his unfortunate Chorus to be massacred by the exasperated Taurians.[1] So an opportune head wind drives back the fugitives; but Athéna commands Thoas to let them go and to set the Chorus free.

An unusually exciting plot; and some good characters—the melancholy, bitter Iphigeneia; the loyal Pýlades; the neurotic but resolute Orestes, who mistakes cattle and dogs for Furies. But, not unamusingly, Euripides the rationalist intrudes himself even here. Orestes' Furies are imaginary; Iphigeneia's dream is false, or at least deceiving; and she cannot resist a little higher criticism at the expense of gods who are supposed to like human sacrifices. But these Voltairean touches are not enough to injure what remains, though not a great play, a very pleasing one.

[1] The fate of the Chorus is neglected in the very similar end of *Helen* (p. 303).

HELEN

(412 B.C.)

Passing from hand to hand so passively,
Helen was Helen's secret, Helen's own.

Gordon Bottomley.

Elsewhere in Euripides Helen is a shallow wanton; in this curious semi-burlesque she becomes a Penelope.   He adopts the variant legend that she never went to Troy—a phantom impersonated her.[1]

The scene lies in Egypt, where she has taken refuge at the tomb of good King Prōteus from the suit of his wicked son, Theoclýmenus.   Menelaus arrives in the wet clothes of a shipwrecked mariner; and, after a grotesque encounter at the palace-gate with a shrewish old Egyptian portress, is much amazed to meet Helen, whose phantom-double he has just left safely hidden in a cave.   At first he refuses to believe that all the carnage of a ten years' war has been inflicted for a hallucination.   But an old messenger from the shore announces that the false Helen has just floated skyward and dissolved. Vigorously he expresses his feelings:

Now indeed I see
What a poor and lying trade all soothsay is.
Mere cheats, it seems, are fiery divinations;
Empty, the cries of birds; and he's a fool
Who thinks that fowls of the air can profit men.
For Calchas spoke no word to warn the host,
Although before his eyes his comrades fell
For a mere cloud; no word spoke Hélenus,
Though Troy was sacked for nothing.
Say you: 'But God had *willed* them not to speak'?
Then how serves prophecy?   We should but bring
Our offerings to the Gods, and pray their blessing,
But heed no prophet's art.   Since *that* is found
Simply a snare in life—for when did idler
Ever grow rich by reading signs of flame?
Prudence and judgment are the wisest seers.

(744–57.)

---

[1] This version is also briefly alluded to at the end of *Electra*.   It goes back to Stēsíchorus (c. 610–550) who, says the famous story, having written a poem on Helen's faithlessness, was blinded by her anger (for she was worshipped as a goddess at Sparta and elsewhere).   He then recovered his sight by composing a palinode or recantation (Plato, *Phaedrus*, 243 A), which began:

A lie, a lie is the tale they tell!
No galley's benches bore thee to Ilios' citadel.

Elsewhere (*Republic*, 586 C) Plato likens the sensual in their vain struggles for pleasure to the hosts that warred for a phantom Helen.

Helped by Theónoë, the wicked king's saintly sister, Helen now plays the same trick as Iphigeneia among the Taurians. She tells Theoclýmenus that Menelaus is lost at sea; she will wed the Egyptian; but first, by Greek custom, she must perform her drowned husband's funeral rites off shore. When Theoclýmenus finds that Menelaus has escaped with Helen after knocking the Egyptian escort on the head, he prepares in fury to kill his sister as accomplice; but is prevented by an epiphany of Helen's divine brothers, Castor and Polydeuces.

It has been not unplausibly suggested that this strange piece, with its defence of Spartan Helen, its gibes at soothsayers, its picture of the world's most famous war being fought for a spectral chimera, was, like Aristophanes' *Lysistrata,* a plea for peace with Sparta in the war-weary years after the shattered dream of Sicilian conquest.

THE PHOENICIAN WOMEN
(c. 410–409 B.C.)

This play (apparently much interpolated) tries to be a sort of 'omnibus' of Theban legend. Incorporating too much, it bursts.[1]

When it begins, Polyneices is already investing the city to dethrone his brother Éteocles. But in this version Oedipus is still alive, a blinded prisoner; and so is Jocasta, who in a vast and frigid prologue catalogues all the woes of Thebes since its founder, Cadmus. Then, in the vividest scene of the play, she arranges a meeting between her warring sons; but it only embitters them. Éteocles reveals himself as ambition incarnate.

> Mother, I speak my heart without concealment.
> I, were it in my power, would break my way
> Far as earth's verge, where rise the sun and stars,
> Or deep beneath it, could I only win
> That greatest of all gods, high Sovereignty. . . .
> Therefore come sword, come fire!
> Harness my chargers, with chariots fill the plains!
> Never will I resign my royal throne!
> For if man *must* do wrong, then it were best
> Do wrong for Sovereignty, right in all else.
>
> (503–6, 521–5.)

---

[1] So Agathon tried to crowd into one play all the events of the fall of Troy (Aristotle, *Poetics*, ch. xviii).

The first lines of this were to be echoed by Shakespeare's Hotspur; the last two (according to the shocked Cicero) to be a constant quotation on the lips of Caesar.

Then episode tumbles over episode, in alternations of pathos and bathos. Creon's son, Menoeceus (another recruit to Euripides' swollen army of martyrs), sacrifices himself for the victory of Thebes. The Theban brothers kill each other. Jocasta stabs herself over their bodies. Antigone vows she will bury Polyneices despite Creon; then accompanies the blind Oedipus into exile. With one thousand seven hundred and sixty-six lines (including accretions) the play is unusually long: few will say it seems short. And some will feel at the end of it as if they never wished to hear of Thebes again. Swinburne grew childishly ribald at the expense of poor Mrs Browning and her 'Euripides the human, with his *droppings* of warm tears.' Certainly 'droppings' seems an understatement. But such rivers of them as flow here yield nothing electrifying. One sickens of being as systematically harrowed as if one were a field. The tragedy reads like the work of a tired and depressed old man, stumbling on mechanically; yet soon he was to break the ties that held him, a prophet without honour, in Athens and to find new life in the wilds of Macedon.

ORESTES
(408 B.C.)

Like *Electra*, this is a pitilessly unpleasant play; but it is dramatic and exciting—indeed there are said to be more quotations from it in Antiquity than from all Aeschylus and Sophocles combined.

Clytemnestra has been murdered; to-day Argos is to decide whether Orestes and Electra shall be stoned for it. Meanwhile they are blockaded in the palace—Orestes asleep after a fit of frenzy, with Electra watching at his side. Their one hope is their uncle Menelaus, who has just sailed home with Helen. Here Helen has again become a heartless fribble; Electra, with the lynx-eyes of hatred, watches her cutting her tresses to offer on Clytemnestra's grave.

> Did you see how she merely snipped the tips of them,
> To keep her looks? The woman she always was!
>
> (128–9.)

Orestes wins little sympathy from Menelaus and is savagely attacked by his grandfather Tyndareus, father of Helen and Clytemnestra. Why did Orestes not seek justice by law? (Euripides modernizes the situation,

regardless of anachronisms.)   Then Orestes and Pýlades plead before the
assembly; but the only grace they can win is suicide for brother and sister.
Electra, begging Orestes to kill her, wrings from him only the embittered
answer:

> Enough is my mother's blood.   I will not kill you.
> Find your own death, whatever way you will.

> (1039–40.)

Pýlades suggests that they at least repay the shuffling Menelaus by murdering Helen first.   Electra adds the proposal that they seize Helen's daughter,
the innocent Hermione, as hostage for their own lives.   Orestes is as
delighted by her courage as Macbeth by his wife's:

> O woman's body, that outshines thy sex,
> But heart that is a man's!

> (1204–5.)

The shrieks of Helen are heard; her cowardly Phrygian attendants
scatter in panic; the palace is in flames; the distracted Menelaus sees Orestes
on the battlements, his sword at Hermione's throat.   But suddenly Apollo
intervenes.   He has already saved Helen—she shall become a goddess
succouring seamen in distress; Electra shall wed Pýlades; and Hermione
Orestes (after he has stood his trial at Athens).

Apart from this bizarre and incongruous ending, the play is a realistic
struggle of deliberately unattractive characters—Electra, affectionate but
savage as in the piece that bears her name; an Orestes who provides another
of Euripides' practised studies of minds diseased; and a Menelaus who is a
toad.   The end is a miracle; but from the rest of the drama the miraculous
is rationalized away, and the Eumenides of Aeschylus here become figments
of a sick imagination.

Like *Ion*, this work leaves the impression that Euripides sometimes
wrote his plays both for thinkers and for the multitude; but his epilogues
(like some of his prologues) for the multitude alone.   Hardly an out-
standing work; but not a dull one.

THE BACCHAE
(*c.* 407 B.C.)

If the red slayer think he slays,
Or if the slain think he is slain,
They know not well the subtle ways
I keep, and pass, and turn again.

Emerson.

The Bacchae is for us, in a sense, the epilogue of Greek tragedy itself, dedicated to its patron, Dionysus. For many years Euripides the realist had warred with Euripides the romantic: here the two meet in a kind of final reconciliation.

Exiled to half-civilized Macedonia, where the women, like Queen Olympias, the mother of Alexander, still worshipped Dionysus with a wilder ecstasy, wreathing live snakes about them, the old Euripides perhaps realized as never before the value of vitality and the force of unquestioning faith. And so he wrote a play about 'enthusiasm'—recalling at moments a medieval mystery, at moments a religious revival, at moments a witches' sabbath.

That some scholars should have supposed it a religious recantation, while others judiciously hedge, seems strange—except that some minds are made so uncomfortable by freedom of thought that, if they cannot convert sceptics living, they try to do it after their deaths. I see no more reason to believe that Euripides was converted into a devout pagan than to believe that Cadmus was converted into an actual serpent. Are we to imagine the most compassionate of poets throwing his belated grain of incense to a vindictive deity that makes mothers rend their own living sons in pieces, and then surveys the result well pleased—when even the fanatic Chorus are visibly shocked and shaken?[1] Euripides had not recanted like Racine; but his mind had grown broader and deeper. At seventy-seven that is remarkable enough.

Through a long life Euripides had struggled to enlighten men; in return they had distrusted, disliked, made mock of him; now his grey hairs were going down to a foreign grave. Such were the results of trying to make men think; it was something to think about.

The problem is eternal. It is not hard to be critical, to undermine beliefs, to start men asking questions. But to make them find sane answers

---

[1] Cf. the denunciation of Apollo in *Andrómache* (p. 283):

> The God remembered,
> Like some bad man, only his ancient grudge.
> And where, then, lies his wisdom?

—that is less easy.   Men think they think; but their thought is largely the shuttlecock of passion, desire, or fear.   Who can master Dionysus?

Besides, may it not be that life is too terrible, except for the strongest nerves, to face without intoxication?   That, for many, freedom from chains becomes an intolerable burden of responsibility?

The late Lord Keynes in *My Early Beliefs* has recorded the attitude of the early twentieth-century intellectuals among whom he moved: 'We were among the last of the Utopians. . . .   We were not aware that civilization was a thin and precarious crust.'   They believed, as Euripides had believed, in reason and human reasonableness.   And so that Bacchanal D. H. Lawrence hated them as savagely as Dionysus hated Pentheus.   Impulse, instinct, ecstasy, destruction, were what Lawrence wanted; and the world was soon to have them abundantly.

The Bacchae is the tragedy of fanaticism.   Euripides is not converted to it; he is horrified by it; but he recognizes, at last, its terrible power.   Here the theme of *Hippolytus* is carried further.   In that play, Aphrodite is Nature in her ruthless fecundity; Artemis is Nature in her lonely aloofness: here Dionysus is Nature in her blind instincts and impulses, her intoxication, and her callousness.   Wisdom will not worship Dionysus—he is, as Agāve found, a beautiful devil; wisdom will not try to extirpate him— he is, as Pentheus would not see, the basic energy of life.   One must try to render to reason the things that are reason's, and to instinct and impulse the things that are theirs.   It is never easy; often impossible.   But had the eighteenth-century Enlightenment and the Romantics understood *The Bacchae*, each might have avoided some of the folly and unhappiness brought by their opposite extremes.   And when Freud shook his head with misgiving over the discontents and maladjustments of civilized man, he was only amplifying, with far profounder knowledge, the conclusion hinted in *The Bacchae*.   Caliban lives in every individual and every community; he is equally dangerous if let loose or starved in chains; he can—perhaps— little by little be tamed.   Meanwhile Caliban is doubly dangerous because he seems at times to speak with the magic voice of Ariel.[1]

---

[1] I have tried to deal with this more fully in *The Decline and Fall of the Romantic Ideal*, chs. ii–iii; *Literature and Psychology*, chs. vi–vii.

THE BACCHAE

DIONYSUS
CADMUS
AGĀVE, his daughter
PENTHEUS, King of Thebes, her son

TEIRESIAS
CHORUS OF MAENADS
A GUARD
TWO MESSENGERS

[*Before the Palace of Pentheus at Thebes. On one side, the vine-grown tomb of Sémele, among still smouldering ruins.*]

Dionysus. Here to this Theban land to-day I come,
   Dionysus, son of Zeus,
   Borne Him by Cadmus' daughter Sémele,
   Who for her midwife had the lightning's flame.
   With my form divine exchanged now for a mortal's,
   Once more I stand beside the springs of Dirce
   And the waters of Ismēnus:
   And next the palace I can see the grave
   Where, blasted by the thunder, sleeps my mother
   Amidst her ruined home that smoulders still
   With the unslaked flame of Zeus, and still recalls
   The eternal wrong by Hēra wrought on her.
   Well pleased I am with Cadmus, that he keeps
   That ground untrodden, sacred to his daughter;
   And, by my will, now all its earth is veiled
   Beneath my vine's green clusters.
      From Lydia's golden land, and Phrygia's,
   Through the sun-scorched Persian uplands I have passed,
   Through Bactria's cities and the Medes' bleak marches,
   Through Araby the Blest and Asia's coasts,
   Where by the salt sea's verge her fair-towered cities
   Are thronged by Hellene and Barbarian;
   And now to *this* town first I come in Hellas,
   Having established in those other lands
   My rites and dances, that the earth may know me
   God revealed.
      But, of all Greece, first here in Thebes I raised
   My cry of revelry—flung first on *her*
   My fawn-skin, and armed her with my ivy-wand—
   Because the sisters of my mother said

308

What they, of all, should have been the last to say:
'Dionysus is no true-begotten son
Of Zeus.   By some mortal lover Sémele
Was shamed; then on Zeus she fathered her dishonour—
A trick of Cadmus!'   'So, because she lied
About His love,' they gloated, 'Zeus destroyed her.'
For that I have goaded them in headlong frenzy,
Out of their homes, to dwell mad on the mountain,
Clad in the emblems of my ecstasy;
And, with them, I have hounded forth distracted
The womenfolk from all the hearths of Thebes.
So now with Cadmus' daughters they abide
In the green pine-woods, amid the roofless rocks.
For Thebes must learn, despite her frowardness,
My holy mysteries that she disdains,
Till in men's eyes I have cleared my mother's honour,
Revealed as the son divine she bore to God.
    Now Cadmus has resigned his royal state
To Pentheus, his daughter's child—who wages war
Against my godhead; names me in no prayer;
Thrusts me from all libations.   So to him
And all his Thebans will I manifest
My heavenly birth; and then to other lands,
Once this is set to rights, I will wander onward
To make known what I am.   But if in anger
Thebes shall unsheathe the sword to drag my Maenads
Down from Cithaeron, *I* will head my faithful
And meet the shock of battle.   Such my purpose
In stripping off my own immortal shape
And taking, thus, man's image.
        The Chorus of Lydian Maenads begins to enter, with fawn-
        skins and ivy-wands, pipes and timbrels.
    But you, my women, my wild worshippers,
You that left Lydia's mountain-wall of Tmōlus
To follow me from your barbarian home
As comrades and as fellow-wayfarers—
Take up the timbrels of the Phrygian land,
The Mountain Mother's music and my own,
And make their thunder boom round Pentheus' palace,
Till all Thebes flocks to see!
But *I* will away to the glens of high Cithaeron
And join my Maenads' dances.
                                        [*He goes out.*

Chorus.

From Asia I come, with hurrying feet,
    Where sacred Tmōlus towers on high,
To follow my Lord—ah service sweet,
Labour of love, as my lips repeat
    The Bacchants' holy cry!

Who is abroad?   Who is abroad?
    Who is within now?   Clear the ways,
And hush your tongues, with one accord.
For now to Thy name, O Bacchus, Lord,
    Thine olden hymn I raise.

Ah happy is he and blest,   *strophe* 1.
Who knoweth the hidden rites,
Whose spirit is pure within;
Who high on the mountain crest,
Where soul with soul unites,
Can worship, clean of sin;
Who serves the Mighty Mother,
    Cýbele adored,
And with temples ivy-crowned
And thyrsus whirled around
    Hails Dionysus Lord!

Come, Bacchanals, come, Bacchanals,
    Bring Brómius with you riding
        From the peaks of the Phrygian land!
God born of God, to His native walls
    Bring Him back!—to His home abiding,
        Where wide her highways stand!

Fierce flew the thunderblast   *antistrophe* 1.
Of Zeus, and from the womb
To light of day he came;
The while his mother passed
From travail to the tomb,
Seared by the lightning's flame.
Yet for the life she cherished
    A resting-place unseen
In the thigh of Zeus was found—
With clasps of gold close-bound,
    Safe hid from Heaven's Queen.

So, when the Fates ordained the day,
    Was born of the Son of Crŏnus

A God bull-horned, and crowned
With a serpent-crown; from whence alway
  We Maenads wear upon us
  Wild snakes with our hair enwound.

Thou nurse of our God's mother,   *str. 2.*
  O Thebes, now wreathe thy head
With ivy, with bryony,
  Green leaf and berries red!
Burst into life, to life,
  Crown thee with oak or pine,
And dance!   On the dappled fawn-skin
  Strands of white wool entwine!
Grasp the dread wand—be pure, beware!
Soon shall all Thebes dance *with* us there,
When Bacchus leads his bands believing
To the hills, to the hills!   There wait us, leaving
  Hearth and home, the Theban wives,
Maddened away from loom and weaving,
    Where Dionysus drives.

Hail, haunt of the Curētes,   *ant. 2.*
  Hail, holy cave of Crete,
Where Zeus of old lay cradled!
  This timbrel that I beat—
Thy crested Corybantes
  Contrived its round of hide
To mingle its own wild booming
  Where Phrygia's sweet flutes cried,
And gave it so to Cýbele
To rouse her Bacchants' ecstasy.
Then in the Mighty Mother's land
The crazy Satyrs from Her hand
  Took it, and gave to our dance divine,
Wherewith at His feast our Maenad band
  Makes glad the God of Wine.

                    epode.

Ah sweet to swoon on the mountain, faint with the sacred chase,
    Girt with the skin of the holy fawn,
    Tracking the goat that must be torn—
  The blood to drink, the raw, red flesh of grace,
High in the Lydian, Phrygian hills, where Brómius leads the race.
           Evoi!

With wine, with milk, earth floweth, with the nectar of the bee;
    And bright for all to see
    The flame of pine-wood gleams.
    From the fennel-wand it streams,
    Like incense of the East,
    In the hand of Bacchus' priest,
      Lifted high.
    Dancing as he runs,
    He spurs the laggard ones
    With his wild and mystic cry.
Light on the wind his ringlets leap,
Mid the cries of the Maenads his voice thrills deep:
'On, ye Bacchae, on, ye Bacchae!
    Pride of Tmōlus rich in gold!
Lift your shout to Dionysus,
    Mid the timbrels' thunder rolled.
Praise the God of Joy, rejoicing,
    While your Phrygian chanting shrills
      And the holy pipes are sounding
      Holy gladness, praise Him, bounding—
    Upward, to the hills, the hills!'

Then on leaps the Maenad, light as a foal
In the meadow by its mother, with rapture in her soul.
    The blind Teiresias enters, clad in Bacchic guise with ivy-wreath and fawn-skin.

Teiresias. Who watches at the gateway?   Call forth Cadmus,
Agēnor's son, that leaving Sidon's city
First piled the towers of Thebes.
Go, one of you, and say Teiresias here
Seeks audience.   He knows, himself, my errand—
The compact that I made, myself so old
With him yet older—that we both should don
Fawn-skins, and fasten ivy on our wands,
And crown our heads with springing ivy-sprays.
Cadmus (coming forth in similar attire). Ah dearest friend, even within the palace
I heard your voice—the wise words of your wisdom.
And, see, I am dressed already in the garb
Of this new God.   He is my own daughter's son,
This Dionysus, now revealed divine;
And right it is that we with all our power
Should magnify his greatness.

Where must I dance now? Where must I set my steps,
And toss my hoary head? Tell me, Teiresias!
For we are elders both—and *you* are wise.
I feel I could never weary, night and day,
Smiting upon the ground my ivy-wand.
Ah what a happiness when we forget
That we are old!

Teiresias. Why then, you feel as I.
I too grow young—all eager for the dance.

Cadmus. Shall we not ride in a chariot to Cithaeron?

Teiresias. Nay, it would show less reverence towards the God.

Cadmus. Then *I* will lead you—one old man another.

Teiresias. With magic ease the God will guide us there.

Cadmus. Shall none in Thebes, but we two, dance for Bacchus?

Teiresias. Yes, only we are wise—blind all the rest.

Cadmus. We linger over-long. Come, take my hand.

Teiresias. And here is mine—clasp both our hands in one.

Cadmus. *I* will not scorn the Gods—I am but man.

Teiresias. *We* do not whet our wits on Heavenly things;
We keep our fathers' faiths, as old as time.
No tongue shall overthrow them—
Whatever subtleties keen brains devise!
I know that some will say that I disgrace
The dignity of age, to dream of dancing
With ivy round my brows. But no distinction
The God hath made of dancers young or old—
From all He claims one universal honour
Without respect of years.

Cadmus. Since darkness veils your eyes, Teiresias,
I must be 'seer,' and tell you what approaches.
Now towards the palace there comes hurrying
Pentheus, Echīon's son, to whom I yielded
The sovereignty of Thebes.
How wild he looks! What has he now to say?

> *Pentheus enters with his bodyguard; at first without noticing
> the two old men.*

Pentheus. I chanced to be beyond our Theban borders,
But word was brought me there of evil changes
Rife in the city—that our womenfolk
Have quit their homes, on plea of mystic worship,
And gad about the forests of the hills,
Dancing in honour of this new-made God,
This Dionysus—whoever *he* may be!

I hear there stand amid their congregations
Wine-bowls full-brimming; while, this way and that,
Into the lonely places, one by one,
They creep to lie with lovers. 'Bacchic worship'
They call it—but indeed, far less they honour
Bacchus than Aphrodite!

   Those I have caught lie now in the public prison,
With fettered hands, well watched by my own guards;
The rest I have yet to hunt from off Cithaeron.
But once I have fitted *them* with iron shackles,
There shall be an end to these foul ecstasies.

   Further, they say there is a stranger here,
A juggling wizard out of Lydia;
His yellow ringlets pleasantly perfumed—
Cheeks flushed with wine—and in his eyes the graces
Of Aphrodite. Day and night he haunts
Our young girls, luring them with revelations
Of mystic joys. But once within these walls
I have him fast, then I will make an end
Of all his wand-wavings and tossing tresses,
By hewing head from trunk.
The fellow dares to call this Dionysus
'God'!—to pretend he was sewn within the thigh
Of Zeus!—though Zeus consumed him with His lightning,
And *with* the child its mother, for her lies
In claiming Zeus had loved her.
Whoever this stranger be—the mad blasphemer!—
Has he not earned the hangman's grisly noose?

                                     [He notices the two old men.

   But here's another marvel! Look, the prophet
Teiresias, tricked out in dappled fawn-skins!
And my mother's father—what a sight for laughter!—
Waving a fennel-wand! I cannot bear it,
Old sir, to see such folly at your years!
Off with that ivy-wreath! Grandfather, come!
Throw down that thyrsus! *You*, Teiresias,
Have urged him on to this. Was it your hope,
By bringing men to worship this new God,
To have more birds to watch, more fees to win
By divination from burnt-offerings?
I tell you, were it not for your grey hairs,
Well chained you should have sat amid the Maenads,
For spreading rites perverse. For when the wine

Gleams ruddy at a feast where women meet,
  I doubt the wholesomeness of their devotions.
Chorus-leader. What, stranger!—dare you scoff at piety!—
  At Cadmus, sower of the Giants' seed!
  Shall the son of Echīon sully his own race?
Teiresias. For a clever speaker, with a fair occasion,
  Not hard is eloquence.   Your tongue is nimble,
  As if you were also wise; yet in your words
  Wisdom is not!   A facile orator,
  Full of assurance yet devoid of sense,
  But poorly serves his city.
      This new divinity that moves your laughter—
  I have not words to say how high exalted
  His might shall be through Hellas.   In man's life
  Two powers, young sir, stand foremost.   First, Demeter—
  Earth, if you will—(no matter for the name),
  Who grants to men all sustenance that's dry;
  And, after her, the son of Sémele
  Hath come to bring them, as a counterpart,
  The liquid of the grape; that medicines
  Our sad humanity for all its sorrows,
  When the juice of the vine has filled them, bringing sleep
  And deep oblivion of daily cares.
  Toil knows no other balm; to the Gods themselves
  This God is poured in offering—so by Him
  All Heaven's blessings reach the sons of men.
      Why must you scoff to hear that He was sewn
  Within the thigh of Zeus?   Let me expound
  The whole fair truth.
  When Zeus had snatched him from the lightning-flame
  And to Olympus brought the babe, as God,
  Then Hēra sought to hurl him forth from Heaven,
  But Zeus in His wisdom ordered otherwise.
  For from the ether compassing the world
  He brake a fragment, and to Hēra gave
  That '*sky-born*' shape as hostage,
  And from her anger so saved Dionysus.
  Thence, with the passing years, men fabled him
  '*Thigh-born*' from Zeus; out of a twisted word
  Building a legend, since this son of Heaven
  As an airy semblance lay in Hēra's power.
      This God, too, is prophetic.   Ecstasy
  And mania hold, indeed, much mantic virtue;

And when the flesh of men grows filled with Him,
He makes them, in their madness, prophesy.
He hath taken, too, a portion of the power
Of Ares; for, when armies ranged for battle
Ere the first spear-thrust flee dissolved in panic,
This too is a madness sent by Dionysus.
Ay, the day comes when at Delphi itself,
Across the height that crowns its double crags
With His pine-torches thou shalt see Him leap,
Shaking and brandishing His holy wand—
Yea, mighty through all Hellas. Hear me, Pentheus!
Dream not that force can rule the affairs of men,
Nor, if thou thinkest so, in thought so blinded
Think there lies wisdom. Welcome Him to Thebes!
Pour Him drink-offerings—enwreathe thy brows—
And yield to His ecstasy!

It is not Dionysus can compel
Our women to be chaste. That must be sought
In their own hearts. No Bacchic revellings
Can ever stain the soul of her that's pure.

And think how *you* are happy when men crowd
Your gates, and Thebes cries glory to the name
Of Pentheus: so, I doubt not, Dionysus
Delights in being honoured.
And therefore I and Cadmus (though you mock him)
Will crown our brows with ivy and go dance—
Two grey old men, and yet go dance we must.
No words of thine shall make me war with Heaven.
Stark mad thou art, past power of drugs to cure—
Nay, it must be some drug that makes thee mad.
Leader. Old seer, thy words are worthy of Apollo!
And wise thy reverence for our mighty Lord.
Cadmus. My son, Teiresias advises well.
Abide with us, dwell not outside the law.
For now thy words are whirling; thy wisdom, folly.
Even if, *as* you say, he is no God,
Do not deny him—make a fair pretence
That he *is* the true-born son of Sémele.
So let her seem the mother of a God,
And bring new honour to *us* and all our house.
Remember how miserably Actaeon died,
Torn high among the hills by the ravening hounds
His own hands reared, because he bragged himself

A mightier hunter than Queen Artemis.
Share not *his* fate!　Come, let me bind thy head
With ivy.　Join in honouring Dionysus.

Pentheus. Hands off!　Begone and revel with your god,
But smear not on *me* the infection of your folly!
As for this tutor of your senselessness,
On *him* I will wreak my justice.　Go someone—
Quickly!—seek out his seat of augury;
With levers heave it up and fling it headlong,
In uttermost confusion overturned.
And scatter the holy bands that bind his brow,
To wind and tempest.　That will vex him most.
　　　You others, through the streets of Thebes track down
This womanish stranger that among our women
Spreads his contagion and pollutes their honour.
If ye can catch him, hale him here in fetters
To find a just death by stoning—bitter end
To all his Theban revels!

　　　　　　　　　　　[*Some of Pentheus' guards go out.*

Teiresias.　　　　　　　Reckless fool,
You know not what you say.　Even before,
You were beside yourself—and now stark mad!
Come, Cadmus, let us go and beg the God,
For this man's sake (although grown now so savage)
And for all Thebes, still to forbear His anger.
Take up your ivied staff and follow me.
Try to stay up my weakness, as I thine.
For two old men to fall—what ignominy!
And yet no matter!
The service of Lord Bacchus is our duty.
But, Cadmus, beware lest on your house this Pentheus
Bring sharp repentance.　I say it not as prophet;
It is enough to look upon his actions—
A fool, with tongue of folly!

　　　　　　　*The two old men go out; Pentheus and his remaining guards
　　　　　　　enter the palace.*

Chorus.　　　　Holiness, Lady of Heaven,　　　　　*strophe* 1.
　　　　　　　Holiness whose wing
　　　　　Over the earth soars golden,
　　　　　　　Hast heard what said the King!—
　　　　　Heard how that tongue unholy
　　　　　　　Mocked with its blasphemy
　　　　　Him who in Heaven's hall,

Where feast the Blest, of all
Stands forth supreme, the Son of Sémele!—
        Yea, Him that gave the dances
            Where all our souls unite,
        The fluting and the laughter
            Of hearts He maketh light,
When the high Gods pass the wine-cup
            Or when, at feasts men keep,
        On brows enwreathed with ivy
            His bowl sheds sleep.

    The mouths that foam unbridled,   *antistrophe* 1.
        The madness scorning law,
    There is one end awaits them—
        Destruction, evermore.
    But the Peace of Understanding
        Shall fear no troublous days,
    No strife her house divide;
    For, though far off enskied,
Well the Immortals watch all human ways.
    Folly is this world's wisdom,
        And pride past man's estate.
    Too brief our days. Too fondly,
        Pursuing hopes too great,
    Men lose the good beside them
        For visions vast and vain—
    Schemers blind in counsel,
            Crazed in brain.

    Ah to flee to Cyprus,   *str.* 2.
        Aphrodite's isle,
    Where the Loves go flitting,
        That men's hearts beguile,
    Where the fields of Paphos grow
    Green from the far-off rainless flow
        Of hundred-headed Nile!
    Bear me, bear me, Dionysus,
        Lord of dance and joy, afar
    To the slopes of dread Olympus,
        Muse-beloved Pīéria!
    There the Graces, there Desire
                Aye abide;
    There the Maenad too may worship
        Thee, my Saviour, undenied.

Well our Lord loves revel,   *ant. 2.*
  Well He loveth Peace—
Her that, bringing riches,
  Biddeth youth increase.
Rich and poor His hand divine
Blesses with the gift of wine,
  Till their sorrows cease.
But He hates all them that make not
  Bliss of life their single prize
Through the days, the nights of gladness;
  Still He loves the humbly wise,
Who reject the clever scoffer's
      Subtlety.
What the common folk and simple
  Think and do, sufficeth me.

Guards lead in Dionysus: Pentheus reappears from the palace.

Guard. Pentheus, the errand that you charged us with
Is done—and here is the quarry that we caught,
A gentle creature, that did not even flee!
Of his own will he held out both his hands
And waited there.   Easy he made my errand.
Ruddy as wine, his cheek still kept its colour,
As, with a smile, he bade us take and lead him.
I felt ashamed, and said: 'By no will of mine
I seize you, stranger.   These are Pentheus' orders.'

  But as for the Maenads that you caught and shut,
Fast chained, in our common prison—they are vanished!
Freed from their fetters, through the mountain glades
They dance with loud cries to Brómius divine.
For, of themselves, the gyves slipped from their ankles,
The bolts slid back untouched by human hand.
Marvels indeed this stranger has brought to Thebes!
The rest, my lord, your judgment must decide.

Pentheus. Let go his hands.   Now that I have him snared,
Whatever his swiftness, he shall not escape me.

  Indeed your looks are not unhandsome, stranger,
At least for women (and for *them* you come).
Never from wrestling grew those flowing ringlets—
Lovelocks low-curling all about your cheek.
And what a white complexion, kept with care
In pleasant shades, where never sun should burn it!
A comely fellow, that quests the Queen of Love!
First tell me—what's your country?

Dionysus. Gladly I tell it. That is easy said.

　　You must have heard of the flower-grown slopes of Tmōlus?

Pentheus. I have—the heights that girdle Sardis city.

Dionysus. There lies my home. My land is Lydia.

Pentheus. How comes it, then, you bring these rites to Hellas?

Dionysus. Bacchus Himself so taught me, the son of Zeus.

Pentheus. Is there some Zeus there, that begets new gods?

Dionysus. No, the same Zeus as here loved Sémele.

Pentheus. In dream did your God constrain you? Or awaking?

Dionysus. Yes, face to face. And gave me His holy rites.

Pentheus. What manner of holy rites?

Dionysus. *That* none may know, except the initiate.

Pentheus. What profit are they to the worshippers?

Dionysus. You may not hear it—though well worth the hearing!

Pentheus. Ah, you are cunning to make me curious.

Dionysus. His rites abhor the heart irreverent.

Pentheus. You say you saw the God? And in what likeness?

Dionysus. Such likeness as He pleased. Not mine to choose.

Pentheus. Once more, well parried—with mere empty words!

Dionysus. To ignorance, the wisest words seem folly.

Pentheus. And was it first to Thebes you brought your God?

Dionysus. All the barbarian lands dance in His worship.

Pentheus. Being duller, far, than Hellenes.

Dionysus. Wiser in this; though different their customs.

Pentheus. Is it by day or night ye celebrate?

Dionysus. Mostly, by night. Night hath solemnity.

Pentheus. Ah yes, for women, here is shrewd corruption.

Dionysus. Foulness can be contrived no less by day.

Pentheus. You shall pay dearly for your curséd quibbles!

Dionysus. And you for your blindness and your blasphemy.

Pentheus. How bold our Bacchant is!—and skilled in speaking!

Dionysus. Tell me my doom now—what dire penalty?

Pentheus. First, I will shear away those delicate tresses.

Dionysus. My hair is holy. I keep it for the God.

[A guard cuts it off.

Pentheus. And hand me over, next, your sacred staff.

Dionysus. Take it yourself. It is Dionysus' own.

[Pentheus takes it.

Pentheus. Your body we shall keep in close confinement.

Dionysus. The God Himself shall free me, when I will.

Pentheus. He *may*, when you are safe among your Maenads!

Dionysus. He is here—beside me—seeing what I suffer.

Pentheus. And where then? Nowhere that eyes of mine can see.

Dionysus. With *me*.   But *your* impiety is blind.

Pentheus (to his guard). Seize him!   This is contempt of me and Thebes.

Dionysus. I, sane, to ye, grown senseless, say: 'Forbear!'

Pentheus. And *I* say: 'Bind him'—with a better right!

Dionysus. You know not what you live for—do—or are.

Pentheus. I?—Pentheus, son of Agāve and Echīon.

Dionysus. Unhappiness lives in your very name.

Pentheus. Go!   Shut him in the stables hard at hand—
Let him contemplate their darkness!
There you can dance!   As for these women here
That follow you, as your accomplices,
They shall be sold to bondage—or myself
Will turn their hands from thumping the hide of timbrels
To labour at my loom.

Dionysus. So be it, I go.   What is not fated me,
I cannot suffer.   Yet shall Dionysus,
Whom thou deniest, for this sacrilege
Hound thee to retribution!
For, wronging *me*, thou hast led *Him* in chains.

> *The guards lead Dionysus away.   Pentheus re-enters the palace.*

Chorus.   Daughter of Achelōus,   *strophe.*
                    Dirce, maiden and queen,
                Washed of old in thy waters
                    The babe of God hath been,
                That day when his Heavenly Father
                    Forth from the quenchless fire
                Snatched the child and laid him
                    In the thigh of his own sire.
            'Come,' He cried, 'come, Dithyrambus,
                    In thy father's womb lie sealed.
            By that name all Thebes shall know thee,
                Bacchus, whom I have revealed.'
                Why then, O blessed Dirce,
                    When here with wreath on brow
                I dance, wilt thou reject me—
                    Deny me—shun me now?
            Nay, by His own vine's clustering grace,
            To Bacchus yet thou shalt turn thy face!

                This Pentheus once begotten   *antistrophe.*
                    Of Echīon, son of earth,
                This scion of earth and dragon—
                    His rage well shows his birth!

No mortal, but a monster,
Savage and grim to see
As the red Giants that challenged
The high Gods' sovereignty!
Soon about me, Bacchus' servant,
Shall the tyrant's bonds be tied;
Even now the priest, our comrade,
Shadows of his prison hide.
Our martyrdom that preach Thee,
O Lord, canst Thou behold?
Rise up, O Dionysus,
And shake Thy staff of gold!
Come Thou from Heaven's height to seize
This murderer in his blasphemies.

Where art hidden, Dionysus?   *epode.*
Leadest Thou Thy mystic band
Through beast-haunted glens of Nysa?—
Where the Crags Corycian stand?—
Or amid the forest-coverts
Of Olympus, where of old
With his harp by hill and hollow
Orpheus drew the trees to follow,
Drew the beasts of wild and wold?
Blest art thou, Piéria,
Cherished by the God of Gladness;
He shall bring His holy madness
For thy dancing, from afar,
With His Maenads round Him whirling,
Over Axius swiftly swirling,
Over Lydias, fairest river,
Where the steeds graze in their pride,
Of all happiness the giver
To the dwellers by his tide.

Dionysus (*within*). Ho!
Hark to my voice now, harken,
O Bacchanals, O Bacchanals!
One of the Chorus. Whence comes this sound around me
Of the voice of God that calls?
Dionysus (*within*). Ho, again I call to ye—
The Son of Zeus and Sémele.
Another. Ah my Master, ah my Master!

Hither, hither!—join with us,
  Brómius, Brómius!
Dionysus (*within*). Spirit of Earthquake, upheave thou the land!

                                         [*The earth trembles.*

Another. Ah, ah!
  Swiftly now shall Pentheus' hall
  Shudder to its final fall.
Another. There within moves Bacchus—now!
  Worship Him!
Another.   To Him we bow.
Another. Look, where the palace-columns rise,
  The marble lintel splits and falls!
  Loud and clear behind its walls,
  'Victory!' our Master cries.
Dionysus (*within*). Thunderbolt, fall glittering!
  Kindle the palace of the King!   [*Lightning.*
One of the Chorus. See the sacred tomb where slumbers
  Sémele!—high round it glare
  Heaven's fires that, since they smote her,
  Smouldered there.
  Cast ye down, with bodies trembling!
        Down, ye Maenads!   From on high
  To this house, all things confounding,
        Sure the Son of God draws nigh.
     They prostrate themselves and Dionysus enters.

Dionysus. Lie ye on the earth prostrated, with your terrors thus aghast,
  Asia's daughters?   Sure, ye saw it, how Lord Dionysus cast
  To the earth King Pentheus' palace?   None the less, with better cheer,
  From the dust upraise your bodies—tremble now no more with fear.
Leader. Ah thou saving light and glory of our joyous ecstasy,
  How my heart, that was so lonely, gladdens now at sight of thee!
Dionysus. Was your courage, then, so broken, when the guards led me
                      away
  To the dungeon of King Pentheus, darkened from the light of day?
Leader. Could I help it?   Hadst thou perished, who was left to save me
                      still?
  How wast thou delivered—tell us!—from that man of evil will?
Dionysus. I alone, without an effort, made my own way back to light.
Leader. Had he not, then, bound together both thy hands with cords
                   drawn tight?
Dionysus. Thus it was that I befooled him. Binding me, indeed, he
                   seemed,
  Yet he never grasped nor touched me, feeding but on fancies dreamed.

In the stable where he shut me, as it chanced, a bull he found;
Knees and hoofs, he sought to bind it, with a rope fast knotted round.
Wildly panting in his frenzy, deep he gnawed his nether lip,
While I calmly sat beside him, from his body watching drip
Streams of sweat—so hard he laboured.   Then it was that Bacchus
                                                                came—
Made the palace quake, and kindled on His mother's tomb the flame.
Fearing that his hall was burning, hither, thither rushed the King,
Shouting madly to his servants, calling to his men to bring
Water, while with idle efforts all his henchmen ran and cried.
Then, persuaded I had vanished, all his labour cast aside,
In he rushed to search the palace, snatching up a blue sword-blade.
What there followed next, I know not.   But it seems that Bacchus made
In the court a phantom like me.   Then on that bright shape of air
Pentheus sprang and hewed and stabbed it, passionate to slay me there.
Next, Lord Dionysus smote him with a new indignity,
Toppling all his house to earthward.   Ruined it lies for him to see—
Bitter end to my enchaining!   Dropped now from his fainting hand
In the dust his sword is lying.   Fool, that dared in fight to stand
Man with God!   But I, arising, passed from out his royal hall,
Calm and undisturbed, to join ye, heeding Pentheus not at all.
Hark!   If I am not mistaken, near the door his footstep rings.
Forth he comes!   What will he say now, after these strange happenings?
Unperturbed I will await him, stormy though his anger be.
Wise the heart that, still unshaken, keeps its equanimity.

Pentheus (*opening the palace-door*). Monstrous!   The stranger I had
    confined in durance,

    Has slipped from out my grasp!   [*Seeing Dionysus.*
    Ha!
    Here is the fellow.   What means *this?*   How come you
    Walking abroad in the court before my palace?
Dionysus. Stay now!—and give your rage an easier pace.
Pentheus. How come you here at large—my prison broken?
Dionysus. Said I not—heard you not—that One would free me?
Pentheus. And who then?   Still these strange, new-fangled speeches!
Dionysus. He that has given men His clustering vine.
Pentheus. A famous feat—for Dionysus' shame!
        [*One or more lines probably missing.*]
    (*To his guards.*) Shut every gateway in the city-wall.
Dionysus. What use?   Can even walls confine the Gods?
Pentheus. So wise, so wise!—except where wisdom's needed.
Dionysus. I have the wisdom that is needed most.

                            [*A messenger enters.*

　　But, first, hear what this fellow has to tell,
　　Who brings some message for you from the mountain.
　　We will await your pleasure; not escape.
Messenger. King Pentheus, sovereign of this Theban land,
　　I come now from Cithaeron, where year-long
　　Endure the pure white-glistening drifts of snow.
Pentheus. And now what urgent news have you to bring?
Messenger. I have seen the wild women—those that fled from Thebes,
　　With white feet in their frenzy darting hillward;
　　And come to tell you, sire—all Thebes as well—
　　How strange their doings—more than miracles!
　　But first I would know *this*—dare I speak freely,
　　Or shall I curb my tongue?
　　For I fear, my lord, the quickness of your anger,
　　Knowing your temper sharp and but too kingly.
Pentheus. Say on, I grant thee full impunity.
　　Anger should not be spent on honest men.
　　But the worse news you bring about these Maenads,
　　The heavier punishment I shall exact
　　From their instigator in these evil arts.
Messenger. Our herded beasts were breasting the hill-summit
　　Just as the sun rose warm across the world,
　　And there I saw three bands of Maenad dancers—
　　Autónoë headed one, Īno another,
　　Agāve, your own mother, led the third.
　　There they all lay, with limbs relaxed in sleep,
　　Some pillowing their backs on boughs of pine,
　　Some with their heads reclined on heaps of oak-leaves,
　　But modestly—and not, as *you* say, maddened
　　With cups of wine and frenzies of the flute,
　　And through the forests making lonely love.

　　　But then your mother heard our horned beasts lowing;
　　Swift to her feet she leapt, among the Maenads,
　　And cried their holy cry to waken them.
　　Then, flinging from their eyes the weight of slumber,
　　They too sprang up—a marvel of ordered grace—
　　Old wives and young, and maidens yet unmarried.
　　Loose on their shoulders they tossed out their hair
　　And drew their unclasped fawn-skins closer round them,
　　Girdling the dappled hides with living snakes,
　　That licked their faces.　Mothers that had left
　　Their babes at home, were suckling in their arms
　　With their white milk the fawns of forest deer,

Or wild wolf-cubs.   With leaves of oak or ivy,
Or flowering bryony they wreathed their hair;
Then one would strike her wand against a rock
And forth would leap a jet of dew-bright water;
Another dashed her staff against the ground
And the God sent a gush of wine in answer;
While others, if they craved a draught of milk,
Had but with finger-tips to scrape the earth,
And forth a white stream came flowing; or ivy-wands
Dripped honey sweet as from the honeycomb.
Hadst thou been there, and seen such sights thyself,
Thyself had worshipped Him thou persecutest.

    Then all we herders there of sheep and cattle,
We laid our heads together in dispute
About these marvels and these miracles.
Now with us was a glib, street-haunting townsman,
Who made us all a speech: 'What say you, fellows
That live among the high and holy mountains,
Shall we capture Queen Agāve, Pentheus' mother,
Amid her revels?   *That* would please the King.'
To us his plan seemed clever—so in ambush
Amid the undergrowth we hid and waited.
But now it was the appointed hour of prayer,
And waving ivy-wands they moved to worship,
Crying with one voice: 'Iacchus, Brómius, Son
Of God in the highest!'   All the mountain there
Went mad with ecstasy, and all its beasts—
All leapt to life in one wild, whirling dance.

    Now Agāve, as it chanced, sprang past my ambush,
And out I jumped to fling both arms about her;
But shrill she shouted: 'Ha, my hunting-hounds,
Here are men hunting *us*!   Up!—follow, follow,
With your wild wands to strike them!'   Then *we* ran
From their fierce, rending clutches; but they instead
Fell with bare hands upon our herds at pasture.
You might have seen one catch a great-uddered heifer,
Wild-bellowing, in her grip—and others tearing
Whole cattle limb from limb, while high in Heaven
A rib, or a cloven hoof, would soar and fall,
Or hang, red-dripping, from the fir-tree branches.
Ay, lordly bulls, with fury in their horns
In other days, were now dragged headlong down,
Battered and hauled by a hundred girlish hands,

And all the flesh torn quicker off their bones
Than, my good lord, you'd wink your royal eyelids.
   Then, like a flight of birds, downward they swooped
Towards the low fields that, by Asōpus' stream,
Yield their rich harvests to the men of Thebes.
On Érythrae and Hysiae at the foot
Of Mount Cithaeron, like a marauding army,
They burst in tumult, plundering, ravaging,
Haling the very children from the hearth.
And all that they set upon their shoulders—bronze,
Or iron—clung fast, and fell not to the earth—
No need of ropes to hold it; on their hair
They carried fire—it burnt not.   Then the rustics,
Seeing themselves pillaged, flew in rage to arms.
And now there came the fearfullest sight of all.
For, sire, no spear could draw blood from a Maenad.
Yet every thyrsus that they hurled in answer
Struck home—till our peasants turned their backs in flight,
Men before women!   Sure, it was God's hand.
Then to their haunts the Bacchae turned again,
To the water-springs their God had made for them,
And washed away the blood, while their tame serpents
Licked from their faces all the stains of war.
   Master, whoever this new God may be,
Pray welcome Him to Thebes—for strong His arm!
Ay, and they say He is the very same
As gave to men the care-consoling grape.
Now without wine—why, there would be no love,
Nor any other pleasure left in life.
Leader. I tremble to speak so free before the King—
   And yet it *shall* be said.
There lives no God more great than Dionysus.
Pentheus. This Bacchic wantonness, like some wild fire
Closes upon us—to our shame in Hellas.
No hour for weakness!   (*To a guard.*) To the Electran Gate
Go you, bid all my warriors muster there—
My shielded spearmen and swift-mounted riders,
And all that draw a bow or bear a buckler.
For we march against the Bacchae!   Past endurance
To suffer what *we* suffer—men from women!
Dionysus. You do not listen, Pentheus, to my words;
   But ill though you have used me, yet I warn you—
Vain to unsheathe your sword against a God.

Better be quiet.   For Brómius will not bear it,
That you hunt the Maenads from His holy mountains.

Pentheus. Preach not at *me*!   You have escaped to freedom—
Keep it!   Or must I hale you again to justice?

Dionysus. I should sacrifice to Him; not thus in rage
Kick at the pricks—a man defying God.

Pentheus. 'Sacrifice'?   That I will!—the blood of women,
Spilt, as deserved, in havoc through Cithaeron.

Dionysus. You will flee!—with all your army.   What dishonour!
Bronze shields in rout before the wands of women.

Pentheus. This fellow is indeed unconscionable.
Free or in chains, nothing can stop his tongue.

Dionysus. Sir, everything might yet find happy ending.

Pentheus. How?   If I grow the slave of my own slaves!

Dionysus. I can bring these women home—no need of arms.

Pentheus. Ha?   Now you spin some cunning plot against me.

Dionysus. How 'plot'?   When now I would contrive to save you.

Pentheus. Ye are leagued and sworn to keep these rites of Bacchus.

Dionysus. Yes, *that* indeed I have sworn to Dionysus.

Pentheus. Bring me my armour.   You have talked enough.

Dionysus (*fixing on him a stare of fascination*). Ah!
Would you like to see them gathered on Cithaeron?

Pentheus. I would indeed!   Though it cost me gold uncounted.

Dionysus. What?   Have you such a passionate desire?

Pentheus. It would anger me to see them drunk with wine.

Dionysus. And yet you would *like* to see that sight, though bitter?

Pentheus. For sure!   Could I watch beneath the firs, in quiet.

Dionysus. Though you come by stealth, still they will track you out.

Pentheus. There you speak truth.   I will go openly.

Dionysus. Shall I take you?   Will you venture?

Pentheus. Take me at once!   I would not lose a moment.

Dionysus. Then you must wear a trailing robe of linen.

Pentheus. What!   I, a man, to rank myself with women!

Dionysus. For fear they kill you, if they see a man.

Pentheus. Well said again!   Long since, you have shown your wisdom.

Dionysus. In that I have been taught by Dionysus.

Pentheus. How shall I follow, then, this good advice?

Dionysus. I will come and dress you, there within the palace.

Pentheus. But how?   In woman's clothes!   I am ashamed.

Dionysus. Is it gone, your wish to spy upon the Maenads?

Pentheus. What *is* this dress that you would put on me?

Dionysus. First, long and flowing tresses on your head.

Pentheus. And after that?   How must I be disguised?

Dionysus. A headband; and a robe to reach your feet.

Pentheus. And is there more than this?

Dionysus. An ivy-wand; and then a dappled fawn-skin.

Pentheus. I *could* not bring myself to dress as woman!

Dionysus. Then you must fight the Maenads. Blood will flow.

Pentheus. True, true! I *must* go, first of all, as spy.

Dionysus. Wiser, at least, than seeking ill by ill.

Pentheus. But how shall I pass unseen the streets of Thebes?

Dionysus. By lanes deserted. *I* will lead the way.

Pentheus. Anything sooner than let these Maenads mock me!
   We will go in. . . . I'll think what's best to do.

Dionysus. Whatever you will; I still am at your service.

Pentheus. Well, I'll within; and either march in arms
   Or take your counsel.   [*He enters the palace.*

Dionysus. Women, this man walks now into the net.
   He shall find the Maenads—and the death he earns!
      Now, Dionysus—for Thou art not far—
   The rest is in Thy hand. Grant us revenge.
   Infatuate him first with giddy frenzy—
   For never in his right mind will he wear
   These woman's clothes. He cannot come to it,
   Until his reason's gone.
   I long to see him made a mockery
   To Thebes, as he treads her streets disguised as woman—
   Fine end to all his blustering menaces!
   But now I must go and drape him in the dress
   That he shall wear upon the road to Hades,
   When his mother's hand has killed him!
   So shall he know at last the Son of Zeus—
   That Dionysus is a God indeed,
   To Man most gentle, yet most terrible.   [*He enters the palace.*

Chorus.   Once again, until the morning,   *strophe.*
           Shall I dance where feet flash white,
       While my face, flung back towards Heaven,
           Drinks again the dews of night?—
       As a fawn goes gaily leaping
           Where green pastures smile around,
       When she foils the dreaded hunter,
           Breaking with a headlong bound
       O'er the net where ambush lies,
       While in vain the huntsman cries,
           Holloing on each eager hound?
        Swift as storm, by river-meadows

On she gallops, undismayed,
Glad of thickets no man knoweth,
Glad of green young life that groweth
    In the long-tressed woodland's shade.

What is wisdom?   What is fairer
    Gift of God in human eyes
Than to bow, with stronger arm,
Hated heads that sought our harm?
    Fair is fame, and dear its prize.

Slowly Heaven's power moves onward,   *antistrophe.*
    Yet unfailing finds its goal,
Bringing still to retribution
    Him that with insensate soul
Honours pride without compassion,
    Or denies the Gods his praise.
Subtly hid, though Time be laggard,
    Still They track the sinner's ways.
Better not to set at naught
(Not in deed, nor even thought)
    Customs come from ancient days!
Faith is mine (it costs not dearly)
    That for aye these things endure—
Heaven's will (whate'er be Heaven),
And the laws that Time hath given
    And that Nature planteth sure.

What is wisdom?   What is fairer
    Gift of God in human eyes
Than to bow, with stronger arm,
Hated heads that sought our harm?
    Fair is fame, and dear its prize.

Happy it is to come to harbour   *epode.*
    Safe at last, though tempests lower;
Happy to see the end of labour;
Neighbour still surpasses neighbour,
    One in riches, one in power;
Hopes beyond all telling
    The hearts of men have sought—
Some that find fulfilment,
    Some that come to naught;
But best I hold, upon life's way,
The happiness of day to day.

Dionysus (*reappearing from the palace*). You that so crave to see forbidden things,
So eager after evil—come you forth,
Pentheus, before the palace. Let me see you
Clothed as a woman, as a maddened Maenad—
You that would spy on your mother and her band.
Indeed you might be one of Cadmus' daughters!

Pentheus (*emerging in the dress of a Bacchant*). Why, now I seem to see
two suns in Heaven—
Two Theban cities, each with its seven gates.
And you—you seem to stride like a bull before me,
With horns upon your head. Were you indeed
A beast? For *now* you seem become a bull.

Dionysus. The God walks with us—He before was angry,
But gracious now. You see what you *should* see.

Pentheus. How do I look? Is this not just the bearing
Of Ino? Or Agāve, my own mother?

Dionysus. You are like them to the life.
But come, this lock is straying out of place—
Not as I set it, underneath your headband.

Pentheus. Indoors I disarranged it, as I tossed,
In Maenad dance, my tresses back and forth.

Dionysus. But I whose task it is to attend upon you
Will set it to rights again. Lift up your head.

Pentheus. Yes, order all. For I am in your hands.

Dionysus. Too slack your girdle. And your robe's long folds
Do not fall straight to the ankle.

Pentheus. True, on the right. Here on the left most fairly
It flows to the very heel.

Dionysus. Ah you will thank me as your best of friends,
When you see the Maenads, after all, so sober.

Pentheus. Must I hold my thyrsus in right hand or left?
Which is more like a Bacchant?

Dionysus. The right. And in time with your right foot you raise it.
Good, that your mind is changed so!

Pentheus. Why now, could not these shoulders heave aloft
Cithaeron's mountain-mass, with all its Maenads?

Dionysus. Ay, if you chose. This is a healthier mood.
Before, your soul was sick.

Pentheus. Shall we take crowbars? Or shall I uplift
The summit by sheer strength of arm or shoulder?

Dionysus. Ah do not wreck the haunts of the mountain-nymphs,
The bowers where Pan sits piping!

Pentheus. Well said! I must not by brute force defeat
Mere women—enough to hide among the firs.

Dionysus. Hide? In such hiding-place thou shalt be hid
As fits a peeping spy of Bacchanals!

Pentheus. Ah yes, I doubt not, couched among the thickets,
Like birds, they couple in love's sweet embrace.

Dionysus. But now you go to keep a good guard on that!
Maybe you will catch them—if you be not caught!

Pentheus. Now lead me on, straight through the midst of Thebes.
For I alone am man enough to dare this.

Dionysus. You are alone her champion. You alone!
Therefore there waits you this doomed agony.
Follow! In safety I will lead you there—
But another brings you home. *Pentheus.* You mean my mother?

Dionysus. Yes, watched by all men's eyes. *Pentheus.* For *that* I go.

Dionysus. You shall be borne aloft. *Pentheus.* Such luxury?

Dionysus. Ay, in your mother's arms. *Pentheus.* But that were softness!

Dionysus. Softness indeed! *Pentheus.* Indeed not undeserved.

[*He staggers out.*

Dionysus. Thou portent of clever cunning, how portentous
The end that waits thee—thou shalt find thy glory,
Exalted high as Heaven!
Stretch out your hand, Agāve!—and you, her sisters,
Daughters of Cadmus! Here your young King comes,
To his crowning struggle; but I it is who win—
And Dionysus! Time shall show the rest.

[*He follows Pentheus,*

Chorus.   Swift hounds of Madness, now turn ye flying   *strophe.*
                    To the hills where the daughters of Cadmus be,
                         And to frenzy goad them now
                    Against this madman that ventures prying,
                         In woman's guise, on their revelry,
                              Couched high on crag or bough.
                    There shall his mother, first of all,
                    Mark him, and shrill to her Maenads call:
                         'Who is yon Theban there?
                    To the hills, to the hills, what man comes peering
                         At *our* hill-revels? What mother bare
                              This creature? Whence his breed?
                    No man! But a whelp of a lioness' rearing,
                         Or scion of the Libyan Gorgon's seed.'

Come forth, O Justice, come with sword in hand!
　　Home to the heart-root thrust
Echīon's son, this godless, lawless, ruthless
　　　　Child of dust!

Fool, that wars with wanton spirit　　　　　　　*antistrophe.*
　　And lawless anger against the rites
　　　　Of Thy mother and of Thee!
O Dionysus, he shall merit
　　Death, for his blinded heart that fights
　　　　Invincibility.
So shall he learn.　But peace they find
Who bow before God with a soul resigned.
　　　　I envy not the wise;
Things greater and surer my own heart chooses,
　　That lead at the last to life's best prize;
　　　　Let me give my nights and days
To honour the Gods, while my soul refuses
　　　　To walk with the wicked on evil ways.

Come forth, O Justice, come with sword in hand!
　　Home to the heart-root thrust
Echīon's son, this godless, lawless, ruthless
　　　　Child of dust.

Come, Lord!　As lion with eyes of flame, or steer,　　*epode.*
Or dragon many-headed, show Thee here!
Hunt Thou our hunter, Dionysus!—hurling
　　With a calm smile Thy deadly noose that falls
About the victim's neck, amid Thy whirling
　　　　Bacchanals!

Messenger (*entering*). Ah house once happy in the eyes of Hellas,
　Home of the old Sidonian king who sowed
　The Dragon's earth-born seed!
　Slave though I am, how I must mourn for thee!
Leader. How?　Is there news from the Maenads on the mountain?
Messenger. Echīon's son, King Pentheus, lies there dead.
Leader. Glory to Thee, Lord Brómius,
　That hast revealed Thy godhead thus!
Messenger. What's this!　What words are these!　Rejoicing, woman,
　At the ruin of my master?
Leader. No Greek am I!　In barbarian strain
　I chant; for no longer I dread your chain.

Messenger. But think you Thebes has so lost all her manhood
    That now—
Leader. Dionysus!—it is He—
    Not Thebes—that holds my loyalty!
Messenger. In you, it is pardonable—and yet, O women,
    Vile to exult at others' suffering!
Leader. Tell me! Say! How did he win
    Death, that sinner, in his sin?
Messenger. When we had left the last of our Theban homesteads
    And passed beyond the waters of Asōpus,
    We came among the ridges of Cithaeron,
    Pentheus and I—for my lord had bid me follow—
    With that same stranger who should show us all.
    Then first we halted in a grassy glen,
    Crouching with silent lips and noiseless feet,
    That we might see unseen. There wound a gorge
    Walled close with precipices, torrent-pierced,
    Dark with the gloom of pines; and there they sat,
    The Bacchanals, with busy happy fingers—
    For some were setting on their faded wands
    New coronals of ivy; others, eager
    As steeds new-loosed from beneath the painted yoke,
    Chanted their worship's wild antiphonies.
    But the doomed Pentheus, since he saw but ill
    That multitude of women, said: 'Good stranger,
    From here my vision cannot reach these Maenads
    At their pretended revels;
    But, if I climbed some tall fir on the cliff,
    I *could* view clearly their abominations.'
    Soon as he spoke, I saw that stranger do
    A miracle. A fir that towered to Heaven
    He seized by the top and lower, lower, lower
    To the black earth he bowed it; till the stem
    Curved like a full-bent bow, or rounded wheel
    When the wheelwright's cord marks out its circling rim.
    So powerfully the stranger drew to earth
    That mountain-bole, with might of more than man.
    Then he perched Pentheus there, astride a bough,
    And let the fir straighten itself again—
    Gently, for fear it should fling loose the King.
    So to high Heaven, once more, high towered the tree,
    And mounted on its summit sat my lord.
    But ah, the Bacchanals could see him better

Than *he* saw *them*—and scarcely was he revealed
Seated aloft, when, lo, our guide had vanished.
Then pealed a voice from Heaven (sure, it was
The God Himself), that cried: 'Women, behold,
I bring you this mocker both of you and me
And all my holy things—take your revenge!'
And, as He spoke, there towered from Earth to Heaven
A mighty pillar of unearthly flame.
Hushed hung the sky, hushed lay the forest-glen—
Not a leaf moved, no cry of beast was heard.
But they, with that shout still ringing in their ears,
Confused as yet, leapt up and peered about them.
Again the summons rang; and Cadmus' daughters,
Hearing that manifested voice of God,
Came rushing side by side, as swift as doves—
Agāve, his own mother, with her sisters,
And all the Maenads—down the stream-swept glen,
Down the ravine, wild-leaping, God-possessed.
But when they saw my lord aloft the tree,
At first they pelted him with showers of stones,
Climbing a tower of crag that fronted him.
Others hurled branches broken from the firs
And others darted thyrsi through the air—
Grim marksmanship! And yet they toiled in vain,
For higher up than all their rage could reach
Poor Pentheus sat, resourceless and alone.
Then with great oak-limbs shivered from their trunks,
Instead of iron, they levered at the roots.
At last, when all their labour found no end,
Agāve shouted: 'Gather round the tree
And grip its girth, my Maenads! That this beast,
This clambering beast, may not escape our grasp
To betray the mystic dances of our God.'
With that, innumerable hands laid hold
Upon the trunk and heaved it from the ground;
Then from his lofty seat crashed headlong earthward
King Pentheus, uttering shrill scream on scream
(For well he saw his evil hour at hand).
His mother was the first that leapt upon him
In that red sacrifice. He tore away
The headband from his hair, that she might know him—
Poor Queen—and spare her son. Touching her cheek,
'Mother,' he cried, 'it is I, yes, I, thy son—

Pentheus, the child of thee and of Echīon!
O pity, mother, pity!—do not murder
Thy son for this poor folly I have done.'
    But foam flowed from her lips, wild rolled her eyes,
And Dionysus held her soul possessed;
Blind and infatuate, she heeded not,
But seizing his left arm, and bearing hard
With her foot against his flank, she wrenched away
His shoulder—it was a deed past human strength,
Yet the God made it easy for her fury.
And Ino straining on the other side
Helped tear him, while Autónoë behind
Pressed forward with her fellows—all was howling,
With yells of pain from him, while yet he breathed;
From them, mad shrieks of triumph.   One bore away
An arm; and another snatched his sandalled foot.
His ribs were stripped of flesh.   With fingers crimson
They tossed between them fragments of the King.
    So there he lies dismembered—part beneath
The mountain-crags, part in the leafy forest;
And hardly shall man find him.   But his mother,
Into whose hand that tortured head has fallen,
Bears it upon her ivy-wand, impaled,
For she dreams it a mountain-lion's.   While her two sisters
Remain yet with the Maenads, she alone
Is hurrying back through mid Cithaeron hither,
Down into Thebes, proud of her ghastly trophy,
Calling to Dionysus as 'fellow-huntsman'—
Comrade in all the glory of her kill;
So little knowing all her triumph is tears.
    But I will shun this scene of misery
And go, before Agāve's coming home.
Surely restraint and reverence for Heaven
Are the better way—indeed, the truest wisdom,
For all that follow them.

                                                    [*He goes out.*

Chorus.   Come now and dance in the praise of our Lord,
                Come ye and lift, for the fate abhorred
        Of Pentheus dragon-born, your chant on high.
                    In woman's weed enwound,
                    His staff with ivy crowned,
                    For the House of Hades bound,
        Our Bull Divine hath led him forth to die.

Maenads of Thebes,
Proud rings, as yet, your chant for victory won;
But the end thereof is tears to shed.
Fair triumph, in truth, to cast that arm blood-red
About her son!

Leader. But see, here comes Agāve, Pentheus' mother,
Towards the palace, with wild-rolling eyes.
Greet we this revel of our Lord of Joy.

Agāve enters, with her son's head.

Agāve. Maenads of Asia!   *Leader.* And what wouldest *thou*, O?
Agāve. From the hill-crest
A garland of ivy new-cut we are bringing.
God smiled on our quest.

Leader. Welcome, then, welcome, comrade in worship!

Agāve. And I caught, without snare,
This cub of a lion of the mountain-wild.
Look on it!   There!   [*She holds out the head.*

Leader. And where in the waste?
Agāve. Cithaeron—*Leader.* Cithaeron?
Agāve. —saw us kill what we chased.
Leader. And who was the killer?   *Agāve.* I, first of all!
'Blest be Agāve!' our Maenads call.
Leader. What others?   *Agāve.* The daughters—
Leader. The daughters?   *Agāve.* Of Cadmus.
After me, *after* me, *they* struck as well.
Nobly, most nobly this hunting befell.
Come, share in my banquet.   *Leader.* What!   Share it, thou lost one!

Agāve. Young is the bull.
See, on his cheek, how softly curling
The down grows full.

Leader. Indeed it has hair, like a beast of the wild.

Agāve. A master of skill
Is Bacchus the hunter.   Ah how He hallooed us
On to the kill!

Leader. Ay, such are His ways.

Agāve. You praise me?   *Leader.* I praise you.
Agāve. And Thebes too shall praise.
Leader. And Pentheus your son?   *Agāve.* He shall acclaim
His mother, Agāve, the lion-slayer's name.
Leader. Past measure!   *Agāve.* Past measure!
Leader. Art happy?   *Agāve.* I triumph,
For the great, great deeds that *we* have done,
The trophies that our hunt has won.

Leader. Then, wretched woman, show your countrymen
  This glorious prize that you are bringing home.
Agāve. Dwellers in fair-towered Thebes, come, see my prize—
  This trophy of the beast that we have slain—
  We, Cadmus' daughters—not with hunting-nets,
  Nor with thonged javelins of Thessaly,
  But with our own white hands.   Why do men boast
  The kills they make with all their useless weapons,
  When *we* have caught this beast with our bare hands,
  And torn him piecemeal too!
  Where's my old father?   Quickly, send him here.
  And where is my own son Pentheus?   Let him rear
  His ladder high against the palace-cornice
  And nail there this lion's head I have made my prize.
        Cadmus enters with servants carrying a bier.
Cadmus. Follow me, men, before the palace here,
  With your disastrous burden—Pentheus' limbs,
  That I have gathered up with toil untold,
  Seeking their scattered fragments, piecemeal flung,
  Through the dim forests of Cithaeron's glens.

     For tidings reached me of my daughters' frenzies
  When I, with old Teiresias, returning
  From the Maenads on the hills, had entered Thebes.
  So I retraced my steps, back to Cithaeron,
  To bring again my child whom they have murdered.
  There I saw Íno, and Autónoë
  Who once to Aristaeus bore Actaeon,
  Raving, poor wretches, still among the woodlands;
  But as for Agāve, I was told she dances
  With maddened steps towards Thebes—and true it was!
  For here I see her—vision terrible!
Agāve. Father, a splendid triumph is yours to boast of !—
  That you, of all men living, have begotten
  Daughters most glorious—all three of us,
  But me above the rest, that have left behind me
  Shuttle and loom, and risen to higher things—
  To hunt wild beasts bare-handed!
  Look!—in my arms I bear this prize of valour
  To be hung aloft upon your palace-wall.
  Take it now, father.   And proud of my brave hunting
  Summon your friends to banquet.   Blessed thou,
  Most blessed, in the triumph we have won!
Cadmus. Oh grief intolerable to look upon,

Unutterable!—curst hands whose triumph was murder!
Here's a fair offering you bring the Gods,
That you should call our Thebes and me to banquet!
Alas for your misery, and alas for mine!
Ah Dionysus has destroyed us—justly,
And yet too cruelly—His own kith and kin!

Agāve. How surly is old age, and sullen-eyed!
Oh that my son, when in the chase he joins
The youth of Thebes, were a hunter like his mother!
But warring against the Gods is all he knows.
You should rebuke him, father. Call him, someone,
Call him to come, and see my happiness.

Cadmus. Alas, alas—when you know what you have done,
What anguish then, my children! Could you keep
Your blindness always. happy ye would not seem,
And yet not all unhappy.

Agāve. But what is not well done? What is it grieves you?

Cadmus. First lift your eyes up, to this sky above us.

Agāve. Well then? And what's to see there?

Cadmus. Seems it the same to you? Or somehow changed?

Agāve. Brighter than once it was. And more translucent.

Cadmus. Still does the same wild tumult sway your spirit?

Agāve. I do not know your meaning. Yet, somehow,
I feel a change—as if my mind returned.

Cadmus. Can you listen to me, then?—and answer clearly?

Agāve. I have forgotten, father, what we talked of.

Cadmus. Into whose house, once, did you come as bride?

Agāve. Echīon's—who sprang, they say, from the Dragon's teeth.

Cadmus. And what son did you bear him?

Agāve. The son that has blessed our union?—it was Pentheus.

Cadmus. Whose face is *that* you hold, then, in your hands?

Agāve. A lion's—at least, so said our huntresses.

Cadmus. Look straight at it—*that* is not hard to do.

Agāve. Aie! What is this? What am I carrying?

Cadmus. Look at it longer, till the truth grows clear.

Agāve. Ah misery, I see the worst of sorrows.

Cadmus. Has it *now* a lion's likeness?

Agāve. Wretch that I am! It is the head of Pentheus!

Cadmus. Long I have mourned him, while you knew him not.

Agāve. But who has killed him? How came he in my hands?

Cadmus. Ah bitter truth, untimely recognized!

Agāve. Speak! My heart trembles; dreading what's to come.

Cadmus. *You* killed him—with your sisters.

Agāve. Where did he perish? In our home? Or where?

Cadmus. Where, in past days, his own hounds tore Actaeon.

Agāve. But why did my poor son go, then, to Cithaeron?

Cadmus. To mock at Dionysus, and your worship.

Agāve. But how did *we* come, then, to be there ourselves?

Cadmus. Ye all were mad—all Thebes possessed with frenzy.

Agāve. I see it now. Dionysus has destroyed us!

Cadmus. In vengeance for your insults. You denied Him.

Agāve. Father, where does it lie—his dearest body?

Cadmus. With toil and pain I gathered what I bring.

Agāve. His torn limbs laid in decency together?

            [*Some lines—perhaps three—seem missing.*]

Agāve. But with my madness what had *he* to do?

Cadmus. Like you, he was irreverent to the God,
   Who therefore has involved us all in ruin,
   Both ye and him—with all our royal house
   And me, who never called a son my own,
   But now must see this child of your womb, poor daughter,
   Most cruelly and foully murdered! Ah my son,
   Child of my child and light of all this house,
   And pillar of my hall, and dread of Thebes!
   Once, in thy sight none dared insult my age—
   So swift thy vengeance came.
   But now I must pass to exile, all dishonoured—
   I, the great Cadmus, that in the furrow sowed
   This Theban race and reaped so fair a harvest.
   Ah dearest!—for even in thy death, my child,
   Thou shalt be numbered with my best beloved—
   Never again, with hand laid on my beard,
   Shalt thou embrace me—call me grandfather—
   Or ask: 'Old man, does anyone offend you,
   Troubling your heart with insult or injustice?
   Tell me—he shall be punished.'
   But now—unhappy you, and wretched I,
   Wretched thy mother, miserable her sisters!
   If there is any man contemns the Gods,
   Let him look on Pentheus' fate and bow to Them.

Leader. Cadmus, I pity you. Your grandson's death
   Was well deserved; but bitter indeed for *you*.

Agāve. Father, you see how my life is overturned.

         [*Another passage missing, during which Dionysus appeared from Heaven.*]

Dionysus. . . . Thou shalt become a serpent, and thy wife

Harmonia, that once, though Ares' daughter,
Wed thee, her mortal lover,
With thee shall wear the beast-like form of snake.
And both—so saith the oracle of Zeus—
Mounted upon an ox-drawn chariot,
Shall lead a barbarous horde innumerable,
To plunder many a city;
Until, when they have sacked Apollo's shrine,
Homeward they make calamitous retreat.
But thee and her shall Ares save at length,
And bring ye living to the Blessed Land.
    Thus say I, Dionysus, who call 'father'
No mortal man—but Zeus! Had ye not turned
So wilfully from wisdom, happy now
Ye might have been, blessed by the Son of God.

Cadmus. Ah Dionysus, mercy! We have sinned.
Dionysus. Ye learn too late. *Then,* when ye should, ye would not.
Cadmus. We do confess it. Yet too harsh Thou art.
Dionysus. Ye had blasphemed me, who was born a God.
Cadmus. But Gods in Their anger should not be as men.
Dionysus. My Father, Zeus, hath willed this long ago.
Agāve. Ah we are doomed, old father! Hopeless exile!
Dionysus. Why linger, then, since all these things must be?

        [He ascends to Heaven.

Cadmus. Daughter, to what a pitch of misery
  We all are come!—unhappy you, your sisters,
  And wretched I, that in my age must live
  Exiled among barbarians, and lead,
  By Heaven's will, their motley hordes on Hellas—
  Ay, with my Heaven-born wife, Harmonia,
  In savage serpent-shape must head wild spearmen
  Against the altars and the tombs of Greece!
  And even then
  I must find no peace from sorrow—never cross
  The roar of Acheron to lie at rest.
Agāve. And I, my father, exiled far from thee!
Cadmus. Ah vain, poor child, to fling thy arms about me,
  As a young swan clasps the old, grown frail and hoar.
Agāve. Where shall I turn, cast out from my native land?
Cadmus. I know not, child. Your father cannot help.
Agāve. Farewell, my home! Farewell, dear land!
  I go from my roof, lonely and banned,
  For evermore.

Cadmus. Where Aristaeus went before,
 My child, go there.

Agāve. I grieve for thee, father. *Cadmus.* And I for thee—
 For thy sisters, too, in their despair.

Agāve. Ah, upon thee and all thy line
 Bacchus hath turned too brutally
 His wrath divine.

Cadmus. Because in Thebes ye had done Him shame,
 Dishonouring His holy name.

Agāve. Farewell now, my father. *Cadmus.* And farewell still,
 Poor child, that art like to fare so ill.

Agāve. Take me, my friends, where my sisters wait,
 Like me, for the exile's weary fate.
 May I come where
 No curst Cithaeron looks on me!—
 Far from my sight let Cithaeron be,
 And Maenad rites from my memory—
 For *those* let others care!

    Father and daughter go out different ways.

Chorus.   In many a shape is the Gods' will wrought,
    And much They accomplish that none foreknows.
   What men deemed sure, They bring to naught,
    And what none dreamed of, They dispose.
    Such now this story's close.

IPHIGENEIA AT AULIS
(c. 407 B.C.)

I was cut off from hope in that sad place,
*   Which men call'd Aulis in those iron years:*
My father held his hand upon his face;
*   I, blinded with my tears,*

Still strove to speak: my voice was thick with sighs
*   As in a dream. Dimly I could descry*
The stern black-bearded kings with wolfish eyes,
*   Waiting to see me die.*

Tennyson.

This play, left unfinished by its author, has now two beginnings—first a prosaic prologue of the usual type; then a spirited dialogue between Agamemnon and an old servant in the starlit darkness of the Greek camp opposite Euboea—one of the best night-pieces in Greek poetry from Sappho to Theocritus.

Agamemnon. What is yon star that swims now above us?
Servant. Sirius, next to the seven Pleiads—
    Still in his course he holds the mid-heaven.
Agamemnon. Not a sound in the stillness—no cry of a bird,
    No call of the sea.   Not a whisper of wind
    Along Euripus shore.
Servant. Why do you start, King Agamemnon,
        Forth from your tent?—
    When all lies at peace on the coasts of Aulis
    And on her wall the warders are still?
    Let us go in.
Agamemnon.   Old man, how I envy
    You and all those that, like you, travel
    Unknown, unhonoured, the roads of life!
    But the great in their glory I envy less. . . .
Servant. A lamp you have kindled to cast its light
        Across the gloom,
    And you write on that tablet your hand is holding
    And then erase what is written there;
    You seal it fast, you tear it open,
    You fling it from you upon the floor—
        Tears on your face,
    Wild with distraction as one whose senses
        Are all but gone.

(6–19, 34–42.)

343

Agamemnon, bidden by Calchas to sacrifice his eldest daughter Iphigeneia to Artemis if he would have a fair wind for Troy, had reluctantly written to Clytemnestra to bring the girl as bride for Achilles. But now his mind has veered—the old servant is to take a letter warning Clytemnestra not to come. But at once the messenger is waylaid by the suspicious Menelaus, who angrily attacks his brother for this double-dealing. In mid-quarrel Clytemnestra and Iphigeneia arrive. Agamemnon bursts into tears that soften even Menelaus. But too late. The army demands the sacrifice; and Agamemnon here is no King of Kings, but rather in the plight of many a popular politician: 'I *have* to follow them, because I am their leader.' Hardly has Iphigeneia flung her arms about her anguished father than Clytemnestra encounters Achilles outside the royal quarters and hails the bewildered young hero as her son-in-law. The truth is out; and at her prayer the angry Achilles promises, if she cannot move Agamemnon, to defend the girl's life. But mother and daughter appeal to Agamemnon in vain; and Achilles returns with the news that the whole army, even his own Myrmidons, are howling for the victim's blood —and for his own, if he interferes. None the less he is ready to die for her. Then the simple girl rises to the crisis, like Jephthah's daughter in Tennyson. (Aristotle found this change unreal; but it seems psychologically sound.) She will not have Achilles killed for her. If others can die for Greece, so can she. Before her quiet heroism the vanity of Achilles himself turns to affectionate admiration. He will still be close to her at the altar, in case her heart should fail. So she goes to her death—though at the last moment Artemis is to save her by substituting a hind (as Isaac was replaced by the ram in the thicket) and bear her away to serve as priestess among the wild Taurians of the Crimea.

The play lacks the depth of *The Bacchae*; but the old poet had produced few plots so dramatic in the modern sense, few characters more natural. It does not give the modern reader much idea of Greek drama at its best; but it is one of the easiest Greek dramas for a modern to enjoy.

THE CYCLOPS

(date quite uncertain)

This is our only complete example of a satyric drama—'tragedy at play.' It travesties Odysseus' famous adventure with Polyphemus; adding a Chorus of satyrs (led by Silēnus), who have been shipwrecked on the Sicilian coast and forced to tend the Cyclops' sheep. When Odysseus appears in search of food and water, the roguish Silēnus is

delighted to sell his master's provisions for wine; then, when Polyphemus
enters, brazenly pretends that Odysseus robbed him. The giant, after
devouring two of Odysseus' men, is made drunk and has his eye burnt
out, while the cowardly satyrs excuse themselves from helping as they had
promised; though they are glad enough to bait the blinded monster, till
they finally escape with Odysseus.

A farce relying on horseplay more than humour; but with more comedy
in it than might perhaps have been expected from the writer called by
Aristotle 'the most tragic of the poets.'

Rhēsus

Euripides wrote a play so named. But it is disputed whether this is his
genuine work—probably early; or spurious—perhaps a fourth-century
chamber-drama, meant only to be read. It is in any case more readable
than some of his better-known pieces. The whole action takes place at
night and dramatizes *Iliad* x. Hector, hoping to annihilate the defeated
Greeks at dawn, sends Dŏlon on patrol. Rhēsus, the proud King of Thrace,
son of a Muse and the River Strymon, arrives to the help of Troy; and,
reproached by Hector for his late coming, boasts he will crush the Greeks
unaided. But Odysseus and Diomed have waylaid Dŏlon and learnt the
Trojan password; with Athena's help they steal into the camp and kill
Rhēsus asleep. Thanks to the password, Odysseus eludes the Chorus
of Trojan guards; and finally the Muse, Rhēsus' mother, laments for her
dead son.

With less than a thousand lines, the piece has plenty of action, a vigorous
rhetoric, and some real poetry; as when Athena pictures the famous horses
of Rhēsus:

> And, near at hand, to his Thracian chariots
> Are tied his white steeds, gleaming through the gloom,
> Splendid as shines the swan's wing on her stream;
>
> (616–18.)

or when the yawning sentries wait for relief at dawn:

One. Clearly I hear the nightingale
　　　By Símoïs' bed
　Mid battle-reddened rushes wail,
　Like the voice of many harp-strings, for the child her hand struck dead.
Another. Already on Ida the sheep are straying—
　I catch the sound of a shepherd's playing
　　Far across the night

Another. Sleep-bewitched, my eyelids meet—
  Never slumber falls so sweet
    As ere the break of light.   (547–56.)

After twenty-five centuries these last three lines may still stir vividly, for some, their memories of modern war.

FRAGMENTS OF LOST PLAYS

Poetry

Whose youth no song of the Muses hears,
Dead is he to the vanished years,
Dead for the years to come.

                    (Nauck, *Tragicorum Graecorum Fragmenta*,
                                        p. 687, fr. 1028.)

Athleticism

  Now of ten thousand curses that plague Hellas
None is more pestilent than this breed of athletes,
Who never yet have learnt how men should live,
And could not though they would. . . .
Oh, they go brave in youth, the strutting ornament
Each of his city.   But once grim age has clutched them,
Then see them slinking threadbare, out at elbows.
It gets no praise of me, our Grecian way
Of gathering in multitudes for *their* sakes,
Making the honour of such useless sports
Excuse for banqueting.
For what stout wrestler, or what nimble runner,
Or discus-thrower, or brave jaw-bone-breaker,
Profits his country by the crown he wins?
Will they go grappling in the grip of war,
Quoits in their hands?   Or in the clash of shields
Will boxers' punches fell an enemy?
None meddles with such fooleries, when he faces
Steel!   Keep your wreaths to honour wiser heads—
For good men, temperate leaders of their land,
Whose words can put a curb on reckless doings,
And quell strife or sedition.   *These* are gifts
To bless alike our country and all Hellas.

                    (*Autolycus*, Nauck, fr. 282.)

Love

An idle thing, and bred for idleness,
Is Love. In mirrors and in fair-dyed tresses
His joy lies—toil's his terror. This my proof—
Love troubles not the man that begs his bread:
On those whose purse is full He wreaks His power.

(Danaë, fr. 322.)

Love turns to a poet
Even the heart that was but dull before.

(Sthéneboea, fr. 663.)

Woman

Fearful the violence of the raging sea;
Fearful the force of torrent and of flame;
Fearful is penury, and a thousand ills
There are beside; but none so fell as woman—
No written word has power to say how evil,
No tongue has power to tell it. If any God
Created them, *He* was an evil genius—
That let Him know!—and hater of mankind.

(Fr. 1059.)

Auge the Priestess defies Athena

Spoils of dead men, wreckage of slaughtered bodies,
Gladden Thine eyes—Thou findest nothing *there*
Unclean! But *this* is terrible to Thee,
That I have borne a child!

(Auge, fr. 266.)

Children

Dear to our eyes, O lady, is this sunlight
And fair the wide sweep of the windless sea,
Life-giving streams, or earth grown green with spring.
I could name many another loveliness;
But nothing there is so bright, so beautiful,
As, for a childless heart long gnawed by sorrow,
Are little children blossoming at home.[1]

(Danaë, fr. 316.)

[1] Compare *Andrómache*, 418–20:

> Children, after all,
> Are very life to us; the childless heart
> That scorns them, suffers less; and yet enjoys
> Only a miserable happiness.

(And contrast p. 241.)

Human Blindness

Why then, in the seats of the mighty high enthroned,
Do ye claim to know the truth of heavenly things,
Ye professed masters of these mysteries?
Who boasts to comprehend divinity,
Has not more knowledge—merely speciousness.

(Philoctētes, fr. 795.)

Justice

A. Dream you that men's misdeeds fly up to Heaven,
And then some hand inscribes the record of them
Upon God's tablets; and God, reading them,
Deals the world justice?   Nay, the vault of Heaven
Could not suffice for God to write men's crimes,
Nor He Himself avail to punish them.
Justice is here beside you, had ye eyes.
B. Lady, the Gods deal out their punishment
To whatsoever men They chance to hate.
Evil to Them is nothing.

(Melanippe, fr. 506, and Nauck, p. 935, fr. 489.)

Bellérophon and the Gods

Dares any say that there are Gods in Heaven?
Nay, there are none, are none!—save for the fool
That still must cling to tales of ancient time.
Think for yourselves—I do not ask ye take
My word on trust.   I say men tyrannous,
With tongues that break all oaths, and robbers' hands,
Fill earth with massacre and sacks of cities;
And, though they do it, prosper more than those
Whose days are spent in peace and piety.
I know of little cities, fearing God,
That yet must bow to wicked greater states,
Crushed by brute weight of spears.
And very sure I am if one of you,
Instead of labouring for his livelihood,
Should try to live at ease by prayers to Gods,
He soon would find there *are* none.   Faith is built
Upon mere Fortune's favours and disasters.

(Bellérophon, fr. 286.)

Life and Death

Who knows if this that we call 'death' be life,
And 'life' in deed be death?   We only know
That sick are all men living; but the dead
Are whole at last and freed from all our ills.

(Phrixus, fr. 833.)

Wiser it were to gather and lament
For every babe that enters this sad world;
But when man dies and all his trouble's over,
Bear him with joy and blessings from his home.

(Cresphontes, fr. 449)

FRAGMENTS OF OTHER TRAGIC POETS

Critias (*c.* 460–403)

Critias, whose mother was Plato's cousin, became a disciple of Socrates; but afterwards made himself infamous as leader of the oligarchs and quislings who, backed by a Spartan garrison on the Acropolis, instituted a reign of terror after the fall of Athens in 404.   Early in 403 he died in battle against the democratic rising of Thrasybūlus.

Origin of Religion

A time there was when man's life knew no order—
A bestial thing, where violence was lord,
Where good men found no recompense for goodness,
The bad no punishment.
And then, I take it, human wit invented
Laws to chastise the evil that men did,
That so at last Justice might reign supreme,
With Insolence her slave.
But since, although the laws now set a curb
On open outrage, still men sinned by stealth,
Methinks some shrewd and subtle politician
Contrived the Gods; that so above the wicked
Terror might hang, even if secretly
They sinned in act, or even word, or thought.
Thus came religion first into the world—
The faith that there exists a God eternal,

Whose wisdom sees and hears and knows and pays regard
To all these things; for His immortal nature
Catches the least light breath that mortals whisper,
Perceives their slightest deed.
Therefore, however hushed thine evil purpose,
It is not hidden from the all-wise Gods.
By such a doctrine did this sage induce
Belief most wholesome, though indeed he blinded
The eyes of Truth with falsehood.
And for the habitation of the Gods
He chose that place which men would feel most awesome,
The source of human terrors, yet no less
Of blessings that lighten still their troubled life—
The firmament of Heaven.   For thence proceed
The lightning-flash, the dreaded roll of thunder,
The glory of the stars whose spangled beauty
Time the wise craftsman made; thence too there shines
The sun in his molten splendour, thence to earth
Descends the moistening rain.
So then this first contriver fenced men round
With terrors, settling God within the world,
With wise persuasion, where beseemed Him best,
And quenched, with fear of Him, iniquity.
And thus, I hold, were mankind first persuaded
That there exist in Heaven beings divine.

(*Sīsyphus*, Nauck, p. 771, fr. 1.)

Unknown Tragic Poets

The Queen of Candaules

Now when I saw
Gyges before my eyes—no fantasy!—
I feared within our gates some plot of murder
(Recompense that so often waits on kings);
But when I marked Candaules was awake,
What had been done, I knew—and *who* had done it!
And yet, in spite of the turmoil in my heart,
As if I had noted nothing, back I choked,
In secret silence, the cry of my dishonour.
There on my bed I tossed, with thought on thought,
While sleepless still, and endless, passed the night.

But when arose the shining star of dawn,
The harbinger of day's first glimmerings,
From bed I aroused my lord, and bade him forth
To deal his people justice—on my lips
Persuasion's ready plea, that suffers not
A king who loves his folk, night-long to slumber.
But now to summon Gyges. . . .

(*Proceedings of the British Academy,* vol. xxxv, 1950.)

'Neiges d'antan'

Where lie those ancient glories? Where is Croesus
The mighty Lord of Lydia? Where is Xerxes,
That yoked the great neck of the Hellespont?
In the House of Death, and of Oblivion.

(Nauck, p. 909, fr. 372.)

Disillusion

Poor Virtue, empty name!—I gave my life
To thee, as real—that wast but Fortune's slave!

(p. 910, fr. 374.)

God

Confound not God with mortals; dream not He
Is made of fleshly substance like to theirs.
Thou knowest Him not. He manifests Himself
Now in the guise of water, now of darkness,
Or flame with onslaught unapproachable;
Sometimes He wears the likeness of wild beasts,
Or wind, or cloud, or lightning—thunder—rain.
To Him the sea is servant, and the rocks,
The springs, the gatherings of mighty floods;
The mountains tremble at Him, and the earth,
The ocean's vast abysses and the heights
Of the great peaks, whenever falls on them
The dread look of their Lord. For power almighty
Is His, and the glory of all-highest God.

(p. 127, fr. 464.) [1]

---

[1] Attributed by Clement of Alexandria (c. A.D. 150–c. 215) and Justin Martyr (c. A.D. 100–c. 165) to Aeschylus.

World-conflagration

For surely, surely it shall come, the day
That ends the world—when from the golden face
Of Heaven shall burst forth its pent-up fires,
And everything from earth to sky shall blaze
In the mad fury of one full-fed flame.
Then, when it dies away, there shall have vanished
The vast abyss of ocean—earth be void
Of all her cities—not a bird shall fly
Across the charred wreck of the firmament.
Then He who all destroyed, shall all restore.

(p. 360, fr. 1027.) [1]

[1] Attributed by Justin Martyr to Sophocles.

NOTES ON EURIPIDES

HIPPOLYTUS

The House of Athens

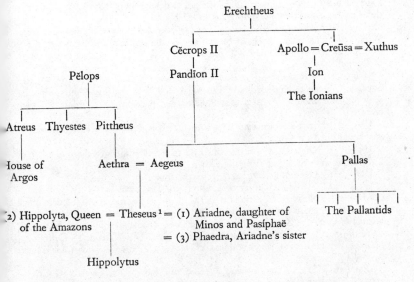

[Page 246] *Pontic surge.* The Black Sea.

[Page 247] *A shrine beside the Rock of Pallas.* In historic times a shrine of Aphrodite stood on the S. side of the Acropolis, near a monument to Hippolytus.

[Page 247] *Blood of Pallas' sons.* See genealogical table. These cousins of Theseus, the Pallantids, fell in disputing with him the throne of Athens.

[Page 247] *Poseidon.* According to one version, Theseus' real father (cf. Zeus and Hēracles).

[Page 249] *Mountain Mother.* Rhea or Cýbele, mother of the gods (p. 113).

[Page 249] *Corybants.* Priests of Rhea, who performed orgiastic dances in armour (p. 356).

[Page 249] *Dictynna.* A Cretan goddess, later identified with Artemis.

[Page 251] *Ah for some cool spring.* These day-dreams of the unhappy Phaedra are among the earliest utterances of the Romantic spirit.

[Page 251] *Lady of Limne. Limne* means 'marsh,' 'lagoon.' There was in Troezēn a temple of Artemis Limnaia.

[Page 251] *Enétian.* The Eneti or Veneti (whence 'Venice') were a tribe, famous as horse-breeders, living from *c.* 950 B.C. at the head of the Adriatic.

---

[1] By one account his true father was Poseidon.

[Page 254] *Bull of Crete.* When Minos broke his vow to sacrifice to Poseidon a bull which the god had sent from the sea, Poseidon infatuated Minos' queen, Pasíphaë, with a mad passion for it. So was born the half-human Minotaur, which was shut in the Labyrinth and killed there by Theseus.

Euripides wrote his *Cretans* on the subject of Pasíphaë and, with typically misplaced ingenuity, makes his heroine defend herself against her angry husband on the ground that her behaviour must have been a divine visitation—what possible attraction could there be in a bull?—'Was he so handsome in his clothes?' (D. L. Page, *Greek Literary Papyri*, I, 74–5.)

[Page 254] *Sister.* Ariadne, who saved Theseus from the windings of the Labyrinth by giving him a ball of thread, fled with him from Crete; but was deserted on Naxos, where Dionysus loved her.

[Page 255] *Even honest women, Fight how they may, can still grow passionate.* With Euripides, character itself begins to become destiny, and drama to move into the theatre of the soul. (Cf. the passion of Racine in contrast to the action of Corneille.)

[Page 255] *I cannot think it is defect of reason.* Better psychology than the Socratic 'Virtue is Knowledge.' Euripides, followed by Ovid, puts a similar view in the mouth of Mēdēa, maddened by passion to murder her own children.

[Page 255] *And our own sense of pride. . . .* It is doubtful whether these four bracketed lines are genuine.

[Page 257] *Céphalus* of Phocis, husband of Prŏcris and great-grandfather of Odysseus, was loved by Eōs, the Dawn.

[Page 259] *Oechalia's daughter.* Íole (p. 163).

[Page 259] *Sémele,* daughter of Cadmus (p. 227), was loved by Zeus. Incited by the jealous Hēra, disguised in the shape of her old nurse, Sémele made Zeus swear to grant her a wish, then asked to see him in his full glory. She was burnt to ashes; but Zeus saved the unborn Dionysus, sheltering the infant in his own thigh till it was ready to be born. (See *The Bacchae.*) Originally, perhaps, Sémele was an *earth*-goddess (cf. Novaya *Zemlya*—'New *Land*') from Anatolia.

[Page 261] *My tongue it was, but not my heart, that swore.* Curiously enough, this line is said to have provoked an uproar in the theatre, as immoral (though actually Hippolytus is going to die sooner than unseal his lips). If the story is true, it suggests that the Athenians (like most of us) did not find Hippolytus very sympathetic; for far more immoral things have already been said by the nurse.

Later, the line was even brought up against Euripides in a lawsuit (Aristotle, *Rhetoric*, iii, 15).

[Page 261] *To multiply mankind, . . . by other means.* A famous passage, imitated by Milton in Adam's invective against Eve (*P.L.,* x, 888–908). It may be recalled that the same foolish wish was expressed by Sir Thomas Browne; though it did not deter him from marrying and having ten children.

[Page 261] *A stupid woman.* This curious theory of the preferability of stupid wives was shared (and practised) by Talleyrand, on the dubious ground that a fool could compromise only herself.

[Page 263] *To hide all you have heard.* An example of the awkwardness of Choruses. The women of Troezēn have the odious role of seeing an innocent man perish because they must not speak. (The Chorus of *Ion* are able to show more sense, p. 291.)

[Page 264] *Erídanus.* The Po. Phaethon, son of the Sun-god and Clýmene, vainly trying to drive his father's chariot through Heaven, crashed into this river; his grieving sisters were changed into poplars, and their tears into amber.

[Page 264] *Hesperides.* These daughters of Hesperus, the Evening Star, or of Atlas, guarded in the far west, at the foot of Mount Atlas, the garden with the golden apples given by Earth to Hēra when she wedded Zeus.

[Page 264] *Mūnychus.* The hero who gave his name to the small harbour of Mūnychia, E. of Peiraeus.

[Page 265] *A Woman's Voice.* This may be the Nurse.

[Page 269] *Orpheus.* Believers in the cult known as 'Orphism' (from its supposed founder Orpheus) held that, when the wicked Titans had torn in pieces and devoured the infant Dionysus, Zeus blasted them with his lightning; from their ashes sprang mankind, who were thus partly evil, partly divine. Orphics abstained from flesh (probably from belief in transmigration); and hoped by purification and initiation to improve their lot in the next world. In the great period of Greece they are generally mentioned with a certain contempt.

[Page 270] *Sīnis . . . Scīron.* Sīnis was a robber on the Isthmus of Corinth, who tore travellers asunder by fastening them to two down-bent fir-trunks, then letting the trees go; Scīron followed a similar occupation just west of Megara, making travellers wash his feet, and kicking them over the Scīronian Cliff to feed a tortoise below. The young Theseus, travelling from Troezēn to seek his father in Athens, meted out to both ruffians the fate they had inflicted on others.

[Page 275] *Asclēpius' crag.* The Acropolis of Epidaurus.

[Page 280] *One man She in Her turn holds dearest.* Adonis; though in the usual version he is killed by a boar, not by the arrows of Artemis.

For the later legend that Artemis made Asclēpius restore Hippolytus to life, then bore him away to her grove of Aricia in Italy, by the Lake of Nemi, where he reigned as Virbius, see Frazer, *Golden Bough,* I, ch. i. It appears that originally Hippolytus was the male consort of Artemis, as a Mediterranean mother-goddess; standing to her as Adonis to Aphrodite, Attis to Cýbele. Curiously enough, he finally became a Christian martyr, Saint Hippolytus; who like his prototype was dragged to death by horses.

THE SUPPLIANT WOMEN

[Page 289] *Like the tall ears.* Compare the story that Thrasybūlus, despot of Miletus, consulted by an envoy from Periander, despot of Corinth, on the best means of maintaining autocracy, walked in silence through a cornfield symbolically smiting off the tallest ears. (A similar anecdote is told of Tarquin at Rome, with poppy-heads in place of corn-ears; and modern totalitarian states have shown that the principle still applies.)

THE TROJAN WOMEN

[Page 296] *Mýconos.* One of the Cyclades.
[Page 296] *Caphēreus' headland.* The S.E. cape of Euboea.
[Page 297] *Amyclae.* A city some 3 miles S. of Sparta.

THE PHOENICIAN WOMEN

[Page 303] On the play hangs a story which shows the hold of tragedy on Athenian imaginations (as well as the hysterical tendency of their democracy to stage tragedies in real life). Before the naval battle of Arginusae (406 B.C.) the Athenian general Thrasyllus dreamt that he and six of his fellow-commanders acted *The Phoenician Women*, while the enemy leaders acted Euripides' *The Suppliants*; the Athenian team was victorious, but like the Seven Champions they lost their lives. In the ensuing battle the Athenian fleet prevailed; but Thrasyllus and his colleagues were executed at Athens for failing to rescue the crews from twenty-five of their own disabled ships.

THE BACCHAE

For genealogical table, see p. 227.

[Page 308] *Sémele, Dirce, Ismēnus.* See pp. 354, 226.

[Page 308] *Hellene and Barbarian.* A curious anachronism, anticipating later Greek trade and colonization.

[Page 309] *Tmōlus.* This mountain, S. of Sardis, had vineyards on its lower slopes.

[Page 310] *Cýbele* (see p. 113) is not unnaturally linked with Dionysus; for she is ultimately one of the ancient mother-goddesses of the Near East, and he one of its son-gods.

[Page 310] *Brómius.* 'The Roarer'—a suitable name for a god of savage ecstasy, kettledrums, and earthquakes, himself often incarnated in bull or lion.

[Page 311] *Haunt of the Curētes . . . cave of Crete.* Legend told that, when Crönus took to devouring his children, his wife Rhea gave him a stone in place of the infant Zeus, whom she hid in a Cretan cave; there her ministers, the Curētes or Corybantes, drowned the child's cries by clashing arms and beating kettledrums.

[Page 312] *Teiresias . . . Cadmus.* There is a touch of comedy, though only a touch (the play is too grim for more), in these two figures of an older generation, confronted by a young fanaticism. Cadmus, the pathetic old ex-monarch, has an innocently Machiavellian idea that the new religion can be exploited to raise the prestige of the royal family; while Teiresias the prophet plays theologian and sophistically decants this new wine into the old bottles of his orthodoxy. None the less, in actual history, a policy of similar compromise was successfully adopted towards Dionysus by Delphi; and by Rome towards enthusiasts like Saint Francis.

[Page 313] *Pentheus* is later to become pathetic; but at his entrance, like Creon in *Antigone*, he at once strikes a sinister note of insolence and tyranny. There is indeed no really sympathetic character in the whole play; though some win sympathy in the end by the disproportionate barbarity of their punishment.

[Page 315] *Sky-born . . . thigh-born.* This represents an equally imbecile pun in the Greek—*homēros*, 'hostage,' and *ho mēros*, 'the thigh.' As Racine observed in a marginal comment: '*Cela est bien tiré par les cheveux.*' Doubtless Euripides meant it to be.

[Page 316] *Ares.* Because Dionysus, like Pan, can strike armies with 'panic.'

[Page 316] *At Delphi itself.* Apollo was supreme at Delphi for nine months in the year; but in the three winter months he gave place to Dionysus. It was during this period that Dionysiac worshippers danced with torches on the uplands of Parnassus.

[Page 316] *Actaeon.* There were several other versions of Actaeon's offence; including the familiar story that he chanced on Artemis bathing.

[Page 317] *Pentheus . . . repentance.* There is a similar play in the Greek on *Pentheus* and *penthos,* 'grief.'

[Page 318] *Paphos . . . Nile.* The likeliest explanation of this strange combination seems that of Professor Dodds, who points out that modern Cypriot peasants have long believed the water of their rather brackish springs to come from beneath the sea; and suggests that their ancient predecessors thought it to flow from the Nile. (This belief was certainly held about the little stream of Inōpus on remoter Delos. Cf. the spring of Arethusa at Syracuse, which was supposed to be connected with the River Alpheius in the Peloponnese.)

[Page 318] *Piéria.* The Muses' native district, N. of Olympus.

[Page 319] Pentheus proceeds to examine the disguised god with the imperious ruthlessness of an Inquisitor questioning a heretic. Not the least dramatic thing in *The Bacchae* is the gradual turning of the tables, until the judge is, as it were, hypnotically dominated by his victim.

[Page 320] *Flower-grown . . . Tmōlus.* Saffron was made from its crocuses.

[Page 320] *Tell me my doom now. . . . The God Himself shall free me.* Horace (*Epistles,* i, 16, 74–9) adapts this passage to symbolize the sage's defiance of tyranny and adversity.

[Page 321] *Achelōus,* largest of Greek rivers, is here thought of as the father of inland waters in general.

[Page 321] *Dithyrambus.* An obscure word, generally applied to the choric dance in Dionysus' honour—perhaps its original meaning; then, as here, it is used as a name of the god himself. Probably Euripides has in mind the false etymology—'he that comes twice to the gate' (of birth); with allusion to Dionysus' second birth from the thigh of Zeus.

[Page 322] *Nysa.* Dionysus' holy mountain, to which a dozen different locations were assigned.

[Page 322] *Corycian.* The cave of that name was high on the uplands of Parnassus (p. 229).

[Page 322] *Axius . . . Lydias.* Macedonian rivers, now Vardar and Mavronero.

[Page 323] Ingenious critics have supposed that this earthquake only occurs in the imaginations of the Chorus. But such an idea is not drama. The miracle is never denied (contrast the explicit hallucinations of Pentheus mistaking the bull, and the phantom in the courtyard, for Dionysus): if it is not again referred to, that is presumably because Euripides saw no need.

[Page 325] *Cithaeron where year-long . . . snow.* Strange that Euripides could be so inaccurate about a peak within sight of Athens. Cithaeron (4,620 feet) loses its snow in spring. But Greeks are apt to be curiously shy of snow. I have been warned at Kalamata that snow would be a metre deep on the Langada Pass to Sparta, when in fact there were only a few small patches at the col.

[Page 325] *Suckling . . . fawns.* Cf. the old idea that witches suckled familiars in animal shape. Similarly the gathering of women on the mountains with a single priest (*Baccheus*), representing Dionysus, curiously recalls Witches' Sabbaths.

It makes an interesting study in decadence to compare this fine description of the Maenads with the precious and voluptuous version of Chaerēmon (middle of 4th century) in his *Oeneus* (Nauck, p. 786, fr. 14). There the Bacchanals lie asleep by moonlight in flower-beds; one revealing a naked breast, another a bare thigh 'where Love, despairing, imprinted kisses.'

[Page 327] *Electran Gate.* On S. of Thebes, facing Cithaeron.

[Page 329] *I could not bring myself to dress as woman.* Diogenes Laertius (ii, 78) says that Plato quoted this line when Dionysius of Syracuse invited his guests at a banquet to don a purple robe and dance in turn. But Aristippus of Cyrene, a less rigid moralist, put on the robe and danced, capping Plato's quotation with the earlier lines of this play (p. 316):

> No Bacchic revellings
> Can ever stain the soul of her that's pure.

[Page 329] Pentheus' assumption of woman's clothing is perhaps based on similar practices in Dionysiac ritual. Here it may also symbolize his gradual loss of personality under the fascination of Dionysus.

[Page 331] *The God walks with us.* Apparently Pentheus sees a double image of Dionysus as well as of Thebes; one of these two Dionysus-images is horned, and marches in front, like a bull leading the herd.

[Page 332] *In such hiding-place thou shalt be hid.* In full view, on the fir-tree's top. These diabolical ironies of Dionysus might be spoken as asides; but Pentheus seems by now too demented for that to be necessary.

[Page 334] *A fir that towered to Heaven.* Pausanias (fl. *c.* A.D. 150) describes two statues of Dionysus, supposedly made from this fatal tree, as still standing in the market-place of Corinth (ii, 2).

[Page 337] *Agāve ... with her son's head.* After the disaster of Crassus, the triumvir, at Carrhae in 53 B.C., the unfortunate Roman's head was brought to the Parthian king at his son's marriage-feast and used by the actor Jason of Tralles (S.E. of Ephesus) in a performance of this scene from *The Bacchae*—a grim symbol of Greek decadence.

[Page 337] *What! Share it ... !* Even the fanatic Chorus begins to feel sickened.

[Page 340] *Father, you see how my life is overturned.* Here there seems to be a gap of fifty lines or more. Later references, and adaptations in the Byzantine Passion Play *Christus Patiens* (11th–12th century), suggest that Agāve lamented (in excessive detail) over her son's mangled body; then Dionysus appeared from Heaven, justifying the past and foretelling the future.

[Page 340] *Thou shalt become a serpent.* A bizarre conclusion, though it inspired the lovely lines on Cadmus and Harmonia in Arnold's *Empedocles*. Dodds suggests that (1) Harmonia was originally a Mycenaean snake-goddess; (2) the exile of her and Cadmus reflects the expulsion of the old Mycenaean dynasty from Thebes; (3) the barbarian tribe concerned is the Enchēleis in Illyria, on the coast of which Cadmus and Harmonia seem later to have been worshipped (possibly because the Greeks found there traces of Phoenician settlement).

[Page 341] *Gods in Their anger should not be as men.* This one line, repeating a fundamental text of Euripides' rationalism (cf. pp. 283, 286, 306), might alone confute those who see *The Bacchae* as a recantation.

[Page 342] *Aristaeus.* Agāve's brother-in-law and father of Actaeon. The allusion remains obscure; and there may be another gap at this point.

ĪPHIGENEIA AT AULIS

[Page 343] *Not a sound . . . warders are still.* Concentrated by Racine in the famous line of his *Iphigénie*:

> *Mais tout dort, et l'armée, et les vents, et Neptune.*

FRAGMENTS OF LOST PLAYS

[Page 346] *Athleticism.* There is a similar indictment of it in Xenóphanes (c. 565–470 B.C.). (Diehl, *Anth. Lyr. Graeca*, i, p. 55; *Greek Poetry for Everyman*, p. 257.)

[Page 347] *Auge the Priestess* bore to Hēracles the child Tēlephus, whom she hid in Athena's temple—a profanation which caused a famine in the land. The child was found and exposed, but suckled by a hind; later he became King of Mysia (p. 446).

[Page 349] *Lament For every babe.* Compare Hardy's 'Mad Judy.' (*Collected Poems*, 1920, p. 138.)

FRAGMENTS OF OTHER TRAGIC POETS

[Page 350] *The Queen of Candaules.* This strange fragment from a papyrus of the 2nd or 3rd century A.D. was published in 1950. It clearly comes from a dramatization of the story told by Heródotus (i, 8–13) about Candaules, King of Lydia; who, in his infatuation for his queen, forced his favourite bodyguard Gygés to hide in the royal chamber so as to see her beauty when she undressed. But the queen noticed Gyges as he crept out; and next day gave him the choice between killing this husband who had shamed her, or being put to death himself. Gyges chose to survive, killed his master, and became King of Lydia (680 B.C.).

Internal evidence possibly points to a date for this tragedy early in the fifth century[1] (it could even be by Phrynichus); though it might belong to the fourth century, or even to Hellenistic Alexandria.

It is in any case extraordinary to find a Greek tragedy on the fate of a barbarian king of the seventh century. Personally, I find it sharpens my regret that Attic dramatists did not do more in this vein, instead of monotonously confining themselves to the same eternal round of mythological themes.

[Page 351] *Disillusion.* Dio Cassius says these two lines were quoted by Brutus before killing himself on the field of Philippi. (Plutarch in his *Brutus* mentions him as quoting also a line of Euripides' *Mēdēa*.)

---

[1] See D. L. Page, *A New Chapter in the History of Greek Tragedy*, 1951.

PART TWO

GREEK COMEDY

INTRODUCTION

Laugh and be well ; monkeys have been
Extreme good doctors for the spleen.

Matthew Green.

ORIGINS AND DEVELOPMENT

COMEDY, curiously enough, is the child of religion.   So is Tragedy ; but
that seems less surprising.   Yet, after all, to the moods of man Nature
herself appears a thing of moods, now grim, now gentle, now gay, now
sinister ; as Meredith knew :

> Earth in her heart laughs looking at the heavens,
>   Thinking of her harvest : I look and think of mine.

But also :

> Overhead, overhead
> Rushes life in a race,
> As the clouds the clouds chase ;
>   And we go,
> And we drop like the fruits of the tree,
>   Even we,
>   Even so.

And since Nature brings both birth and death—the joy of her inexhaustible fertility, the melancholy of her insatiable massacres—it was understandable that the Nature-worship of primitive Greece should embody
both aspects—both Dionysus the mystic Destroyer, who is himself destroyed, and Dionysus the giver of intoxicated exuberance.   Comedy
(*kōmoidia*) is 'the song of the revellers'—of merry mummers for whom
grossness was not merely amusing, but a religious ritual to arouse Nature's
fecundity.   And since the primitive temperament is not only gross but also
aggressive, these early mummers were not only indecent, but also scurrilous
—revelling in battles of abuse, as medieval Scots poets relished 'flytings.'

In its early days Greek comedy falls into two main divisions—the non-
choric comedy of Sicily and the choric comedy of Athens ; which, like
tragedy, is specially linked by certain threads of tradition with the Attic
deme of Icăria, but seems influenced by the Dorians of Peloponnesus and
of the nearer Mĕgara on the Isthmus.   Of Sicilian comedy, whose great
figure is the long-lived Epicharmus (*c.* 530–440 B.C.), little need be said ;
for little survives.   Epicharmus, like Molière, had serious interests as well.

He wrote on medicine and ethics; and a tetrameter of his embodies what remains one of the wisest of mottoes:

> Still be sober, still be doubting—such the muscles of the mind.

His thirty-five or forty comedies, in literary Doric, seem to have been farcical, but not personally satirical like Attic Old Comedy (which is indeed an important ancestor of literary satire). Apparently some of these pieces burlesqued mythology, mocking Poseidon as a fishmonger, or Hēracles as a glutton; some dramatized controversies, like our medieval *Owl and Nightingale*; some mimed aspects or figures of ordinary life, such as sightseers at Delphi or a social parasite.

The origins of Attic comedy were already obscure to Aristotle; he supposed it to have arisen from phallic processions and dances. But, until the fifth century opens, comedy has left even dimmer traces of its growth than tragedy. For long it seems to have been acted, both at the Lēnaea in January and at the Great Dionysia in March, only by volunteer amateurs; at the Dionysia it did not become an officially organized contest till 486; at the Lēnaea, not till about 442.

The typical, though far from invariable, form of Old Comedy seems to have been as follows:

(1) Some character has a bright idea. For instance, a man thinks of stopping the war by flying to Heaven on a beetle; or a woman by organizing a women's strike.

(2) There enters a Chorus, sympathetic or hostile.

(3) There is a set debate (*agōn*) about the idea.

(4) The Chorus turns and addresses the audience in a *parabasis*—perhaps a relic of the mockeries flung at bystanders by the old phallic mummers.

(5) A series of farcical episodes arises from putting the original idea into practice.

(6) All ends in a revel scene—feast or wedding; a further relic of the primitive merrymaking.

One curious result of the ritual element in Old Comedy is the unequalled licence it enjoyed in personal abuse. About the time of the Samian revolt (440) a law was passed against attacks on individuals; but it was repealed in 437. Another ineffective attempt *may* have been made after the Syracusan disaster. Cleon, again, retaliated on Aristophanes by impeachment. But nothing could long muzzle fifth-century comedians. Even the Olympian Pericles had to endure public derision in the theatre; just as even Caesar, driving in triumph through Rome, had to hear his legionaries chanting the traditional mockeries of their general and bidding the citizens beware of 'the bald adulterer.' After all, the Gods are jealous; perhaps Nemesis might be placated by jeers at the greatest in their greatest hour. At all events the Athenian Demos must be allowed to laugh at its leaders; even if it re-elected them to-morrow. Only when the end of the fifth century brought the end of Athenian greatness (404), did it end also the reckless freedom of her comic poets.

The fourth century produced something more like our idea of comedy. As in tragedy, the Chorus shrinks; as in tragedy, there is a growth both of realism and of romance. The old fantasy is replaced by the lifelike; the old obscenity by an interest in love. The actors no longer make themselves grotesque with paunch and phallus. To what grammarians have called 'Middle Comedy' there are assignable more than fifty playwrights and eight hundred plays; of which only fragments remain, apart from Aristophanes' *Plutus*.

To the New Comedy which followed, time has been almost as merciless. Its seventy playwrights are likewise lost except for fragments; but at the beginning of this century Egypt yielded long passages of the greatest among them, Menander. It seems paradoxical to find a comic form moulded by tragic influence. By the end of the fifth century Attic tragedy had declined still more than comedy; yet the literary parent of Menander was the realistic and romantic Euripides.

In New Comedy the lyric has almost disappeared and the Chorus dwindles to a band of revellers, who may provide an occasional interlude as much divorced from the action as the music of a modern *entr'acte*. In easy-running iambics, these plays picture the curiously artificial entanglements of a series of private lives. For public spirit has faded. Athenians no longer, as in Pericles' day, love their city like a mistress. At Aegospotami in 404 Athens had lost her dominance; at Chaeronēa in 338 and Crannon in 322 she lost even her independence. The age of Epicurus is at hand—cultivated, disillusioned, even cynical, yet humane; seeking in love or society the means of passing in happiness, or at least in tranquillity, the fleeting brevity of individual existence. Indeed fragments of Middle and New Comedy give the impression that this drama must have dwelt on cooks and dinners with a minuteness unparalleled in literature. Little wonder if Demosthenes had hard work goading his countrymen into the field against Macedon. For there is a strong flavour of decadence about some of these rosebud-gatherers.

> But where the land is dim from tyranny,
> There tiny pleasures occupy the place
> Of glories and of duties; as the feet
> Of fabled fairies, when the sun goes down,
> Trip o'er the grass where wrestlers strove by day.
>
> (Landor)

None the less some of Menander's characters are gentlemen—a kind of creature that would seem never to have come within the ken of Aristophanes. Their two worlds are as different as the art of Jane Austen from that of Hogarth.

But though charmed at times by the dialogue, we may be maddened by the plots of this new kind of comedy, with their damnable iteration of themes now long banal—pertly intriguing servants, girls in trouble made honest women, long-lost infants recognized from trinkets, and so forth. Aristophanes, far cruder but far more forcible, has never been repeated; Menander has often been outdone. All the same, he has been outdone precisely because the kind of comedy which he and his fellow-playwrights produced proved a pattern for the far-off future—for Terence and Shakespeare, Molière and Congreve, Sheridan and Wilde. Indeed those who wish for a less fragmentary idea of Menander's qualities may well read the adaptations of New Comedy by Terence (c. 195–159 B.C.); even if Julius Caesar in a verse-fragment denies him Menander's force. And I know no better summary of the finer side of Greek drama in its last phase than the words of Sainte-Beuve on its Roman imitator: 'Térence est le contraire de bien des choses, il l'est surtout de la dureté, de l'inhumanité, de la brutalité— de ce qu'on court risque, à mesure qu'on avance dans les littératures, d'ériger insensiblement en beauté et de prendre pour la marque première du talent.'

In the age of Joyce and D. H. Lawrence, and of aesthetes celebrating the artistry of bullfights, that passage has lost none of its force.

THEATRE AND PRODUCTION

The main details are as for tragedy (p. 9) and only a few differences need be noted. The stage-building generally represented two or more houses; in Old Comedy the actors became normally restricted to three, as in tragedy, with occasional extras; but the Chorus numbered twenty-four,[1] instead of twelve or fifteen. Where the tragic actor was heightened and padded to heroic size, his comic counterpart in the fifth century was made grotesque, not only by his mask, but also by an exaggerated belly and rump, often with phallus as well.

The normal number of plays competing in the official contest was five; but this was reduced to three during the Peloponnesian War (431–404 B.C.). Three comedies could conveniently be acted in the afternoons of the three days given to tragic tetralogies. (How matters were arranged when there

---

[1] It played a livelier part than in tragedy, might have to present crowd-effects, and sometimes, as in Lysistrata, had to comprise opposing factions, which needed to be of a certain size.

were five comedies is not clear.) Poets wishing to compete applied, as in tragedy, to the archon—the archon *eponymos* for the Dionysia, the archon *basileus* for the Lēnaea. Money-prizes were awarded, as for tragedy. In general, however, the poets of comedy seem to have had a lower prestige in the fifth century than those of tragedy—whether or not it is true that no member of the Areopagus might compose comedies (Plutarch, *Glory of the Athenians*, ch. v).

ARISTOPHANES

(c. 450–c. 385 B.C.)

Ah messieurs, quelles canailles que ces Grecs, mais qu'ils avaient donc de l'esprit!

Viguier (lecturing on Aristophanes).

ARISTOPHANES entered young on a dramatic career that was to last some forty years and produce some forty comedies, of which we possess eleven. He wrote with a good deal of purpose; and he realized that the propagandist must not be afraid of repetition. Four of his plays are appeals for peace; largely combined with satire of war-mongering demagogues. In *The Acharnians* (425) an Athenian farmer successfully concludes a private peace of his own; *The Knights* (424) belabours the bellicose Cleon; the hero of *Peace* (421) flies to Heaven on a beetle's back to find where Peace is, and gets her pulled up from her prison; the heroine of *Lysistrata* (411) reaches the same end by organizing a Panhellenic strike of wives. Only less vexatious, in the poet's eyes, than his countrymen's fondness for wars abroad was their passion for lawsuits at home. The hero of *The Wasps* (422) with much difficulty cures his old father of a mania for sitting on juries. *The Birds* (414), though much of it remains pure fantasy, perhaps touches both themes. Its hero quits Athens because of its intolerable litigiousness; and the city he founds in the clouds may well reflect Athenian day-dreams of wider and wider empire.

Next to war with other Greek states, Aristophanes hated what he considered decadence. He saw his country threatened with material ruin by militarism, with moral decline by the new trends in thought and literature. *The Clouds* (423) assails Socrates as the arch-sophist. Of course it is a caricature; but less, perhaps, than it is conventional to pretend. The Socrates of the play is many years younger than the Socrates of Plato or Xenophon; we know that in earlier days he did turn to natural science; and, more important, though it may be excellent for the mature mind to question everything, it by no means follows that it is so excellent for the man in the street to have all his values discredited, with no assurance that they will be replaced by others better or as good. Even Socrates' disciples sometimes turned out ill enough—Alcibiades helped to ruin Athens, Critias and Charmides to saddle her with an oligarchic tyranny after her ruin.[1] Both Socrates and Plato seem to underestimate (much more than Euripides) the part that the irrational does, and must, play in human behaviour. It is

[1] Paul Bourget has drawn in *Le Disciple*, with a certain melodrama, the danger of corrosive philosophies. But I know no evidence that Socrates ever felt about *his* disciples' misdeeds the anguish of Adrien Sixte over Robert Greslou.

this faulty psychology that vitiates the communism of Plato, as of Marx—neither writer realized the incorrigible poison of power. And it was communism of Plato's kind that Aristophanes turned to ridicule in *The Women's Assembly* (c. 392–389?). Meanwhile he had also unceasingly burlesqued the other great innovator of his day, Euripides, as an affected, quibbling dramatist, obsessed with sex; especially in *The Thesmophoriazūsae* (411) and *The Frogs* (405).

Aristophanes regretted the simpler Athens of Marathon and Salamis, the Athens of Aeschylus; it was a reasonable view. He detested self-styled 'intellectuals' as persons who merely found clever arguments for silly opinions; it is still a possible view. Yet his preaching seems to have made few converts. Athens laughed, then went on as before. So did the war. So did the lawsuits. So did the power of Cleon, the fame of Euripides. If Aristophanes contributed to any real result, it was perhaps, in some degree, to the execution of Socrates. Not a very happy triumph. Still, that was more than twenty years after *The Clouds*; and might well have happened even if *The Clouds* had never been written.

Why did Aristophanes produce so little practical effect compared, say, with Voltaire or Ibsen? Because he had less intellect? Because his own mouth was none too clean? It seems more likely that he was simply too negative and trying to swim backwards against the stream, where they were more positive and looked forward. Easier to hasten the future than restore the past.

Here indeed Aristophanes contrasts strikingly with his great counterpart—Rabelais; who was indebted to the Athenian, but seems to me a shrewder and more original mind. In his own day Rabelais risked more by his bold tongue than Aristophanes—Cleon was less dangerous than the Sorbonne; but Rabelais was fighting successfully for a future liberation of the human spirit. It is not simply that Rabelais battled for what was coming to life against what was decaying; bad things can come to life, good things decay. Nor is it even that Rabelais was in the main on the side of light, health, and sense; so, often, was Aristophanes. It is that Rabelais, with equal grossness, yet seems a more effectual, more vital, more daring thinker. Aristophanes has been called a great moralist; but here there seems a touch of learned cant.[1] No doubt Aristophanes liked at times to picture himself with a mission and a message. But his farces over-simplify life's intricacy; at times he looks unpleasantly like Priapus leering from a pulpit; he remains rather an entertainer than a real influence, where greater writers have been both.

Perhaps he himself lost confidence. His last extant comedy, *Plutus*

[1] True, St John Chrysostom (d. 407) is said to have slept with twenty-eight plays of Aristophanes under his pillow. Fielding, on the other hand (though no Puritan), thought both Aristophanes and Rabelais seemed to have no object but 'to ridicule all sobriety, modesty, decency, virtue, and religion out of the world.' So relative is taste.

(388), turns from the hope of reforming men to a fantasy of reforming a
god.   It is a sort of Morality Play, where the blind Deity of Wealth has
his sight restored, so that he can bestow his riches with more justice.   It
marks the end of the Old Comedy.   Gone are the old political outspoken-
ness, the reckless personalities, the snatches of lyric beauty from the Chorus;
the Chorus itself has thinned to a shadow.

The fame of Aristophanes rests on his fifth-century work; but one may
be allowed at least to ask if his fame has not sometimes been exaggerated.
Clever he is at inventing plots that make his theses into vivid parables; his
characters, though broad types (in more senses than one), have often plenty
of life; and his bursts of pure poetry are as startling as if through the win-
dows of some disreputable tavern were suddenly heard a nightingale trilling
in the moonlight.   On the other hand, his fun is apt to go on too long;
and much of it now seems poor enough fun.   At times one sickens at the
conscientious giggles of professors.   And where they constantly praise
him as 'excruciatingly funny,' readers less partial may find him so in a
more literal sense, as they sigh through page on page of seedy puns and
tedious jokes on faeces, phalli, and fleas.   No doubt comedy had sprung
from a fertility-ritual, where indecency was essential—a sort of magic
moral manure; but to explain a thing is not necessarily to enjoy it.   The
psychologist recognizes in Aristophanic humour the primitive anal erotism
that marks the infancy alike of race and individual; but that does not make
it any less boring for modern minds that are not (as, of course, many are)
still infantile.   Aristophanes criticizes his rivals' stale jests.   His Dionysus
complains:

> I come home from the theatre,
> After I've heard some of their witticisms,
> More than a twelvemonth older.

> (*Frogs*, 16–18)

But he might more often have remembered that himself.

Of course it is the common fate of wit and humour often to travel badly
across the ages.   We can hardly wonder if much 'Attic salt' has lost its
savour; even Shakespeare sometimes revels in witticisms that now seem
grovelling.   Yet this is not invariably so.   The wit of the eighteenth
century at its best, as in Johnson, Walpole, or Sheridan, Montesquieu,
Voltaire, or Talleyrand, keeps a brilliance untarnished still.

The modern world knows Greek poetry too little: it is no remedy to
praise it too much.   That is self-defeating.   Some things in '*le farceur
Aristophane*,' as Voltaire too disdainfully called him, are still very much
alive; but much is dead—and better dead.   Perhaps the most admirable
thing about the Old Comedy of Athens is really, for us, not the plays, but
the amazing freedom of thought and speech that those plays imply.   The
Athenians did indeed, in a moment of political passion, execute Socrates

at seventy, though only after giving him plenty of chance to escape (in Plato's Republic or in half of modern Europe he would have been liquidated long before): but, with only an occasional call to order, they tolerated Aristophanes. In our own world, with its gangs of censors snipping in bureaus and police spies sniffing under doors, that at least is something to look back to, and up to, with admiration and regret.

THE ACHARNIANS
(Lēnaea, 425 B.C.—first prize)

When in the House M.P.s divide,
If they've a brain and cerebellum, too,
They've got to leave that brain outside,
And vote just as their leaders tell'em to.

W. S. Gilbert, *Iolanthe.*

Aristophanes had begun his dramatic career in 427; in his second play, *The Babylonians* (426), he had boldly attacked the bellicose Cleon and had been counter-attacked by that demagogue with an impeachment; in *The Acharnians* of 425 he denounces the war with Sparta but, for the moment, leaves Cleon alone.

Dicaeopolis, a war-weary citizen attending a meeting of the Assembly, is disgusted because no one discusses peace; the time is wasted over futile reports from ambassadors who evade war-service on comfortable missions to barbarian kings. Then he hits on the bright idea: 'I will make a separate peace for myself.' At once he does so (the Old Comedy never lets itself be cramped by prosaic considerations of the possible); but this brings about his ears a furious Chorus of fiery old charcoal-burners from the Attic village of Acharnae, who have suffered particularly from Spartan invasions and feel towards Sparta much as French Lorrainers were apt to feel towards Germany. Dicaeopolis undertakes to plead his cause before them with his neck on a chopping-block; but to excite his judges' compassion he decides to borrow from Euripides (whose lachrymose realism Aristophanes detested) one of the many sets of rags of which that tragedian keeps a whole wardrobe for his heroes. Euripides' house stands in the background; and the busy dramatist is persuaded to let himself be rolled out for a moment by the mechanism for revealing interiors (*eccyclēma*).

Dicaeopolis. But by your knees, Euripides, I beg you,
    Give me some rags from that old play of yours.
    I have to make a long speech to the Chorus
    And the penalty, if I speak ill, is death!

Euripides. Which rags do you mean?   The ones that Oeneus here [1]
Once acted in, unfortunate old man?

Dic. Not Oeneus' rags.   Someone more luckless still.

Eur. Those of blind Phoenix?   *Dic.* No, not Phoenix either.
Someone it was more wretched still than Phoenix.

Eur. What rags and tatters can the man be after?
Is it those, perhaps, of beggared Philoctētes?

Dic. No, someone far—yes, *far* more beggarly.

Eur. Do you want the filthy clouts in which was dressed
This limping fellow here [1]—Bellérophon?

Dic. No, not Bellérophon.   But he I mean
Was also lame, glib, whining, plausible.

Eur. I know!—the Mysian, Tēlephus?   *Dic.* Yes, he!
Give me, I beg you, just the clouts he wore.

Eur. Boy, hand him out the rags of Tēlephus [2]—
They're lying just above Thyestes' tatters,
And under Īno's.   *Slave.* There you are—now take them.

(414–34.)

Thus accoutred, Dicaeopolis pleads to the Acharnians that the war-guilt was not all on one side, nor Sparta unprovoked.   Part of the Chorus is convinced, part not; but finally all are won over, when Dicaeopolis has worsted in a verbal battle the hectoring fire-eater Lámachus (afterwards to fall before Syracuse).   There follows the usual string of episodes—a starving Megarian comes to sell his daughters disguised as pigs; a Boeotian bringing game and Copaic eels is repaid by Dicaeopolis with an animal unknown in Boeotia, but too common at Athens, a public informer. Finally, while Lámachus is brought back wounded from a frontier-skirmish, Dicaeopolis reels home drunken from his peace-time revelry, with a flute-girl under each arm.

It remains a deeper question whether Aristophanes was really best serving the cause of peace against war by picturing the one as a rather degraded kind of cakes and ale, the other as 'blood, tears, and sweat.' Foolish though *this* war was, human nature does not always work quite so simply.

---

[1] It looks as if some of the dresses hung on dummies, perhaps labelled?

[2] And yet, so differently are human beings affected by the same things, the noble bearing of this same Tēlephus in his beggary so moved the Theban Crates (*c.* 365–285) that he gave away his great possessions and became a poor Cynic philosopher (Diogenes Laertius, vi, 87).

The Knights

(Lēnaea, 424 B.C.—first prize)

The Noble Lord who rules the State—
The Noble Lord who cleans the plate—
The Noble Lord who scrubs the grate—
They all shall equal be!

W. S. Gilbert, *The Gondoliers.*

Here Aristophanes renews his assault (though the play hardly mentions his enemy's name) on the detested Cleon; who, by capturing a Spartan force cut off on the island of Sphactēria in the bay of Pylos (Navarino), had just risen to new heights and received among other distinctions the right to a front seat in the theatre, from which he may have watched this vilification of himself as the most odious of charlatans.

The comedy opens with two slaves (representing the rich conservative Nĭcias and his fellow-general Demosthenes) lamenting that their master, the testy old Demos (the People), has come wholly under the thumb of another, newly acquired slave, the tanner Páphlagon—a name suggesting at once barbarism and bluster. Stealing this rogue's collection of private oracles—for fifth-century Athens was already no less 'superstitious' than that of St Paul, as the Syracusan expedition was to show—his rivals find it predicted that Páphlagon is to be succeeded in his turn by an even lower rascal, 'a seller of black puddings' (most simply rendered by 'sausage-seller'). At once they pounce on a passing sausage-seller and hail him as saviour.

Demosthenes.   Hi, good fellow!   Here!
  You, my dear friend!   You blessed sausage-seller!
  Come up!   Our saviour—saviour of our country!
Sausage-seller. What is it?   What's your business?   *Dem.* Come here,
                listen
  What luck you're in, what high prosperity!
Nĭcias. Run!   Make him put down his table; and explain him
  This revelation of the oracle.
  I'll go and keep an eye for Páphlagon.   [*Exit.*
Dem. Come, put your tackle first upon the ground,
  Then bow in reverence to Earth and Heaven.
S.-seller. Hey!   What's the matter?   *Dem.* O man of wealth and for-
                tune—

Nobody, now; to-morrow high and mighty!
O sovereign of this happy land of Athens!

S.-seller. Good fellow, let me wash my guts in peace
And sell my puddings; instead of laughing at me.

Dem. 'Guts,' you poor fool! Look here.
You see these people—rows on rows?   [*Pointing to the audience.*

S.-seller.   I see 'em.

Dem. You shall be lord and master of them all,
Their Market, and their Harbours, and their Pnyx;
Trample the Council, purge the Generals,
Handcuff, imprison, make love as you please
In the Town Hall!

S.-seller.   Who!—I?

Dem.   Yes, *you*, I tell you!
And there's still more to see. Up on your table!
Now look at all these islands round about us.

S.-seller. I see 'em.   Well?   *Dem.* Their ships, too, and their
                    markets?

S.-seller. Be sure I do.   *Dem.* Why, aren't you in luck's way!
And now just cast one eye towards Caria,
There on your right, and your other eye towards Carthage.

S.-seller. 'Luck's way' indeed!—if I'm to twist my neck!

Dem. Nonsense, all these are for your hands to deal in.
For you are destined, says this oracle,
To achieve greatness.   *S.-seller.* Say, what's turning *me*,
A sausage-seller, to a personage?

Dem. But in this very thing your greatness lies—
In being a rogue, and impudent, and vulgar.

S.-seller. I don't see *I* deserve such elevation.

Dem. Oh curse it, what's this talk of not 'deserving'!
I begin to think some decent quality
Burdens your conscience.   Were your family
Gentlemen?   *S.-seller.* No!—Heavens above, not they!—
Scum of the earth!   *Dem.* Ah, I congratulate you!
That's a good start indeed for public life.

S.-seller. But, sir, I haven't any education—
Just know my alphabet—and *that* damned badly.

Dem. That's your one drawback—knowing it even badly!
Not educated men, not honest men,
Are qualified for Leaders of the Masses,
But ignorant scoundrels.   So don't you neglect
These promises the voice of Heaven makes you.

                                        (147–94.)

Now Páphlagon enters and assails his rival; but is assailed in turn by the Chorus of Knights (belonging to a cavalry corps of a thousand, formed about 450 B.C. and composed, since they provided their own horses, of rich youths who naturally hated the proletarian Cleon). The sausage-seller, after outbidding Páphlagon before the Council, repeats his triumph before Demos himself, is appointed steward, and restores his old master, as Mēdēa Aeson, to lusty youth; also to a sane realization that peace and plenty are better than futile war. Páphlagon is condemned to sell sausages at the town gate and drink bath water.

One of Aristophanes' cruder plays. It remains an extraordinary monument of free speech; but hatred of individuals—whether it is Swift falling on Marlborough, or Pope on Hervey, or Hugo on Napoleon III—seldom provides very happy inspiration. One should hate things; not people. Still, this picture of demagogues who bribe their own supporters from the public revenues has a certain relevance to-day to the free democracies, as *Antigone* to the totalitarian state.

It may astonish some modern readers, bred in the faith that wars are all caused by the wicked rich, while the virtuous proletariat are all pacific philanthropists, to find at Athens the war party on the left, the peace party on the right. But the anti-democratic Sparta was naturally more congenial to the richer than to the poorer. And, as in eighteenth-century England, the country party suffered more from the war, while the maritime and mercantile town population often gained.

Fate has a grim way of adding to comedy a tragic irony of its own. Two years later, in 422, Cleon was killed playing general against the Spartans in Thrace; nine years after that, Nīcias and Demosthenes were put to death, perhaps with torture, by the victorious enemy after the disaster at Syracuse.

THE CLOUDS
(Great Dionysia, 423 B.C.)

If you're anxious for to shine in the high aesthetic line as a man of culture rare,
You must get up all the germs of the transcendental terms, and plant them
everywhere.
You must lie upon the daisies, and discourse in novel phrases of your com-
plicated state of mind,
The meaning doesn't matter if it's only idle chatter of a transcendental kind.

W. S. Gilbert, *Patience.*

For the moment peace seemed returning—in 423 a year's truce was agreed with Sparta. Aristophanes could pass to some other theme. He chose pseudo-intellectualism.

In its original form, now lost, his play was placed only third. Aristophanes, considering it his best work, was understandably galled and wrote this surviving revision, which remains, of all his comedies, one of the most interesting to the modern reader. For us, his politics date; we have no longer a passion for sitting on juries, still less (most of us) for going to law; communism has got beyond a joke; and in general we see no religious virtue in obscenity. But we are still interested in Socrates; and we still have among us pseudo-intellectuals not wholly unlike Aristophanes' caricature [1]—the type of clever persons who spent the twenties of this century deriding all past standards, especially 'Victorianism'; then, in the thirties, flirted with Russian 'Marxism' under the illusion that it was genuine communism and, while detesting fascism and Nazism, screamed against the armaments which alone could resist them; and now are fellow-travellers, or surrealists, or existentialists, or -ists of some other fashion. Accordingly *The Clouds* seemed the best of the plays to translate here in full: though I must own that I should have been sorry to imitate the enthusiastic Mme Dacier in reading it through two hundred times before doing so.

No doubt it remains most unfair to the best of the Sophists, who were sometimes distinguished figures; and above all to Socrates, who seems freely to have criticized them, did not take fees like them, and, so far from claiming omniscience, professed omninescience [2]—a modesty which,

[1] Cf. Baldwin's remark that the 'intelligentsia' stands in the same relation to the intelligent as 'gents' to gentlemen.

[2] There may be truth in the story preserved by Aelian (*Var. Hist.*, ii, 13) that Socrates was so unperturbed by the first performance of *The Clouds* that, hearing some aliens whispering: 'Who *is* this Socrates?', he stood up for the audience to see, and so remained till the end of the play. Johnson was less patient. It will be remembered that, when Foote, 'the Aristophanes of the English stage,' purposed taking *him* off in the theatre, the Doctor ordered a double-thick oak cudgel and sent word to the comedian he would 'go from the boxes on the stage, and correct him before the audience.'

unfortunately, he is sometimes very far from preserving in the pages of Plato. But the unfairness is understandable. Socrates and Euripides were the two typical representatives at Athens of the new freedom of thought and criticism of life; the philosopher's personal eccentricities, often as odd as Dr Johnson's, made him an obvious butt, not only for Aristophanes, but for other comedians like Cratinus and Eupŏlis; and however much he might disclaim any dogmas of his own, his influence was undermining the traditional beliefs of his country. He may well have educated some of his young men beyond their intellectual means. There is more than mere frivolity in the comment that an unknown poet of the New Comedy puts in the mouth of a *hetaira*:

> A Sophist better than a courtesan? . . .
> *We* are no worse at teaching youth than they.
> Compare Aspasia, friend, and Socrates.
> She had, you'll find, for pupil—Pericles,
> While *he* had—Critias!

> (Kock, *Comicorum Atticorum Fragmenta*,
> iii, 431, frs. 121, 122).

Probably Athenian decline was inevitable; but that was less evident in the days of Aristophanes; nor would it have been very heroic to accept the prospect with passive resignation.

THE CLOUDS

STREPSÍADES
PHEIDIPPIDES, his son
SOCRATES
HONEST ARGUMENT
DISHONEST ARGUMENT
PĀSIAS, a creditor

AMYNIAS, another creditor
CHAEREPHON
CHORUS OF CLOUDS
DISCIPLES OF SOCRATES
A SLAVE
A WITNESS

[*Night. In the background two houses—that of Socrates and his disciples and, opposite, that of Strepsiades. He and his son are lying on pallets in front of it.*]

Strepsíades. O-oh! O-oh!
Lord Zeus in Heaven!—*what* a length the nights are!
Endless! Will daylight never, never come?
And yet I heard the cock crow ages back.
But still the servants snore. They wouldn't have *dared*
In the old days!
Oh curse the War!—one bore upon another.
Can't even punish my own servants now!
And then this worshipful young son of mine,
He doesn't wake at nights—just lies ensconced
In five great sheepskins pulled about his ears,
With belly rumbling.
Well, if it's got to be, let's snuggle down
And snore together.   [*He lies down; only to toss again.*
                    But *how?*—Oh curse it!—bitten
By all these debts—stables—extravagances,
Thanks to my son here? For the long-haired darling
Just rides and drives, and even in his sleep
Dreams still of horses; while I go to ruin,
Watching the moon whirl round the days for payment,
And the interest running up. Do you hear me, boy?
Let's have a light. And fetch me my account book.
I want to read my list of creditors,
And reckon up the interest.   [*A slave brings lamp and list.*
                    Let me see—
What do I owe now? Pāsias—twelve minas.
Why 'Pāsias—twelve minas'? What on earth?

378

Ah yes, to purchase that Corinthian racer.

A razor for my throat would have been better!

Pheidippides (*asleep*). You're fouling, Philo! Keep your own side, can't

you!

Streps. Yes, *there*'s the very root of all the evil!

Even asleep, he only dreams of horses.

Pheid. (*asleep*). How many laps of the course will the chariots run?

Streps. On pretty evil courses *you*'ve been driving

Your poor old father!   (*Reading.*) But after Pāsias?

What 'toil and trouble' next?

'Light car and wheels.   Three minas.   Amynias.'

Pheid. (*asleep*). Give the horse a roll, then you can stable him.

Streps. God, sir, you've 'rolled' me—out of all I have!

What with sentences to pay, and creditors

That threaten executions.

Pheid. (*waking*).   Really, father!

What's wrong with you!   You toss the whole night long.

Streps. My pillow's full of biting common pleas.

Pheid. In Heaven's name, *do* let me get some sleep!

Streps. Oh, sleep away!   But all these debts, I warn you,

One day will fall on *you*!

Phew!

Now may Hell take that cursed matchmaker

Who put me on to marrying your mother!

I led the very loveliest country life,

Untidy, slovenly, lie-as-you-please,

All rank with olive-cakes and bees and sheep,

Until I married—

Plain country-bumpkin—that proud city dame,

That niece of Megacles, son of Megacles,

That spoilt, blue-blooded, hoity-toity lady.

On our very wedding-day I came to table

Full of the healthy smell of figs and fleeces,

New wine and rude abundance—she beside me

All saffron, scent, high living and loose kissing,

Extravagance and sex and venery!

She'd work, it's true—but all to cut a figure.

'Wife,' I would say, and show her my old cloak,

'You do not cut according to our cloth.'   [*The lamp goes out.*

Slave. Master, there's no more oil left in the lamp.

Streps. Oh dear, why light that drunkard of a lamp!

Come, let me make you howl.

Slave.   What should I howl for?

Streps. For using that great, fat wick.

So afterwards, when this son of ours was born,
Then I and my good lady at once began
To squabble what to call him. For she wanted
To tag some horsey '-ippus' to his name—
Callippides, or Xanthippus, or Charippus;
But *I* was for calling him Pheidonides
After his grandfather—a frugal name.
A long dispute it was; but in the end
We compromised upon 'Pheidippides.'
And then she'd take the boy and pet him, saying:
'Ah, when you're big, my child, and robed in crimson
You drive your chariot to the Acropolis!—
Like Megacles!' And I in turn would answer:
'Ah, when you drive your goats from the top of Phelleus,
Well wrapped in a good sheepskin, like your father!'
But no, he wouldn't listen. And so he's brought
All my estate to a galloping consumption.
But now that I've lain awake all night to think,
I've hit on *one* way out—divinely clever!
If only I can persuade him, I am saved.
But the first thing is to wake him. How can I
Most pleasantly, I wonder?
Pheidippides, Pheidippides my dear!

Pheid. What is it, father?

Streps. Kiss me, my boy, and give me your hand upon it.

Pheid. (giving his hand). There! But what *is* it?

Streps.   Son, do you really love me?

Pheid. Sure as Poseidon there (*pointing*) is God of Horses!

Streps. Oh no, no Gods of Horses! Why, it's he
That's brought my ruin.
But if, my boy, you really and truly love me,
Do as I say!

Pheid.   But *what* am I to do?

Streps. I want you to throw off your present habits,
And come and study what I'm going to advise.

Pheid. Go on! What *is* it you want?

Streps.   You'll do it?

Pheid.   Yes,
By Dionysus!

Streps.   Well, look over there.
You see that little gate? That dear little house?

Pheid. Why, yes, I see. And what may *they* be, father?

Streps. That's the Reflectory of learned spirits.
There live the fellows that can demonstrate
The heaven is nothing but a vaulted oven
Enclosing *us*—and we're the coals inside.
Now *they* can teach one (if one pays their fee)
To win all controversies—right or wrong.

Pheid. Who *are* they, though?

Streps.　　　　　　　　Their proper name escapes me.
They're—thought-precisians—perfect gentlemen!

Pheid. Ugh, a bad lot!　*I* know—those quacks, you mean,
Those barefoot, pale-faced people—all the set
Of Socrates, poor devil, and Chaerephon!

Streps. Hi!—hold your tongue!　Don't talk like a childish fool.
If you care at all for your father's daily bread,
Just join them, will you?—and give up your horses.

Pheid. By Dionysus!　Never!　Not though you gave me
All the fine Phasians that Leōgoras breeds!

Streps. O well beloved, but do, I beg you, *do*
Go there and learn.

Pheid.　　　　　　And what would you have me learn?

Streps. They keep there, so it's said, two arguments—
One worse, one better (whatever *that* may be).
And one of them, they tell me—yes, the worse one—
Can make its case, although less just, prevail.
If only you'll learn this *un*just argument.
Of all the debts I owe—on *your* account!—
I need not pay my creditors one penny.

Pheid. Ah no, I can't!　I couldn't face the Knights
With my complexion spoilt and gone to pieces.

Streps. Then by Demeter I'll no longer feed you—
You and your thoroughbreds and chariot-horses!
Out of my house, then!—and to Hell with you!

Pheid. Oh, Uncle Megacles'll never leave me
To live without a *horse*!　I'm going indoors,
And I don't care *what* you say.　　　　　　　　　[*Exit.*

Streps. Well, *I*'ll not take things, either, lying down.
I'll go myself instead, with Heaven's help,
To their Reflectory and take the lessons.
Yet how should *I*—with *my* old, blunted wits,
And memory gone—
Learn all their quibbles and their straw-choppings?
Still, go I must.　What use is loitering here,
Instead of knocking?　(*He knocks.*)　Boy!　Do you hear me?　Boy!

Disciple (within). To Hell with you! Who is it knocking there?

Streps. Strepsíades, son of Pheidon, from Cicynna.

Disc. (opening). God, what a clown!—so inconsiderately
To kick our door! Do you know you've made miscarry
A new idea that just had been discovered!

Streps. Oh pardon me! I live far out in the country.
But tell me, do, what *was* it that miscarried?

Disc. We're not allowed to say, except to students.

Streps. Oh never fear, then—tell me! Here am I
Just come to study in your Reflectory.

Disc. Well then. (But, mind, it's a sacred mystery.)
Socrates *was* just asking Chaerephon
How many flea-foot lengths a flea could jump.
For one first bit the brow of Chaerephon
And then it jumped on the head of Socrates.

Streps. And how did he measure it?

Disc.   Oh, most cunningly.
He melted wax and then, catching the flea,
Dipped its two feet in—so, as the flea grew cold,
It was wearing Persian slippers. Off he pulled them
And with their help was measuring the distance.

Streps. Good God in Heaven!—*that* was subtlety!

Disc. What would you say to another deep idea
Of Socrates?

Streps.   What was it? Tell me! Please!

Disc. He was asked by Chaerephon the Sphettian,
Whether the note of gnats, in his opinion,
Came from their mouths, or their posteriors.

Streps. And what, then, was the Master's view of gnats?

Disc. He said the intestinal ducts of gnats
Are narrow; so, down this constricted passage,
The blast is forced towards the posterior,
And then, emerging on the wider tail,
By the forced draught makes it vibrate a note.

Streps. Ah, so the gnat can use its tail as trumpet.
What a magnificent anal analysis!
A man that even knows a gnat's intestines—
Why, *he*'d win any case you brought against him!

Disc. But the other day a most important theory
Was wrecked just by a lizard.

Streps.   How could *that* be?

Disc. During the night the Master was observing
The courses and revolutions of the moon;

And while he stood gaping upwards, from the roof
  A lizard let fall its droppings full upon him.
Streps. A lizard on Socrates!   How most amusing!
Disc. Last evening, too, we'd nothing left for supper.
Streps. Aha!   And did he juggle you a meal?
Disc. As if for geometry, he scattered ashes
  Upon a table; then he bent in two
  A spit, as if to serve for compasses—
  And hooked a cloak out of the wrestling-school!
Streps. Why honour the great Thales any more?
  Quick, quick, friend, open your Reflectory!—
  Show me your Socrates!   I long to be
  His student.   Open, open!   [*The interior is revealed.*
  Great Hēracles, but what queer fish are these?
Disc. Why so surprised?   What do you think they're like?
Streps. Pale as those Spartan fellows caught at Pylos.
  But why are these here poring on the ground?
Disc. *They* are in search of subterranean things.
Streps. Truffles?   Don't waste such cogitation here;
  I know where great big fine ones can be found.
  But what are these doing, with their backs bent double?
Disc. Plumbing the deeps beneath the Bottomless Pit.
Streps. But why does the stern of each peer up to Heaven?
Disc. Learning astronomy on its own account.
  Get in, you fellows—or the Master'll catch us.
Streps. Stop, stop a moment!   Let me impart to them
  A little piece of business of my own.
Disc. Ah, but they mustn't waste too long outside
  In the open air.   [*Exeunt other disciples.*
Streps. (*pointing to two statues*). In God's name, what are these?
Disc. This is Astronomy.
Streps.   And what is this?
Disc. Geometry.
Streps.   And what's the use of that?
Disc. To measure out the land.
Streps.   For colonies?
Disc. No, the whole world.
Streps.   A man of the world you are!
  That's a most useful, democratic notion.
Disc. And here—do you see?—is a map of all the earth.
  Look, here is Athens.
Streps.   Athens?   I don't believe you!
  I can see no juries sitting.

Disc. But, I assure you, it *is* Attica.

Streps. Then where are my fellow-demesmen of Cicynna?

Disc. Oh, somewhere there.   And here, you see, there lies
   The long stretch of Euboea.

Streps. Ah yes, poor thing—stretched on the rack she was
   By us and Pericles!   But where is Sparta?

Disc. Sparta?   Why, here.

Streps.   But that's most terribly close!
   Turn your great minds to move her *far* away.

Disc. It can't be done.

Streps.   God, then you'll smart for it!

   Socrates appears above, hanging in a basket.

   But who's this fellow hanging in the basket?

Disc. The Master.

Streps.   Why, what 'Master'?

Disc.   Socrates.

Streps. Hi, Socrates!   (*To the disciple.*)   Come, you!   Give him a shout.

Disc. Call him yourself!   I'm busy.   [*Exit.*

Streps. Hi, Socrates!   Hi, Socrates my pet!

Socrates. Why do you call to me, ephemeral creature?

Streps. First be so kind as to tell me what you're doing.

Socr. I tread on air—my thoughts descry the sun.

Streps. Why mount a basket to decry the Gods,
   If you *must* do it?   Why not from the ground?

Socr. Never could I have learned,
   Rightly, the nature of the things of Heaven,
   Unless I lifted up my mind, and merged
   Its subtle essence with its kindred air.
   Vain all my labour, if from earth below
   I studied things above.   The earth perforce
   Attracts the vital fluid of our thought.
   The same thing happens, too, with watercress.

Streps. What's that!
   Thought attracts fluid into watercress?
   Come down to earth now, Socrates my pet,
   And tell me the things I've come to ask about.

Socr. (*descending in his basket*).   And what are *they*?

Streps.   I want to be taught to speak.
   Interest and creditors are merciless—
   I'm ruined and ravaged, and my goods distrained.

Socr. How slipped you unawares so deep in debt?

Streps. I caught a frightful, most consuming horse-pox.
   But teach me, please, of your two arguments,

The one that bilks all payments.
What fee you like!   I swear by the Gods to pay.
Socr. Swear by the Gods indeed!   Now, first, no Gods
Are current coin with *us*.
Streps.   What *do* you use, then?
Iron, like Byzantium?
Socr.   But would you learn,
Clearly, the *real* truth of things divine?
Streps. Why, yes, by Zeus!—if things divine exist?
Socr. And have communion with the holy Clouds,
The powers *we* worship?
Streps.   Yes, indeed I would!
Socr. Then sit you down upon this sacred couch.
Streps. Here I am, sitting.
Socr.   Now then, take this garland.
Streps. But why a garland?   Heavens, Socrates,
You will not make a sacrifice of *me*,
Like Áthamas?
Socr.   Oh no, we use this ritual
For *all* initiates.
Streps.   But what do *I* get?
Socr. You'll be a polished rogue, a perfect rattle,
Fine flour of subtlety.   Only keep still!   [*He sprinkles Strepsiades with
                                                                    meal.*

Streps. By Zeus, you speak the truth!—with all this sprinkling,
I shall turn to a perfect flour-sack!
Socr. Let the old man cease, and hold his peace, and hearken to my
      prayer.
Lord on whose breast all Earth doth rest, O infinite space of Air!
O Ether resplendent!   O powers transcendent, ye Clouds that lighten
      and thunder!
Ladies, arise, look from the skies on your sage that waits in wonder!
Streps. Not yet!   Not yet!   I shall get wet.   I must wrap me against the
      weather.
Oh curse the thought!   From home I brought not even a cap of
      leather!
Socr. Ye Clouds adored, sail forth abroad, to *him* your beauties show;
Whether ye shine on the peak divine of Olympus white with snow,
Or with your dance the Nymphs entrance, where the gardens of Ocean
      smile;
Whether ye hold your urns of gold to catch the flow of Nile,
Or the snowy head of Mĩmas tread, or skirt Maeōtis' lake;
This offering that here I bring, with benediction take!

strophe.

Chorus of Clouds (*behind the scene*). Ye Clouds that fleet onward for aye,
    Lift up before men's view your shapes of light and dew.
      Up!—from the thunders of Ocean, our father, mount high in the air.
           Up!—to the forested hill-tops away!
             And gathering there
        Look on the mountain-peaks distantly looming,
          Rivers divine with their hurrying roar,
        Lands that they water, like gardens blooming,
          Rollers that thunder in surf on the shore.
        Lo now, the eye of the Heaven upspringing
          Casts his unquenchable splendour of light;
        Now from our forms incorruptible flinging
        Mantles of mist and vapours clinging,
          Gaze we on Earth far outspread to our sight.

Socr. Ah now 'tis clear that ye give ear, great Clouds whom we adore,
    (*To Streps.*) Did you hear their song, as they sail along, and their thunder's awful roar?
Streps. Blest Ones, I adore ye and fall before ye. My belly would fain reply
    To the thunder's roar. For I'm frightened sore, and all a-quake am I. . . .
Socr. Have done, have done! With such poor fun let clowning comedians please.
    You hold your tongue! Here comes in song a swarm of deities.
Chorus.   O maiden bringers of rain,   *antistrophe.*
        Let us arise and go where sunlight-smitten glow
        The lovely walls of Pallas and the proud Cecropidae;
          Where the rites none dare reveal again,
            Are wrought in mystery,
        And pilgrims throng the hallowed portals,
          And shrines of the Gods with gifts are dressed,
        And temples tower, with their carved Immortals,
          Amid processions of the blest,
        With wreaths and revels and offerings burning
          Through all the round of the circling year;
        And Brómius graces the spring returning,
        And music of choirs sets the senses yearning,
          And droning of pipes delights the ear.
Streps. But who are these, good Socrates, that utter a chant so splendid?
    For God's sake, say—of what race are *they?* Some heroines God-descended?

Socr. Pish! Here draw nigh the Clouds of the sky—great powers for
   'men of leisure.'
  'Tis they have lent us argument, and thought, and reason's measure,
  Verbosity and quackery, deceit and confutation.
Streps. That's why what they utter so set a-flutter my heart with per-
   turbation?
  It too would learn to twist and turn, and talk in vapoury phrases:
  Where one splits a straw, I would split it more, and counter each plea he
   raises.
  Therefore I long (if it is not wrong?) to see those shapes most holy.
Socr. By Parnes' height they come in sight. Look, now! I see them
   slowly
  Sink through the air.
Streps.   Quick, show me where!
Socr.   A mighty company,
  By wood and dale, aslant they sail. They come!
Streps.   I cannot see.
  What mean you? Where?
Socr.   By the entrance there.
Streps.   Yes . . . *some* dim shapes arise.
     The Chorus of Clouds dances in.
Socr. Well, anyhow you must see them *now*—or you've pumpkins in your
   eyes.
Streps. Good God, I see! Ah blessed ye! They fill the dancing-floor!
Socr. And were *you* so blind, that you never divined that these were Gods
   before?
Streps. By God, I thought that clouds were naught but vapour and moisture
   and mist.
Socr. Good Heavens, no! By the gifts They bestow whole hordes of
   frauds exist—
  False prophets, and then quack medicine-men, and fops beringed and
   curled,
  Dithyrambists, too, with tongues askew and nonsense Heaven-hurled,
  Whom They with pleasure support in leisure, for chanting in Their praise.
Streps. So *that*'s why their songs are filled with throngs of 'wild cloud-
   hosts ablaze,'
  'Dank creatures of air,' or 'tossing hair of the hundred-headed Titan,'
  Or 'birds crook-clawed that swim abroad, where the Heavens thunder
   and lighten,'
  Or 'vapours that yield the dew of the field.' And then with a rich
   collation
  Of turbot rare, or fat fieldfare, they are paid for their celebration.
Socr. Thus They repay it. And who shall gainsay it?

Streps.   But why does each Cloud-goddess—

If such they be, in verity—why wear they women's bodies?

For the clouds I know have never looked so.

Socr.   How then do they look to *you*?

Streps. I cannot tell you very well—like fleeces afloat in the blue,

With never a sign of the feminine.   But *these* have great big noses.

Socr. I will question *you*.   Now answer true.

Streps.   Ask on, as your mind disposes.

Socr. When you looked at the sky, did you ever descry a cloud in Centaur's guise?

While others appear like a wolf or a steer, or a leopard?

Streps.   And that implies?

Socr. Just that They fill what form They will.   If They see some man of
hair,

Shagged and unshorn as a savage born, like Xenophantes' heir,

To parody such loons as he, They take that Centaur-shape.

Streps. And what do they do, if Simōn's in view, for the public gold agape?

Socr. In imitation of *his* peculation, They turn to wolves that prey.

Streps. And was it thus, for Cleonymus, that just the other day

They looked like deer?—because in fear he flung away his shield?

Socr. And now that each sees here Cleisthenes, as *women* They come revealed!

Streps. (*bowing down to the Chorus*). Hail Ladies divine!   Oh be it mine,
great Queens in the Infinite crowned,

If ever man heard, to hear your word to Heaven's height resound.

Chorus-Leader. All hail, greybeard, thou many-yeared seeker for terms of
art!

(*To Socrates.*) High priest of wit and hairs to split, say now, what seeks
your heart?

For there is none but you alone, of sages Heaven-discerning,

We honour thus—save Pródicus (*him* for his mind and learning,

And you for your stalking, stately walking and the glances you cast
beside you,

And your feet left bare to the biting air, and your pride in us that guide
you).

Streps. O Earth beneath, what words they breathe!—solemn, portentous,
holy!

Socr. Said I not these were the true deities, all other faiths mere folly?

Streps. But in Earth's name!   You will not claim there's no Olympian
Zeus!

Socr. Zeus!—a mere fable!   Have done with your babble!

Streps.   What next will you deduce!

Then pray explain who makes it rain.   Let's hear your confutation.

Socr. The Clouds, of course!   'Tis proved by force of clearest demon-
stration.

For just tell *me*, did you ever see Zeus make it rain *without*?

Yet He *ought* to do, from a sky of blue, with never a cloud about.

Streps. Quite true, by Apollo!   Yes, that must follow.   What a clever
proof to give!

I fancied, I, that Zeus on high made water through a sieve.

But whence, reveal, the thunder-peal, that frightens me past bearing?

Socr. Upon my soul, just Clouds that roll.

Streps.   How, man of reckless daring?

Socr. When, filled with the weight of a watery freight, through Heaven
They go riding

And sagging there with the rain They bear, They shock together col-
liding,

They split in sunder with claps of thunder, by mere Necessity.

Streps. But by whom are They driven across the Heaven?   By Zeus it,
sure, must be.

Socr. Mere aberration!   The sky's rotation.

Streps.   I'd never heard that—never—

That Zeus was dead and, in His stead, Rotation reigns for ever.

But you have not taught by what is wrought the thunder's crash and
roar.

Socr. Did you not hear how I made it clear, by what I said before?

Clouds dense with water together batter, and thence their thunderous
tone.

Streps. And yet, in brief, prove your belief.

Socr.   By experience of your own.

You have known at least, at Athena's feast, your loaded belly
grumble;

Then did it not, with broth all hot, on a sudden roar and rumble?

Streps. By Apollo, indeed!   Just after my feed comes a terrible pertur-
bation

And that spoonful within makes a thunderous din—an incredible crepi-
tation. . . .

Socr. Why, then I tell ye, if your little belly can make so loud a sound,

Shall the infinite air above us there not vent a roar profound?

Yes, 'rumbling thunder' and 'grumbling under' are like in sound as
sense.

Streps. But whence comes the glare of the lightning there, with its bright
magnificence?—

While some by its flashes are scorched to ashes, and some it singes
merely?

From Zeus is sent that punishment on perjured sinners.   Clearly!

Socr. You moss-grown fool, of an outworn school! Moonstruck antiquity!

   If you think Zeus cares when a man forswears, why goes Theōrus free?
   Why spares He thus Cleonymus?   Why should Simōn escape?
   Yet His hand divine strikes His own shrine, or 'Sunium, Attica's cape,'
   Or a tall oak's crest.   By what possessed?   Can an oak do perjury?

Streps. I cannot tell.   You speak so well.   What, then, can lightning be?

Socr. When a wind that's dry ascends the sky and in the Clouds is pent,
   By Necessity, as you must see, it swells their integument,
   Like a bladder at first; and then they burst, with such compression
      loaded,
   And the air freed thus, by its impetus, is spontaneously exploded.

Streps. By Zeus, I recall, at His festival, the very same proceeding.
   For there with me was my family, and I roasted a paunch, not heeding
   To make a slit in the skin of it; and swelling on a sudden
   In my face, all hot, there burst the lot and fouled my eyes with pudden.

Leader. O man that aspirest—that desirest   our   wisdom's   high
      possessing,
   In Greece how great, and in Athens' state, how rich shall be thy blessing,
   If thou hast but reflection, *and* recollection, and a persevering heart,
   That does not baulk to stand or walk in the service of our art—
   If it is bold to bear the cold, nor cares if breakfast come,
   And can resign licence and wine, *and* the gymnasium—
   If in thy mind first rank's assigned (like a man of intelligence)
   To counsels of state, and high debate, and battles of eloquence.

Streps. If you want to find a stubborn mind, and care-worn sleeplessness,
   And a stomach of thrift that can make shift to dine on herbs and cress,
   You need not fear—you'll have them here.   No anvil's more resistant.

Leader. Will you hold, as we, that there are but three divinities existent?—
   All else disown but the Clouds alone, and Tongue, and the Void of Space?

Streps. I will not greet them, although I meet them—those others—face
   to face;
   No wine will I bring, no offering—not a single incense-grain!

Leader. Then, what you will, we shall fulfil.   You shall not ask in vain,
   If you revere and hold us dear, and sharpen well your wit.

Streps. Oh mistresses, I ask but this—a trifling benefit.
   Make me best to speak, of any Greek—by a hundred mile the best.

Leader. What you have sought, you shall be taught.   You shall be skil-
      fullest,
   When they convoke the Attic folk, at passing all your measures.

Streps. Oh, not *decrees*!   I seek not these.   They're *not* among my
   pleasures.
   My object's *this*—to evade justice, and baulk each creditor.

Leader. What you would gain, you shall obtain. Small favours you implore!
   Take courage, friend! Do but attend to our ministrants' tuition.
Streps. I will obey; just as you say. So desperate my position,
   So sharp my needs, from Corinth steeds and my marriage of perdition!

> Now let them do their very worst,
> With blows torment this body of mine,
> With cold or squalor, hunger or thirst—
> Ay, flay my hide as a skin for wine,
> So long as I leave my debts unpaid,
> And rise to seem in every eye
> Voluble, shameless, unafraid;
> An impudent forger of every lie,
> A fox, a pettifogging cheat;
> Brazen to bully, smooth to wheedle,
> Cunning at law for all deceit;
> A twisty trimmer as sharp as a needle,
> Who will do aught to eat!
> If they will but win me such names as these,
> They may do whatever they like with me—
> Ay, if they please,
> By God they may mince me to sausages,
> To serve in their Reflectory.

Leader.   Here's a fellow can endure!—
       Ever ready, full of daring, spirit high.
  If you learn what you are taught, I can promise you for sure,
       Your fame shall top the sky.
Streps. But what's the lot in store for me?
Leader. At my feet you still shall find
  Happiest life of humankind.
Streps.   Such fortune shall I really see?
Leader. Yes, crowds shall wait, assembled, before your gates for you,
  Wild to have a hearing, to gain an interview;
    Consulting your acuity
    On suits where thousands form your fee.
  (*To Socrates.*) So take the old man and follow your plan, to polish his
    education.
  Set out to find his powers of mind and ratiocination.
Socr. Come now, and tell me of your character.
  That known, I then can bring to the attack
  Our latest engines and contrivances.
Streps. God! You don't mean to besiege me and assault me?
Socr. No, but I need some brief details about you.
  Is your memory good?

Streps.   Good Heavens, yes and no.
  As creditor, there's nothing I forget:
  As debtor—why, there's nothing I remember!
Socr. And have you any natural gift for talking?
Streps. Not talking—but I *am* quite good at *taking*.
Socr. Then how do you hope to learn?
Streps.   No fear, I'll manage.
Socr. Look! If I throw you some deep proposition
  On themes celestial, mind you snap it up.
Streps. What, must I gobble wisdom like a dog?
Socr. A very illiterate and barbarous fellow!
  I fear, old man, you sadly need a flogging.
  Come tell me now, supposing someone beats you,
  What do you do?
Streps.   Why, first I take a beating.
  I wait a little, then take witnesses.
  Then, in a flash, I take him into court.
Socr. Come now, take off your cloak.
Streps.   Have I done wrong, then?
Socr. No, but all strip who pass within this portal.
Streps. But I'm not searching here for stolen goods!
Socr. Doff it, I tell you. No more trifling!
Streps. (*taking off his cloak*).   Say now,
  If I'm diligent and keen in all my studies,
  Which of your students shall I most resemble?
Socr. You?—you will be another Chaerephon.
Streps. Oh horrible—look like a living corpse!
Socr. Have done with chatter! Follow me inside
  And waste no time about it.
Streps.   But give me first
  A honey-cake, in case I meet with monsters.
  I'm frightened now as if I were descending
  Into Trophōnius' cavern.
Socr. Get on! Enough of hanging round the door.
           The two descend into the dark interior.
Chorus.   Go!—and we all must wish good speed
                    To a heart so bold.
                    He merits to succeed,
                    A man that, grown so old,
                    Although his years are sinking
                    Yet dares to undertake
                    Ideas of a younger tone, unshrinking
                    For wisdom's sake.

They turn to the audience.

Leader. O my hearers, *I* will tell you, now, the simple verity—
Be my witness Dionysus, who has bred and nurtured me!
May I be acclaimed as victor and as poet true-inspired,
Sure as *I* thought *you* judicious, weighing well what you admired,
And this play, so deeply laboured, of my comedies the best.
So I brought it out before you, let you taste it earliest—
All in vain, for I was beaten!—put to most unworthy shame,
By the work of vulgar scribblers! And on *you* I throw the blame—
You that are no foolish judges—you for whom I laboured so!
Still, I will not yet abandon those of you whose taste I know.
For since first, in this same theatre, men to write for whom is pleasure
Gave my Modest Son, and Wanton, praise in full and generous measure
(*Then* I was a maiden poet, dared not show the babe I bred,
So exposed it, and another nursed my bantling in my stead;
None the less ye nobly reared it, brought it to its full estate)—
From thenceforward I have warrant of your judgment, and its weight.
So to-day this piece, its sister, like Electra in the play,
Comes to seek some kindred spirits, wise to judge her worth as they;
She will know at sight the tresses crowning once her brother's brow.
Note too how the girl is modest, she that comes before you now—
With no gross appendage on her . . . for the mirth of boys half bred;
She brings no licentious dances, jokes about the bald of head,
No grey pantaloon that, talking, interrupts his part to hit
With his stick the other actor, just to mask his barren wit.
She does *not* rush, loudly shrieking, on the scene with torches' flame;
All her trust is in good verses, and the worth herself can claim.
　　Such I am, as man and poet, with no long-haired affectations.
I do *not* attempt to fool you with old hackneyed situations.
My brain always lies in labour with new themes for you to see,
Never twice alike and, always, full of ingenuity.
I, when Cleon's power was greatest, in his belly rammed the clown;
Yet I scorned to jump upon him, after fate had struck him down,
While these fellows, without ceasing, once they thought they'd got a hold,
At Hyperbolus the wretched, and his mother, scoff and scold.
It was Eupŏlis began it—thrust on you his *Maricas*;
From my *Knights* he dared to steal it—spoiling what he stole, the ass!—
Foisting in a drunken beldam, Phrynichus' old fantasy,
Eaten by the ocean-monster—just to dance indecently!
Then there came Hermippus likewise—parodied Hyperbolus;
At Hyperbolus the others volley plays as scurrilous.

One and all, from *me* they plunder my old adage of the eels:
I will never try to tickle those to whom such stuff appeals.
But all you that hear me gladly—you that love my new ideas,
Shall be praised for wit and judgment, through the length of coming years.

Chorus.   Lord enthroned in the Heavens o'er us,   *strophe.*
                                Whose sovereign might none may withstand,
                        I call Thee first to hear our chorus,
                                Zeus!   And Thee, whose ruthless hand
            Makes tremble, with its trident the sea-wave and the land!
                        And hear Thou too our voices praising,
                                Our own great sire, all-nurturing Air!
                        And Thou, whose coursers Heaven-blazing
                                Make the wide earth glitter fair,
                        Godhead greeted in the skies
                        By mortal and immortal eyes!

Leader. Most enlightened of spectators, turn your minds to what we tell.
    For—we say it to your faces—you have used us far from well.
    Us alone you never offer slaughtered beast or cup of wine,
    Though we guard you well and truly, more than any power divine,
    Watching still the weal of Athens.   If your folly votes to sail
    On some crack-brained expedition, then we thunder or we hail.
    Once when you elected general him all Heaven disavows,
    That curst Paphlagonian tanner, terribly we knit our brows;
    Dread our threats, 'with thunders rolling and with lightnings flashing
        thick,'
    On her path the Moon was darkened and the Sun turned down his wick,
    Swearing that no more henceforward he would shine to give you light,
    If you sent the ranks of Athens under Cleon to the fight.
    None the less he *was* your chosen.   For, they say, on Athens lies
    Still the curse of evil counsel.   Yet though *you* are so unwise,
    Still the Gods amend your follies, turn your errors for the best.
    So here too we can foretell you how your fortunes shall be blest—
    Just condemn this cormorant Cleon, fat with theft and stolen fee,
    To be clapped with greedy gullet choking in the pillory!
    If ye do this, notwithstanding all ye have done ill before,
    As in ancient days for Athens all shall yet go well once more.

Chorus.   Next, to Thee our praise be given,   *antistrophe.*
                                Phoebus who art throned divine
                        Where Cynthus' horn towers high to Heaven!
                                Artemis, our praise be Thine,
            Whom Lydia's daughters honour in Thy gold Ephesian shrine!

      Praise to Thee, our land's defender,
        Pallas, Aegis-bearing Queen!
      Praise to Thee, whose torches' splendour
        On Parnassus' crags is seen,
      Lord of the Delphic Bacchanals,
      Voice that still to revel calls!

Leader. When we started out together, here to meet you, on our way,
   As it chanced, Selēne met us and she asked us all to say,
   After duly greeting Athens and her loyal confederacy,
   That you have provoked her anger, treating so discourteously
   One that seeks all ways to serve you—and with deeds, not specious lies.
   First, a drachma's worth of torches, monthly, you economize
   Thanks to *her*; for of an evening, going out, you all can say:
   'Boy, no need for buying torches. There's a lovely moon to-day.'
   And in other ways she aids you. But 'tis all in vain, says she,
   For you keep the days all wrongly—mix them higgledy-piggledy.
   So, she says, the Gods grow angry—rage against her, one and all,
   When your blind miscalculations make them miss a festival,
   Turning homeward disappointed, all the promised dinner lacking.
   When you *should* be sacrificing, you sit judging suits, and racking;
   Or, again, when we Immortals celebrate some solemn fast,
   Mourning for the day when Memnon, or Sarpēdon, deathward passed,
   Then you come with *your* libations, and your laughter! That is why,
   When Hyperbolus was chosen for the sacred embassy,
   We of late puffed off his garland—we, the Gods—to teach the loon,
   That his days of life henceforward should be governed by the moon.

Socrates reappears.

Socr. Never—by Chaos, Air, and Respiration!—
   Never have I set eyes on such a bumpkin,
   So stupid, dunderheaded, and forgetful.
   The lightest chips of ratiocination
   He loses before he learns them. But no matter—
   I'll call the fellow out of doors to daylight.
   Strepsíades! Take up your bed and come.
Streps. (*emerging with his pallet*). Bring out my bed? The bugs inside
     won't let me.
Socr. Quick, put it down!—and listen!
Streps.   There you are. . . .
   But why should I learn things everybody knows?
Socr. Never you mind! Lie down in bed and—
Streps.   What?

Socr. Meditate deeply on your own affairs.

Streps. Oh not in bed, please!   If I must lie down,
  Do let me meditate upon the ground!

Socr. No other way but this.

Streps. (*getting into bed*).   Oh misery!
  What damages I'll have to pay these vermin!

Chorus. Let thy thoughts twist and wriggle; reflect and rock thy head,
                    And grow not weary.
                If baffled, turn thy thoughts instead
                    To a new theory.
  Let no care-charming slumber upon thine eyes be shed.

Streps.   Ow!   Ow!

Leader.   What ails thee?   What irks thee?

Streps. Wretch that I am, I'm dying!   From the bed
  The enemy creep out to exverminate me.
            All along my ribs they're preying,
                Now my very lifeblood's shed.
            Round my loins the things are straying,
            And my buttocks they are flaying.
                They will leave me dead!

Leader. Be not overmuch annoyed.

Streps.   How!   Is *this* not hard?
                    Lost my gold; my shoes are lost;
                    Lost, skin and life!   So trouble-tossed,
                    Even sleep I must avoid—
                        Sing here on guard,
                    Till I myself am near destroyed!

Socr. Come, fellow!   You're not thinking?

Streps.   What!   Not I?
  By God, I am.

Socr.   What have you thought of, then?

Streps. Whether these bugs will leave an inch of me.

Socr. To Hell with you!

Streps.   Good sir, I'm there already!

Socr. You must not flinch.   Come, wrap the bed-clothes round you.
  You must excogitate some fraudulence,
  Some fine prevarication.

Streps.   Ah, if someone
  With all these sheepskins only could perspire me
  With a real gift for fleecing!

Socr. Come, let me see now what the man is doing.
                                    [*He peers under the coverlets.*
  Hey!   Are you sleeping?

Streps.   By Apollo, no!

Socr. Got hold of anything?

Streps.   Good Heavens, no.

Socr. Surely of *something*? . . .

Cover yourself again.   Get *some* idea!

Streps. Of what?   *You* ought to tell me, Socrates.

Socr. First think what you desire, and tell me that.

Streps. But I *have* told you that—ten thousand times!

It's just my debts—how to avoid repayment.

Socr. Come now, wrap up, and subtilize your thought,

Survey the whole, analyse, subdivide

Each detail point by point.

Streps.   Poor, wretched me!

Socr. Calm now!   Keep calm!   And if a point defeats you,

Leave it a moment—then with mind refreshed

Re-view the matter, poise it in the balance.

Streps. Oh Socrates, dear pet!

Socr.   What now, old man?

Streps. I have a notion of appropriation.

Socr. Propound it, then.

Streps.   How think you, if I—

Socr.   What?

Streps. Suppose I hired a Thessalian sorceress

To pull the moon, one night, down from the sky,

And shut it up inside a rounded box

(Like they keep mirrors in), and kept it there?

Socr. What good to you would *that* be?

Streps.   Can you ask?

Why, if no moon should ever rise again,

I need not pay my debts.

Socr.   And why not pay?

Streps. Because they're borrowed till the next new *moon*.

Socr. Fine!   And now here's another pretty problem.

Suppose a suit against you for five talents.

How, tell me, could you quash it?

Streps. How?   How?   I cannot say.   But let me think.

Socr. Do not constrict your thoughts in a narrow circle,

Centred about yourself—let them soar to Heaven,

Like a cockchafer, thread-bound by the foot.

Streps. I have it now!—the cunningest subterfuge,

You must yourself admit it.

Socr.   Well, say on.

Streps. You must have seen at the apothecaries'

That pretty kind of stone—that's all transparent,
And used for kindling fire.

Socr.   A burning-glass?

Streps. That's it.   Suppose I got a glass like that
And, as the clerk was writing out the suit,
I stood behind him, so, on the sunward side,
And melted what he'd written?

Socr.   By the Graces,
A pretty notion!

Streps.   Ah how pleased I am!
To think I've quashed a suit for five whole talents!

Socr. Quick, now, and snap this problem.

Streps.   Well, what *is* it?

Socr. As a defendant, how would you save your case,
If it went against you for want of witnesses?

Streps. Quite easily and simply.

Socr.   How?

Streps.   Why, thus.
While there was still one case upon the list
Ahead of mine, I'd run and hang myself.

Socr. You talk mere twaddle.

Streps.   Heavens, but I *would*!
No one can sue me dead.

Socr. You drivel.   Go!   I will not teach you longer.

Streps. But why?   For Heaven's sake, good Socrates!

Socr. But you forget things just as soon as learnt.
What was, for instance, your first lesson?   Say.

Streps. Come, let me see, what was it first?   What first?
About that thing we use for kneading flour?
Dear me, what *was* it?

Socr.   Get you gone to Hell,
Most stupid and sieve-headed of old dotards!

Streps. Oh me, poor wretch, what ever shall I do?
I'm ruined unless I learn a twisty tongue.
O Lady Clouds, give me some good advice.

Leader. Old man, we should advise you, if you have
A grown-up son,
To make him come and study in your place.

Streps. Why, yes, I have a fine young gentleman.
But *he* won't study.   What's to become of me?

Leader. But *you* allow it?

Streps.   Yes, for he's strong and lusty,
His mother a high-flown dame with grand connections.

Still, I'll go after him.   If he refuses,
I'll throw him—nothing shall stop me—out of doors.
But wait a moment while I run inside.   [*Strepsíades runs into his house.*
Chorus (*to Socrates*).   See with what gains we bless you!   Of all in
                    Heaven, *we*
              Alone could do it.
          Whatever your commandment be,
              He will pursue it:
So wild the expectations of his blind fatuity.
              But gobble your profits while you may;
For frail are such occasions, and fast they pass away.

          Socrates goes in.   Strepsíades reappears with his son.

Streps. No more, by all the Fogs, my house shall hold you.
    Off!—to your Uncle Megacles!—and gnaw
    His marble columns.
Pheid. In the name of goodness, what's the matter, father?
    By Zeus of Olympus, you have lost your wits.
Streps. Hark to him!   Hark to him!   'Zeus of Olympus.'   Fool,
    At years like yours, still to believe in Zeus!
Pheid. What are you laughing at?
Streps.   To think that you
    Are both so young and yet so antiquated.
    Come closer to me, boy, and let me tell you.
    I'll teach you something to make a man of you.
    But breathe no word of it to living soul.
Pheid. What is it then?
Streps.   Just now you swore by Zeus.
Pheid. I did.
Streps.   Now see how wonderful is learning.
    There *is* no Zeus, Pheidippides!
Pheid.   Then who—
Streps. Rotation's cast him out and reigns instead.
Pheid. Oh pooh!   What drivel!
Streps.   But it's true, I tell you.
Pheid. Who says so?
Streps.   Socrates, true son of Mēlos,
    And Chaerephon, who knows the tracks of fleas.
Pheid. Have you come to such a pitch of craziness
    That you trust these lunatics?
Streps.   Oh hush, my boy.
    You must not slander men so intellectual,
    So subtle—*and* so economical

That never one of them has had his hair cut,
Put oil upon his skin, or visited
The bathhouse for a bath.   While *you*, as if
I was a corpse already, have washed me clean
Of all my livelihood!
So come at once and study in my place.
Pheid. What good can anyone learn from such a set?
Streps. Learn!   You can learn the sum of human wisdom.
You'll find at least what a dolt and clown you are.
Just wait a moment.   [*He runs into his house.*
Pheid. Good God, my father's mad.   What *shall* I do?
Bring him to court and have him found insane?
Or tell the coffin-makers that he's senseless?
Streps. (*reappearing with a cock in one hand, a hen in the other, and holding up
the cock*).   Now then!   Look here!   What do you think this is?
Pheid. A chicken.
Streps.   A chicken; very good.   And this? (*Holding up the
hen.*)
Pheid. A chicken.
Streps.   Both the same!   Ridiculous!
Never say that again.   You must call *this* (*showing the cock*)
A chicken, and this one a 'chickenette.'
Pheid. 'A chickenette'!   Is *this* your precious knowledge
Learnt at the feet of these same sons of earth!
Streps. This and much more.   But everything I learnt,
It slipped my mind again—I grow too old.
Pheid. And just for that you've gone and lost your cloak!
Streps. I didn't lose it—it got lost in thought.
Pheid. And what have you done, then, with your shoes, you madman?
Streps. Like Pericles, 'in the good cause I gave them.'
But up!   Away!   Let's hurry.   Humour your father
In *this*—and *then* commit what sins you like!
Why to be sure, when you were six years old,
A little lisping boy, I humoured *you*—
My very first obol earned as juryman
Bought you a go-cart at the feast of Zeus.
Pheid. Take it from *me* that one day you'll regret it!
Streps. Splendid!   You will! (*Running over to Socrates' house.*)   Here,
Socrates!   Come here!
Come out of doors.   I've coaxed my unwilling son
And here he is!
Socr. (*appearing*). I see he's still a youngster
And not well tried in our uplifting methods.

Pheid. You'd be well tried, uplifted to a gallows!

Streps. To Hell with you! How dare you curse the Master!

Socr. Just listen to him! What a booby's accent—
   Drawling with mouth agape about the 'gaallows'!
   How could *he* learn to evade a condemnation,
   Cite witnesses, invalidate a charge?
   Yet even Hyperbolus learnt it—for a talent!

Streps. Never mind, teach him! He's a natural genius.
   Why, as a little fellow, just so high,
   At home he modelled houses, carved out boats,
   Contrived his little go-carts out of fig-wood;
   Yes, he would chop from peel of pomegranates
   Such frogs as you'd not credit.
   Let him just learn your pair of arguments—
   The better, whatever it is, and then the worse one,
   That beats the better, though it *is* dishonest;
   Or, if not both, at all events the bad one.

Socr. Then he shall learn from each of them in person.
   I will be gone.

Streps.   Only make sure of *this*—
   That he can baffle every honest plea.

> *Socrates and Strepsiades withdraw. The two Arguments enter;
> perhaps brought on in cages, dressed as fighting cocks, and flying
> at each other when released.*

Honest Argument. Come on! Before the audience now
   Show, if you dare, your brazen brow!

Dishonest Argument. Wherever you will. With a crowd to hear,
   I'll smash you the faster, never fear.

Hon. A. Smash *me*! What are *you*?

Dishon. A.   An argument.

Hon. A. The worse!

Dishon. A.   No matter. I'll leave you rent
   To shreds, although you claim you're truer.

Hon. A. And how so clever?

Dishon. A.   By bringing newer
   Syllogisms and sophistries.

Hon. A. (*pointing to the audience*). True, your tricks flourish, thanks to
                      these
   Fools—

Dishon. A.   No, not fools but wise are they.

Hon. A. I'll annihilate *you*.

Dishon. A.   And how then, pray?

Hon. A. By speaking justly.

Dishon. A.　　　　　　　　　　With this conclusion
I crush you—Justice is mere illusion.

Hon. A. Illusion!

Dishon. A.　　　　　　Why, yes!　Where does Justice dwell?

Hon. A. With the Gods above.

Dishon. A.　　　　　　　　　　Then perhaps you'll tell
Why Zeus has not perished, if Justice reigns,
For putting his own old father in chains.

Hon. A. Ugh!　Worse and worse depravity!
A basin, quick!　It sickens me.

Dishon. A. You drivelling old decrepitude!

Hon. A. And you're a libertine and lewd—

Dishon. A. What a nosegay of roses!

Hon. A.　　　　　　　　　　A buffoon without bridle!

Dishon. A. You wreathe me with lilies!

Hon. A.　　　　　　　　　　A wretch parricidal!

Dishon. A. What golden opinions you heap on my head!

Hon. A. In better times you'd have felt them like lead.

Dishon. A. But now it does good to my name—not evil.

Hon. A. Shameless you are!

Dishon. A.　　　　　　And *you*'re primeval.

Hon. A. You make our youth,
Corrupted now, forsake the schools.
Yet one day Athens shall see the truth
And how you have mistaught the fools.

Dishon. A. You're horribly shabby.

Hon. A.　　　　　　　　Magnificent
Are *you*!　Yet you called yourself 'as poor
As Telephus' once; and you begged!—content
With only a walletful to gnaw,
Of pettifogging argument!

Dishon. A. How clever I was—　*Hon. A.* How infatuate—

　　　　　　　　　　　　　　　[*They both speak at once.*

Dishon. A.—in the days you recall!　*Hon. A.*—are you, and the state
　　　　　　　　That lets you live
　　　　　　　　To make our youth degenerate!

Dishon. A. (*pointing to Pheidippides*).　You shan't teach *him*, you primitive!

Hon. A. I must, if his salvation matters
And he's not to grow just a fool that chatters.

Dishon. A. (*to Pheidippides*).　Come *here*!　Let this maniac go his way.

Hon. A. Hands off him!—or dearly you shall pay!

    Leader. Enough of this recrimination.
      State your older education,
        You—and *you*, your new.   In turn.
      After hearing each oration,
        He can choose from which to learn.

Hon. A. I consent.
Dishon. A.   And *I* consent.
Leader. Who then begins the argument?
Dishon. A.   *That* I permit him.
  Whatever the reasons he may find,
  Thence I will make me arrows to hit him,
  With notions and quips of the latest kind;
  Till in the end, if he dares to speak
  One syllable more, he shall be stung
  To death—close-riddled, eye and cheek,
    By the barbs of my hornet-tongue.

                                    strophe.
Chorus. Now shall this pair of rivals, with their eloquent invention
    Of phrase and thought adorning their high sententious theme,
  Prove which of them is master in argument's contention,
  While all the fate of wisdom is staked on this dissension,
    Where meet our friends together in one last clash supreme.

First, you that once crowned with virtues renowned the men of olden
    days,
Those truths impart that stir your heart, and tell us of your ways.
Hon. A. Now shall be told, in times of old how youth was reared and bred,
  When flourished the cause of *my* just laws and temperance was not dead.
  First, never a word of chatter was heard—for boys that was the rule;
  In disciplined order the lads of each quarter would stream to the harpist's
    school,
  Uncloaked together, whatever the weather—although like meal it
    snowed.
  Modestly seated, they all repeated, learning by heart, an ode:
  'Far, far away the harp-strings play' or 'Pallas, sacker of cities'—
  Keeping the while the manly style of our fathers' ancient ditties.
  And if some loon dared play buffoon with precious affectations,
  Such as to-day, in Phrȳnis' way, fill song with complications,
  By many a blow he was made to know he was murdering the Muse.
  In the wrestling-school it was the rule that every lad should choose,
  When he took his seat, a pose discreet, not shameless nor ill-bred . . .
  And then at table no boy was able to take the radish-head,
  Nor to snatch there at his elders' fare—parsley or anise—or sit
  Crossing his knees, or love delicacies, or yield to a laughing fit.

Dishon. A. Pooh, how antique!   You might as well speak of the grasshoppers of gold

In our fathers' hair—of stale bards that were—old fusty feasts—

Hon. A.   But hold!

By such ancient ways it was mine to raise the men of Marathon.

But now the young by *you* are flung thick mantles to put on—

I choke as I glance at our youth that dance in our Athena's feast,

Each shivering waist with a shield embraced, not honouring *Her* in the
least.

Therefore, young man, choose *you* my plan—my cause is better far.

Follow my paths, and shun the baths, and hate the agora.

Dare to feel shame at what brings blame; blaze up, if mockers jeer you;

And yield your place with a proper grace, when older men come near you.

Honour their worth that gave you birth, and never earn disgrace;

Be your heart the shrine where the shape divine of Conscience keeps her
place.

Wait not before a dancer's door, lest while you gape at that,

An apple tossed by a wench that's lost should lay your honour flat.

What your father shall say, do you obey, nor mock him as 'patriarch
perished'

With thankless sneers—by his ageing years your fledgling youth was
cherished.

Dishon. A. If you take for truth what he says, good youth, by Bacchus,
you will get

As big a dunce as Hippocrates' sons (those pigs!)—and a 'mother's pet.'

Hon. A. No, bright of breast—youth's flower at its best—in the wrestling-
school you'll stay,

Not hale through the streets your prickly conceits, as the young men do
to-day,

Nor yet be brought before a court for some pettifogging greed,

But in Academe, where the olives gleam, on the track you'll try your
speed—

A friend at your side, straight, true, and tried—head bound with the
milk-white reed,

Your blithe youth blent with the honeysuckle scent and the blossoming
lime-tree boughs,

Till your heart shall sing with the joy of spring, when the plane to the
elm-tree soughs.

> *If* to my counsels you give ear,
>   *If* you store them in your thought,
> Then yours, from year to year,
> A brawny chest and a skin that's clear,
>   Shoulders broad and a tongue that's short. . . .

But if you live like the modern young,
　　Then you shall win
A pigeon chest and a pallid skin,
Shoulders too small, too long a tongue . . .
　　And an endless reach in public speech.
That foul is fair he would persuade you,
　　And better, worse;
He will not rest till he has made you
　　Loose as Antímachus, as perverse.

antistrophe.

Chorus. O follower of Wisdom in her glorious exaltations,
　　How fair your pleading blossoms with the flower of modest ways!
Happy the men that lived so, in bygone generations!
Come now, you clever master of specious calculations,
　　Produce your paradoxes. For *he* has won our praise.

You will need some cunning answers to meet the case we've heard,
If you would not be beaten, and derided as absurd.
Dishon. A. Why, all the while I've listened, my heart was like to choke
With arguments confuting every word he spoke.
'The worse cause'—so they call me, the men of intellect,
Because I first contrived the way to cavil and object
Against what stands established by justice and the laws.
This is a power worth thousands—to take the worser cause
And yet, by clever pleading, no less to win one's suit.
Now for his boasted training—see first how I refute
His stupid banning of warm baths. For why should not
A man, I ask, prefer to bathe in water that is hot?
Hon. A. Because that cursed habit makes him effeminate.
Dishon. A. Ah there I have you on the hip—now just you wait!
Pray tell me, of all the sons of Zeus, who was the best
In strength of spirit, think you? In labours manliest?
Hon. A. Never a better man than Hēracles, I hold.
Dishon. A. Then what of 'Hēraclean baths'? None gives that name to cold.
Yet who hád heart so virile?
Hon. A.　　　　　　　　　　　Such are the things they say,
To fill our baths with striplings, chattering all the day,
And leave the schools of wrestling abandoned to neglect!
Dishon. A. And then from public places you would bar them! I object.
Is public speaking evil? Then what has Homer meant
By making his ancient Nestor, and his wise men, 'eloquent'?
Such mastery of the tongue—this fellow here denies
The young should ever learn it. And I—I say he lies.

And temperate, too, he bids them be—both views absurd!
What man was ever better, I ask, that *you* have heard,
For the temperance he practised?   Prove if I speak amiss!

Hon. A. Many!   The Gods gave Pēleus his sword divine for this.

Dishon. A. A sword!   A fine advantage to the poor wretch for his pains!
The lamp-making Hyperbolus, by vileness, counts his gains
In gold beyond all telling.   *He* did not need a sword!

Hon. A. But Thĕtis, for his continence, took Pēleus as her lord.

Dishon. A. And then she went and left him.   The man was too polite,
No passionate bedfellow with whom to pass the night.
Rough handling pleases women.   You relic of the past!

(*To Pheidippides.*) Think, if your choice is continence, what pleasures
            must be cast
For ever, young man, behind you and what you forgo hereafter—
Feasting and wine and women, gaming and love and laughter.
And then, with these joys forbidden, what use is life to you?
Enough!—and think of the shifts that Nature drives us to.
You slip, and you fall in love—a little intrigue—you're caught—
Ruined, with never a word to say!   But if you're taught
By me, you can follow your humour, laugh, wanton, stick at naught.
For if you're caught in a love affair, you simply tell
Her husband you are guiltless.   For has not Zeus as well,
Many a time, been vanquished by women and by love?
How then should you, poor mortal, be stronger than God above?

Hon. A. If radish and ashes are his fate, what subtle plea
Can save him from being branded as a shameless debauchee?

Dishon. A. And if he *is?*   Say, how is he the worse?

Hon. A. Upon the contrary, what deeper curse?

Dishon. A. If here I prove you wrong, what will you say?

Hon. A. I'll hold my tongue.   How not?

Dishon. A.   Then tell me, pray,
For Counsellors, whom do we take?

Hon. A. Why, debauchees.

Dishon. A.   Yes, no mistake!
What sort of man turns tragic poet?

Hon. A. Why, debauchees.

Dishon. A.   And well you know it.
Whom do we choose as orators?

Hon. A. Why, debauchees.

Dishon. A.   You've lost your cause.
Even to *you* that must be clear?
Now turn to the spectators here.
Look at them well.

Hon. A.   I do, I do.

Dishon. A. And what see you?

Hon. A. By Heaven, the greater part of these

   I see, are only debauchees.

   (*Pointing.*) Here's one I know—and another there—

   And that one with the lanky hair.

Dishon. A. Then your reply?

Hon. A. Good God, you have the victory!   (*Running over towards the*

   Reflectory.)

   O libertines, now take from me

   My cloak, for I

   Desert to your majority.

      He goes in, pursued by his opponent. Socrates and Strepsiades reappear.

Socr. (*to Strepsiades*). Now then! Do you want to take your son away,

   Or will you have me teach him how to speak?

Streps. Oh teach him, drub him soundly, and remember

   To whet me well his tongue; with one edge sharp

   For petty lawsuits, and the other side

   Trenchant to deal with things of larger scope.

Dishon. A. No fear, we'll make a perfect sophist of him.

Streps. A poor sick wretch, more likely!

Leader. Off with you all! (*To Strepsiades.*) I think, you will repent it.

      Strepsiades re-enters his house, the other two disappear into the Reflectory.

   (*To the audience.*) Now it's time to tell the judges, if in justice they accord

   Favour to our cloudy Chorus, what shall be their due reward.

   First of all, at every season when you wish to cultivate,

   We will rain upon your acres, while your neighbours have to wait;

   Next, we'll keep a watch unfailing on your vineyards, fruit, and grain,

   That no drought shall ever harm them, no excessive storms of rain.

   But if mortal does dishonour to our race, of Heaven born,

   Let him heed the retribution that shall fall upon his scorn.

   All his lands shall yield him nothing, neither sustenance nor wine.

   For when first unfolds the blossom on his olive or his vine,

   We will nip them, we will smite them, as with bullets from a sling.

   If he's making bricks, and building, we will pour; and clattering

   From our hands, the hail shall shatter all the tiles above his head.

   If he celebrates his marriage, if his friends or kinsmen wed,

   All night long we'll send a deluge. He may wish he had his birth

   Far away in rainless Egypt, rather than misjudge our worth.

Streps. (*reappearing from his house*). Four days to run, then three, then

   two, then one;

   And then the day that, past all other days,

   I fear and dread and most abominate,

Falls sheer upon me—last day of the month.
For every man that I owe money to,
Vows he will sue me to my utter ruin,
Though all I ask's so small, so reasonable:
'Sir, don't claim *that* part yet; and part defer;
And part remit.' They swear, if things go thus,
They'll never get their payment; cursing me
As rogue, with threats to bring me into court.
Let them bring me, if they want to! Much I care,
If my Pheidippides has learnt to speak.
Now I shall know—I only need to knock
At the Reflectory here. Boy! Boy, I say!

Socr. (*opening*). Good day, Strepsíades.

Streps.   The same to you.
First, pray accept this bag. (*Handing a bag of meal.*)
The Master must have his honorarium.
And now my son, whom late you took as pupil—
Say, has he yet acquired that art of speaking?

Socr. He has.

Streps.   Well done, O Queen Duplicity!

Socr. So now in any suit you can win your case.

Streps. Even if witnesses can swear I borrowed?

Socr. The more the better!—though there are a thousand!

Streps.   'My voice at its loudest shall ring on high.'
          Weep, petty usurers, weep and cry,
With your principals, your compound interest!
Never again shall *you* hold *me* oppressed,
          So fine a son have I,
          Whom in these walls they rear
          With a tongue of two-edged splendour,
Dread of my foes, stay of my house, defender
          Of his father from all fear.
          Run, call him forth to meet me!
          'O son, come out to greet me,
          To your father's words give ear.' [*Pheidippides emerges.*

Socr.   Here comes your son.

Streps.   My darling boy!

Socr.   Take him, begone!   [*He withdraws.*

Streps.   O son beloved, Oh joy, Oh joy!
What a pleasure it is to see you look so pale!
Yes, now indeed you have a denying air,
A disputatious aspect; all the flower
Of native impudence, that still seems asking:

'What's that you say?'—the poise that makes a knave
Seem innocent, the injurer the injured;
In fact, a face of purest Attic mould.
So now come save me, as you ruined me once.

Pheid. What is it, then, alarms you?

Streps. The day called of the old moon and the new.

Pheid. Is there a day at once both old and new?

Streps. Well, that's the day they threaten they will sue me.

Pheid. They'll lose their suits then. It's impossible
For one day to be two.

Streps.   Impossible?

Pheid. How could it be, unless it's possible
For the same woman to be old and young!

Streps. Well, that's the law.

Pheid.   I don't believe they know
Themselves the law's true meaning.

Streps.   Then what *is* it?

Pheid. Old Solon had a democratic heart.

Streps. What's that to do with the old moon and the new?

Pheid. Why, he ordained that summonses should fall
Upon *two* days; but that all court deposits
Be paid on the *new*-moon day.

Streps.   If that were so,
Why speak at all of *old* moons?

Pheid.   My good sir,
So that upon the *first* day all defendants
Might come to terms, if willing; and if not,
Begin their troubles when the new moon came.

Streps. But then the magistrates should take deposits
From litigants upon the new-moon day,
Not the day of old-and-new.

Pheid.   Well, I suppose
They're like the tasters of the public feasts—
They're in such haste to pocket those deposits,
That they 'taste' them one day sooner.

Streps. Splendid! (*To the audience.*) Poor idiots, why gape you
there,
Stupid as stones, piled up in rows like jars,
Flocks of dumb sheep, the prey of us the clever!
Now for a little ode of panegyric
On the triumphs of my son here, and myself.
(*Sings.*) Thee, Strepsiades, we bless
     For thy great ingeniousness,

> For the son that is thy heir.
> So my demesmen will confess,
> And my friends declare,
> Envying you, triumphant in every case you plead.
> But I've a banquet for you, son.   Come in, and feed!

> *They enter the house.   The creditor Pāsias appears, with a witness.*

Pāsias. What!   Must a man forgo his own good money?
Never!   Far better have refused him *then,*
Unblushingly, than land in all this trouble.
For now, to get my lendings back again,
I have to drag you here as evidence
And make an enemy of my own demesman.
But never, while I live, will I disgrace
My Attic blood.   And so I hereby summons (*knocking at the door*)
Strepsiades—

Streps. (*coming out*). And who's this fellow here?
Pās.—for the day of old moon and new.
Streps.   Bear witness now,
He has summonsed me for *two* days.   And for what?
Pās. Twelve minas, that you borrowed when you bought
That dapple-grey horse.
Streps.   A horse!   Just hear the man!
When everyone knows I loathe all equitation!
Pās. Why, yes, by Zeus!   And you swore by Heaven to pay.
Streps. Why, no, by Zeus!   *Then* my Pheidippides
Had not yet learnt the unanswerable plea.
Pās. And now, do you tell me, you'll disown your debt?
Streps. Or else what good would his instruction be?
Pās. You'll swear, then, by the Gods, you owe me nothing,
At the place I shall appoint you?
Streps.   By which Gods?
Pās. By Zeus, Poseidon, Hermes.
Streps.   Yes, by Zeus!
And pay three obols for the joy of swearing!
Pās. To Hell with you for such rank shamelessness!
Streps. (*feeling the paunch of Pāsias*). Just tanned with salt, he'd make a
    useful wineskin.
Pās. Mock me, indeed!
Streps.   He'd hold a good four gallons.
Pas. Now, by great Zeus and all the Gods, for this
You yet shall pay!
Streps.   'The Gods'—what a joy to hear him!
He swears by Zeus—what a jest to those who know!

Pās. Ah, the day comes you shall atone for this! . . .
  So you won't pay me?

Streps.   Never, while I know it.
  Now hurry up and take yourself from here.
  Out of my doorway!

Pās.   Very well, I'll go
  And pay my deposit for a suit against you.
  Or strike me dead!

Streps.   You'll only lose that too,
  As well as your twelve minas.   Well, I'm sorry. . . .

          *Pāsias goes out and a second creditor, Amynias, limps in, having
          had a driving accident.*

Amynias. Ah miserable me!

Streps. Hey, who's this fellow moaning?   Can it be
  Some querulous deity of Carcinus?

Amyn. Why ask me who I am?   A man of sorrows.

Streps. Then go and mind your business.

Amyn. O Fate relentless!   O thou evil Fortune,
  Wrecking my chariot!   Pallas, Thou hast destroyed me!

Streps. What harm, then, has Tlēpólemus done to *you*?

Amyn. Friend, do not mock me.   Make your son **repay**
  The money he has borrowed.   All the more,
  Since I have met disaster.

Streps. Money!   What money?

Amyn.   What he borrowed of me.

Streps. Borrowed?   I think you *have* met with disaster!

Amyn. By God, I have—my horses threw me down.

Streps. Horses?   You drivel, as if ass-ass-inated.

Amyn. Drivel!—to want my money back again!

Streps. You cannot be quite right.

Amyn.   What's that you say!

Streps. You look as if your brain had had a shock.

Amyn. You look to *me*, by God, as if you soon
  Would be in court, unless you pay me!

Streps.   Say,
  Do you think that Zeus, each time He rains, employs
  New water?—or does the sun suck up again
  The water that has fallen, back to Heaven?

Amyn. I neither know nor care.

Streps. How is it right, then, that you should be paid—
  A man so ignorant of higher things?

Amyn. If you can't produce the money, pay at least
  The interest it has borne.

Streps.   Has 'borne'!   What monster
   Is this you're talking of?
Amyn.   Why, well you know,
   As time runs on, by the month or by the day
   The debt grows bigger and bigger.
Streps.   Very pretty!
   Say, do you think the sea is any bigger
   To-day than once it was?
Amyn.   God, no!   The same.
   Things would be wrong, if it grew bigger.
Streps.   Then,
   Most miserable man, if all the sea,
   With rivers running in, still grows no bigger,
   What right have *you* to make your money grow?
   Come, prosecute your exit from my house.
   (*Calling to a servant.*) Bring me my goad.
Amyn.   I call all men to witness—
Streps. (*goading him*). Away with you!   At once!   Be off, you racer!
Amyn. Is this not rank assault?
Streps.   Now hop!   For I
   Will sting your rump, my blood-horse, without mercy.
   Aha, it stirred you?   *That* has got you going—
   You and your wheels and pairs!   [*He chases Amynias out.*
Chorus. Such is the love of evil!   That ill passion   strophe.
                    Has led astray
             This old man here in shameless fashion
                    To pocket the money he ought to pay.
                 And so, for certain, we shall see
                    This day some sudden chance befall
                    To make him—arch-sophistical
                       Although he be—
   Regret those scoundrel courses that bring calamity.

                                                      antistrophe.
                 He will find that he has triumphed in his endeavour,
                       Pursued so long,
                    To have his son trained to be clever
                       And champion the cause of wrong;
                    Skilled to baffle, as absurd,
                       All that plead in justice' name;
                       A rogue by any touch of shame
                          Undeterred.
   Yet soon he may be wishing his son could speak no word.
        Strepsiades runs out of his house, pursued by his son.

Streps. Ow!   Ow!

  Help, kinsmen, help!   Neighbours and fellow-demesmen,
  Help, I beseech you!   I am being basted.
  Ah misery!   My poor headpiece!—and my jaw!
  Vile wretch, would you strike your father!
Pheid.   Yes, my father.
Streps. Listen!   He owns he beats me!
Pheid.   Certainly.
Streps. You wretch, you brigand!—oh, you parricide!
Pheid. Go on and call me names!   Yes, call me more!
  Didn't you know I love to be abused?
Streps. You libertine!
Pheid.   Yes, strew on me your roses.
Streps. To strike your father!
Pheid.   And by Zeus, I'll prove
  That I was *right* to strike you.
Streps.   Abomination!
  How could it ever be 'right' to strike your father?
Pheid. I'll prove it now and leave you quite confuted.
Streps. You'll prove me *this*!
Pheid.   Why, nothing easier.
  Choose now which argument you want to take.
Streps. 'Argument'?   What do you mean?
Pheid.   The worse or better?
Streps. Heavens, I've had you taught to controvert
  All justice, with a vengeance, if indeed
  You're going to demonstrate it right and proper
  For fathers to be beaten by their sons!
Pheid. Yet I think I shall so convince you, that yourself,
  Once you have heard, will have not a word to answer.
Streps. Indeed, I long to hear what you can say!
Chorus. Time now, old man, to bring your thoughts to bear   *strophe.*
                          On victory.
              Without some firm assurance, he'd not dare
                          So wantonly.
              Something emboldens him—his fearless air
                          Is plain to see.
  But first of all we ask of you, explain to us the Chorus,
  How did this battle come about?   Now set it clear before us.
Streps. Well, as you wish, I will describe how rose this altercation.
  We had sat down together there to enjoy our celebration,
  And first I told him: 'Take the lyre, and let our feast be cheered
  With the song of old Simonides, of "how the Ram was sheared."'

But 'Oh, it's out of date,' he snapped, 'for drinkers when they fill
  Their cups, to harp the while and sing, like women at the mill.'
Pheid. And was not *that* good cause enough for thumping you, old sinner—
  Bidding me sing, as if you had a grasshopper to dinner!
Streps. Language like that!—in my own house I had to undergo it!
  And then he called Simonides 'a pitiable poet'!
  Still for the nonce I swallowed it, though hardly knowing how;
  And so I said to him again: 'Then take a myrtle-bough
  And speak a piece of Aeschylus.' At once he cried in scorn:
  'I reckon him, your Aeschylus, beyond all poets born,
  A millstone-venting blusterer, mere jargon, noise, and yelling.'
  At that indeed, you may suppose, I felt my stomach swelling;
  Yet on my rage I clenched my teeth, and said: 'Then spout a bit
  From one of your newfangled school, that are so full of wit.'
  So then, Apollo save us all, he sang from Euripides
  Some tale of a brother making love—to his sister, if you please!
  Now *that* was more than I could stand; and so I turned to flay
  The boy with terms of round abuse. And then—as is the way—
  With taunt on taunt we both let fly; till up at last he jumped
  And flew at me, and throttled me, and smashed and thrashed and thumped.
Pheid. And did you not deserve it well, blaming that master-mind,
  Euripides!
Streps.   'Master,' indeed! Oh *what* names I could find
  For *you*!—but I'd be thumped again.
Pheid.   By God, and rightly too!
Streps. How 'rightly'! When I bred you up, Oh shameless, shameless
  you!—
  So watchful still to know your wants from every lisping cry.
  Every time you whimpered 'brou,' there with a drink was I;
  And every time you screamed 'mamma,' I brought a piece of bread,
  And the moment that you cried 'cacca,' out through the door I sped,
  With you in my arms, and held you there. And now you choke me
  dead! . . .
Chorus. I doubt not, all young hearts, as he begins,   *antistrophe.*
      Beat eagerly.
    For if, for acts like these, his pleading wins
      Acquittal, we
    Shall not henceforward rate their elders' skins
      As worth one pea!
  Now, engineer and architect of new and cunning phrase,
  Bestir yourself to find a plea will justify your ways.
Pheid. How sweet to meet with notions new, of high intelligence,
  And look down on morality, from one's own eminence!

In days when I applied my mind only to horsemanship,
I couldn't bring three phrases out, before my tongue would trip.
But since my parent put an end to frivolous tastes like these,
Versed as I am in subtle terms and logic's niceties,
I trust to prove it's ethical to punish one's own father.
Streps. Heavens! Go back to horses, then. Indeed I would far rather
Pay the keep of a four-in-hand, than be pummelled till I'm dead.
Pheid. Let me resume my argument, where you broke off the thread.
First tell me—when I was a boy, did you ever give me blows?
Streps. Indeed I did, with loving care.
Pheid.   Why then, sir, pray disclose
Why *I* to-day should not treat *you* with similar affection,
And buffet *you*, since love entails this species of correction?
Why should immunity from blows be granted, pray, to you
And not to *me*? By right of birth am *I* not free-born too?
    Should sons be flogged, and yet unflogged the sire?
Ah, you may plead, it is the rule a child must learn by pain?
But I reply—old men grow back to childhood once again.
It's far more just for old than young to suffer this infliction,
Because they have far less excuse for any dereliction.
Streps. It's nowhere *done*—to castigate a father, as you mention.
Pheid. It was some man like you or me first founded this convention.
He must have argued into it the ancients of our race—
Why should not *I* establish *now* a new rule in its place,
Enjoining sons to give their sires the needful castigation?
(All floggings fathers gave *before* my new law's promulgation
We do remit—for past blows struck we will not ask to strike them.)
Consider, too, the ways of cocks, and other creatures like them,
And how they beat their fathers, all—in what way is their nature
Other than ours?—except, of course, they have no legislature.
Streps. If to adopt the ways of cocks is the end of your researches,
Why not go on to dine on dung, and roost the night on perches?
Pheid. That does not follow!—Socrates would *never* have assented.
Streps. Well, don't beat *me*! For if you do, hereafter you'll repent it.
Pheid. And how comes *that*?
Streps.   As I've the right to punish *you*, one day
    You'll beat your son—if you have one.
Pheid.   But then I never may!—
And lose my pains—then *you*'ll have scored, off *me*, before you die!
Streps. (*turning to the audience*). Friends of my age, I must admit there's
    force in his reply.
I find it not unfair to make the youngsters this concession—
It's only just that elders too should smart for a transgression.

Pheid. Consider now a further view.

Streps.   As I love my life, I hear you.

Pheid. And after all you've just been through, maybe 'twill rather cheer you.

Streps. Come on then.   Tell me what it is, that I shall find repaying.

Pheid. I'll beat my mother, as well as you.

Streps.   What's that!   What's that you're saying!

Why, this just goes from bad to worse.

Pheid.
                              But how if, justifying

The worser case, I prove it right to beat her, past denying?

Streps. (*exploding*).   What next!   I don't care whether

                              In the bottomless pit, if so you please,

                              You fling yourself, and Socrates,

                              And your 'worse case'—all together!

O Clouds, O Clouds, all this is just your doing—

All for confiding my affairs to *you*!

Leader. You've nobody but your own self to blame,

Because you chose to follow shady courses.

Streps. Why did you not take such a tone at first,

Instead of leading on a poor old rustic?

Leader. This is our way, whenever we see a man

In love with evildoing;

We always lead him onward to disaster,

Until he learns to reverence the Gods.

Streps. Ah Clouds, it was ill done—yet not unjustly.

For I was wrong in trying to withhold

My debts.   But come, dear boy, and help me now

To annihilate that cursed Chaerephon

And Socrates, who duped us.

Pheid. Oh no, I could not harm my own instructors.

Streps. Yes, yes!   Respect the Zeus of fatherhood.

Pheid. The Zeus of fatherhood!   You're out of date.

Does Zeus exist?

Streps.   He does!

Pheid.
                              He doesn't!   Why,

Rotation's cast him out and reigns instead.

Streps. It doesn't!   Though I thought it, loving so

My dear Pot-ation here.   (*Pointing to a large mixing-bowl, perhaps out-
     side the Reflectory.*)   Fool that I was,

To reverence a god of earthenware!

Pheid. Then stay, and rave, and drivel to yourself.   [*He goes out.*

Streps. Ah 'rave' indeed.   How raving mad I was,

Trying to cast out the Gods—for Socrates!   [*He addresses a figure of
                                                  Hermes in the street.*

Hermes beloved, do not be angry with me!
Do not destroy me!   Pardon me my folly—
My head was turned by all their chattering.
Now give me your advice—shall I indict
And prosecute them all?—or what do you think?
Ah, you are right—best keep off litigation
And, without more delay, give to the flames
The house of all these babblers.   Xanthias!   Here!
Come out!—with a ladder—bring a pickaxe with you!
Then scale the wall of their Reflectory
And, as you love your master, smash the roof
Until you bring their home about their ears.

> *The slave Xanthias climbs with his pickaxe, followed by Strep-*
> *siades.*

Quick, someone!—a lighted torch.   I'll be revenged
This day on some of them,
For all the cunning of the charlatans.

First Disc. (*rushing out*). Oh!   Oh!
Streps. Come on, good torch, now show a lively flame.
Second Disc. What are you doing, fellow?
Streps.   Doing?   Only
Chopping a little logic with your rafters.
Third Disc. Horror!   Who is it sets our home afire?
Streps. Yes, it's the man you cheated of his cloak.
Third Disc. Hi!   Murder, murder!
Streps.   That's just what I want—
Unless my pickaxe disappoints my hopes,
Or I go tumbling off and break my neck.
Socr. What are you doing—you there on the roof?
Streps. I tread on air—I contemplate the sun.
Socr. Oh terrible!   I shall be suffocated.
Chaerephon. And I, unhappy wretch, be burnt to cinders.
Streps. What, then, possessed you to blaspheme the Gods
And pry about the station of the moon?
Down with them, pelt them, smash them—for many reasons,
But most of all that they have wronged the Gods.

> [*Exeunt pursuers and pursued.*

Leader. Lead on to the exit.   For to-day
We have done not so ill in the part we play.

THE WASPS

(Lēnaea, 422 B.C.—second prize)

Though all my law is fudge,
Yet I'll never, never budge,
But I'll live and die a judge.

W. S. Gilbert, *Trial by Jury.*

Athenian juries were drawn from a body of six thousand citizens, aged over thirty, divided into sections of five hundred and paid for each day's session at the rate of one or two obols under Pericles, increased by Cleon in 425 to three. This system was popular with the jurymen; less popular with the subject allies, who had often to bring cases to Athens.

The play begins with two slaves, Sosias and Xanthias, blockading inside his house their old master, Philocleon (Love-Cleon) by order of his son Bdělycleon (Loathe-Cleon), who wants to cure his father of his mania for sitting on juries. The old man makes frantic attempts to escape. Now he emerges from the chimney, pretending to be smoke; now, on the pretext that his donkey must be sold, he comes out clinging beneath its belly, like Odysseus beneath the ram. But always he is intercepted. Next enters the Chorus of old jurymen, dressed as wasps with huge stings; they encourage Philocleon to gnaw his way out through the nets that surround the house; but again he is foiled. Then follows a set argument between father and son before the Chorus. Philocleon dilates on the juryman's happy sense of power and self-importance, as litigants grovel before him; and then there are the fees. But Bdělycleon crushingly points out that the jurymen are merely duped by the ruling demagogues who, from a public revenue of two thousand talents, toss them a beggarly hundred and fifty. Philocleon is overcome and the Chorus converted. But the old man is miserable with his occupation gone. So a domestic trial is staged for him, in which the house-dog Lăbes (representing a certain general, Lăches) is indicted for stealing Sicilian cheeses. At its close Philocleon is tricked into putting his vote into the urn of acquittal—a horrible lapse at which he swoons.

> How can I bear this burden on my conscience?—
> Acquit a prisoner! *What* will become of me?
> Gods that I honour, pardon me my sin.
> All a mistake—quite out of character!

> (999–1002.)

In consolation, Bdělycleon promises to take his father into society. Meanwhile in the choric address to the audience (*parabasis*) the waspish

418

old jurymen recall, like Falstaff and Shallow, the great doings of their youth; and Aristophanes makes one of his sudden changes from horse-play to poetry, as he remembers Marathon.

> We that walk with tails so deadly, *we* can claim that we alone
> Are the true-born sons of Athens, seed that from her soil has grown.
> Bravest we of all her manhood, once in war we served her best,
> When the Persian sought to sack her, sought to burn and blast our nest,
> Smothering the walls of Athens with the reek of smoke and flame.
> Sallying forth at once to meet him, serried shield and spear, we came,
> And, with lips in fury bitten, man to man we met their line,
> Sharp as if our throats had swallowed sourest vinegar for wine.
> Hiding all the sky above us, whizzed their war-shafts on the wing;
> *Yet* we, by the help of Heaven, hurled them back towards evening.
> Overhead, before the battle, soared an owl; and with a cheer
> *We* swept after, grimly thrusting their great trousers with the spear,
> Just as fishers spear the tunny.   Little wonder if they fled,
> Stung so sore in cheek and forehead; so that even now 'tis said,
> Wheresoever men are gathered, in barbarian lands afar:
> 'Nothing lives with manlier valour than a wasp of Attica.'
>
> (1075–90.)

The play ends, less excellently than it began, with the monstrous high spirits of Philocleon at his party, where he carries off the flute-girl, assaults everyone he meets, and challenges all the world to dance against him.

It will be recalled that Racine, irritated by a personal experience of the legal mind, adapted *The Wasps* into *Les Plaideurs*—a play at which Paris looked dubiously till Louis XIV was pleased to signify: 'We *are* amused.'

Peace

(Dionysia, 421 B.C.—second prize)

Once more we meet a war-weary Athenian—Trygaeus (Vintager); who, recalling how Aesop's beetle and Euripides' Bellérophon flew to Heaven, decides to do likewise and beg Zeus for peace.   The mount he chooses is a large dung-beetle and the play opens with his two slaves feeding up the creature, on which Trygaeus duly ascends, with anxious appeals to the stage mechanist not to let him drop.   But the Gods, disgusted by Greek war-madness, have quitted Heaven for remoter altitudes, leaving behind only Hermes, as caretaker, and War, who has buried Peace in a pit and is

making ready to pash all Hellas in his giant mortar.   Trygaeus sets about
rescuing Peace, aided by a Chorus of Attic farmers as war-sick as himself.

> Long enough we've waited,
> Marching far and near,
> Worn to death and baited,
> '*From* Lyceum,' '*To* Lyceum' dragging shield and spear.
>
> (354–7.)

Finally, though *some* helpers from other Greek cities do not pull their
weight, Peace is hoisted out of her prison, along with her handmaids
Opōra (Harvest) and Theōria (Holiday).   But the charm of the play lies
in the lyrics lavished here by Aristophanes on the simple happiness of
country life.

Chorus. Day that all the good have sighed for, and all honest husbandmen,
    I salute you!—how I'm longing just to greet my vines again,
    Just to go and bid good morning to my fig-trees in a row,
    That in younger years I planted!   What a weary while ago! . . .

> Call to memory, my comrades,
>   All our old life's happy ways,
> All that Peace used once to bring us—
>   Ripened figs and myrtle sprays.
> Call to mind the cakes we nibbled
>   And the new wine, sweet and strong,
> And the leaves of olives blowing
> And, by well-heads, violets growing—
>   Craved so long.
> Joys in life the happiest,
> For them all let Peace be blest!
>
> (556–9, 571–81.)

Trygaeus himself is betrothed to Opōra.   Then, after a *parabasis* of the
Chorus extolling the poet, the play returns to earth and tails off, as so frequently, in a series of farcical scenes, showing how Trygaeus deals at his
marriage feast with a meddling oracle-monger, with weapon-sellers ruined
by the peace, and so forth.   Better than these clownings is the second
parabasis, where the Chorus paints delightfully a wet spring afternoon on a
farm in Attica.

Ah there's nothing near so pleasant as when sowing's safely done,
Then, while God rains softly on it, some good neighbour calls to one:
'Now we have a bit of leisure, what's to do, Comarchides?'
'God's so kindly with this weather,' then I answer, 'if you please,

I should like a little drinking.   Wife, three quarts of beans, and wheat!
Set them on the fire a-roasting.   Bring us out some figs to eat.
And let Syra shout to Manes: "Leave your work and come away!"
Anyhow, it serves no purpose, trying to prune the vines to-day,
Or to dig the earth about them—all the ground is sodden through.
Someone get the thrush, to cook it, and the pair of siskins too;
There's some beestings in the larder.   And there are four hares to bring.
(That's to say, unless our ferret [1] stole the lot last evening.
For most certainly I noticed some strange din and clatter there.)
Three of these, boy, for our eating: one is for my father's fare.
Ask Aeschínades to give you some ripe-berried myrtle-boughs;
Call Charínades, moreover, as you pass before his house.

> Let him join us in our mirth,
> Seeing God has blessed the earth,
> Blessed the labour of our ploughs.'

(1140–58.)

Here at least Ancient and Modern can join hands.

THE BIRDS

(Dionysia, 414 B.C.—second prize)

Ye wanderers from a mighty State,
Oh, teach us how to legislate—
Your lightest word will carry weight
In our attentive ears.
Oh, teach the natives of this land
(Who are not quick to understand)
How to work off their social and
Political arrears!

W. S. Gilbert, *Utopia, Limited.*

In 421 Athens and Sparta had concluded the Peace of Nīcias, for the optimistic term of fifty years.   But, possessed by some strange megalomania, Athens undertook a new war in Sicily which was to rekindle the old war in Greece and bring her own ruin.   In 414, when the Athenian expedition was about to besiege Syracuse, Aristophanes produced this extravaganza of besieging Heaven itself.   Some have seen in it a satire on Athenian ambition; but, if so, it was a very veiled satire; and *his* satire was not in the habit of going veiled.   It seems rather as if he were not so much mocking his countrymen for their mood of fantasy as, in his own way, sharing it as well.

[1] Kept instead of cats.

Two elderly citizens, Peisetaerus [1] (Persuasive) and Euelpides (Hopeful), sick of the perpetual litigations of Athens, hit on the idea of seeking a quiet life among the birds; whose legendary king, the hoopoe Tēreus, was once a man himself, and allied to Athens by marriage with an Attic princess. Further, Peisetaerus has a plan for aggrandizing the birds; by building a bird city they can wall off Heaven from the sacrifices of earth, as the Athenians were about to try to wall off Syracuse from the outer world. They meet the hoopoe; and he summons his subjects.

> Hoo-poo-hoo-poo-hoo-poo-oi!
> Ee-o, ee-o!   Gather, gather, gather O!
> Birds of a feather, come flock together—
> Come from the fields that the farmers sow,
> Tribes without number that eat their barley,
>   Peckers of grain,
> Darting and chirping, softly, clearly,
>   As ye settle and rise again,
> Searching the furrows, chattering cheerly
>   Your sweet strain:
>   Tio, tio, tio, tio!
>
> You that gather in gardens O,
>   Upon the ivy-bough,
> Or peck the mountain fruit of wild olive and arbute,
>   Flutter in haste to my summons now.
>   Triotó, triotó, totobrix!
>
> Hither, you that in the marshes, where the reedy channels run,
>   Snap the stinging midges!   You that dwell within
> Meadows fresh and dewy, fair fields of Marathon!
>   Hither, hither, speckled one,
>   Francolin, francolin!
>
> You that over the surges' thunder
>   Flit in the halcyons' company,
> Hither, to hear of this latest wonder,
>   Hither, whatever your kind may be,
>   Long-necked birds!
>
> For there's come a shrewd old man,
>   With notions new,
> Starting a strange and novel plan;
>   Come and listen, all of you.

[1] This seems a likelier form than 'Peisthetaerus.'

> Hither, hither, hither now.
> Toro, toro, toro, tix,
> Kikkabau, kikkabau,
> Toro, toro, toro, toro,
>   Lí-lí-lix!

(227–61.)

At first hostile, the Chorus of Birds are in the end enthusiastically convinced. Part of their *parabasis* to the audience ranks justly among the most famous passages of Aristophanes.[1]

> Now hearken, mankind, dim creatures and blind, like the leaves' frail generations,
> Ye feeble in act, of clay compact, ye shadowy, strengthless nations;
> Ye dream-like things, devoid of wings, poor phantoms of a day,
> We bid ye hear—give careful ear to *us* that endure for aye,
> Us dwellers on high, that age not nor die, whose wisdom lives eternal;
> And we will bestow the truths we know about all matters supernal.
> Of Birds, and the birth of the rivers of earth, of the Gods we can speak with precision,
> Of Chaos and Hell.   And then ye can tell old Pródicus: 'Go to perdition!'
> At first nor air nor earth was there, nor sky—but the depths unbounded
> Of Hell without light, of Chaos and Night; but then in Hell's gulfs unsounded
> An egg without father—a wind-egg, rather—was laid by the black-winged Night;
> And from it at last, as the seasons passed, grew Love, the world's delight.
> From his golden wings the splendour springs; like the eddying winds he races;
> And next from the womb of Chaos' gloom, in Tartarus' endless spaces,
> Us Birds he bred, and hatched, and led into the light of existence.
> Yet still no sign of the Powers Divine—till Love mixed the world's consistence.
> *Then* came to the birth both Heaven and Earth, and Ocean, as all things blended,
> And the Blest upon high, that cannot die.   But we Birds are far longer descended,
> Of all the Blest the ancientest.   We are children of Love, past denying.
> It is easy to tell—we are winged as well; and *with* the winged Loves we go flying;
> And many a swain that sighed in vain, of a fair face gains possession,
> In spite of the pride that long denied, by *our* strong intercession;

---

[1] There is a version by Swinburne in his *Studies in Song*.

For he prospers his suit by the gift of a coot, or a cock or a goose or a
    quail.
Ay, all things the best, wherewith mortals are blest, they come of us Birds
    without fail.
For first we show how the seasons go, autumn and winter and spring,
And *then* ye know it is time to sow, when the crane flies chattering
Towards Libya's shore; then the skipper can snore, by the chimney his
    rudder leaving,
And Orestes takes note to get him a coat for his winter nights a-thieving;
But next in sight there wheels the kite, that warns of spring to follow,
As the time draws near your sheep to shear; and then in turn the swallow
Bids ye dispose of your winter clothes, for lighter—could Apollo
Better divine?   Or Ammon's shrine, or Dōdōna, better guide ye?
It is *we* that tell, when ye buy or sell, if gain shall then betide ye;
When ye seek your bread, or turn to wed, ye ask us what comes of it. . . .
Is it not clear a Bird's a seer as sure as Phoebus the prophet?

(685–722.)

    Peisetaerus and Euelpides are duly naturalized with feathers; and the
birds start building Nephelococcygia—Cloud-cuckoo-city. After Peisetaerus has driven off with contumely various officious helpers from earth,
such as a poet, an oracle-monger, a town-planner, and a legislator, the city
is completed. Iris, sent by Zeus to complain to mankind about the ces-
sation of sacrifices, is intercepted and sent back to Zeus with the audacious
message that if he is recalcitrant, Heaven shall be burnt about his ears.
More busybodies arrive from earth, seeking naturalization—a son who
wishes, as birds can, to kill his father; another poetaster; a professional
informer; but they too are sent about their business. Then Prometheus,
hidden from Heaven's eye by a large umbrella, deserts to Peisetaerus with
news that the Gods are starving and about to sue for peace—Peisetaerus
must demand, not only the sceptre of Zeus, but also the hand of his daughter
Basileia (Dominion). The divine embassy follows—Poseidon, Hēracles,
and a comic Thracian deity. The greedy Hēracles is bribed with food,
the terms are accepted, and the wedding follows, leaving Peisetaerus master
of the universe. Aristophanes was too happy in his dream to end it with a
disillusioned awakening, like those of poor Piers Plowman in the dank
daylight of the Malvern Hills. But his next extant play was to come down
to the earthiest earth.

LYSISTRATA
(Lēnaea, 411 B.C.)

Each newly joined aspirant
To the clan—to the clan—
Must repudiate the tyrant
Known as Man—known as Man—
They mock at him and flout him,
For they do not care about him,
And they're 'going to do without him'
If they can—if they can!

W. S. Gilbert, *Princess Ida.*

When *The Birds* was written Athens was fighting for empire; but now
for existence. Once more Aristophanes pleads for a reasonable peace.
The Knights is an extreme example of the political freedom allowed to the
Old Comedy; *The Birds*, of its religious licence; *Lysistrata*, of its sexual
audacity. The women of Greece are to stop the war by refusing to make
love—one of the earliest of recorded strikes and, I suppose, the first inter-
national one. For a moment Aristophanes talks like the Euripides he
detested, about the frivolity of women's lives. *Now* let them at least
turn that frivolity to account.

Calonīce. What *could* we women do that's sensible
   Or splendid?—we that sit
   Painted and prettified in saffron dresses,
   In our outlandish frocks and fancy shoes?
Lysistrata. It's just to these very things I look to save us.

(42–6.)

After convincing the female delegates from other Greek cities, Lysistrata
seizes the Acropolis and its treasury with a force of Athenian women. A
semi-chorus of old men marching up to burn them out is repelled by a
semi-chorus of old women with water-jugs. Lysistrata herself has an
encounter with one of the ten Commissioners of Public Safety appointed
after Syracuse (historically Sophocles was among them); and again the
argument takes at times a Euripidean seriousness of tone.

Lysistrata. All through the war that raged before, we sat and tolerated
   Day after day, in our patient way, what you *men* decreed and debated.
   Never a mutter you let us utter. Yet *we* felt disapproving—
   Well we knew of the things you do. As we sat at home, unmoving,

Well we noted how you had voted some quite calamitous folly.

We would ask with a smile, though all the while our thoughts were
    melancholy:

'When the people met, to-day, to set new words on the treaty-slab,

What *did* you decide?' Then my husband cried: 'For God's sake, hold
    your gab!

That's *our* affair.' So I left it there.

Stratyllis (an old beldame).   Never would *I* have obeyed him!

Commissioner. If you didn't do it, you'd dearly rue it.

Lys.   So I sat there and never gainsayed him.

But the very next week we'd hear men speak of some still worse decree—

'Husband!' we'd cry, 'how *could* you try this imbecility?'

And then with a scowl my man would growl: 'If *you* don't mind your
    spinning,

I'll break your head. The war,' he said, 'we men will see to winning.'

Com. A sensible view, by Heaven, too!

Lys.   How 'sensible,' wretched man?—

When we had, in your eyes, no right to advise, though you muddled
    every plan?

So came the day when we heard you say, aloud, in the public street:

'Not a man to lead, in our country's need!' 'Not a man!' the other'd
    repeat.

Then we felt it right for us wives to unite, to bring Hellas salvation.

And do it straight. What use to wait? Why more procrastination?

So if in turn you'll sit and learn the wisdom we put before you,

If you will hold, like us of old, your tongues, we may restore you. . . .

Com. Women, that bear in war no share!

Lys.   You dolt, our share is double—

Double, and worse, for us the curse! Do you think it was no trouble—

The sons we bore, then sent to war?

Com.   No painful memories, pray!

Lys. And all the time of a woman's prime, that *should* be happy and
    gay,

Alone we have lain, through each long campaign. Oh, never mind us
    wives!—

But the girls that sit—I rage at it—at home, young wasted lives!

Com. Well, what about men? Don't *they* age, then?

Lys.   My God, but not like these!

Back from the fight, though his hair be white, a man gets a bride with
    ease.

But brief the hour of a woman's flower, and once that hour has fled her,

Good-bye to men! She may sit *then*, telling fortunes *who* will wed her.

                                        (507-28, 588-97.)

Lysistrata gets the better; but is troubled by signs of blacklegging among her followers under the strain of this austerity. She rallies them, however; a Spartan envoy arrives; and the comedy ends with the usual revelry. In some of its scenes this astonishing play shows a crudity both tedious and barbarous. It is not a matter of morals, but of an insensitiveness that appeals to-day less to the uncivilized than to the decadently overcivilized. And yet, in essentials, Aristophanes never wrote a work so serious.

THE THESMOPHORIAZŪSAE

(Dionysia, 411 B.C.)

I know not mercy—men in women's clothes!
The man whose sacrilegious eyes
Invade our strict seclusion, dies.

W. S. Gilbert, *Princess Ida.*

This play, like *Lysistrata,* is dominated by women; but it turns from politics to literature. Before the house of his friend Agathon, tragic poet and aesthete, there enters Euripides, with a kinsman (generally but doubtfully identified, by analogy with another lost play, as his father-in-law, Mnēsílochus). For the women of Athens are celebrating the October feast of the Thesmophoria, in honour of Demeter and Persephone; and Euripides has heard that they are to discuss murdering him for the misogyny[1] of his plays. So he begs the effeminate Agathon to go, disguised as a woman, and defend him. Agathon refuses; but 'Mnēsílochus' obligingly lets himself be shaved, dons woman's clothes, and attends the meeting (as at Rome in 62 B.C. Clodius, the lover of Caesar's wife Pompeia, slipped into the women's celebration of the Bona Dea at Caesar's house). The scene changes to the women's assembly, where a speaker quickly opens the debate.

It is not, ladies, by our Goddesses,
To obtrude *myself* I rise. But I am grieved,
Deeply distressed, to see this many a day
How every sort and kind of calumny

---

[1] Misogyny may seem a strange charge to bring against the poet of Alcestis, Polýxena, Andrómache, Creûsa, and Íphigeneia; but Rogers well points out in his introduction to this play that Stobaeus (c. fifth century A.D.), compiling for his anthology a section of 'Attacks on Women'—sixty-four passages in all—takes none from Aeschylus and only two from Sophocles, but from Euripides thirty-five or thirty-six. Compare pp. 261, 347.

Is ignominiously spattered on you
By this same vegetable-woman's son,
Euripides.   With what does he not besmirch us?
Wherever actors, Chorus, audience,
Gather together, *when* has he spared his slanders?—
Calling us all man-hunting chamber-plotters,
Tipplers and traitresses and chatterers,
Rotten all through, the worst of all man's curses.
The moment, now, they quit the theatre benches,
Our husbands glance at us suspiciously
And poke about to find a hidden lover.
We can't do anything we used to do—
Such frightful things he's made them think of us.
If a woman twines a garland, it must follow,
At once, she is in love! . . .
Is a girl poorly?   Quick her brother mutters:
'I don't much like the look of her complexion.'
Why, if a wife that's never had a child
Would like to palm one off upon her husband,
We can't do even *that*!—they sit and spy.

(383–401, 405–9.)

Most inexcusable of all, husbands now get complicated keys to stop
housewives pilfering from larder or cellar.   And a second speaker complains that her trade in religious wreaths has been ruined by the man's
atheist plays.   Now rises the disguised 'Mnēsílochus.'

Of course I too—sure as I love my children—
Detest the fellow (or I should be mad).
But still we *should* talk frankly here together.
We're all alone—there's no one to betray us—
Why should we blame him and resent it so
(Being what we are), if he has seen and told
Just two or three of all our thousand lapses?

(469–76.)

He then relates escapades so outrageous as to rouse general uproar.   The
effeminate Cleisthenes, allowed entrance as practically a woman, brings
word of Euripides' plot; and 'Mnēsílochus' is searched and exposed.   Now
follow ingenious parodies of four plays by Euripides.   As the Tēlephus of
Euripides saved himself in the Greek camp by seizing the infant Orestes for
hostage, so 'Mnēsílochus' seizes and stabs a wineskin hugged by one of the
women; as the Oeax of Euripides wrote news of his brother Palamēdes' fate

on oar-blades cast into the sea, so 'Mnēsílochus' writes appeals for help on slabs of wood. The Helen of Euripides was found and rescued by Menelaus in Egypt; so 'Mnēsílochus' acts Helen, and Euripides enters disguised as Menelaus, but is repulsed by the arrival of magistrate and Scythian policeman. The Andromeda of Euripides, chained to her rock, was rescued by Perseus; so 'Mnēsílochus,' bound to a plank by the policeman, acts Andromeda, while Euripides enters as Perseus, but is again foiled by the policeman's vigilance. Finally Euripides makes terms with the Chorus of Women: if they will let him save his kinsman, he will cease slandering their sex. He then disguises himself as an old hag and brings a dancing-girl to lure away the Scythian, while 'Mnēsílochus' finally escapes. Considering the energy here attributed to Euripides, it is a little astonishing to recall that he was at this date aged no less than seventy-four!

An amusing play in parts, which implies a keen literary sense in its audience; though I am afraid I cannot equal the enthusiasm of Professor Norwood, who compares it in turn to *The Gondoliers, A Midsummer Night's Dream, Man and Superman,* Meredith, Villon, and Chaucer.

The Frogs
(Lēnaea, 405 B.C.—first prize)

Once more the theme is, largely, Euripides—now dead in distant Macedon at nearly eighty. Dionysus, as patron of tragedy, cannot bear the degeneracy in which his death has left the art. The God has just been at sea with the Athenian fleet:

> And there a-shipboard, reading to myself
> *Andromeda,* I felt a longing for him
> Stab sudden at my heart—you can't think how.
>
> (52–4.)

So Dionysus decides to carry off Euripides from Hades, as his brother Hēracles carried off the hound Cerberus and the captive Theseus; equipped with club and lion-skin, and followed by his slave Xanthias, he knocks for advice at Hēracles' door.

Dionysus. No more of that! Tell me the quickest way
  Down to the House of Hades. Mind it's one
  That's not too hot nor cold.
Hēracles. Which shall I recommend you? Which, I wonder?
  There's one that goes by way of Rope and Stool.
  You hang yourself. *Dion.* Ah no! That's simply stifling.

Hēr. Then there's a beaten track, a fine short cut,
  By Pestle and Mortar.   *Dion.* Oh, hemlock you mean?
Hēr. Precisely. *Dion.* Ah, but that's too cold and bleak.
  At the first step you feel your shins go numb.
Hēr. Shall I tell you of a *fast* route, all downhill?
Dion. Good Heavens, yes!   I never was a walker.
Hēr. Go down to Cerameicus.   *Dion.* And what then?
Hēr. Climb up the lofty tower that stands there.   *Dion.* Then?
Hēr. Just watch the start of the torch-bearers' race,
  And when the onlookers begin to shout:
  'Go!   Let 'em go!'—why, then you let go too.
Dion. Where?   *Hēr.* From the top!

(117–33.)

Finally Dionysus and Xanthias prefer the route used by Hēracles himself.   Dionysus, forced to row Charon's boat across the Infernal Lake
(the orchēstra), is tormented by a Chorus of deceased Frogs, endowed by
Aristophanes with some of his old lyrical lilt.

> Lift your voices!   Send them ringing,
>   Gay as once on sunny days,
> Through the rushes diving, springing,
>   Through the sedgy waterways;
> Or as when pool-deep we tumbled
>   From the raindrops pattering o'er us,
> And from far below there rumbled
>   Up our hubble-bubble chorus:
>   Brékekekéx ko-ax ko-ax.

(241–50.)

Xanthias rejoins his master after running round the lake shore; they
meet a somewhat incongruous Chorus of Mystics; then knock at Pluto's
door, where the porter Aeăcus furiously taxes Dionysus, whom he mistakes for Hēracles, with the theft of the dog Cerberus.   The frightened
Dionysus persuades Xanthias to change clothes with him.   Then a maid,
mistaking Xanthias for Hēracles, invites him to feast with Persephone;
loth to miss this party, Dionysus changes back into the costume of Hēracles; only to be assailed by two infernal landladies, whom Hēracles had
left unpaid after eating vast meals and stealing their rugs.   Again Dionysus
hurriedly changes clothes.   After more horse-play of this rather rudimentary
kind, the Chorus speaks a *parabasis* urging on the audience political unity
and reconciliation in face of their country's danger.   (Athens fell next year.)

This made a great impression at the time and gained the play the unusual honour, for a comedy, of a second representation.

But now sounds of tumult are heard.

Xanthias. By Zeus, our fellow in rascality,
  What's all this noise inside?—this bellowing
  And calling names?
Aeäcus. Oh that's Euripides and Aeschylus.
Xanth. Eh?
Aeäc. Great doings are afoot among the dead—
  Great doings—a riot between two hostile mobs.
Xanth. But why?   *Aeäc.* We have a long-established custom,
  In all the fine arts and the noble crafts,
  Whoever is the master in his calling,
  Takes all his dinners in the Public Hall,
  Next to the throne of Pluto—   *Xanth.* Ah, I see.
Aeäc.—until there comes some master of his art
  Yet greater.   *Then* the former must give way.
Xanth. But why has this, then, upset Aeschylus?
Aeäc. He occupied the chair of Tragedy,
  As being its greatest poet.   *Xanth. Now* who holds it?
Aeäc. When first Euripides descended hither,
  He kept exhibiting his skill before
  All the pick-purses and the clothes-stealers,
  House-breakers, parricides (we've crowds of them
  In Hades here).   And when they listened to him,
  His pleas and counter-pleas, his twists and turns,
  They went clean mad, and thought him unsurpassed.
  So then his head got swollen and he claimed
  The throne from Aeschylus.

(756–78.)

There follows the celebrated 'flyting' between Aeschylus and Euripides, judged by Dionysus as connoisseur, which occupies some six hundred lines—more than a third of the play.   It remains one of the most extra-ordinary relics of antiquity—imagine a modern music-hall audience listen-ing for the best part of an hour to a versified discussion on the relative merits of Shakespeare and Milton, or Corneille and Racine!   I own to thinking it would be better if briefer; but it leaves the impression of a general interest in poetry, and a verbal memory for it, unparalleled in any modern community.   None the less some critics, humanly prone to think there is nothing like criticism, have perhaps taken with a rather owlish over-seriousness what is largely light-hearted fooling.   It is not criticism to say one verse outweighs another because it has a heavy river in it; the whole point of this is its gay nonsense. It is not criticism to sling mere abuse like 'Creator of beggars and stitcher of tatters' or 'Purveyor of loves incestuous to the stage'; it merely recalls the gibberings of journalists at the first appearance of Ibsen's *Ghosts*. Indeed Aristophanes says little here that he had not said before. He attacks Euripides as by turns a squalid realist and a decadent aesthete, where Aeschylus had been a moralist in the grand style. Naturally there are memorable moments, as when Aeschylus exclaims:

> But I scorned to draw some shameless whore like Phaedra or Sthéneboea;
> A woman in love!—by Heaven above, in *my* plays you'll not see her.
>
> (1043–4.)

We remember; but we are not persuaded. Aeschylus *had* drawn, with surprising frankness, the love of Achilles and Patroclus; and, tiresome tyrant as Love has often become in the theatre, who dreams of sacrificing *Hippolytus* or *Antony and Cleopatra*, *Phèdre* or *Hedda Gabler*?

Dionysus himself is left at the end in a very human dilemma: 'I find one clever: I enjoy the other.' Finally he takes Aeschylus, who cedes his first place, till his return, to the mild and modest Sophocles.

But it is vain to cry: '*Debout les morts!*' In this year 405 the genius of Attic tragedy had breathed its last for ever; and, though Aristophanes could not know it, the genius of Old Comedy also.

THE ECCLESIAZŪSAE (392 or 389 B.C.) and PLUTUS (388 B.C.)

These two latest plays show a depressing decline. The first, *The Women's Assembly*, treats of communism. Plato's *Republic*, with its unpleasantly totalitarian Utopia, had not yet been published; but Aristophanes had apparently got wind of its ideas, or of others like them. The opening is passable—led by Praxagora, the women attend the Assembly disguised as men and, by a snap vote, decree a gynaecocracy, which then communizes property and women. Naturally what amused Aristophanes most was the community of women; but the later scenes, with their amorous hags, show a grossness that seems to me merely revolting.

Plutus, since Byzantine days, has been dear to schoolmasters, as being, like *The Clouds*, comparatively decent. But its idea of establishing a welfare state by restoring the sight of the blind God of Wealth is wearisomely fumbled. 'It is idle to be assiduous in the perusal of inferior poetry.'

MENANDER
(342–341 — 292–290 B.C.)

MENANDER, 'star of the New Comedy,' was born within a twelvemonth of Epicurus. He seems himself to have been something of an Epicurean, in the modern sense—Suidas (tenth century A.D.) describes him as passionately addicted to gallantry, and Phaedrus (first century A.D.) as a dandy—

> Drenched with perfume, in a long-trailing robe,
> With delicate and languid pace he came.

But he must have laboured. After learning from his uncle Alexis, the comic poet, and from Theophrastus, the philosopher of the *Characters,* he produced in thirty-three years over a hundred plays. For the poet whose most famous line is the familiar 'Whom the Gods love, dies young,' did not live to be old; being drowned, it is said, at fifty-two while bathing at Peiraeus. He won only eight prizes; but, like his admired Euripides, he was compensated by posterity for the coldness of contemporaries (who preferred his rival Philēmon). Aristophanes the grammarian (*c.* 257–180 B.C.) put Menander second only to Homer—a verdict which the surviving remains make, for me, at the least surprising. Plutarch (*c.* A.D. 46 —after 120) sets him high above Aristophanes 'at whose jokes one's gorge rises'! Even in A.D. 472, on the eve of the Dark Ages, Sidonius Apollinaris amuses himself in barbarized Gaul by writing a comparison of Menander with Terence.

Of Menander's development of comedy something has been said (p. 365). As an example of his best work I have translated here a scene from *The Arbitrants* (a play of which rather more than half was recovered from an Egyptian papyrus in 1905). For it seems to me admirable in its natural humanity and its racy dialogue [1]—as if Greek drama in its old age had at last realized, as never before, the value of brevity and speed. And apart from literary interest it gives a Theocritean glimpse of fourth-century peasant life (where even charcoal-burners seem well up in tragedy).

At a woman's nocturnal festival Pamphila, daughter of the testy old Smicrines, was violated by the young Charisius, who had been drinking. Four months later, by one of the coincidences so frequent in New Comedy, the young pair were married, without recognizing each other. Five months

---

[1] Quintilian (x, 1, 70) admired the scene, rustic though it is, as a brilliant piece of forensic pleading.

after that, Pamphila had a baby boy; and, not knowing it was her husband's child, secretly exposed it, with trinkets round its neck by which it might perhaps one day be known.   Charisius, however, got wind of the birth; and in his anger, though too fond to divorce Pamphila, left her for the harp-girl Habrótonon.   This wild behaviour has reached the ears of his father-in-law Smicrines, who comes to visit his daughter, perhaps with a view to divorce; leaving her house, he finds two peasants, Davus, a shepherd, and Syriscus, a charcoal-burner, quarrelling over the trinkets of the baby, which Davus has found.   And so, all unknowing, the irritable old gentleman becomes arbiter in the case of his own grandchild.

Syriscus. You're shirking what is fair.   *Davus.* Blackmailing wretch!
Syr. Why should you have what isn't yours?   *Davus.* We need
    A judge between us.   *Syr.* Right!   *Davus.* Let's take an umpire.
Syr. But who?   *Davus.* All's one to me.   (*Aside.*) Just serves me right.
    Why *did* I share with you?
Syr. (pointing to Smicrines as he comes out of Charisius' house).
                      Will you have *him*
    For judge?
Davus.   Why, yes, for luck!
Syr. (to Smicrines).   Would you, kind sir,
    So may God bless you, spare us just a moment?
Smicrines. You!   And for what!   *Syr.* We have a difference.
Smicr. What's that to *me*?   *Syr.* We want a judge that's fair.
    If there's nothing to prevent you, be so kind
    As to decide between us.   *Smicr.* Gallows-birds,
    What call have *you*, then, fellows dressed in goatskins,
    To walk round talking law?   *Syr.* But, father, please!
    It's only a small thing, soon explained.   For God's sake,
    Do it, and don't despise us.   For it matters
    That always, everywhere, justice should win;
    And everybody, when it comes his way,
    Should work for *that*.   It touches all our lives.
Davus. (aside). I'm matched against a fellow with a tongue!
    Why, why did I go shares!   *Smicr.* Then you'll abide—
    Promise!—by my decision?
Both the others.   Sure!
Smicr.   I'll hear you.
    What's to prevent me?   (*To Davus.*) You, the quiet one, first!
Davus. I must go back a bit, to make all clear,
    And tell you what happened before I dealt with *him*.
    Good sir, maybe about a month ago,
    I was herding my flock, alone in the woods near by,

And there I found a baby lying abandoned,
With a necklace on it and that sort of things—
Just trinkets.   *Syr. That*'s our quarrel!   *Davus.* He interrupts me!
Smicr. If *you* go thrusting in, with this stick here
I'll break your head.
Davus.   Quite right!
Smicr.   Go on, then.
Davus.   Well,
I picked it up.   I took it home with me.
I meant to rear it.   *That* was my idea,
But in the night (as always happens), thinking,
I considered with myself: 'What call have *I*
To bother rearing babies?   Where am *I*
To find the money?   And why look for troubles?'
That's how I felt.   Next day I went out herding
At dawn—and *he* came up to where I was
(He's a charcoal-burner), looking round about
For old tree-stumps to saw.   I knew him well,
So we got talking.   Seeing me so gloomy,
'What's wrong,' he says, 'with Davus?'   'Wrong!' I said;
'I'm meddlesome.'   And then I told him all,
How I found the child and took it.   Then at once,
Before my tale was done, he started begging,
With 'Bless you, Davus!' every other word,
'*Do* give the child to *me*!   As you hope for luck,
For liberty!   For I've a wife,' he says,
'And she's just had a baby—but it died';
                              Pointing to Syriscus' wife.
Meaning her here, with the baby in her arms.
Smicr. Did you ask this?   *Davus.* Syriscus!   *Syr.* Yes.   *Davus.* All day
He pestered me.   So, as he begged and prayed,
I promised it.   I gave it.   And he left me
With a thousand blessings.   Yes, he took my hands
And kissed them.   *Smicr. Did* you?   *Syr.* Yes.   *Davus.* So off he went.
But now, of a sudden, with his wife he meets me
And claims the things the child was wearing then—
Trifles, mere trash worth nothing!—claims to have them,
And takes it hard, when I refuse and say
By rights they're mine.   *I* claim he should be grateful
For getting what he asked for.   Why should *I*,
Because I won't give all, be brought to book?
Now *if* he'd found them, walking *with* me there,
And we'd gone halves in luck, they *would* have been

Part his, part mine.   (*To Syriscus.*) But all alone I found them,
Without you—yet you think it fair to take
The lot, and leave me nothing!   Cut it short—
I freely gave you something of my own;
If you're content, then keep it; if you're not—
If you've regrets, then hand it back again.
Don't cheat me, nor be cheated.   But don't think
You can take the lot—part as a gift, and part
By putting force upon me.   There!   I've done.

Syr. Has he really done?   *Smicr.* Haven't you ears?   He's done!
Syr. Good!   And now *my* turn!   Yes, he found the child,
All by himself.   And everything he says,
Father, is quite correct—just as it was.
I don't deny it.   Beg and pray I did,
To have the baby.   All he tells is true.
But then a shepherd, one that works with him,
Told me he'd chattered—there were ornaments
He'd found upon the child.   The child himself,
Good sir, comes here to claim them.
(*To his wife.*) Here, wife!—the baby!   (*He takes it.*)   See, he asks you,
    Davus,
For his tokens and his trinkets.   For he says
They were given for his person, not your pocket.
And in his prayer I join him, being now
His guardian—as you made me, when you gave him.
            He hands the child back to his wife.
Oh sir, I think that now it is for *you*
To judge if these golden things, and all the rest,
As given by its mother, whoever she was,
Should be kept safe for the child, till it's of age;
Or this purloiner of others' property
Should have them, as the finder.   (*To Davus.*) Why, you ask,
When I took the boy—why didn't I claim them then?
But *then* I had no right to speak for him.
And I'm not asking *now* for anything
That's personally mine.   'Go halves in luck'!
Don't talk of 'finding,' when you're wronging someone—
This is no lucky 'find'; it's downright *theft*!
(*To Smicrines.*) And, father, think of *this* too.   He may be,
This boy, above our station.   Though brought up
By work-people, he may have higher aims
And, rising to his own real character,
Dare something noble—go off lion-hunting,

Or running in the Games, or taking arms
(You've been, I'm sure, to tragedies and know
About such things). Just think of Nēleus (was it?)
And Pélias—those heroes, *they* were found
By an old goatherd, leather-clad like me;
And when he saw they were of better blood,
He told them all, of how he found and reared them,
And gave them back a wallet full of tokens;
Through *that* they found the truth about themselves
And rose from simple goatherds to be kings.
Supposing Davus had taken what was theirs
And sold it for a dozen drachmas profit,
Those noble princes, of so high degree,
Would have been unknown for ever.
Father, it isn't right that I should feed
His body, while Davus goes and makes away
With all his future hopes. Why, through such tokens
A lad's been stopped from marrying his sister,
Or found his mother and delivered her,
Or saved a brother. *All* life's so uncertain,
Father, one *must* take every care beforehand;
Foreseeing all such chances, if may be.
'If you don't like it,' says he, 'give him back!'
He thinks that puts him in a strong position.
It isn't justice. (*To Davus.*) Rather than hand me over
What is the child's, would you try to take him too
And play the rogue more safely a second time,
Because good luck has saved some things of his?
(*To Smicrines.*) That's all I have to say. Judge as you think.

Smicr. That's quickly done. All that was found with him
    Belongs to the child. And that's my verdict.

Davus.   Good!
    But what of the child, then? *Smicr.* God! I won't award him
    To *you,* that cheat him—no, to his rescuer,
    That set his face against your trying to cheat.

Syr. Now blessings on you! *Davus.* Heaven save us all!
    A monstrous judgment! I, that found the lot,
    Stripped of it all, for one that never found it!
    Must I hand over? *Smicr.* Yes! *Davus.* A monstrous judgment,
    So Heaven help me! *Syr.* Come, be quick about it.

Davus. O Hēracles, how I'm treated! *Syr.* Come, your wallet!
    Open and show us—*that*'s where you keep them. (*To Smicrines.*) Wait
    A moment—please!—till he gives them!

Davus.   What possessed me
  To let him judge!   *Smicr.* You jail-bird, come, hand over!
Davus (*relinquishing the trinkets*). A shame it is!
Smicr.   Have you got the lot?
Syr.   I think so.
Smicr. Unless, as I gave my sentence, seeing he'd lost,
  He swallowed something?   *Syr.* Hardly that, I think.
  Good luck, good sir!   I only wish all judges
  Would do their job like *you.*   [*Smicrines goes out.*
Davus.   Oh Hēracles,
  What foul unfairness!   Never a worse decision!
Syr. You played the scoundrel.   *Davus.* Scoundrel yourself!   Look out
  And take good care you guard those trinkets for him.
  You may be sure I'll keep my eye upon you.
Syr. Oh go to Hell!   And now, wife, take the things
  And carry them in to our young master's here.

                                                        (1–160.)

  How natural this is, and human, and humane!
  While Syriscus and his wife are going through the trinkets, Charisius'
slave Onēsimus recognizes a certain ring—which Pamphila had snatched
from her violator—as his master's.   But he hesitates to tell; already he has
got into trouble once by informing Charisius about Pamphila's child.
Habrótonon persuades him to let her have the ring.   She may be able to
find out (1) if Charisius is really, as it looks, the child's father; (2) who, if
possible, is the mother.   After various complications, the truth emerges,
husband and wife are reconciled, and the crusty Smicrines placated; while
Onēsimus and Habrótonon are probably freed and wedded.

OTHER PASSAGES FROM MENANDER

Character

Onēsimus. Do you imagine, Smicrines, the Gods
    So leisured that they daily can dispense
    To each man good and evil?
Smicrines.   What do you mean?
Onēs. I'll make it clearer.   In the whole world, say,
    There are a thousand cities—in each one
    Dwell thirty thousand citizens.   Think you
    The Gods assign to every single one
    His ruin or salvation?   *Smicr.* How indeed!
    You'd make the life they lead a busy one!

Onēs. 'But,' you may say, 'do the Gods then take no heed
Of all our lives?' Yes; for in each of us
They have implanted our true character
As captain of our soul, who never leaves
His post. One man he saves; and ruins another,
Who serves him ill. *This* god guides each of us
To prosper, or to fall. And, would you prosper,
Be neither fool nor clown, to lose his grace.

(*Arbitrants*, 872–87.)

Greek Reason

The Greeks are *men*, and not devoid of reason—
Whatever they do, they do it with reflection.

(Kock, *Comicorum Atticorum Fragmenta*, 1880, iii, 185, fr. 617.)

Coup de Foudre

By Athena, sirs, I cannot find an image
To express what happened to me,
Think as I may of what brings swift destruction.
A whirlwind? While it gathers strength, approaches,
And strikes, and whirls away—why, it's an age!
Or shipping a heavy sea? *That* still gives time
To cry: 'Zeus save us!—catch hold of the rigging!'
You still may breathe to wait a second wave,
And then another, grabbing a piece of wreckage.
But as for *me*,
Soon as I touched and kissed her—I was sunk.

(iii, 159, fr. 536.)

'Ripeness is all'

Him I call happiest,
My Parmeno, that quickly gets him back
From whence he came, once he has gazed, untroubled,
Upon life's solemn pageants—stars and clouds,
Water and flame, and the sun that lights us all.
Whether you live but few years, or a hundred,
These will not change—and to the end of time
You will not look on sights of greater glory.

Consider, then, our span of days on earth
As it might be some fair—some foreign city—
With crowds and stalls, fun, dicing, pickpockets.
Leave early—and you'll slumber in your inn
Better provided for the road before you,
And free of enemies.
But he that lingers, loses and grows weary,
Till, bowed with years and burdened with his needs,
Bewildered, fleeced, among malignant faces,
He takes that last long road in bitterness.

(iii, 138, fr. 481.)

Fragments of Other Comic Poets

OLD COMEDY

Cratinus (c. 484–419 B.C.)

Mocked by his junior, Aristophanes, in *The Knights* as a senile tippler, he retorted by defeating *The Clouds* next year (423) with a comedy about his own bibulousness. (See G. Norwood, *Greek Comedy*, 1931, ch. iii.)

Wine and Song

On wine the gracious fancy of the bard goes galloping:
On water he'll not think of *one* good thing.

(Kock, Comicorum Atticorum Fragmenta, 1880, i, 74, fr. 199.)

Eupŏlis (flourished c. 430–410 B.C.)

A younger rival of Aristophanes, he claimed to have helped in *The Knights* and was accused by Aristophanes of plagiarism. He attacked Cleon, Hyperbolus, Socrates, Alcibiades. Suidas (tenth century A.D.) says he fell at the Hellespont; after which the Athenians forbade poets to be sent on active service. (See G. Norwood, *Greek Comedy*, ch. v.)

Pericles

A. Of all men born he was most eloquent.
When he came forward, like a champion runner
He could give, easily, a ten-foot start
To other orators.

B. Quick, as you say!   And yet, besides his quickness,
There sat upon his lips a strange persuasion.
He left men spellbound.   As with *no* other speaker,
His hearers felt, fixed in their hearts, his sting.

(Kock, i, 281, fr. 94.)

Demagogue

Syracósius, whenever he makes a speech,
Is like a mongrel mounted on a wall—
Yaps from the platform, running to and fro.

(i, 315, fr. 207.)

MIDDLE AND NEW COMEDY

Eubūlus (flourished *c.* 375)

Women

Curse on the cursed fool that was the second
To marry a wife!   For I can't blame the first.
I suppose he hadn't learnt the curse they are;
But the second knew all right! . . .
Most hallowed Zeus, should *I* speak ill of women!
Good God, let me perish sooner!   There's no treasure
That can compare with them.   And if Mēdēa
Was a bad woman, still Penelope
Was just a marvel.   Say you, Clytemnestra
Was also wicked?   But how good, Alcestis!
Someone may censure Phaedra.   But by Heaven
There was that noble . . .
                              Dear, dear me,
How quickly my worthy women have run out!—
While still I have a whole long list of bad ones.

(Kock, ii, 205, frs. 116–17.)

Love

Who was the first of men that drew or moulded
Eros with wings?
The man was only fit for drawing swallows;
Little he knew about the ways of Love!

For *he*'s not light, nor easy to be quit of,
When once a man has caught the malady,
But desperate heavy.   How should such a thing
Have wings!   If any said so—utter nonsense!

(ii, 178, fr. 41.)

Amphis (Middle Comedy)

Plato

O Plato,
How little you know except of looking gloomy,
With lofty-lifted eyebrows like a snail!

(Kock, ii, 239, fr. 13.)

Country Life

Then is not solitude a thing of gold?
The countryside is like a father, helping
(As none else will) to veil life's neediness;
But the city is a theatre where misfortunes
Crowd before all men's view.

(ii, 241, fr. 17.)

Anaxilas (Middle Comedy)

Suspicion

Why you are more distrustful than a snail,
That, when he travels, takes his house as well.

(Kock, ii, 274, fr. 34.)

Mnēsímachus (flourished *c.* 365–360 B.C.)

Sleep

Our sleeps, that are Death's Lesser Mysteries.

(Kock, ii, 442, fr. 11.)

Xenarchus (Middle Comedy)

Silence

What happy creatures, then, are grasshoppers,
Whose females haven't even the tiniest voices!

(Kock, ii, 473, fr. 14.)

Antíphanes (c. 388–c. 311 B.C.)

A foreigner for whom Demosthenes obtained Athenian citizenship, he
is credited with 260 or even 365 plays (an imposing output, though nothing
to Lope de Vega's).

Destruction

'He has got married.'   '*What* is that you say!
Got *married*!   Why, I left him alive and walking.'

(Kock, ii, 108, fr. 221.)

Woman

For one thing only will I trust a woman—
Once she is dead, not to come back again;
But trust her in nothing else, till dead indeed.

(ii, 119, fr. 251.)

There's Many a Slip . . .

Anyone that, born a mortal, fondly calculates that he
Can in life have sure possessions, trusts an utter fallacy.
One has all his coffers emptied by some public contribution;
One, involved in litigation, comes to total destitution;
Chosen general, one goes bankrupt; one, providing cloaks of gold
For his Chorus, as *chorēgus*, shivers ragged in the cold;
Or, as triërarch, you're broken; or, as trader, in the waves
Lose your all; you may be murdered, sleeping, walking, by your slaves.
There's no wealth you can be sure of—only what you chance to pay
In the purchase of enjoyment, as there passes day by day.

Even *that* is none too certain.   Spread although your table lies,
Someone may, when least you think it, snatch it all before your eyes.
Out of all you own each moment, you can count as surely won
Not a thing except the mouthful that your teeth have closed upon.

                                                    (ii, 98, fr. 204.)

Alexis (*c.* 372–*c.* 270 B.C.)

An Italiot Greek from Thurii, naturalized at Athens, and the uncle of
Menander, he lived over a hundred years and is credited with 245 plays.

Profiteers

A new law, now, he's bringing in—pure gold!—
That fishmongers henceforth must sell their wares,
Not seated, but all standing; and he says
Next year he'll make it 'hanging'!

                                                    (Kock, ii, 342, fr. 126.)

Husbands

We married men alone
Must face an audit of our lives, not yearly,
But every mortal day.

                                                    (ii, 393, fr. 262.)

A Servant's View of Philosophers

Why do you chatter, tossing stupid phrases
From Academe, Lycēum, or Odēum—
Mere sophists' gabble?   There's no good in that.
Oh Sicon, Sicon, let us drink—drink deep—
Be merry while we have a soul to cosset!
Come, Manes, roister!   Belly's best of all;
That's your real father, and your mother too.
Your lofty actions, embassies, commands
Are a bluster of empty boasts, as good as dreams.
Once your hour comes, then God'll strike you cold,
And leave you nothing but what you've drunk and eaten.
The rest is dust—your Codrus and your Cïmon,
Your Pericles and all!

                                                    (ii, 306, fr. 25.)

Philēmon (c. 361–c. 262 B.C.)

A Syracusan naturalized at Athens and a rival of Menander; more successful with his contemporaries, less so with posterity. 'Tell me, Philēmon,' said Menander to him once, 'do you not blush each time you have defeated me?'

Euripides

If, as some say, my friends,
In very deed the dead had consciousness,
I had hanged myself to see Euripides.

(Kock, ii, 519, fr. 130.)

God

God wills not you should know Him—what He is;
Then impious you,
Seeking to know Him, that would *not* be known!

(ii, 526, fr. 166.)

NOTES ON COMEDY

ARISTOPHANES

THE ACHARNIANS

[Page 372] *Oeneus*, King of Calydon and father of Meleager, Tydeus, and Dejaneira, was dethroned and ill-used by the sons of his brother Agrios, but later avenged by Tydeus' son, Diomed.

[Page 372] *Phoenix* was accused by his stepmother, who had failed to seduce him, to his father Amyntor, who blinded him. He then fled, doubtless in rags, to Pēleus, who had him healed by Cheiron the Centaur and made him Achilles' tutor.

[Page 372] *Philoctētes* sailed against Troy, but was marooned by the Greeks on Lemnos (p. 214).

[Page 372] *Bellérophon* tried to ride Pegasus to Heaven, but was thrown and lamed.

[Page 372] *Tēlephus*, King of Mysia, was wounded in a battle against the Greeks by the spear of Achilles. As an oracle revealed that his wound could only be cured by the spear that made it, he came disguised as a beggar to the Greek camp.

[Page 372] *Thyestes, Ino*. Thyestes was presumably ragged when driven into exile by his brother Atreus (p. 103). Ino, being possessed by Dionysus with Bacchic frenzy (see *The Bacchae*), disappeared so long that her husband Athamas married again; but, finding she was alive, he brought her back into his household disguised as a handmaid.

THE CLOUDS

[Page 378] *Can't even punish my own servants*. Because discontented slaves could desert to the enemy; later in the war Thucydides speaks of 20,000 such desertions.

[Page 379] *Biting common pleas*. The Greek says literally: 'There's a demarch (type of local magistrate) biting me in the bedding.'

[Page 379] *Megacles*. A common name in the aristocratic Athenian family of the Alcmaeonidae, to which belonged the reformer Cleisthenes; the mother of Pericles; and the mother of Alcibiades (whom Pheidippides here may be meant in part to recall).

[Page 380] *Pheidonides*. With a play on *pheidein*, 'spare,' 'economize.'

[Page 380] *Phelleus*. A Greek work meaning 'uplands'; it is not clear whether here it is a common noun, or the proper name of an Attic locality.

[Page 380] *Poseidon*. The god who gave Athens the horse, as Athena gave the olive (p. 217). He seems to have been the deity of Minyan invaders from the north (*c*. 2000 B.C.), who owed their success in part to horses and chariots. (See C. Seltman, *The Twelve Olympians*, pp. 143–4.)

[Page 381] *Pays their fee*. A particularly dishonest gibe; for Socrates, unlike the sophists, took *no* fees.

[Page 381] *Chaerephon.* A disciple of Socrates. According to tradition it was he that asked the Delphic oracle if any man were wiser than Socrates, and received the answer:

> Wise, Sophocles; wiser, Euripides;
> But wisest of all men is Socrates.

Unlike many of his fellow-disciples, he was a democrat and shared the fortunes of Thrasybūlus; but he died before the condemnation of Socrates in 399.

[Page 381] *Phasians.* It is disputed whether 'Phasians' means 'horses' or 'birds' (pheasants). Horses seem more in Pheidippides' line; and the Irish illogicality of being bribed with horses to give up horses is nothing against it here.

[Page 382] *Made miscarry.* It will be recalled that Socrates was the son of a midwife, and often compared himself to one, since by interrogation he brought his hearers' ideas to birth.

[Page 383] *Scattered ashes.* Ashes or sand being used, instead of a blackboard, for geometrical demonstrations. It was while poring over a sand diagram that the great Archimedes was cut down by a Roman soldier at the fall of Syracuse (212 B.C.).

[Page 383] *Thales* of Miletus (*c.* 640–546 B.C.), the father of Ionian philosophy, who thought all things arose from water.

[Page 383] *Spartan fellows caught at Pylos.* In 425, to the amazement of Greece, 292 Spartiates surrendered to Cleon and Demosthenes on the island of Sphactēria in the Bay of Navarino.

[Page 384] *Euboea . . . stretched on the rack.* The island was reconquered by Pericles, after a revolt, in 447–446 B.C.

[Page 384] *Watercress.* As watercress draws the moisture from the earth so the earth draws the vital fluid from the mind.

[Page 385] *Iron like Byzantium.* Presumably Byzantium had introduced small coins in iron. In a trading city there could be no question of iron becoming the *sole* currency, as at Sparta.

[Page 385] *Athamas,* a Boeotian king, deserted his wife Nephele (Cloud) for Ino, daughter of Cadmus. When Ino instigated him against her stepchildren, their mother Nephele, who had returned to Heaven, demanded the sacrifice of Athamas himself; but Hēracles saved him at the altar.

[Page 385] *Air . . . Ether.* In the Levant there is often a more striking contrast than in N. Europe between the cloudy or stormy lower atmosphere ('air') and a radiant upper sky ('ether'). *E.g.* from a distance, the lower half of Olympus may be seen black with tempest, while its upper half glows with unearthly sunlight. (See C. Seltman, *The Twelve Olympians,* pp. 182–3.)

[Page 385] *Mīmas.* A headland near Chios.

[Page 385] *Maeōtis.* Sea of Azov.

[Page 387] *Parnes* (4,630 feet) is on the Boeotian frontier and twelve miles N. of Athens.

[Page 387] *Aslant they sail.* Presumably, with the head of the cloud in advance of its foot. Mr. G. M. Young calls my attention to Ruskin's appreciation of this trait in *Modern Painters,* Part VII, ch. iv.

[Page 387] *False prophets.* Lit. 'Thurian prophets.' In 443, when Athens colonized Thurii in S. Italy, on the site of Sybaris, one of the leaders in the undertaking was the seer Lampon, whom Aristophanes satirizes elsewhere.

[Page 387] *Hundred-headed Titan.* Typhōs or Typhon (p. 41).

[Page 388] *Xenophantes' heir.* A dithyrambic poet, Hieronymus.

[Page 388] *Cleonymus, Cleisthenes.* Two constant butts of Aristophanes; the first threw away his shield at the Athenian defeat of Delium (424), where Socrates distinguished himself by his calm; the second was a notorious effeminate (cf. p. 428). For Cleonymus cf. *The Birds*, 1473 ff., where the Chorus describes the Cleonymus tree, which grows 'far from the town of Good Heart,' has shields for leaves, and drops them all each autumn.

[Page 388] *Pródicus* of Ceos. One of the most distinguished of the sophists, and author of the famous myth of The Choice of Hēracles.

[Page 390] *Gymnasium.* Gymnasia were not only places of exercise, but also haunts of disreputable loungers. It is from this second point of view that Strepsíades must give them up.

[Page 392] *Take off your cloak.* As a fee for Socrates. Strepsíades mistakenly infers he is to be beaten.

[Page 392] *Searching for stolen goods.* To prevent objects being 'planted,' searchers for stolen goods in a house had to strip before entering.

[Page 392] *Trophōnius' cavern.* The dead hero Trophōnius gave oracles in a cave near Lebadēa in Boeotia. Worshippers descending into it took honey-cakes to appease the serpents there. They then fell into a trance and saw visions so awesome that not for months after the ordeal could they smile again.

[Page 393] *O my hearers.* Here begins the *parabasis* (address of Chorus to audience). The first part seems to belong to Aristophanes' revised version. For here Cleon (killed 422) is spoken of as dead; contrast p. 394, where he is still alive.

[Page 393] *Let you taste it earliest.* Possibly because it had not been previously acted at Peiraeus, or elsewhere outside Athens.

[Page 393] *Modest Son, and Wanton.* Characters in Aristophanes' first play, now lost, *The Banqueters* (427).

[Page 393] *Another nursed my bantling.* The play, like several others by Aristophanes, was produced in the name of Callistrātus.

[Page 393] *Like Electra.* In Aeschylus (p. 106). As Electra found her brother's tress, so this play hopes to find the applause of its predecessor.

[Page 393] *Gross appendage.* The phallic symbols commonly worn by the Choruses of Old Comedy.

[Page 393] *No long-haired affectations.* Aristophanes was bald.

[Page 393] *Cleon* fell ingloriously when his force was routed by the Spartan Brasidas outside Amphipolis in Thrace (422).

[Page 393] *Hyperbolus.* A lamp-maker, demagogue, and constant butt of Old Comedy, he succeeded Cleon as leader of the left-wing war party; but was banished in 417, murdered in 411.

[Page 393] *Eupōlis* (fl. c. 430–410) was one of the three chief writers of Old Comedy, along with Cratīnus and Aristophanes. His *Maricas* was produced in 421.

[Page 393] *Phrynichus* (fl. c. 430–400; not to be confused with Phrynichus the *tragic* poet, elder contemporary of Aeschylus) in some comedy unknown had travestied Perseus' rescue of Andromeda; replacing the heroine by a hag.

[Page 393] *Hermippus,* another comic poet (fl. c. 435–418), attacked Pericles, Aspasia, and Hyperbolus.

[Page 394] *Adage of the eels.* In *The Knights* (864–7) Cleon was likened to eel-fishers, because he troubled the public waters so as to fish in them.

[Page 394] *Paphlagonian tanner.* Cleon (p. 373).

[Page 394] *Curse of evil counsel.* The story was that, when Athena defeated Poseidon in their contest for Athens (p. 446), the angry god laid on the city the curse that its counsels should be evil; but Athena nullified this by ordaining that these evil counsels should yet turn out well. (Unfortunately in the next few years that was no longer to come true.)

[Page 394] *Cynthus.* The holy hill of Delos (370 feet).

[Page 395] *Keep the days all wrongly.* Měton the astronomer had introduced in 432 a reformed system for correlating lunar months and solar years; this change may easily have caused confusion in the dates of festivals.

[Page 395] *Memnon.* Son of the Dawn, slain by Achilles at Troy.

[Page 395] *Sarpēdon.* Son of Zeus and King of Lycia, slain by Patroclus.

[Page 395] *There you are....* Here follows in the original a passage of feeble and largely untranslatable humour in which Socrates tries to instruct the stupid Strepsíades in prosody and philology; in particular, in a scheme for reforming the language by abolishing the anomaly of words that are masculine in form, but feminine in gender. *E.g. alectryon* ('cock' or 'hen') should be given a feminine form *alectryaina*—as if a female chicken were to be called a 'chickenette,' or a female 'fowl' a 'fowless.' Similarly *cardopos* ('kneading-trough'), being feminine, should acquire a feminine termination—*cardope.* One may be reminded of the orthographical quirks of Robert Bridges.

[Page 396] *Exverminate.* In the Greek there is a pun on *Korinthioi* ('Corinthians') and *koreis* ('bugs').

[Page 397] *Thessalian sorceress.* Thessaly was famous for witches, who were credited with a peculiar fondness for drawing down the moon.

[Page 398] *Melted what he'd written.* Being, of course, on wax.

[Page 398] *Thing we use for kneading flour.* With reference to *cardopos* ('kneading-trough') above.

[Page 399] *Socrates, true son of Mēlos.* An allusion to Diagoras of Mēlos, the famous atheist, who lived in Athens at this time and fled in 415 to avoid execution.

[Page 400] *Like Pericles.* Pericles (*c.* 446), having secretly expended ten talents on bribing the commanders of an invading Spartan army, simply told the Athenian Assembly that he had employed them 'for the public good.'

[Page 401] *Socrates and Strepsíades withdraw.* Possibly the two actors taking these parts (*if* there were only three actors in all) had now to play the two Arguments. But Strepsíades *may* remain present.

[Page 402] *Zeus ... old father in chains.* The argument used by the Erīnyes in *The Eumenides* (p. 108).

[Page 402] *Tēlephus.* One of the ragged wretches of Euripides (p. 446).

[Page 403] *Phrȳnis* of Mitylene (fl. *c.* 450), a musician of a more modern school. At conservative Sparta the authorities are said to have hacked away the two strings he had added to the older seven-stringed lyre.

[Page 404] *Mock him as 'patriarch perished.'* Lit. 'call him Iápetus' (the equivalent of Methuselah). For this Titan, father of Prometheus and Atlas, see p. 113.

[Page 404] *Hippocrates' sons* are frequently mocked by the comic poets for their swinishness. Their father is probably the general (nephew of Pericles) who fell in the defeat of Delium (424).

[Page 404] *Academe.* A garden and gymnasium, sacred to the hero Academus, a mile N.W. of the Acropolis.

[Page 405] *Antímachus.* Some effeminate decadent.

[Page 405] *Hēraclean baths.* The original baths of Hēracles were the hot springs that still flow at Thermopylae ('The Hot Gates'). Athena was said to have created them to refresh Hēracles after his labours.

[Page 406] *Pēleus*. In one of the many legends on the same theme as the story of Potiphar's wife, Pēleus, having refused the love of Hippolyte or Astydameia, Queen of Iolcus, was denounced by her to her husband Acastus. By him Pēleus was left unarmed to the beasts of Mount Pēlion; but the Gods, or Cheiron the Centaur, saved him by the gift of a sword.

[Page 406] *And then she went and left him*. Tradition told that Thētis really left Pēleus and returned to her native sea because, when she was laying their infant son Achilles in the fire, to make him immortal, Pēleus caught sight of it and cried out in dismay.

[Page 406] *Radish and ashes*. The punishment for a detected adulterer was thrusting a radish up the fundament and sprinkling with hot ashes.

[Page 408] '*My voice at its loudest shall ring on high.*' Borrowed from *The Satyrs*, a comedy of Phrynichus. The last two lines of this speech ('O son,' etc.) are based on Euripides' *Hecuba*.

[Page 409] *The day called of the old moon and the new*. The last day of the lunar month (when interest fell due) was called 'the day of old and new *moon*,' because on it the moon ceased waning and began to wax again. Pheidippides merely quibbles that a day cannot *itself* be both old and new.

[Page 409] *Tasters of the public feasts*. Apparently there were officials appointed for this duty.

[Page 411] *You shall atone for this*. After this I have omitted nine lines in which Strepsíades poses his creditor with the same tedious problem about the masculine termination of the feminine noun *cardopos*, 'kneading-trough' (p. 449).

[Page 411] *Carcinus*. A derided tragic poet whose plays were full of lamenting deities. The passage that follows contains parodies of tragedies now lost; especially of one by Carcinus' son Xenocles about Tlēpólemus, son of Hēracles.

[Page 411] *Ass-ass-inated*. Corresponding to a pun in the Greek on *ap'onou*, 'from an ass,' and *apo nou*, 'out of your mind.'

[Page 413] *How the Ram was sheared*. Simonides of Ceos (*c.* 556–468) wrote a poem on the defeat at Olympia of an Aeginetan wrestler, Crius ('Ram'). It opened with this pun.

[Page 414] *Grasshopper*. Because cicalas were supposed to do nothing but sip dew and sing.

[Page 414] *Sang from Euripides*. Euripides' *Aeolus*, where Macarius committed incest with his sister Cánace.

[Page 415] *Should sons be flogged, and yet unflogged the sire?* A parody of the words of Admētus' father in Euripides' *Alcestis*, 691 (see p. 237):

Shall *you* then love to live, and not your sire?

[Page 416] *Pot-ation*. The Greek *dīnos* means (1) 'rotation'; (2) 'a large round vessel.'

[Page 417] *Give to the flames*. Grote long ago suggested that this holocaust of Socrates and his disciples was based on the actual fate which overtook the Pythagoreans at Croton in S. Italy. About 450, while the brethren of the sect, now become a powerful oligarchic faction, were assembled in the house of Milo the famous athlete, their opponents fired it, so that only two escaped. This was followed by a general persecution of Pythagoreans in Magna Graecia.

THE BIRDS

[Page 424] *Orestes*. A notorious robber.

THE THESMOPHORIAZUSAE

[Page 428] *Vegetable-woman's son.* Aristophanes repeatedly throws this taunt at Euripides; though actually his mother Cleito was of good birth. Professor Murray suggests that the gibe originated because Euripides' heroine Melanippe had a mother skilled in herbs. This, however, seems a little thin. But one can imagine such a joke arising if, for instance, Cleito tried—perhaps too pushingly—to market some of her farm produce in Athens. (Her husband, the poet's father, was a merchant.)

THE FROGS

[Page 430] *Feel your shins go numb.* Cf. Plato's account in his *Phaedo* (117 E–118 A) of the effect of the hemlock on Socrates—chill and numbness ascending from the feet. (Physically, the description curiously resembles Mrs Quickly's account of Falstaff's death in *Henry V*.)

MENANDER

[Page 437] *Nēleus . . . Pélias.* Tyro bore to Poseidon two sons, Nēleus (father of Nestor) and Pélias (the evil uncle of Jason and father of Alcestis). Their mother exposed them; but they were saved by a herdsman and recognized when they grew up; Nēleus becoming King of Pylus, Pélias of Iolcus. There were tragedies on the subject by Sophocles and others.

BIBLIOGRAPHY

(A few further books for the ordinary reader)

THEATRE

A. E. Haigh, *Attic Greek Theatre*, new edition by A. W. Pickard-Cambridge, 1907.
R. C. Flickinger, *The Greek Theater and its Drama*, 4th edition, 1936.
A. W. Pickard-Cambridge, *The Theatre of Dionysus in Athens*, 1946.
A. W. Pickard-Cambridge, *Dramatic Festivals of Athens*, 1953.

GREEK TRAGEDY AND COMEDY

J. A. Symonds, *Studies of the Greek Poets* (1873), 3rd edition 1893.
G. Murray, *Ancient Greek Literature* (1897), reprinted 1927.
G. Norwood, *Greek Tragedy*, 1920.
F. L. Lucas, *Tragedy*, 1927, 2nd edition 1957.
A. W. Pickard-Cambridge, *Dithyramb, Tragedy and Comedy*, 1927, 2nd edition 1962.
Sir John Sheppard, ch. v of *Cambridge Ancient History*, vol. v, 1927.
G. Norwood, *Greek Comedy*, 1931.
H. D. F. Kitto, *Greek Tragedy* (1939), 3rd edition 1961.
D. W. Lucas, *The Greek Tragic Poets*, 1950, 2nd edition 1959.
T. B. L. Webster, *Later Greek Comedy*, 1953.
John Jones, *On Aristotle and Greek Tragedy*, 1962.
A. Lesky, *Greek Tragedy*, Eng. translation 1965.
A. Lesky, *History of Greek Literature*, Eng. translation 1966.

AESCHYLUS

Translations

Prose. H. Weir Smyth (Loeb Library), 1922.
Verse. E. D. A. Morshead, 1881–1908.
G. Murray, 1920–39.
(*Agamemnon*) L. Macneice, 1936; Sir John Sheppard, 1952.

Criticism

Sir John Sheppard, *Aeschylus and Sophocles, Their Work and Influence*, 1927.
G. Murray, *Aeschylus*, 1940.

SOPHOCLES

Translations

Prose. R. C. Jebb (1904), reprinted 1928.
Verse. R. Whitelaw (1883), 2nd edition 1897.
G. Murray (1911–48). (*Antigone, Oedipus the King, Oedipus at Colonus, Trachiniae.*)
Sir John Sheppard (1920–49). (*Electra, Oedipus the King, Oedipus at Colonus.*)
E. A. Watling (1947–52).

Criticism

Sir John Sheppard, *Aeschylus and Sophocles, Their Work and Influence*, 1927.
T. B. L. Webster, *Introduction to Sophocles*, 1936.
C. M. Bowra, *Sophoclean Tragedy*, 1944.
A. J. A. Waldock, *Sophocles the Dramatist*, 1951.
G. M. Kirkwood, *A Study of Sophoclean Drama*, 1958.

EURIPIDES

Translations

Prose. D. W. Lucas (1930–51). (*Alcestis, The Bacchae, Electra, Ion, Medea.*)
Verse. A. S. Way (Loeb), 1916.
G. Murray, (1902–31). (*Alcestis, The Bacchae, Electra, Hippolytus, Iphigeneia in Tauris, Medea, Rhesus, The Trojan Women.*)
Sir John Sheppard (1923–5). (*Helen, Cyclops.*)

Criticism

G. Murray, *Euripides and his Age* (1913), 2nd edition 1946.
F. L. Lucas, *Euripides and his Influence*, 1924.
G. M. A. Grube, *The Drama of Euripides*, 1961.

ARISTOPHANES

Translations

Verse. B. B. Rogers (Loeb), 1924. (Also with text and commentary, various dates.)
(*The Frogs*) G. Murray, 1908.
(*The Birds*) G. Murray, 1950.

Criticism

G. Murray, *Aristophanes*, 1933.

MENANDER

Translation

Verse. F. C. Allinson (Loeb), 1921.

Criticism

T. B. L. Webster, *Studies in Menander*, 1950.

INDEX OF TITLES